Psychiatry and Ethics

PSYCHIATRY AND ETHICS

BY

MAURICE LEVINE M.D.

INTRODUCTION BY *Margaret Mead*

BIOGRAPHICAL NOTE BY *George L. Engel* M.D.

GEORGE BRAZILLER *New York*

Note to the Reader

All case histories described are presented with complete concealment of the patients' identity in order to maintain the strictest confidentiality.

Published simultaneously in Canada by Doubleday Canada, Limited.
All rights reserved.
For information, address the publisher:
George Braziller, Inc.
One Park Avenue, New York 10016

Standard Book Number: 8076-0642-1
Library of Congress Catalog Number: 72-81354
First Printing
Printed in the United States of America

•

Acknowledgments

The various essays by Maurice Levine in the present book appeared originally in the following magazines:

American Journal of Orthopsychiatry, Vol. XVII, 1947, Maurice Levine, "Psychiatry for Internists."

Archives of General Psychiatry, Vol. 26, No. 1, January, 1972, Maurice Levine, "A Memo from ML."

The Family, Vol. XVI, No. 5, July, 1935, Maurice Levine, "Psychoanalytic Comments on Community Planning."

Journal of Medical Education, Vol. 35, No. 3, March 1960, Maurice Levine, "Oedipus, Cain and Abel, and the Geographic Full-Time System."

The American Journal of Psychiatry, Vol. 128, No. 5, November, 1971, George L. Engel, M. D., "In Memoriam" (used as Preface to Part II of the present volume).

The Journal of Medicine, Cincinnati, Vol. 20, No. 6, August, 1939, Maurice Levine, "The Diagnosis of Normality."

To my wife,
children and grandchildren,
who have been extraordinarily helpful
in many happy and productive ways—
a three-generation alliance.

Contents

PART II

SELECTED PAPERS AND LECTURES

NOTES AND BIBLIOGRAPHIES

Introduction

•

This book might have been called, and indeed Maurice Levine's whole life might have been called, psychoanalysis at work. Some very active verb is needed to convey the contrast between the way in which he thought about, talked about, and wrote about human life and the physician in the midst of life and death, and the more usual reflective and remote role of psychoanalysis. He was a psychoanalyst in every sense of the word. He had gone through the whole long exhausting initiation, he became a training analyst, and he kept analytic cases going in the midst of an exacting administrative life. But somehow the break between life and work which is characteristic of most psychoanalysts and most psychoanalytic writing was not there. The walls of the consulting room held their secrets—indeed he was far more demanding of confidentiality than many analysts—but the posture of the analyst, attentive to the slightest nuance in the patient's voice and acutely perceptive, did not necessarily alter outside the consulting room. For Maurice Levine life was all of a piece and his own roles, as physician, husband and father, teacher and friend, were permeated with the same sunny lucidity, the same perceptive tolerance for human weakness and the same imaginative expectation that somehow the humanness in other persons would come through—in whatever predicament they found themselves. For him we all shared the same human predicament, and there were, in fact, no hierarchical relationships between the saved and the damned, the physician and the patient, the father and the child, only hierarchies of responsibilities, and he himself was always willing to shoulder the largest part.

When a psychoanalyst also sets the style of a school of psychiatry, the outside observer has a chance of understanding more about what psychoanalysis is all about. The broad categories of ego, the individual's posture toward the outside world; libido, the surge of impulse-life within him; and superego, the archaic and experiential conscience, have become so much a part of the background of our thinking, while at the same time the process of psychoanalysis itself remains mysterious to all of those who have not undergone it, that the special triumphs of psychoanalytic procedure and insight are often overlooked. Maurice Levine's style in psychiatry, in teaching and therapy, the subjects about which he chose to write, and this last book, in which he took insight out of the consulting room to offer certain of its precious properties to the active world, all reveal his sense of the extra dimension given to understanding human behavior by the analytic practice itself.

He writes here always as a physician, always as one who accepts the nature of man as illuminated originally by Freud and perennially enlightened by each clinical case, and by each slip of the tongue, each pun, each temporary slump or fit of depression or spasm of enthusiasm. But although Freud and his students and disciples all write extensively about behavior, there is something about their writing which suggests that there are depths—whether these be called the death instinct, obsessional neurosis, sado-masochism, or repetition compulsions—indicating that man can plumb safely only within the special circumstances of the protected consulting room, where the highly trained analyst sits and takes upon himself the aggression, the terror, and the terrible ambivalence each human being carries within himself, a compound of ancient compromises between man's animal heritage, his growing capacity for ethical behavior, and the vicissitudes of childhood and helplessness.

When Maurice Levine started his teaching and as he developed the school of psychiatry at the University of Cincinnati, he set up no mysterious walls between the analyzed and the unanalyzed, no taboos about who could work together, no restrictions upon the analyst as a commentator on a problem speaking in front of an analysand or rules on who could socialize together. And in the same way in his writing, he assumes nothing—nothing of the abysmally threatening and unknowable, or knowable only to be hastily suppressed—which stands like a screen between the analyzed and the unanalyzed in practice and in literature. His was a department of psychiatry within which residents were to come to learn about human behavior, and especially about the kind of behavior that occurred in settings where illness was a principal preoccupation. Eventually some of those young residents might decide to be one kind of psychiatrist—a kind who would sit in a consulting room and listen intently to the most minute associations of a troubled mind; some would deal with disturbed children and some would become advisers to professionals who were themselves working with individuals, as teachers, nurses, social workers, surgeons. Their futures were expected to be diverse; their present was a shared concern which enveloped every act in luminous responsibility.

It is this kind of shared concern, this sense that the most esoteric experience has immediate implications for the behavior of other human beings, not only for analyst and analysand, not only for physician and patient, but for all of thinking mankind and womankind that is evident here. What he is saying he makes very clear, so clear that it is easy to miss the sophistication. Throughout he recognizes that readers, like students and patients, have their own psychological blocks and hang-ups which will distort and disturb their ability to understand. But the book is also permeated with Maurice Levine's patience, his willingness to try to say something over once more or in another way to make it clearer. It is—as was almost all his writing—the published part of a two-way process, in which the reader can feel the writer including him, in the extra earnestness with which he is taken into account. This gives his writing a special flavor—the kind of flavor which history sometimes gives to words spoken in passionate recognition of the presence and the importance of the audience on a great occasion. We feel this when we read the Gettysburg Address, as one who can put himself in the place of the Americans whom Lincoln addressed, or Martin Luther King's speech, "I Have a Dream," as one of those who experienced the march on Washington in high hopes in the summer of 1963. It was with such a passionate preoccupation with a moment, and what it meant to all of us, that Maurice Levine wrote his last "Memo from ML" to the people whose happily offered blood was coursing through his veins and keeping him alive a few weeks longer. In this memo he takes those to whom he is writing through his own fears and hopes; he lays down the law lightly, when he speaks of having games of table tennis again: "And when we play, anyone who won't try his best to beat me, because I am older, or because I have leukemia, or because he 'may be the cause of my death,' should not play with me. Until I say don't, I want the games to be competitive.

"But also if I am feeling tired, we will postpone the game or merely hit the ball around, practicing some strokes." [1]

Sentence by sentence he took us all in, anticipating the response of each, speaking with us, not at us.

This is the special quality that is found in all of his papers, a few of which have been included for background in the second part of this volume. His important book, *Psychotherapy in Medical Practice*, now in its eighteenth printing, grew out of and remains as one half of a dialogue with every type of community worker, as well as with physicians and psychiatrists. It contains also a sense of that invigorating and indomitable desire to teach which made George Engel describe Levine's responses to the new chairmanship of a department of psychiatry as those of "a hungry child to a dish of ice cream . . . He wanted students and residents to learn of psychiatry as an all encompassing human endeavor . . . Nothing that could possibly throw light on the human mind was to be overlooked, no topic to stimulate the intellect was barred." [2] And no reader, no matter how naive and callow, was excluded.

So, as in that important book, here too in *Psychiatry and Ethics*, the reader hears a voice, talking carefully, patiently, hopefully, to him in the confident aspiration that—if he takes a little more time, and thinks a little more about what is being said, and about himself if he were acting in the ways that are being discussed—he will learn and will practice what he has learned. Some writing invokes such disparate images that the reader either feeds upon magnificent figures of speech, or falls away in a revery of his own, unrelated to the flow of what is being said. Maurice Levine does not approach his readers in this way; he keeps them conscious of their and his immediate situation. Not a sentence is written for people who are unknown, unknowable, not really there, too old or too young or too unintelligent to understand.

We live in an age in which we have all become preoccupied with what is called communication. Heterogeneous in experience, in training, in vocation and avocation, each seeks, and usually does not find, a way of communicating more acutely, more vividly with other minds. This I found in Cincinnati, as I began to form the habit of taking a new idea, while it was still a bud not yet ready to flower, and presenting it to Maurice Levine and the lively seminar of colleagues and students who crowded together into an antiquated and uncomfortable basement room, where the very walls sang with responsive interest. Here one could be sure to be taken seriously, to be listened to responsively with suspended judgment and hope that the idea would indeed be a good one, to be seen not as a competitor nor a patient nor an authoritative scholar, but as one of all those who labored there together to understand the different new ideas which grew out of new cases, new research findings, new points of view. Something of that eclectic welcome to new material is reflected in the fascinating bibliography which illustrates how Maurice Levine prepared for the Weil lectures, now published here.

His sense of communication, spoken or written, being a process rather than an act, is illustrated too by a memorandum he wrote to his young collaborators—students, residents, faculty—who had participated in the experience of preparing and giving the lectures.[3] He carries them along, back to the lectures again, and onward, and explains that he wished to avoid emphasizing that the things he was saying were controversial or new but welcomed them as sophisticated collaborators. How wise he was is amply illustrated at present by the way in which public clamor in the women's liberation movement takes advantage of the strictures of Freudians against Freudians, as feminists wield their axes in the heat of a battle, entranced with the kind of "adversary system" which Maurice Levine decries. So, if the reader happens upon a point where he quietly gloats over unorthodoxy, he can feel pleased with himself without adding one jot or one tittle to the malignancy of the kind of intra-disciplinary controversies which are destroying our chances of producing a real science of human behavior.

Perhaps even more than the insights into ways of conducting human relations which this book offers, its major contribution is to a style of intellectual conduct, a generous and concerned inclusiveness in which the reader becomes almost as much a part of the argument as the writer. This is the way Maurice Levine always wanted it to be.

Margaret Mead

American Museum of Natural History
New York City
July, 1972

PART I

PSYCHIATRY
AND ETHICS

The study of ethics is fascinating, on its own. The study of the contribution of psychiatry to ethics makes it even more so. But when one adds that such a study may lead to additional ways of coping with the dangers facing the world, in the present and the future, the urgency of such a study becomes compelling.

M. L.

Author's Preface

THE central thesis of this book is that the facts, the concepts, and the insights of psychiatry have had a major impact on the development of man's ethical principles and ethical behavior. In the future, in the further development of ethics, this impact should be even greater. Such an ongoing development of ethics in turn can be of high value in the struggle of mankind to cope more effectively with the extraordinary dangers and with the magnificent opportunities of the 1970s and the 1980s.

The substance of this book, therefore, its presentation of the central topics and concepts of ethics, will indicate time after time the way in which ethics has been profoundly influenced by the facts and the insights of psychiatry. Such an influence is based on a number of sound and cogent reasons. One is the fact that most of the primary data of psychiatry come from the observation of patients who talk as honestly and as fully about themselves as they can, driven to do so by the strongest of motives, their hope for an alleviation of their personal suffering. Therefore the primary data of psychiatry have a high level of relevance, of immediacy, and of reliability. Also, in the struggle of patients to talk as fully and honestly as they can, there often appears convincing evidence of crucial emotional responses and conflicts which are unknown even to the patient himself, but which provide a fuller understanding of his love and his hate, his guilt and his shame, his ethical successes and his ethical failures.

Not only the content of the book, but to some degree even some of its form, some of its patterns of presentation, have their starting point in the field of psychiatry. An example is the emphasis on the relation between reader and author. This pattern of presentation is prompted by the fact that in a center for the learning and teaching of psychiatry, several types of two-way working alliances appear with great frequency. One is the alliance for treatment, the therapeutic alliance, between patient and psychiatrist. A second is the supervisory alliance, between resident-in-training and individual supervisor. Another is the two-way working relation, a mutual alliance, which often develops between an individual resident or between the residents as a group, and members of the faculty.

In such a center, it becomes clear that two types of learning process exist concurrently. One process is the residents' learning of the facts, the concepts, and the skills of a new discipline, a process which in good part is intellectual or cognitive. The other process is the development of the resident-faculty alliance, the interpersonal relation of residents with supervisors and other faculty, a process which becomes highly significant in the learning and maturation of the resident, and which can be called a learning-teaching alliance.

The combination and the interplay of the two processes, the intellectual learning of facts and skills, in the setting of a learning-teaching alliance, is so productive that often I have come to hope that a comparable development will take place in the various other areas in which I become involved. When I gave the series of lectures from which this book subsequently was developed, I knew that the experience would be more productive for the members of the audience and for me if a two-way interaction, a creative alliance, could develop between the audience and myself, in addition to the listeners' growing intellectual understanding of the substance of the lectures.

Later, in the development of this book from the lectures, I was hopeful that the two processes would occur. One would be the process of my expressing clearly enough in the writing the essence of the facts, the concepts, and the insights of psychiatry so that their potential impact on the further development of ethics would become apparent to the reader. The other process would be the development of a two-way working alliance between the reader and myself.

The reader-author alliance has never been described previously, as far as I know. So I decided to do nothing to interfere with its development, and to welcome its appearance, if appear it did. It would have its usual value as one of the two processes which are so effective in the growth of learning. But also if the reader-author alliance did appear, it would provide an immediate and observable example of a two-way working alliance, and so provide a way of clarifying that extraordinarily important concept.

This book, then, had its origin as a series of six lectures on "Psychiatry and Ethics," given under the auspices of the Frank L. Weil Institute for Religion and the Humanities, at the Hebrew Union College in Cincinnati. In the process of becoming a book, this material came to differ from a series of lectures in certain essential ways. In a lecture, the medium of communication is the spoken word. The spoken sentences or paragraphs often are modified extemporaneously as they are given. Their meaning and their impact are further modified by the nonverbal behavior of the lecturer, his tone of voice, his gestures, and his facial expressions. In a book, the medium of communication is the printed word, which must stand on its own. Each page must permit repeated reading and a searching scrutiny. Therefore, in the preparation of the series of lectures for publication as a book, extensive changes were necessary.

The reworking of the material to make it more suited to the needs of a reader led also to the emergence of new ways of presenting several of the essential patterns of ethics. In the first chapter, the crucial concept of self-scrutiny is presented and then is exemplified by the self-scrutiny done by the author about the temptations which appeared in giving the lectures and in writing this book.

In the second chapter, the discussion centers on the reader-author alliance, mentioned above. That material serves to introduce the reader to one of the recurrent themes of the book, the importance of creative alliances as a pattern of ethical behavior.

In addition to the first and second chapters, two other new chapters were added after the lectures were given. One is a Midpoint Summary, as Chapter VI. The other is a Postscript, as Chapter XI. Each of these chapters provides a condensed replaying of the discussion up to the point of the chapter itself. Such a rephrasing and condensation can point up the major thrust of the book, and can provide the reader with a clear-cut set of starting points for his further consideration. Also, the Postscript calls attention to some of the more novel or controversial suggestions of the book.

In this preface, the author wishes to express his sincere appreciation for the invitation to give the Weil Lectures. The author's personal thanks and admiration go to Dr. Nelson Glueck, the illustrious President of the Hebrew Union College, whose recent untimely death is so much to be regretted, and to Dr. Samuel Sandmel, who has been so strong a force in developing the Weil Lectureship.

The author welcomes this opportunity to acknowledge the skill, the helpfulness, and the dedication of Mrs. Dorothy Donohue and Mrs. Patricia Haynes, secretaries and research assistants in the Department of Psychiatry of the Medical School of the University of Cincinnati.

1

The Process of
Self-Scrutiny

A good part of a man's ethics consists of the ways in which he copes with his temptations. Witness Charles Darwin, the great biologist, who writes:

I had, also, during many years, followed a golden rule, namely that whenever a published fact, a new observation or thought came across me, which was opposed to my general results, to make a memorandum of it without fail and at once; for I had found by experience that such facts and thoughts were far more apt to escape from the memory than favorable areas. Owing to this habit, very few objections were raised against my views which I had not at least noticed and attempted to answer.[1]

None of us would have doubted the quality of Darwin's observations, his thoroughness, his memory, his logic, and his scientific achievements. Yet he came to recognize his own temptation, and the high value in his work of coping with it.

Darwin recognized that often he forgot observations or thoughts if they seemed to contradict his general results, and that he had to make immediate notes of such observations. The high quality of his work is based not only on his perceptive observations, his thoroughness, his logic, etc. It is based also on the fact that he recognized in himself a pattern of temptation that might have affected his work unfavorably, and then dealt successfully with that temptation.

From the quotation, it is clear that Darwin became aware of the temptation by observing himself, by using the process called self-scrutiny. Fundamentally this is the need to know oneself, the need to be as honest with oneself as possible, the need to avoid self-kidding.

The process of self-scrutiny is one of the central emphases in the field of psychiatry. Some version of this process will emerge, time after time, in this book, as playing a crucial role in the further development of ethical behavior and of ethical principles.

It is essential to call attention to the level of Darwin's self-scrutiny. He was not looking very deeply into the primitive depths of his personality. He was looking squarely at one of his repetitive bits of behavior, his forgetting of a certain category of facts, and looking, one can suppose, at some of the obvious motivation for his forgetting. He looked, he saw, and he coped with the temptation.

Self-scrutiny at the level used by Darwin, which is the level we can recommend in the further development of ethics, is possible without personal psychoanalysis or psychotherapy. The basic requirement is a persistent drive to see and to evaluate one's assets and one's mistakes, without minimizing them and without exaggerating them, and then to cope with them as well as one can.

Darwin's comments can evoke feelings of empathy and understanding in the reader. Almost everyone has had the temptation to forget facts which contradicted his own ideas, and most everyone, if he recognized the temptation, has had to struggle, more or less successfully, to deal with such temptations. Therefore, the reader's understanding of the process of self-scrutiny and of its value can be fostered by his emphatic understanding of Darwin's struggle and of his success.

The reader will have an empathic understanding of the next example of self-scrutiny, also. He will feel personally involved, in a sense, since the self-scrutiny being reported took place when this book was being written for him. It is the self-scrutiny by the author, revealing some of his own temptations as he began to write this book.

I could have used the self-scrutiny of others rather than my own, to give examples at this point. But it seemed important for me to use myself, since in the report of my own self-scrutiny, I can choose, from many examples, those episodes which will best show the value of the process of self-scrutiny, and which at the same time will deal with topics which are relevant to what I hope will be the reader's growing understanding of other issues in the field of psychiatry and of ethics. Further, when I give examples of my own self-scrutiny, I can give them with touches of humor to lessen the weight of a serious discussion of temptation.

When I report my own self-scrutiny, I can assure the reader that it is authentic, that it actually took place. But it will not be complete. No one should ever publish his self-scrutiny in full. I censor what I write about myself, as I do when I write about others, but I censor it in such a way as to preserve the essential truth and value of the points being made.

There are several other issues to mention. When I report my own self-scrutiny, I shall be talking about myself, which in a way is a risky thing to do. The fact that one is focusing on one's own thinking and feeling may be taken under many circumstances to indicate that one is self-centered. But this is a risk I must take.

Also, when I report my own self-scrutiny, a second danger appears, which is the opposite of the first danger, being regarded as self-aggrandizing. In self-scrutiny, one often uncovers some unpleasant or unattractive feelings or impulses in oneself, which in part one should report, or at least in censored terms indicate their existence. But if one reports unpleasant impulses, one might be thought to be self-depreciating, belittling oneself. Again this second risk is one that I must take.

Most of the examples of my own self-scrutiny occurred during the period in which I was preparing the Weil Lectures. At the time, my predominant feeling was of being deeply appreciative of the honor of being asked to give the lectures. I enjoyed the challenge, the prospect of presenting some new ideas to a potentially responsive audience, and of being stimulated then to rework the material for publication.

In addition, I came to recognize that the experience of being the holder of the Weil Lectureship had evoked in me a number of other responses which were unexpected, and were of a kind which usually are left unspoken and unrecorded. But since the unspoken and unwritten human responses are part of the essence of psychiatric understanding, and since in this instance they happen to be amusing and only mildly unspeakable, I will report them, with a trace of censorship at one point or another.

The first part of this Weil Lecture period of self-scrutiny can be understood most quickly, if we regard it as a continuation of an emergency job of self-scrutiny earlier in the year. At that time I had been asked to give a paper at a meeting of the psychoanalytic society in a nearby city. I was to be on a panel of five psychoanalysts, each of whom had been in practice for thirty years or more. We were to discuss our professional development and to summarize our advice for the younger generation. The program chairman emphasized the length of our experience, and hinted at our inevitable wisdom. The temptation was to accept with pleasure the implication that a long period of training and long experience can provide an automatic assurance that the older man has much to teach, that inevitably he has great wisdom.

This is an example of the kind of seductive temptation which must be faced occasionally by most of us who are members of the older generation. In this emergency, it is essential to take a heavy dose of the medicine of self-scrutiny.

Self-scrutiny and the observation of others make it clear that many of us whose long years of experience might be thought to qualify us as Wise Elder Statesmen, in reality qualify for only a minimal version of that role in life. Length of experience alone may mean merely the accumulation of a mixed bag of unclear observations and uncritical inferences, plus a few time-tested and sharply tested observations and inferences. So in the panel that evening, I recommended to those who might be myth-makers themselves, then or later, and especially to myself, that we use the techniques of a stringent self-scrutiny and of a persistent renunciation of the process of self-kidding. I called the paper "The Myth of the Wise Elder Statesman."

The invitation to give the Weil Lectures tempted me to fantasy again. The previous holders of the Lectureship have been excellent. My admiration for them tempted me to think of them as larger than life. When I thought of myself as their successor, I began to be tempted to regard myself as larger than life-size.

And magic plays a role. The Department of Psychiatry has had thirty-five large picnics during my tenure as Director, and only one of them has been dampened by rain, to the delight of the younger group, who pretend each time that it is my magic omnipotence that does the trick. So my personal Satan went further and suggested that if I am regarded by such competent authorities as omnipotent, why not be convinced also that I am omniscient, a Wise Elder Statesman?

The temptation this time was not too difficult to resolve. I talked to Satan. I began by saying, "Satan, get thee behind me." But then I remembered that over the years I had come to realize that such a comment to Satan was a mistake. If Satan were in back of me, he might hide there in the darkness, biding his time. Translated into psychiatric language, this means that when a temptation is merely repressed, it may continue to have great power, hiding in the dark, in the unconscious part of the mind. So I said, "Satan, get thee in front of me, so I can take a good look at thee (i.e., at the temptations) and decide what's best for myself and for others."

I present this, with tongue partially in cheek, as the first major new ethical principle announced in this book. It can be labeled, "The Transposition of Satan." The principle to be recommended is that one must never say, "Satan, get thee behind me"; instead one must say, "Satan, get thee in front of me." In translation, the new ethical principle is that most often it is advisable for mere mortals to look squarely at their own temptations.

When the process of self-scrutiny is to be as honest as one can make it, the realities of life, of oneself and of the world outside, are to be faced as well as one's temptations. The reality is that I have had extensive experience in my profession, but more important, that I have been in constant contact with younger faculty, with residents-in-training, and with students. They certainly do not regard me as incapable of mistakes. They know that I have certain strengths and various deficiencies. I know, and the others around me would never let me forget, that I am not a figure, either mythologic or human or infrahuman, of genius or wisdom or stupidity, except on the day of a picnic. They would agree that I have a number of facts and ideas worth presenting in a book, and that I know that most of the facts and ideas undoubtedly are the result of the hard work of hundreds of others, in many fields of science, in the humanities, in religion, and in the arts.

The reality also is that I would not pretend that this book provides a thorough or systematic presentation of the field of psychiatry or a thorough or incisive coverage of the field of ethics. In fact, this book presents only a small portion of these two fields, primarily some of the areas in which the two are related.[2]

"Reality-testing" is one of the famous phrases in psychoanalytic understanding. It refers to the process of observing and appraising the facts of life, in order to have a sound basis for judgment and action, and to minimize the distorting effects of wishful thinking and of fearful thinking. A workable ethics must make good use of reliable reality-testing, which in ethical questions must include both a realistic scrutiny of oneself and a realistic scrutiny of others.

Therefore, as part of a workable ethics for myself, it is essential for me to recognize that a very large number of men and women are capable of publishing a book like this, if they choose to spend the extraordinary number of hours in work which eventually leads to having something to say, and then choose to spend the extraordinary number of hours of work which are necessary in the writing and rewriting of the book. More generally, almost any one who reads this type of book, if he or she works hard enough, and self-critically enough, can become a good member of a good team in his own field or his own work. Such a recognition of the realities about oneself and about others is much more solid, more deeply satisfying than is the empty pleasure of a fantasy of being omnipotent or omniscient.

Through such a process of thinking and feeling, my temptation toward grandiosity was settled enough. But then, to my surprise, another temptation appeared which was more subtle and more persistent. This temptation was to avoid an open discussion in this book of the unpleasant, the hidden, the unacceptable aspects of the internal forces in mankind.

At that point I was tempted to whitewash, to bowdlerize, my presentation of the negative or unpleasant portions of the human personality. The ethical parts of the personality often are regarded as positive and pleasant, and elicit approval; the hostile and the sexual portions of the personality often are regarded with disapproval. The temptation was to be on the side of the angels, and to play for the approval of the readers, by understating in the book those parts of the personality which might elicit disapproval.

A long time ago it was noticed that the one who bears bad tidings may be dealt with unpleasantly by those to whom he brings the tidings. In a similar fashion, one who brings tidings about the aspects of the personality which elicit disapproval may find some of that disapproval directed toward himself.

I knew that most readers of a work with this title would be intelligent and perceptive. But it seemed probable that many of them would not expect to read in a book by a member of my generation, written for the intelligent general reader, the kind of open talk, about usually forbidden topics, which often occurs during psychiatric examination and treatment, and in the supervision and the seminars which are part of the learning process in becoming a psychiatrist. But in this book, forbidden topics must appear. If I am to do a solid job of writing about ethics, I must write also about the nonethical, the antiethical, the unacceptable parts of man, which provide one of the basic reasons for the existence of ethical patterns.

Ethics has a defensive function, of controlling or directing or balancing some of the potentially destructive impulses in life, or of preventing a healthy part of life (such as a workable conscience) from becoming a dangerous distortion of itself (such as a rigid, corruptible conscience). These patterns will be discussed later under the rubric of Defensive Ethics.

It follows that in a meaningful discussion of ethics one must refer also to the unpleasant, the unacceptable aspects of life, to misplaced or misdirected sexuality, to unacceptable hostility and destructiveness, to parasitic impulses, to patterns of cruelty and hatred, and to the corruptible parts of the human conscience. In fact, one must refer to the whole gamut of human patterns which, correctly or incorrectly, may arouse anxiety, guilt, shame, horror, and revulsion. Then can one give a sound consideration of ethics, of some of the more highly developed patterns of life, of the Ego as well as the Id, of effective and workable voices of conscience, and of mutuality, friendship, trust, and love, of all those developments which evoke attitudes of approval rather than of disapproval, from the individual himself and from the group, depending in good part on the standards of the culture.

In spite of my recognition of the logic of this approach, I found myself repeatedly wanting to ignore some of the facts I know about human beings, the degree and frequency to which they have dirty or cruel impulses, and the fact that occasionally they behave, or want to behave, in a way which they, as well as others, consider deserving of guilt and shame. I found myself writing sentences that minimized the surging destructive impulses of human beings, writing as if the ethics of purity and cleanliness had won a total victory.

I could have rationalized this stance as others had done in the past, by saying that it was a necessary correction, since Freud or psychoanalysis had neglected or underplayed the ethical aspects of life and overemphasized the unacceptable drives. To some degree, in the early days, in the heroic age of psychoanalysis, there was inevitably some overstatement of the psychoanalytic discoveries of the primitive nonethical drives of human beings. Innovators often overstate their findings. But that period is over.

Gradually and forcefully, my self-scrutiny did its job. Finally, I came close enough to a resolution of my temptation to overstress the ethics of purity and to underplay the unacceptable human forces which make ethics necessary.

Then, my personal Satan appeared a third time, in the form of a temptation from the opposite direction. Now my temptation was to take pride in having just recognized and resisted my resistance, to be proud of my loyalty to psychoanalysis, and to feel secure in being in the mainstream of the work of my group. The temptation now was to demonstrate emphatically that I belonged to the psychoanalytic Establishment, to place a great emphasis on the unacceptable patterns of human beings, and to feel superior to those who might want to emphasize only the ethical, or who wanted to talk only of the Ego rather than of the Id, or who wanted to discuss social problems rather than intrapsychic conflicts. This third temptation was to "sock it to 'em," to shock the readers of the book, with a dramatic statement of the extraordinary perversity, duplicity, and destructiveness of human impulses.

This temptation to overemphasize and dramatize the forbidden must be resisted as much as the temptation to talk of men as being as pure as driven snow. A distortion either way may damage one's clarity of observation and the effectiveness of one's logic.

Time passed, and with self-scrutiny, this temptation too did pass. The temptation to overstate the unacceptable was resolved as much as it needs to be. In fact, it was not difficult, since psychoanalysis, as a discipline, does not emphasize only the unacceptable aspects of life. Far from it. Psychoanalysis also emphasizes the Ego, the acceptable, the social, the cultural, the ethical. To indicate this part of psychoanalysis, I can quote Freud's comment, "Where Id was, there Ego shall be." I can point to his central emphasis, in part quoting Goethe, that "Voice of the Intellect Is Soft" but eventually has its way. I can refer to the discussion by Karl Abraham[3] and by Freud of the fact that in the highest development of man's love for another human being, in his object-love, he can become post-ambivalent, beyond the combination of love and hate called ambivalence, and can become relatively free of using the other only for his own needs. At this level, a man or a woman is as interested in the satisfactions of the partner as in his own.

These are samples of the direct observation in psychoanalysis of profoundly ethical patterns. Psychoanalysis has a relatively well-balanced approach. It still is growing, still is responsive to the finding of new facts. In my experience, it is the most satisfactory way now available of looking at the facts of life, the facts of human psychodynamics. So temptations aside, we will talk about the acceptable, and about the unacceptable, about any facts or factors in human life which are important in the growth of our understanding.

2

The Concept of a Working Alliance

DURING the writing of this book, there was one other temptation which I found most difficult to resist. I felt tempted to say that humor, especially the types of humor I personally prefer, can be regarded as a profoundly important form of ethical behavior. I could think of a dozen ways of presenting that idea with great conviction. One way would be to say that everyone knows that many a situation loaded with destructive feelings has been resolved ethically, after a bit of teasing or humor.

For the time being at least, I renounced the temptation to be revolutionary, to insist that humor is a central pattern of ethics. Since I made that deposit in a bank account of righteousness, I can feel free to use bits of humor, at times, merely because they are enjoyable. At other times I can use humor as a way of making a transition from one serious topic to another, or as a way of making a difficult point more understandable. I can feel free to tease the reader at times, and at other times to tease myself.

As a starter, as a way of linking the first chapter to this second chapter, I can call your attention to the fact that in the first chapter, self-scrutiny was given of just two human beings, Charles Darwin and myself. It would seem that in that chapter I managed to put myself in very good company indeed. In this chapter, I shall be in very good company again.

Most of this chapter will focus, as did the other, on two figures. This time it will be the reader of this book and the author; the reader will have replaced Darwin. And the reader, comparing himself to Darwin, will find that he will be given far more space and consideration in this chapter than Darwin was given in the preceding one.

In the previous chapter, the emphasis was on the author's report of his own self-scrutiny. In this second chapter, the focus will be on the reader as well as the author; it will be on the dynamic interaction, the potential alliance, between reader and author. That alliance will be used as a way of introducing the reader to the general concept of "two-way creative working alliances," a concept which shows promise of being of the highest importance in the further development of ethical principles and of ethical behavior.

The writing of this chapter could have been an easier job, if instead of focusing on the reader-author interaction, I would have chosen a more conventional way of introducing the reader to the concept of the two-way working alliance. I could have started with a general description or a definition of the concept. Or I could have introduced the alliance concept by comparing a number of well-known examples.

But I chose to do this job the hard way, of introducing the concept of the two-way working alliance by focusing on the reader-author alliance as the first example. This is the hard way because the reader-author alliance has not been the focus of attention previously, as far as I know. I shall be introducing a new general topic, the working alliance, by using an example, the reader-author alliance, the evidence for which must be excavated and identified even as it is being used as an example.

I do this, not because I like to do things the hard way, to wear a hairshirt. There will be many opportunities in this book to use the other methods of discussing and clarifying the two-way working alliance in its various forms. This first time around, in this first attempt to present to the reader the basic concept of a two-way creative alliance as an essential pattern of ethics, I want to use an approach which will involve the reader in the process of understanding. When we focus on the reader-author alliance, the concept of a two-way creative alliance can not remain merely as a theoretical construct, since the reader himself is part of the interaction. And the odds are good that this way he will develop a better understanding of the alliance process because he will have had the direct experience of being involved in the process himself.

Further, there is value in seeing oneself as part of a pattern which is being presented as generally valid. One of the important facts of life, which can be phrased as a principle of ethics, is that within certain limits most of the reliable rules of life, and most of the basic patterns of life, probably apply to oneself as well as to others. To give an example, we turn again to the first chapter. The essence of that chapter, in a sense, was that all human beings have temptations with which they must cope. If that is so, then each human being must assume that probably this pattern applies to himself as well as to others. Also, if self-scrutiny can be established as one of the valid and productive processes for the continuing development of ethical behavior, then each individual must consider the possibility that he should attempt to use, or to use more than before, his own pattern of self-scrutiny. The use of self-scrutiny is not a regulation that one must follow, but it is one of the many available and valuable patterns from which one can pick and choose in the development of one's own repertory of patterns of living.

The essential point of this chapter is that the pattern of a two-way creative, working, mutual alliance may be seen to be one of the basic patterns of positive, productive, growth-producing behavior in human beings. If the promise implicit in this concept, which will be discussed time and again in this work, does materialize, it may become a pattern to be urged for most human beings. If so, the reader can assume that the concept of a two-way working alliance can be highly significant for himself as well, and may be a pattern he would pick and choose for himself, as revelant for his own development. It would be worth the effort, then, to have the reader experience the reader-author alliance as it develops.

There is a contrast, an apparent discrepancy, to be mentioned. As I have said several times, the pattern of two-way working alliances is of high importance. But the first example of that category to be discussed, viz, the reader-author alliance, is not one of the important or crucial alliances in life. One can live without such an alliance. Probably one can enjoy reading a book and can learn from it, without developing a reader-author alliance, or with only a faint trace of one. We use this specific alliance as an example, not because it is of high importance itself, but because the recognition of its existence may have a great impact in furthering the reader's understanding of the important general pattern of mutual alliances.

Our understanding of the reader-author alliance can be more effective if we start with its predecessor, the audience-lecturer alliance, which appeared during the series of Weil Lectures. When I began to prepare for those lectures, I realized that a study of the impact of psychiatry on the further development of ethics could make extensive use of the concept of the two-way working alliance. The development of interpersonal alliances is so important a factor in the ongoing work of psychotherapy and of supervision, that it seemed highly probable that we would come to recognize the potential value of interpersonal alliances in the further development of ethical behavior.

Further, in the year preceding my preparation of this material on ethics, I had come to see the importance of the creative alliance phenomenon in other situations. I had begun to use that concept to reach a fuller understanding of such diverse areas as interdisciplinary research, as marriage, as the conflict between the generations, and as the integrative links between medical schools and community hospitals.

With such ideas stirring in me, I started to work on the Weil

Lectures, for an audience which in part consisted of university, hospital, and Hebrew Union College faculty, and the graduate students of many disciplines. Some of them had attended my seminars and lectures previously, and seemed to have liked my approach in the past, even my brand of humor. They knew that I was making a serious attempt to give them a good experience in the Weil Lectures. I worked hard, before and during the lectures, to make them clear and convincing and growth-producing for the listeners and for me. Many of the audience responded by coming back time after time. They listened with obvious interest and attention even though I did not oversimplify the material, and even when I showed my respect for them by expecting them to work with me on the material as I gave it. I tried to make sure that listening to the lecture was not a painful experience. But I made sure also that listening to me was not merely a process of receiving intellectual food which was predigested. I had cooked the dinner of each lecture, but the members of the audience had to do the chewing and the digesting for themselves.

The specific circumstances of these lectures led to the rapid appearance of an ongoing two-way working alliance, which was more observable and more intense than any I had experienced previously. The two-way alliance was so obvious, to the audience as well as to me, that as the lectures proceeded, I was able to use the working alliance between the audience and myself as a way of clarifying the concept of the therapeutic alliance (of patient and psychiatrist), the concept of the supervisory alliance (between graduate student and faculty supervisor), and the overall concept of two-way creative working alliances.

In the audience-lecturer alliance, I could sense the response of the audience, from the size of the group which came voluntarily to each of the lectures, from the way in which they seemed tense or unsmiling at various points, from the comments and questions at the end of the lecture. After the lecture series was over, and I began to convert the lectures into chapters of a book, I had some feeling of regret that there would be less two-way communication, less feedback from future readers than there had been from members of an audience.

Then came an unexpected experience. The lectures had been taped and were distributed by a national educational agency to FM radio stations, chiefly in universities, and were broadcast again. Apparently many listeners respond to such lectures with letters. To my great pleasure, I received a very large number of letters, some approving, some criticizing, some making specific suggestions, etc. I was surprised that this response, a sort of two-way communication, occurred even when the audience and I were not in the same room, in contrast to the situation of the lectures in their original context.

From this experience I have inferred that as an author (at least of a book like this) I can expect that there will be more two-way communication between the readers of the book and me than I had previously expected. Through the book itself I try to communicate facts and concepts about the subject matter of the book. And in that process I communicate my attitudes toward the subject matter, and my attitudes toward the reader. It seems highly probable that in turn, I will hear directly from some of the readers. Some of their comments will affect my thinking, will influence what I will write when I turn again to the process of writing and revising the material of a future book, which is to be on a topic closely related to the substance of the present work.

This is not merely an empty gesture of politeness or of congeniality. The author is thoroughly convinced that even scholarly books should be sensitive to, and responsive to, the ideas and reactions of actual and expected readers. Certainly this book, even though it is based primarily on the author's forty years of work as a psychiatrist and as a supervisor of psychiatrists-in-training, has been improved by a two-way interaction between the author and the readers of segments of it before it was published, and by the two-way communication between the author and the readers of his previous publications.

The communication is two-way in another sense, via the process of empathy and identification. An author must use a modified version of the Golden Rule. He writes for the readers as he would like others to write for him. But also he knows that they differ from him in some ways and so he writes for them, communicates with them, in the way he thinks most productive. If he has succeeded in part in understanding and meeting their legitimate needs, they will respond, and some day he will come to know about some of their responses.

The two-way communication between reader and author should not be overstated. The two are not in the same room, and so the two-way communication often is delayed or uncertain. In the audience-lecturer interaction, the two are in the same room, and the two-way communication often is immediate, strong, and clear. Therefore, the reader-author communication may be less obvious, and less easily observed, than is an audience-lecturer communication.

The reader's participation in the reader-author alliance may begin in a variety of ways. One day as I watched a young man begin to read a book in a small library, I saw a relaxed, easy-going person go through the first ten pages casually. Then the onset of the alliance was signaled by his body posture responding as it might in the game called "Freeze," in which the one on the receiving end of the order must not move from his position, must keep his body posture frozen. In ten seconds or so, the young man in the library relaxed again.

In a conversation with him shortly thereafter, I found that at the freeze-moment he had been responding to the book with an increased intensity of concentration, which for him, often involved an unmoving body posture. At that point the author was discussing an idea which was new to the reader, who felt that the new idea was fascinating, perhaps highly valuable, but exaggerated. This unobtrusive beginning, characteristic of a reader-author alliance, is in contrast to the rather obvious beginning of many an audience-lecturer alliance, such as the sudden onset of complete quiet in the lecture room, with everyone awake, concentrated on the words of the lecturer. A more negative moment is signaled by the shuffling of the feet and restless movements in the audience when the lecturer has forgotten his audience, as he thinks of other things.

Usually some elements of the reader-author interaction come into existence spontaneously, peripherally, perhaps unnoticed. For example, the author's past experience makes him rather certain that when he mentioned his own self-scrutiny in the first chapter, there were both positive and negative responses in his readers. Some readers had a surge of hope, that perhaps this author, or perhaps this field of psychiatry, had something fairly simple and clear and valid to say about ethics, and about the ethical value of self-scrutiny. But other readers may have had a surge of concern, that perhaps the self-scrutiny, as it was given by the author, seemed too easy, and therefore might not be much of a step forward.

The content of the self-scrutiny, the ideas and feelings of the author, may in part have seemed amusing to the reader. The reader may have developed some fellow-feeling with the author, perhaps some interest in the author's approach. He may have had a positive response to the increase in his understanding which grew out of the author's discussion of several kinds of temptation and of the process of coping with temptation.

Similarly, the author's emphasis on the value of two-way working alliances, and on the value of the reader becoming personally involved in the understanding of that process, may have led to some individual responses. The word "involved" is somewhat ambiguous, and some readers may like the idea that the author is trying to get them involved, while others may prefer to have an author use words that are more impersonal.

Also in response to this material, some readers may have become rather hopeful, others hopeful but only slightly so, still others slightly skeptical, and still others very skeptical. Many readers, after these initial pages, probably had two sets of feelings, simultaneously or in quick succession, one set of interest and of hope, and a second set, contradictory to the first, of doubt and of skepticism.

The author's guess is that many of those who have read this first segment of the book, which provides a sampling of my ideas and approach, have developed some personal responses to the book and to the author. With most readers, these responses are relatively minor; with some, the responses are more intense.

My impression is that in many of these responses, there are two components. One is a varying amount of tentative trust. The other is a varying amount of benevolent skepticism. Perhaps both are minimal, merely trace elements. But the author's experience leads him to think that when readers continue to read on, in certain types of books, these two responses are almost always present, in varying amounts.

The phrase, "a combination of tentative trust and benevolent skepticism," can describe one important facet of the spontaneous participation of many readers in the growth of a two-way working alliance with an author. In fact, it seems probable that "a combination of tentative trust and benevolent skepticism" can provide a productive type of preliminary or initial response in many human relations.

Concurrently, some readers may have developed some hope, mixed with skepticism, that a book such as this may come to have some value in their own search for their own ethics, that it may help them to answer for themselves some of their own questions about the development of workable and reliable standards, internal and external. The concept of a creative alliance, and of their participating in the process, may have seemed positive or promising.

With regard to the author's participation so far in the two-way working alliance, one point is that he has an ongoing commitment to a struggle to be as clear, as direct, as logical, and as honest as he can be. Further, he wants his ideas to seem alive and relevant. The fact that these are an essential part of his goals may gradually become apparent to the reader, who then may respond with some pleasure to the idea that the author may in fact prove to be sensitive to the reader's needs and wishes.

By this time, many a reader will have had other responses, positive or negative, as well as some of the responses mentioned above.

In fact, for a moment or more, he may have become aware, to a degree, of the author as a human being, as well as the author of a book. And the reader may have become aware of himself as a human being who is responding with some feelings of doubt and of skepticism, and with some feelings of trust and of hope, as well as being aware of himself as a reader of a book who is using his intelligence to understand the facts, the ideas, and the insights of the book.

We can add to our understanding by returning to a comparison of the reader-author alliance with the audience-lecturer alliance. In a series of lectures, the lecturer and the audience are in the same room, can look at each other when they want to do so, and observe each other's responses. In that setting, it is easy for the lecturer to sense the development of the two-way audience-speaker alliance, from the restlessness or the quiet of the audience at various points, the variations in whispering, the changes in body posture and facial expression, the periods in which there is no coughing, etc. In contrast, in the writing and in the reading of a book, the development of the reader-author alliance is not so apparent or so noisy.

But the author knows from his own self-scrutiny, and from the comments by other authors to him (when they have reason to be frank and open about it) how deeply an author can be involved with his readers. And the author knows, from his own experience as a reader and from the comments to him by readers of his own books and of books by other authors, how deeply a reader can become responsive to, and interact with, the figure of the author of the book he is reading.

In fact, the reader-author alliance, although it is less obvious and less easily observed, often is much more effective and lasting than is the audience-lecturer alliance. The strength and persistence of the reader-author alliance is the result of a number of forces. One is that a reader often feels more equal-equal with the author than does a member of an audience with the lecturer. In a sense, the reader is more independent of the author and feels less controlled by him. A reader can stop reading a book more easily than a listener can leave a lecture. A reader can go at his own pace, and do his reading at a time when he chooses. A reader can interrupt his reading and think through a point, and then return to his reading. In contrast, the listener who wants to stop listening (to think through a point) may be concerned that when he begins to listen again, he will have missed an essential step in the presentation. The reader can reread a paragraph several times; the listener can not take a comparable step unless he has a tape recording.

In Western culture, and perhaps more generally, both readers and authors have a variety of impulses and patterns which are not conducive to the development of an alliance. Strongly competitive impulses are fairly universal. An author may want to show his great knowledge to the reader, to be one up. This could interfere with an author's sensitivity to his readers' needs and it could interfere with a reader's ability to acknowledge that the author has just made a good point in the book. But alongside whatever competitive impulses there exist in author and reader, there exists also a mutuality of interests and a feeling of partnership with regard to working together on the topics of the book.

In the writing and the reading of a book, both author and reader may come to recognize that a team relation has been developing between them, in addition to competitive drives. Both may have come to recognize in the past the high value of team feelings in previous activities, in sports or in human relations. The more successful the author is in expressing himself clearly and vividly in the book, the more the reader will gain from his reading of the book. And the author may know that the more his readers are strengthened by, and the more they receive from his writing, the greater is his own self-esteem, and the greater is the recognition and respect he receives from others.

In a competition, when one shows that he is stronger, he is the winner, the other seems to be weaker, the loser. In the two-way working alliance, when one becomes stronger, the second may become stronger also.

Another factor which explains the effectiveness and the duration of the reader-author alliance may be expressed in symbolic terms. An author has put a great deal of himself in the book. The book is a part of himself. It is his book. But also when the book is being read by the reader, its sentences and its ideas are being absorbed by the reader. It is becoming his book, even though, in a different sense, it remains the author's book. In a way, there is a symbolic partnership in the fact that the book is the author's book and also the reader's book. Hopefully, this represents an active partnership in the job of thinking about, and feeling about, the issues presented and discussed in the book.

The reader-author alliance may be quiet and undramatic, in contrast to the listener-lecturer alliance. Some readers may not have as vivid a living experience of an alliance in the reader-author relation, as they might have had as listeners. Therefore, to add to the reader's awareness of the alliance phenomenon, the author occasionally will describe the audience-lecturer interaction as it occurred at the corresponding point in the lectures. The readers of this book, who surely have attended many lectures, will identify quickly and easily with the listeners at the lecture. In this fashion, the readers of this book can experience vicariously some of the facets of the working alliance which were present in the lecture situation.

It is important to stress the fact that a therapeutic alliance, or a reader-author alliance, or a trustworthy partnership, or a two-way mutual-interest group, must not be a trick to get others to agree with one's ideas or plans. It must not be a sophisticated one-up-man-ship. It is not a skillful salesmanship, valuable as that may be at times. A working alliance, if it is to be regarded as a pattern of ethics, must be based on an actual attempt to form a sort of mutual-interest team, in which some valid and perceptive attention by one member of the team to the interests of the other often leads the second to respond in turn in appropriate ways, to the needs of the first member of the team.

In a two-way working alliance, there are times when one has the impression that the opinions of the others in the alliance should take precedence over one's own even if one is fairly convinced that one's own opinion is more correct. Of course, there are other times when one must persist in one's disagreement, rather than accept the opinion of others. Obviously it is even more desirable, whenever it is possible, to have an active discussion of the issue, and to settle the disagreement in terms of the facts and the logic of the situation.

A clear-cut example of this issue, of an acceptance of the opinions of the others in a potential alliance, occurred in the writing of this book. I had planned to avoid an emphasis on definitions. I know the value of definitions, and in some areas, I am addicted to their use. But I know also that a clear, sharp definition often tends to hamstring the kind of wide-ranging creative thinking which is necessary in the application of the ideas, the facts, or the methods of one discipline to the problems and the issues of another field. I would prefer to have definitions emerge out of the discussion itself, e.g. out of the repeated placement in proximity of apparently unrelated items.

But a fair number of those who spoke to me during the lecture series, or wrote to me in response to hearing the broadcasts from FM radio stations, asked that very early in the lectures I give my definition of ethics (and of several other terms). I hesitated to do so, for the reasons given above. But I decided finally to accept the opinion of those who asked for definitions, because it was the only point mentioned by a large number. Also I decided that if I gave only one definition, that of ethics, it would do no harm. And the definition I shall give is open-ended enough so that there is little chance it will be blocking or restrictive.

I decided to include the definition of ethics in this chapter on the reader-author alliance, since my giving the definition is an example of the many ways in which listeners and seminar-participants and readers actually do have an impact on a lecturer or an author. It is a mistake to think that the impact goes only in one direction, from author to reader, just as it is incorrect to think that in the father-son relation, the impact goes only in one direction, from father to son. For example, many a father these days has intellectual but cold discussions with a son or a daughter. In such a situation, a simple statement such as, "It's good to have a son who likes to discuss these problems," a statement which recognizes the impact of the son's qualities on the father, is worth far more than hours of cold discussion. But it must be an honest statement of fact, by the father to the son. With high frequency, in any two-way alliance, pretense is quickly seen as hollow. My giving a definition of ethics at this point is based on my honest conviction that the request is legitimate and justified.

In giving a preliminary definition of the term "ethics" as it is used in this book, I start with the comment that it rarely seems productive to differentiate between the word "ethics" and the word "morality."[4] It seems best to use one term, "ethics," to refer, first, to those patterns of individual human beings, or of groups, which are restrictive or limiting or inhibiting toward destructive impulses or behavior. Also, we use the term "ethics" to refer, second, to those patterns, in individuals or in groups, which foster the growth of constructive and creative impulses and behavior, in individuals or groups.

For example, when the self-aggrandizement of an individual is of the type which occurs at the expense of other individuals, and damages them unfairly, the self-aggrandizement must be opposed. Those principles or those forces or those forms of behavior are to be called ethical which stand in opposition to self-aggrandizement which occurs at the expense of others. Further, those patterns or principles or forces of behavior are to be called ethical which stand in opposition to the drives in the individual which are destructive or disruptive to the major interests of the individual himself.

It is clear that a working definition of ethics must have several dimensions. One dimension is the cultural, since ethical values and ethical behavior differ from one culture to another. Another dimension is the historical, since ethical values and behavior may vary from one historical period to another. Another dimension is the individual and psychodynamic, since ethical values vary with the age of the individual, his process of maturation, and the degree

to which he is controlled by his conflicts and by unconscious patterns. Another dimension is the biologic, etc.

With this recognition of the multifaceted nature of ethics, it
seems best to start with a rather uncomplicated set of statements,
to which greater depth and clarity may be added in the course
of later discussions. The starting point can be that individual ethics
consists of those principles and those inner drives or patterns which
press the individual toward satisfactions or gratifications or developments which can occur without significant damage to other
human beings (and which at times may foster the interests of
others) and which do not jeopardize other basic needs or satisfactions of the individual himself. Similarly, the ethics of a group
would press it toward group satisfactions or developments which
can occur without significant damage to individual members of the
group, or to subgroups, and which at times may actively foster
the interests of individuals or subgroups. Further, the ethics of
the group must include the avoidance of damage to other independent groups, as well as the avoidance of damage to a larger
group of which the first group is a part, in the course of its own
satisfactions.

A further point in the definition of ethics can be based on the
fact that in general the relations between an individual and a group
to which he belongs can be grossly classified as being of two varieties. The first consists of the mutually helpful and interdependent
relations of the individual and the group. The second consists of
fundamental differences of interest (and therefore the potential for
conflict) between one individual and other individuals and between
the individual and the group.

These two categories in the relation of an individual and a group
can be used as the basis for defining two types of ethics. When
the relation between individual and group is primarily one of
fundamental differences of interest, there develop techniques of
mutual adaptation, techniques which help to assure the survival
of the individual and to assure the survival of other individuals
and of the group. Patterns evolve in which the interests of one side

47

in the conflict are molded to avoid unnecessary damage to the other side or to itself and even to foster the interests of the other side. In this book, the principles and the behavior involved in such techniques are called "Defensive Ethics."

When, however, the pattern is one in which the interests of an individual predominantly are in consonance with, rather than in conflict with, the interests of other individuals and of the group, a different set of responses and techniques is developed. These are patterns or systems of joint behavior, of mutual help, patterns which are expressions of mutuality and partnership, which in their continuing development can be regarded as a Creative Ethics, even more productive than are the patterns of Defensive Ethics.

3

Survival and Ethics

IN recent years there has been a serious question as to whether man can survive in the face of the dangers which now exist and will exist in the years to come. For the first time in history, there is a power which is under human control and which is great enough to decimate the human race, the power of nuclear weapons.

There are serious hazards in the pollution of the air, the water, and the land. There are serious hazards in the increase in the world's population.

The dangers in man's life at this point in history arise from man's extraordinary achievements in the physical sciences and in the technologic application of the discoveries in the physical sciences. The advances in the social and behavioral sciences and in the humanities, and in the technology in those fields, have not kept pace with the advances in the physical sciences and technology. This discrepancy accentuates the danger. We can not be sure that individual men and their nations, their societies, can be trusted with man's new powers, his tools, his weapons. Man may not be ready to do a constructive or even a safe job in the handling of the tools and the processes made available by the achievements in the physical sciences and in their technical applications.

But is is imperative to avoid an overemphasis on man's deficiencies, his failures, and the dangers. We must value highly the great triumphs of mankind in the past hundred years. Using an old figure of speech, we can say that in certain ways, several of the Four Horsemen of the Apocalypse are in retreat. Many diseases have been conquered. The potentiality for eliminating poverty and starvation, were the population increase to slow down, has been achieved. Men have walked on the moon.

Most of us are optimistic enough to think that human forces will prevent the human use of nuclear weapons in widespread devastation. But an optimistic outcome is far from certain, and it is imperative that we become involved in the process of the prevention of nuclear warfare and of the other potential disasters to the human race.

The central issue is that there must be a struggle to match the extraordinary advances in the physical sciences and their technology, by a comparable advance in the biologic, the social and the behavioral sciences. Man's capacity to use or to control the tools which develop from the advances in science and technology must be increased. And the goal must be not only the survival of the human race, but also its survival in the kind of world, in the kind of culture, that will be worth having, for our grandchildren and great-grandchildren.

Along with the advances and the dangers, in science and technology, there have been many changes in individual and group standards, an apparent disruption of many patterns of ethics, in a sense a breakdown of old standards without an adequate replacement by a new set of workable standards. A period that can only be regarded as one of the most severely anti-ethical regressions in human history, the Nazi pathologic state, has occurred. But in general, it would be difficult to document the assertion of a general downhill course in human behavior. There are statistics which seem to show an increase in the rate of certain types of crimes, but there are doubts about the validity of some of the data. In fact, it seems that in certain ways, there has been a highly favorable development of a productively independent attitude in recent years, along with a serious increase in the problems of interpersonal relations. There are many contradictory trends, which are difficult to compare with previous trends.

But even if there is no clear evidence of a loss in man's capacity to cope with dangers, the dangers themselves are much greater. It is safe to say that this is an age of greater uncertainty, greater anxiety, greater alienation, and a far less confident attitude in dealing with the growing complexities of human life. There are many areas of confusion, many ways in which we seem to be stumbling. Many of the apparent certainties of life in the past have become uncertain.

One certain fact is that life is much more complex, not only in the existence of nuclear power and its dangers, but also in the population explosion, the information explosion, the growing role of the computer and other devices, the extraordinary speed of transportation and especially of communication, the urgency and the complexity of the urban crisis, the speed of the cultural changes, and more. Most of these changes, and many others, are the result of positive developments which have great potential value for the present and for the future, as well as dangers. But the capacity of the human race to cope with the increasing complexity, the greater dangers, the severe anxieties, the greater challenges of the future, is being put to a severe test.

As an essential step in the development of man's capacity to cope with, and to master, the problems and the dangers of the present and of the future, there must be a great increase in the scientific understanding of man and an ongoing development of an ethics in contemporary terms. This does not mean that there needs to be a single set of standards to be applied to all human beings. There can be, and must be, a diversity of standards for cultures and subcultures. Eventually there may emerge certain standards applicable to all human beings and acceptable to them. Cross-cultural studies can open the door more widely for an ethics for all mankind. And psychoanalytic studies of individuals of many cultures can speed the growth of a pan-human ethics.

At this point our goal can be much more modest, of participating actively in the struggle toward a more workable ethics for ourselves as individuals, and for our culture. One limited goal can be to have an ethics which is acceptable both to the younger generation and to the older generation.

This process, serious and essential though it is, one that calls for all the sincerity of which we are capable, need not be grim and full of suffering. It can be stimulating, deeply enjoyable, to work this way. Even if we as individuals make only a minor or a minimal contribution, or none, at least we will have had deep satisfaction in the process.

In part, the satisfaction comes from the fact that there are many new facts and concepts to learn, and many old ones to remember. For these new and old facts and concepts, we can draw upon many sources of data, from psychiatry, psychoanalysis, biology, anthropology, and other disciplines.

This is one version of the multidisciplinary approach, used very widely these days. Fortunately, it is a productive approach. The issues to be faced in a discussion of ethics provide so many challenges that it is important to indicate the value and the power of the approach used in meeting the challenges. To give a small sample of the value of multidisciplinary thinking, we can refer to an episode in one of the seminars in the Cincinnati Department of Psychiatry, in which experienced scholars of other disciplines join with psychiatrists in the education of residents-in-training in psychiatry.

During one of the teaching visits of the anthropologist Margaret Mead, she joined me in leading a seminar in which two residents-in-training in psychiatry presented their work with patients, for evaluation and suggestions from their fellow residents, from Dr. Mead and from me. It happened that day that both presenters were white and both their patients were black. Dr. Mead recognized, as did the rest of us, that perhaps as much as is humanly possible, these two residents were successful in dealing with black patients, as with white patients, in a sincerely unprejudiced fashion.

The two residents had only minimal residuals of past distortions.

The goal of training can not be perfection, but the goal must be a very high level of performance, in knowledge, in professional skill, and in ethical standards of interpersonal behavior. There must be an ongoing alertness on the part of the professional staff, white or black, to detect in themselves or in others, any inappropriate emotional responses to patients of either group, white or black, or to patients of other types or categories.

Out of her experience as an anthropologist, Margaret Mead can make observations and suggestions which are of high value in psychiatry. During this seminar she saw a contrast that we had not seen. She saw that one white resident, who had been raised in the deep South, and had had close physical contacts in his childhood with a black nurse and others, showed no trace of hesitation in doing a physical examination of a black patient, but still had minimal, barely perceptible traces of difficulty in developing the essentially equal-equal relation with another human being which is one of the components of the process of psychotherapy. In observing the work of the second white resident, who had been reared in New England, Margaret Mead was able to see the opposite combination. He showed some minimal traces, almost imperceptible, of hesitation in his physical contact with black patients, i.e. in doing a physical examination. But he had no difficulty in developing an essentially equal-equal relation in his psychotherapy with black patients.

Different childhood experiences in different parts of the country may account for certain differences in work patterns. The anthropologist, more quickly than the psychiatrist, may become aware of subcultural and regional patterns. These observations are of value in developing a more fully mature ethical behavior.

Such a multidisciplinary pattern of work leads to a rigorous and stringent study of professional behavior, with the goal of increasing the breadth and depth of professional ethical behavior. It broadens our outlook, by emphasizing the category of subcultural differences which can be important in our understanding and in our work. It calls attention to the fact that in the kind of stringent self-scrutiny which is an essential part of the practice of psychiatry, it is necessary to consider not only the issue of membership in a minority group or a majority group, but also to consider the issue of subgroups within a majority group or a minority group. Differential experiences in the subgroups may play a role in the appearance later of differential patterns of behavior.

Multidisciplinary work is not easy, not always sweetness and light. Each discipline must develop its own special language and the communication between them may be full of misunderstanding. And at times the suggestions from one discipline to another are made aggressively and in a provocative manner. And even a non-provocative suggestion may be regarded as an intrusion.

The risk is clear, and one may be tempted to follow the simple defensive ethical principle, that "discretion is the better part of valor." It would make life simpler and more comfortable. Perhaps it would be best to stifle the impulse to work with other disciplines. At times, when one steps outside one's own field, the workers in the other field are likely to attack vociferously and often justifiably. As a psychiatrist and a teacher, I am much too busy to be able to work directly in the field of anthropology, or animal biology, or mythology, etc. I can make only secondhand judgments. I can read voraciously. I can attend meetings of the other disciplines. I can discuss individual points with workers in other fields. And especially I can play a role in establishing seminars, such as the Perhaps Seminar in the Department of Psychiatry, in which members of other disciplines come to the Department almost every week to present and to discuss the material of their own fields.

Certainly when scholars in other fields talk about psychiatry, and one is tempted to attack, it is necessary to tell Satan, the tempter, to go home, to his own personal hell. Of course if the scholar of another field is wrong, one must discuss the issues; and if he is destructive, one must defend. But at times even a mistake can be productive.

A good example is the story of an extraordinarily gifted scholar of another field who used some of the material of psychiatry and made a mistake in the process. But when his comment is given the consideration it deserves, it is clear that it is a contribution of value.

The eminent philosopher and theologian, Martin Buber, commented that every contact between a psychiatrist and a patient manifests the I-Thou relationship, which is one of the central concepts in Buber's thinking.[5] In his categories, the I-Thou is a high-level phenomenon. Psychiatrists could take this comment as a compliment.

But in a strict sense, Buber's statement is not true. For example, a psychiatrist often is confronted with an exceedingly difficult human-relations problem with a patient during the process of treatment. At such times he may be tempted to respond to the patient not as a "Thou," as another human being with whom a relationship of trust and respect can be established, but rather as an "It," as an object, perhaps human, perhaps not human. At times this may be more than merely a temptation. For a brief period, it may be his dominant feeling, and his tone of voice may be cool or unfriendly.

To caricature the situation, one can say that there are times when the psychiatrist, or any physician, may revert to the fantasy that the ideal patient would be like the cadaver which he dissected as a first-year medical student, or to the fantasy that the ideal patient would be one who had been anesthetized for an operation. A cadaver or an anesthesized patient would be simpler to work on and could not talk back or disagree. Every physician occasionally must struggle against such temptations to simplify his complex and difficult life. By and large he succeeds well enough. Martin Buber's statement would have been more on target if he had said that the psychiatrist was in a lifetime struggle to regard his patients, for therapeutic and for ethical reasons, in an I-Thou fashion, and very often succeeded.

There is a second way in which the Buber statement of the I-Thou relation of psychiatrist and patient must be modified. There are instances in which a psychiatrist may sense that a patient is unable to bear the feeling of friendliness and helpfulness which is characteristic of the usual relation between psychiatrist and patient. The patient may respond as if such a relation is one of dangerous closeness. He may regard human beings as potentially tricky and harmful, and so to be kept at a distance. Another patient may be concerned that he himself may hurt anyone who does not keep his distance. When the psychiatrist recognizes that a patient has such intense anxiety about human relations, he may plan to see the patient only briefly at each contact. In our clinic such a patient may be scheduled for brief interviews with a different psychiatrist or resident-in-training for each appointment. Then the ongoing relation is not to an individual therapist, but to the clinic, providing a more impersonal relation which seems more tolerable. In such instances the relationship is not of the type that Buber would characterize as I-Thou. But one can add that the judgment of the patient's anxieties requiring such a limitation of the I-Thou relationship was based on an I-Thou process at the time of the diagnostic study.

It is clear that Buber was oversimplifying the situation and that his concept of psychiatric work was based on the paradigm of intensive individual psychotherapy. Surely one need not say that Buber's statement about psychiatry was seriously incorrect. Rather his comment had a basic correctness in spite of the fact that his lack of direct experience in psychiatry made his generalization too broad. In fact, his comment can stimulate psychiatrists to a further consideration of their work in the light of Buber's ideas, and so can be regarded as a contribution to the field.

We turn now to the discipline of animal biology for material relevant to the study of ethics. But as soon as we do, we face the danger of generalizing from limited data, and the danger of translating too easily from other animals to man. In that process, we are in danger of repeating the mistakes of the past, when material from the field of animal biology led to waves of optimism and to waves of pessimism about the future of mankind.

When the author studied in Europe toward the end of the 1920s, he heard many discussions of the "pecking order," a concept new to him at the time. These discussions were brought to mind vividly by many pages in the book by Robert Waelder, *Progress and Revolution,* and the review of that book by Lilla Veszy-Wagner.[6]

She speaks of a tremendous wave of pessimism about the loss of hope that in the "natural order" of animal life, there would be full equality of status and influence, and not merely the equality of opportunity and the equality of legal protection. There was a wave of pessimism in the intellectual circles of central Europe when for the first time there was published the account of the pecking order in several animal species, a pattern which since that time has been found to be widespread. The first report by Van Schelderup described the fact that in some species, in the barnyard and outside, a status order developed when animals lived together in a group. The largest and strongest quickly demonstrated his capacity to chase away any competitors pecking for food. The second strongest or most agile was able to push away or peck away or dominate all others except number one. Third place was taken by one who was able to establish his physical superiority over all but the two who were higher in the order, and so on down the list. The important point was that once such an order is established, it is adhered to fairly rigidly, with an occasional attempt on the part of someone lower on a list to displace one who is higher on the list. There are exceptions, in which there is a triangle instead of a straight line in the pecking order, in which A is higher than B and B is higher than C, but in certain ways C is higher than A. The usual pecking order or status arrangement applies chiefly to the obtaining of food, but applies also to priority in sexual partnerships, etc.

In the 1920s many of the European intellectuals were dedicated to a liberal democratic philosophy. They believed in the equality of man, perhaps even in the equality of man at birth, but certainly in the equality of opportunity and potential status for all men. They expected studies of animals other than man to indicate that this was the natural order of things, that infrahuman animals did not have caste or class arrangements, that caste or class or dominance was a purely cultural or economic or political phenomenon.

They were certain that in the natural biologic state, equality would be the rule. The finding of the regular appearance of the pecking order was a serious blow to such a hope for a biologic basis for democratic equality.

There can be a footnote to this story about the pecking order and the pessimism it engendered. The pecking order essentially is a pattern of order and stability even though it does not produce equality. The absence of some such orderly arrangement could result in a constant turmoil, of repeated belligerent tests of strength and superiority, and a chaotic and dangerous series of hostile interactions. Fundamentally the pecking order can be interpreted as the development of a pattern which has great survival value for the group. It prevents the struggles in the group from becoming damaging, even to the killing of members by others of the same species. It provides a *modus vivendi* in which energy can be directed in other ways. Perhaps it helps to assure a high rate of reproduction in animals of greater strength and potential for survival.

In a sense, a status order is a defensive social arrangement, a Defensive Ethics. It may represent the development of order and system as a defense against potentially rampant hostility. But it falls short of what we shall discuss later under the general rubric of a Creative Ethics, of equality, fairness, equal opportunity, and a mutually respecting partnership.

In contrast to the pessimistic response to the reports of the pecking order, a limited degree of optimism seems appropriate when we consider a number of recent developments in the field of biology. Or perhaps instead of speaking of optimism, one should speak of the negating of a previous pessimism, not the pessimism about the pecking order, but the more general pessimism of the post-Darwinian period, and even recently, about man's biologic heritage.

To outline this story, we start inevitably with the work of Darwin. From his work and that of many others, it is clear that man is an animal which is the product of an evolutionary process. In understanding that process, one of the essential ideas is that of natural selection, the survival of the fittest. Darwin emphasized the survival value of competition and strength and adaptation, but he recognized also to some degree the survival value of cooperation, especially in the ants and the bees. After Darwin, the concept of the survival of the fittest came to emphasize almost exclusively the violence of animals toward each other. Such phrases as "the law of the jungle," "nature red in fang and claw," "kill or be killed," became dominant. The general idea was that animals not only killed animals of other species for food, but also killed animals of the same species in a competitive struggle for existence.

This post-Darwinian emphasis on the destructive competitive struggle for biologic survival of the individual and of the species was used in the Industrial Revolution as a justification for destructive economic competition. The biologic struggle for survival was used also to justify the destructive competition of powerful nations, with each other and with the people of their colonies whom they regarded as biologically inferior. A stronger, more powerful individual (or group) was assumed to have the right, biologically, to compete violently with others and to win if he could.

Basically, the concept of animal intraspecies violence, the survival of the fittest, was taken to mean that man's animal heritage consisted essentially of murderous competition. It was assumed that the hostility and killing of man by man was primarily based on his biologic and evolutionary development.

The emphasis, in biologic science, has changed. The post-Darwinian accent on struggle and violence in animal life, with the Social Darwinism that followed its lead, resulted in a corrective movement. There was sharp criticism of Social Darwinism, among others by Julian Huxley and Richard Hofstadter.[7]

Further, studies of animals in their natural habitat, in the wild, have revealed the striking fact that a large number of species of animals live in social groups.[8] In many of these, patterns of cooperation and mutual help are of the essence, far outweighing the destructive competition. The bees and the ants are not the only species which have systems of mutual help. Fish swim in schools because such a cooperative system has survival value, helps to keep them alive. The group living of many animal species is of high value in the species' defense against predatory species and is of high value in the finding of food, both of which have obvious survival value. The end-point of such observations is the recognition that group living, cooperation, and mutual help must be regarded as having a most important place, alongside competition and struggle, as methods for the survival of the individual and of the species. This basic biologic fact, of the survival value of group living, of mutual help, is clearly important for our discussion of man.

At times the emphasis on cooperation and the criticism of Social Darwinism seemed to negate the biologic importance of competition. Now, the consensus seems to include the following points. One is that animals of many species are violent to the point of killing animals of other species, when one species uses the other as a source of food, or when one species defends itself against the attempt of other species to use it as food, or when two species interact in some other conflict-producing situation. Further, an animal may have violent fights with animals of the same species, its own species, almost to the point of killing, in protecting its territory against invaders, or if it is without territory, in trying to invade and take over the territory of another, or in struggles for status or dominance, or in struggles of sexual competition. But most frequently, according to many observers and researchers, animals of one species, even though they fight violently, have what seems to be an innate pattern of defense against killing members of the same species.

This has not been established with finality and varies from species to species. But many reports[9] seem to indicate that in a struggle between two members of the same species, in a struggle that seems to be reaching the point of one killing the other, the one which is losing gives a specific signal, such as turning the head and exposing its neck. The one which is winning responds to the signal. The loser leaves the field of battle, alive.

When there began to be reports of the "avoidance," in many species, of the killing of members of the same species, it seemed possible that man would be found to be the only animal which regularly kills members of its own species. This would be incorrect, an overstatement. It would be less an overstatement to say that man may be the only vertebrate animal except rats which regularly kills members of the same species as part of direct competitive fighting. This phrasing excludes the bees, which kill the drone as part of the insect cycle, it excludes certain insects which eat the young, and it excludes some other instances not related to competitive fighting.

But even the second statement may need to be modified. There are reports that some groups of rats kill each other in competitive fighting. This was reported in contemporary urban life, which in some densely populated areas may not be a good natural habitat even for rats. Also, I have been told that in a recent conference, some evidence was presented of the finding of bodies of individual primates which may have been killed in competitive struggles.

Still further, it seems that in captivity, or in a situation from which there is no escape, or in which a habitual pattern is blocked, animals may kill others of the same species. For example, when lemmings go on their march to the sea, they frequently snap at and bite each other. One study[10] of the lemmings indicated that when the members of the group could keep an adequate distance between them, none is hurt seriously. In one research project, several lemmings were caught during the march to the sea, and were placed overnight in a box which was not quite large enough to permit their usual defensive distancing. By morning, most of the lemmings were dead. Each had bled to death, after being bitten frequently by others of the group, when they could not use their usual pattern of defense, of staying a short distance away from each other.

The evidence is not all in, and judgments are far from final. But so far it seems probable that many or most or all of the vertebrate infrahuman animals in their natural habitat do not kill members of the same species in direct fighting. Man may be the only one which does, or may be one of a small number of species that do.

If this be true, it also is profoundly important. At least it permits

an important correction, which can be phrased as a double negative. It would negate the negative, the deeply pessimistic world-
view that man's membership in the animal kingdom means that man
as an animal is fated to violence, is doomed to continue killing
other men, since all other animals, it was thought, routinely or
frequently killed others of the same species. But if in large part
other animals do not, it becomes possible that the human animal
also has a biologic defense against species-specific killing, the kind
of defense which is characteristic of many other animals, but which
in man is unused or unusable. Or if, as seems more probable, man's
pattern of killing other men is more cultural than biologic in origin,
it would seem that a more fully effective defense in man against
killing other men could develop out of his culture.

Further, if man's killing of other men is found to be in good
part culturally based, the origins of that pattern of killing must be
studied in depth and in breadth. For example, it seems probable
that man's violence in general arises in good part out of the fact
that in man's infancy and childhood there is a prolonged period
of dependence, of relative helplessness and of vulnerability, a
period which is much longer, both in absolute and in relative terms,
than in other species. During this period of relative helplessness,
the child has many positive, constructive experiences, and many
periods of satisfaction and happiness. But during this vulnerable
period, the child goes through many disturbing experiences as well.
During this period, there may be episodes of violent emotions and
conflicts in the child, including periods of explosive anxiety and
hostility.

In this setting in childhood, the primitive defense of projection,
which is one pattern of high importance in man's inhumanity to
man, may have its origin. This sequence in the child may start with
intense rage, which then may lead to intense fear, guilt, and anxiety.
The rage then may be repressed with great intensity. But at
times, the defense of repression alone is not sufficient to contain
the surging drives and emotions. The emergency defense of projection may develop, in which the child goes through a spontaneous

unconscious process which consists of denying or disowning its own rage and attributing it to others rather than to himself. Phrasing the process another way, we can say that the rage and the associated impulse to damage or to destroy is projected outward.

Most children develop the process of projection to some degree, some much more than others. Such children, when they are adults, may visualize strangers (or other groups) as inevitably dangerous. The fact that the strangers or the members of another group are members of the same species, are human beings also, no longer seems important. The members of the other group are regarded as enemies, who may attack at any time.

Of course it is true that strangers, or other groups, are actually dangerous at times. But the process of projection may lead to a great increase in the frequency or in the intensity of the feeling of danger and in the expectation of being attacked. In an interpersonal situation based on or deeply influenced by this pattern, the policy of a preventive showdown or quarrel or confrontation may come to seem urgent and rational when the policy is badly mistaken. And in an international crisis, the use of the policy of a preventive attack or a preventive war may be based on a disastrous misreading of the realities.

The extraordinary importance for later life of the experiences in this early period of life is indicated by studies of other primates. There is convincing evidence, in Harlow's laboratory studies of monkeys, that even in animals which have much shorter periods of dependence than has man, experiences during infancy have profound and lasting effects throughout the rest of the animal's life.[11]

If man's killing of other men is rooted essentially in his early childhood, the eradication of man's killing of man still will not be easy, in fact may be extremely difficult. But it may not be the impossible task it seemed to be, in the thinking of the post-Darwinian period.

So far in our comments about biology we have noted two major trends. One is the finding that cooperation and mutual help is a widespread pattern of survival, along with the competitive struggles which have long been recognized as crucial for survival. The second is the frequency with which competitive struggles within a species include inborn techniques of preventing the intraspecies fights from resulting in the death of the loser.

Another important set of observations has to do with the primates, the animals most closely related to man, including the chimpanzee, the monkey, the gorilla, the baboon and others. Until recently the studies of primates were done with the animals in captivity, in the zoo or in an enclosed colony or in the laboratory. This is a productive setting for some types of studies, but it fails to give a good portrayal of the animal in its natural habitat, the patterns of its usual relations with others of its own species and with the rest of its environment. Captivity, and especially restriction to a small area, has drastic effects, as was seen most dramatically in the biologist's experiment with the lemmings. But now the primates are being studied as they are in the wild, in the free-ranging state, responding to their own biologic needs and patterns, and to the circumstances of their usual environment.

Among the movies of the baboon in its natural habitat, studied closely by Washburn, DeVore, and others, some show the troop of about fifteen baboons at the moment they suddenly became aware of the fact that dangerous predatory animals were about to attack them. The danger was immediate and desperate. The life, the survival, of the baboons was at stake. Their response was instantaneous. One striking point is that the oldest male baboons did not try to escape, did not run away, did not do what might have been safest for each one as an individual. Instead the three rushed in the direction from which the predators were coming and then stood facing them, between them and the rest of the retreating troop of baboons. The three baboons stood their ground, making what we can interpret as frightening gestures and repulsive faces. The three were in imminent danger of death. A baboon is relatively small. The predators were much larger, stronger, more powerful.

It is clear that the behavior of the three baboons increased the risk that they would be killed, and decreased the risk for the rest of the troop. The predators seemed slowed down by the rear-guard action of the elders of the tribe, and the rest of the troop escaped safely. Most often in such a situation the older males escape as well.

The temptation is to shout "Bravo!" and to say that this was profoundly, magnificently ethical, the kind of behavior to be expected of a grandfather. But again we say, "Satan, are you here again?" We must consider this further.

First, one can say that this is not the only situation in which an infrahuman animal behaves in a way which risks its life and simultaneously lessens the risk to others. Perhaps the best known of the older reports is the behavior of a mother bird (females as well as males behave with great courage!) which distracts the attention of attackers from the young in the nest. The mother bird flies around noisily, at times as if one of her own wings were broken, as if she herself might be a helpless prey.

The apparent similarity to certain instances of human behavior is obvious. In human life, an individual who behaves in a way which simultaneously endangers his or her own survival but increases the chance of the survival of others or of the group is regarded as showing one of the highest forms of ethical behavior.

But there are reasons for hesitation in speaking of the comparable behavior in animals other than man as clearly being ethical in the usual sense of the word. There is one point of difference in the behavior of the elder baboons and the comparable behavior in man. This has to do with the process of choice. The baboon in the reported situation of danger may have no choice. He may be responding as he must respond out of an inborn pattern of response to this situation. In the comparable situation in man, the protector can be said to make a choice, or seems to make a choice to fight the attackers rather than to run away. But there remains the solid fact that the social patterns of the baboon troop include one in which even the strongest members of the troop, the top three of their pecking order, will behave in a situation of great danger in a way which jeopardizes their own survival as it increases the chance of survival of the group.

The consideration of the problem of "choice" of behavior leads to several questions and issues. One is whether the definition of ethical behavior must include the fact that the individual chooses that behavior over some other variety of behavior. Certainly there are examples of behavior usually regarded as ethical which do not fit easily into a definition which includes that requirement. A boy who has been trained from a very early period to be a soldier, to sacrifice himself for his comrades whenever he is ordered to do so, or whenever he sees that it is needed, perhaps will always do so, without in a real sense being able to make a choice. At that point he may be unable to choose any behavior other than that of "doing his duty." His behavior in a sense can be called automatic. But it is a variety of automatic behavior which is learned, in contrast to the automatic behavior which we assume to be inborn, in the social patterns of the baboon.

It is conceivable that behavior like that of the baboon could be learned behavior. At least many animals can be taught many kinds of behavior by their human teachers or trainers. But the only clear example known to this author of a younger animal being taught by older members of the same species to carry out a task important for survival is the one reported by Jane Goodall.[12] In this pattern, an older chimpanzee teaches a younger one to make a tool, a sort of spongelike mass of leaves softened by chewing, which can be used to obtain water from a hollow tree. This pattern of teaching and learning appears during a dry period in which water is exceedingly difficult to find any place except in the hollow of a tree, when the water is out of reach of the hand alone, but within reach if the hand is holding the spongelike tool.

The issue of choice as a component of ethics can be considered from another angle. An eight-year-old boy was intensely envious of his baby sister, who, he was convinced, had taken his place in the affection of his parents. As his envy increased, he became exceedingly tense and anxious. At the same time he told the pediatrician about having terrifying dreams about little girls who disappear. Were he to recount the vivid dreams to you, the reader, you would recognize from his detailed description that the disappearing little girls were versions of his sister. But he himself did not recognize the resemblance. The inference seems valid that without his being conscious of his impulses, a part of him wants his baby sister to disappear. But he loved her as well, and most often he behaved toward her in a way that was very protective, as if he wanted to shield her from danger.

The next step in the sequence is that after his tension and anxiety continued for several weeks, he awakened one morning with a severe stiffness, almost a paralysis of both arms, and concurrently he was relaxed and peaceful. Various studies showed no organic, physical, bodily cause for the partial paralysis, which also had the recognizable characteristics of a hysterical paralysis. The odds seemed great that the paralysis was a defense against his unconscious wish to hurt his sister.

Such a defense has an ethical quality, in a sense. There is less danger that the boy might hurt his sister, now that he is sick and can not move his arms. He no longer needs to feel anxious or guilty or tense. In these ways, the defense has a positive value. But it exacts the serious price of the loss of the ability to move his arms, the paralysis.

In this simple defensive ethical sequence, we can not say that the boy made a conscious choice to be paralyzed rather than to continue having a conscious impulse to hurt his sister, about which he was consciously anxious and guilty. Rather the choice, if we use the word, was an unconscious choice about an unconscious impulse.

These considerations and many others seem to call for a definition of ethical behavior that will be broad enough to include automatic behavior, unconscious choice, and unconscious temptations. And it could include simple, perhaps primitive, forms of ethical behavior.

A broad definition of ethical behavior (to amplify the one given at the end of Chapter II) could start with simple social behavior, innate or learned, which has a primary social value, a value for others or for the group, such as a warning signal of impending danger given by one animal to others, a system of mutual help. As the next step, the broad definition would include a social behavior pattern of mutual help such as the one of the baboon troop, which in addition requires that even the strongest of the group behave in a way that subordinates their own interests to those of the group. Then ethical behavior, as the next step, would include social behavior based on the conscious choice of a pattern of social value over a pattern which has only individual value. Perhaps a general definition must emphasize this type of behavior, since ethical teaching most often emphasizes the process of a deliberate and conscious choice of one alternative over another.

Later we shall discuss the fact that a general definition of ethical behavior would go beyond an exclusive emphasis on the fact that ethical behavior is valuable for the group as a whole or for the other members of the group, and see that a general definition would include also an emphasis on having the ethical behavior be of value, whenever possible, to the individual himself. In this type of ethics, high emphasis might be placed both on the individual and his values and on the stability of the group and its values.

The consideration of the question of choice as a component of ethical activity led us to consider some of the issues involved in a further definition of ethical behavior. But we must not be distracted from a recognition of the basic contribution of the description of the social behavior of the baboons and of other species of non-human animals to our central thesis.

The existence of this kind of organized social behavior in animals other than man, whether it is called ethical or not, seems profoundly important. Such behavior indicates that the social patterns in man, which are so valuable, are not to be regarded as psychologic or cultural epiphenomena, superimposed on man's biologic heritage. Rather, the extensive and varied social behavior of the other animals indicates that man's socially oriented patterns may be a part of man's biologic heritage, as well as a part of his cultural heritage, the behavior he learns after he is born. If this be true, the strong forces of violence, of destructiveness, of war, and of other forms of man's inhumanity to man, which perhaps are biologic, cultural, and individual in origin, may be matched within man by the further development of strong counterforces of socially oriented patterns, which also are biologic, cultural, and individual in origin.

To rephrase this, the concept now seems tenable that man's pattern of living in a social order, and of having social customs which govern the relation of one man to other men and to the group (often in the form of ethical standards), is consistent with, and in continuity with, the pattern of living in a social order which is so prominent in the lives of many other animals.

We must not expect that a study of the behavior of other animals will lead to an understanding of the specifics of man's behavior and of his ethics.[13] Each species differs so much that a simple translation is impossible. But we can say with conviction that the study of the behavior of other animals does *not* lead to the conclusion that reliable patterns of ethical behavior are impossible in man simply because he is an animal.

The emphasis on the social life of other animals must not permit us to forget that in animal life there is extraordinary cruelty, predatory attacks, fighting for territory, fighting for dominance, and other destructive behavior. The emphasis rather is on the fact that there is a large variety of attempts to control the violence, especially when it is directed toward members of the same species. And in animal life there seem to be many highly developed patterns of cooperation and mutual help as well as highly developed patterns of competition and violence.

With this in mind, we can avoid the romantic fantasy of the natural animal as the embodiment of innocence, purity, simplicity, and love. And with this in mind, we also can avoid the post-Darwinian distortion that the jungle is a place in which animals are engaged most of their lives in destroying members of the same species and others. That also is a fantasy, a pseudorealistic, pseudosophisticated illusion.

No longer can we rationalize or justify anti-ethical activity by saying that man is an animal, and therefore has only primary and perhaps irresistible impulses to hurt, to kill, to attack, and to dominate. Also, no longer can we say that man's animal heritage means that he cannot have inborn patterns of cooperation. Some day it may be possible to say with certainty that man has the biologic as well as the cultural potential for both such patterns, and that both may play a role in his development.

To recapitulate: The studies of other animals do not lead to a thorough understanding of the behavior of man. That will come only from the study of man himself. But the recent studies of other animals permit us to go forward with our study of man without the gnawing doubt that when we talk of man's cooperation and mutual help, of his socially valuable patterns, of his attempts to control his destructive drives, and of his attempts to consider the well-being of others as well as of himself, we might as well be talking of a being which is not an animal. But now we can speak of man as an animal, and know that when we speak of his helpfulness to others and of his socially oriented patterns, we are speaking of patterns like those which can be found throughout much of the animal kingdom.

With this biologic baseline established, we can turn to the extraordinary ways in which man has developed far beyond the other animals. In the next chapter we shall look directly at man, not only at man as an animal, but also at man as a member of his society and his culture, and especially at man as himself. And we shall look closely at the forces within man, which may be in harmony with each other, but which often are in resounding conflict. It is our study of these forces, the conflict between them and the resolutions of these conflicts, which gives us our best understanding of the agony and the ecstasy of life, of the richness, the fullness, the emptiness, and the heartache of life, and of the creativeness and destructiveness in the life of man. And the issues of ethical behavior and ethical principles play a major role in the understanding of man's conflicts and of man's solutions.

4

Defensive Ethics

I n the last chapter, we focused on the study of animals other than man. In this chapter, we will focus on man, especially on the intensive psychiatric and psychoanalytic study of many patients of many types. The impact of that understanding on our thinking about ethical principles and ethical behavior will become apparent.

Many good books have been written about psychiatry and psychoanalysis. Therefore, one of the challenges in preparing this chapter was to present significant material which would not merely duplicate what can be found in the library. To meet this challenge, I will avoid starting in the usual way, which would be to present the central facts or concepts of psychiatry. Instead I will discuss the kind of thinking about life which has been so amazingly productive in this field, as well as in many other sciences and disciplines.

The type of thinking which deserves such high praise can be outlined most clearly by contrasting it with two simpler, less effective types of thinking. In this presentation, the two less highly regarded types of thinking will be described first. Then the third type of thinking, the most effective variety of the three, will be discussed in greater depth.

There are several phrases which characterize each of the three types of thinking. The first can be called the "Life Is Simple" kind of thinking. It uses stereotypes. It is the one-sided approach. The second type of thinking can be called the "Either-Or." It uses polar opposites. It is the two-sided approach. The third type, the one which deserves the highest respect, can be called the "Dynamic Realistic" kind of thinking. It uses a pluralistic approach.

Inevitably many of those who read a comment which mentions two less highly regarded types of thinking and one which is highly regarded will take it personally and wonder, "Do I use the third type of thinking?" "Is it beyond me?" "How am I doing?"

The question deserves an answer, for the sake of full understanding of the concepts. Even more, the question deserves an answer as part of the working alliance between reader and author.

Fortunately, in this issue, the answer is easy. The words used to describe the third type of thinking may seem weighty and threatening. But it is clear that the third type of thinking is not rare, nor is it unusually difficult. In everyday life, all of us often use the high-level, third kind of thinking. But most of us, under pressure, or because of prejudice, or simply because of lack of information, often slip back into the first or second kinds of thinking.

If that happens, and if one catches oneself doing it, the remedy is clear. One must refuse, congenially but firmly, to let oneself take the easy way out. One must set limits on oneself, must expect a level of performance from oneself which in a way is the essence of a workable ethical system. In spite of rumors to the contrary, psychiatry does not recommend an overly permissive attitude in life. One must say "no," especially to oneself, many times every day. Hopefully one can say "yes" even more frequently. And anticipating one point in the discussion, one can say that in the third kind of thinking one can even more often say, "Yes, if it's the right time, the right place and with the right person."

Now to describe each of the three types of thinking more fully. The first kind is the "Life Is Simple" approach, the one-sided judgment, the quick simplicity. It is the least effective. It may be the expression of a simple prejudice or a preformed opinion. Typical of this kind of thinking are such expressions as: "He is a bad boy"; "She is a good girl"; and "Fever is bad." Another example of this type of thinking is a description of a person in terms of a single character trait, e.g. "Tom Smith is an independent person"; or "John Jones is selfish"; or "Wilson is generous"; or "Mary Brown is oversexed."

Such a simple sentence may be taken as being true at times, if it is recognized as being merely the labeling of an individual by a single fact which appears most frequently, or most obviously. But if one takes more than a quick glance at the facts, each of the simple sentences can be seen to be badly oversimplified, and merely a minor fragment of the truth. Then one can see that other facets of the situation are present also. John Jones, labeled as selfish, may be selfish in a sense, but he can be seen to be more than that. If several words were used, rather than one, they could give a picture a hundred times as valid.

The "Life Is Simple" approach is good enough for casual or unimportant issues, for moments or days of relaxation, and for carefree or careless conversation. But it is unworkable in a situation in which one must think clearly and deal adequately with the facts. For example, when a medical student becomes the youngest member of a hospital team which is responsible for the diagnosis and treatment of patients, he must go beyond the first kind of thinking. He learns that fever is not altogether bad. In fact, most often fever is part of a life-saving, or at least a health-restoring, defense against infection. And he will learn that Mary Brown, whose repeated promiscuous behavior resulted in her being called oversexed, may surprise him, when she trusts him enough to be honest, by telling him that usually she finds that sexual experience is unpleasant.

So the stereotype, the one-angle approach, does not work, when the chips are down. Usually one who has been using it has sensed its shortcomings, and has begun to use the second type of thinking. This second type can be called the "Either-Or" type of thinking. This is the two-sided or bilateral approach, the use of dichotomies.

The observer who in the first type of thinking, had said that "Wilson is generous," now in the second type of observing and thinking, might say that "Wilson is generous but I've seen him be stingy. He seems to be one or the other. He is inconsistent." At this stage the observer can see that life is more varied than he thought. Now he can see at least two sides or two possibilities, and he sees that no amount of wishful thinking can keep it more simple and easy. The observer has made a major step toward a workable testing of reality.

The medical student who is using the second type of thinking knows now at least two facts about fever. First he knows that fever often is favorable, a sign of a protective reaction of the body against germs or other invaders. And the student comes to know as a second fact that occasionally the opposite is true: fever is unfavorable when the temperature mechanism gets out of hand, the temperature goes sky-high, and the patient is in danger of being damaged in that process.

In the second kind of thinking, the usual concept of human nature is that there are two kinds of people, good guys and bad guys. In many TV programs, there must be the good guy, the sheriff, the marshal, the missionary impossible, and then the bad guy, the outlaw, the evil organization, the enemy of law and order, or the enemy of justice.

The two-sided concept of human nature is found not only in a melodrama. In the personal life of many a man, there are important dichotomies, important two-sided polarizations in his thinking and feeling. Many a man, and even more boys, think of women as belonging to two sharply demarcated types. One is the pure, sweet, tender, nonphysical, nonsexual, Madonnalike figure, like mother or sister. The second is the prostitute figure or the promiscuous one, completely sexual, who wants to arouse sexual feelings in men or boys, a woman who is devoid of love and tenderness or ethical and aesthetic feelings, and so is completely unlike the woman of purity.

Such a dichotomy often is based on a boy's hidden anxiety over his own unacceptable impulses. If he is convinced that there is in truth a sharp difference between the pure woman and the sexual woman, he has an automatic pattern which blocks his thinking of a girl or a woman of the first group as having sexual feelings, or as arousing sexual feelings in him, since she is pure and non-sexual. So the dichotomy prevents his feeling anxious or guilty. Parenthetically, a deeply etched Madonna-prostitute dichotomy later may provide a real hurdle for a man when he marries and must accept the fact that the normal equivalent of both types can exist in the same woman.

Such dichotomized attitudes are frequent, in reality. For example, when Gerson Sholom, the historian of mysticism, was Visiting Professor at the Hebrew Union College several years ago, he gave a seminar in the Department of Psychiatry on his research on the life of Shabbatai Zvi, the so-called False Messiah of the seventeenth century. One recorded fact was that Shabbatai Zvi was totally impotent with his wife, whom he respected and loved. They had no children. Later he married a prostitute and was potent. They had several children.

Another example of the second approach can be seen in the progressive development of an observer who, on the basis of experience, no longer can say simply that Tom Smith is an independent person, as he said in the first type of thinking. The observer has come to see that Tom Smith has another side of his personality, that at times Tom's attitude is inconsistent with his usual independence, in fact seems to be a bipolar opposite. The observer has seen that Tom Smith occasionally behaves in a dependent and rather infantile fashion, for example constantly wanting attention from his wife or from the hospital nurses. In the observer's second type of thinking, Tom Smith is regarded as inconsistent or contradictory, with two sides to his character, at times being independent and self-sufficient and at other times being dependent and clinging to others for help and protection.

It is clear from these examples that the Dr. Jekyll and Mr. Hyde story is an extreme example of the "Either-Or" kind of thinking.

We come now to the transition from the second type of thinking to the third type. We can say that inescapably an observer who wants to think clearly has come to see that the "Either-Or," the two-sided approach, superior as it is to the one-sided stereotype, still does not work effectively or fully in many instances. It is good enough for a relaxed enjoyment of most TV programs and of simpler novels, to have the characters be good guys or bad guys; but even this soon palls. The writers of great literature—Sophocles, Shakespeare, Dickens, Goethe, Dostoevsky, the galaxy of dramatists, novelists, poets, and biographers—have recognized the fact, or knew it without thinking about it, that they must go beyond the Either-Or of the good-guy bad-guy portrayal of characters. The basis of great literature certainly is that good guys often are bad, in action or in impulse, in general ways or in specific and idiosyncratic ways, and further that villains in many ways are good guys, and may be heroic. Captain Ahab in Melville's *Moby Dick* is not merely a hero, and not merely a villain.

Further, it is clear that ethics, like literature, can not rest content with the idea that one man is good and another man is bad. It seems apparent that all human beings are both good and bad. Perhaps it is true also that the real enemy in life is not the bad man or the bad group; perhaps the real enemy is the "bad" in all men. But one must add that when a man or a group actually behaves overtly in a destructive way, in important and serious areas in life, that man or that group in actuality does become the enemy.

We return again to the contrast of the second and third types of thinking. The "Either-Or," bipolar approach is much too naive, for literature, for scientific understanding, and for ethics. It can be replaced in most instances by the third kind of thinking, the Dynamic, the one which recognizes the existence of interacting forces in human life. This type of thinking is more realistic, more mature, and more workable.

Several other phrases are of value in clarifying the concept of a third kind of thinking. One is of calling it the use of third alternatives. For example, when the "Either-Or" approach insists that a man is either a good guy or a bad guy, the third kind of thinking would take for granted that these two alternatives are not enough. There are many other alternatives. One is that a man may be partly a good guy and partly a bad guy, most of the time. A woman may be a very good wife in her overt behavior, but in her thoughts and fantasies be full of anger, of hatred, and even of murderous impulses toward her husband. Another alternative is that she may be a good wife in her overt behavior and good also in her conscious thoughts, but unconsciously be full of repressed rage toward her husband.

It is not easy to think about thinking. From my past experience, I would hazard a guess that this book needs a change of pace at this point. So, remembering the reader-author alliance, I can provide the necessary change of pace by including a lighthearted story, which points up some of the practical problems that result from the "Either-Or" approach.

Mr. Jones was the president of a railroad. He decided that the company needed a new lawyer. He talked to the senior partner of a large law firm, who was very pleased to hear that the new client might shift to his law firm a large part of the railroad's law business.

But Jones said that he would do so only on one condition, which was that the lawyer who would be assigned to handle his business must be a one-armed man. Jones gave no explanation, and said that he did not want to discuss it.

The senior partner of the law firm said that one of his best friends was a man who had only one arm, but he was not a lawyer. There was no one-armed lawyer on their staff at the moment, but they would look for one. Finally they found one whom they liked, who had lost an arm in military service. He joined the firm, and he and Mr. Jones worked well together.

The pending railroad case was successful, and Jones decided that he would transfer all of his legal work to the new firm. The atmosphere by this time was very congenial, and the senior law partner thought it was safe now to press the point. He told Mr. Jones that he still was very curious about his insisting that the new lawyer have only one arm. Jones said, "Look, it's simple. I couldn't take it any longer with that other firm. Every time I asked one of the lawyers a question about my business, he would say, 'Well, on the one hand it could be this way, but on the other hand it could be that way.' I just couldn't take it any more. I had to have a one-armed man, a one-handed lawyer. . . . What I really need, of course, is a lawyer who will consider both sides of an issue, and then will give me his considered opinion, his best advice."

To return to our discussion of types of thinking, we can say that most of the time, life is not simple enough for dichotomies, as it was not simple enough for stereotypes. This has implications for ethics. I shall carry this further, by quoting a case, modifying the report in a way that preserves confidentiality but does not change the essential dynamic facts.

The case is that of a fireman who was admitted to the hospital with advanced cancer of the bladder. He was an intelligent man, but he had not had a physical examination during the past six months even though he saw traces of blood in his urine several times a week during the six months, and even though as a fireman he was entitled to medical examinations without cost to himself. He knew intellectually that the cancer-society warnings about such changes were correct, and he knew that blood in the urine deserves serious consideration. Even so, he delayed, with the rationalization that it was only a cold or a scratch or an irritation. Obviously he must have been afraid that he had a serious illness, and we know that some persons who are anxious about physical disease may unconsciously defend themselves from finding out whether they have it or not. But the defense of not finding out can be like the Maginot Line, providing merely a false feeling of security. There are better defenses.

In this man there was a pattern which was even more important than anxiety in causing his delay in asking for medical care. The overriding point was that all through his life his central principle was that a real man must be strong, be unafraid, should not be frightened by a minor illness, should not be anxious about blood.

78

But this pattern, which ordinarily is regarded as valuable and as a good ethical standard, had played a part in leading him to a denial of the danger inherent in urinating blood. When he came for help, he was beyond effective treatment, and he died. His death was due to cancer, but it was due also to the fact that he had delayed coming for help.

Such a death can not be understood sufficiently by asking the typical questions of the "Either-Or" type of thinking, of whether an illness is organic or functional. The understanding must be in terms of a summation or a combination of two sets of facts, not "Either-Or" but "And-And." His death was due to the organic cause, the cancer, *and* his death was due to the personality patterns that led him to delay medical care beyond the point of recovery.

A closer look at this case can throw some light on our thinking about ethics. First, it is important to say that this patient's failure to take care of himself was not based on stupidity, on lack of intelligence, even though he behaved illogically. Rather his failure to take care of himself was based on the dynamics of his emotional life. Part of this process can be visualized as a conflict of ethical standards within himself, a conflict between two voices of conscience, each voice contradicting the other.

One voice of conscience was the expression of a set of ethical principles centering around the need to be strong and brave and to avoid excessive complaining. For the most part, this pattern was workable, realistic, and self-respecting. But in part it was excessive and rigid—related to the persistence of certain unfortunate experiences and responses much earlier in his life. His mother often expressed some contempt, he thought, when she would say that the father was "much too fussy and too scared about his health." So the son, after he was grown, behaved at times as "bravely" as he thought his mother had wanted his father to behave. In part, it would seem, the son had caricatured and exaggerated the mother's attitude. At times, therefore, the son's ethical principle of being brave and of not complaining actually ignored the realities, as in his fatal illness.

We know also, from many other facts and events in his life, that he had a second set of ethical principles. This would be the ethics of living rather than of dying, of preventing an unnecessary death, of wanting to live because one's life has value and meaning to oneself and to others. This set of principles, had it not been opposed by other forces, would have led him quickly to seek early diagnosis and treatment. This pattern of ethics also, for the most part, was workable and realistic. It too had a minor neurotic component, of an occasional excessive anxiety about his own health and that of his family.

This patient, then, had two sets of ethical principles. More important, to some degree the two sets could press him in different directions, could be in conflict. Each set of principles on its own is a fairly good one and deserves our respect. But when two ethical systems co-exist in one man, are contradictory, and have not been integrated, the result may be unfortunate.

If the physician can recognize the conflict of ethical principles, he may help the patient if it is not too late. But if it is too late, the physician still must consider the ways in which, in other patients, a potential conflict between two such ethical systems can be avoided or resolved. He must consider also the ways this pattern can be discussed as a part of the general teaching about ethics.

There are several ways in which the ethics of bravery and of a noncomplaining attitude could be integrated with the ethics of preventing unnecessary pain and disability and death. One solution is to work toward having a flexible combination of the two ethical principles. For example, the pattern of being unafraid and noncomplaining could be dominant most of the time, and the ethics of a foresighted attention to signs or symptoms of possible medical illness could be dominant at other times.

In this resolution of the conflict, the key point must be the realistic consideration by the individual himself of whether a symptom is potentially serious. And there will be times when he can not be certain how to evaluate his own symptoms. To cover this situation, he could have an understanding in advance with his physician, that when he, the patient, is not sure how seriously to take a symptom, he will phone the physician, not to ask for an appointment but to give a brief description of the symptom. Then the two of them can decide if an appointment is necessary.

The discussion of conflicts within the conscience, and their resolution, is an example of the third type of thinking, dynamic, realistic, and integrative. In any discussion of the third type of thinking, the word "dynamic" is prominent. It can serve as a transition word, linking this section to the discussion of the concepts of psychodynamics.

The word "dynamic" stands in contrast to the word "static." The word "dynamics" refers to forces at work. Thermodynamics refers to the forces of heat, hydrodynamics to the forces of water, and psychodynamics to the forces of human drives and emotion and of inner conflict.

To clarify the concept of dynamics, of forces at work, and their interplay, I shall give an example from a fourth field, physiologic dynamics, the dynamics of body processes. When the fluids of the body are studied, one good starting point is that a body fluid can be acid or alkaline. But this is not enough. It would be using the "Either-Or" approach to stop at that point. It would be a static statement. Instead, if the study is to be adequate and productive, the understanding of body fluids must include the fact that there are changes in the acidity or alkalinity, that there are forces working in both directions, some to make the body fluids more acid and others to make the fluids more alkaline. The real focus then is on the degree of power of those forces, and on their reaching an equilibrium, an acid-base equilibrium, at a point which permits good functioning of the organs of the body.

Next, one can add that as part of various illnesses, a child's body fluids may become more strongly acid (a condition called acidosis) which may become dangerous. When that shift occurs, there occurs also one of the most extraordinary events in this, our world. Automatically, there are body responses to the acidosis. The body responses produce a swing in the alkaline direction, to restore the equilibrium, to bring back again the steady state, a homeostasis. If the swing goes too far, toward alkalosis, automatic body responses produce a swing in an acid direction.

This process provides one reason for saying that most of the time one can trust one's body to take care of itself. It is an enormously important fact that in many ways a noxious state, a potentially dangerous state of an organism, will automatically call out responses, defenses, that bring back homeostasis, a steady state, a healthy state. This occurs in temperature regulation, in water regulation, and many other body processes.

Nevertheless, severe illness exists, and at times one must not trust the body to take care of itself. At times the defensive or equilibrating process fails to work well enough, an illness occurs, and external help is needed.

The study of the automatic equilibrating forces of the human body led Walter B. Cannon to use the term "The Wisdom of the Body" as the title of the superb book which describes such processes.[14]

Obviously Cannon is speaking metaphorically, in "as-if" terms. It is "as-if" the body wisely sensed the danger of increasing acidity and averted the danger by setting in motion an opposing force.

The success of that metaphor tempts me to use the metaphor of the "Ethics of the Body." I shall resist that temptation. But in the table of "Defenses, Defensive Ethics, and Creative Ethics," later in this chapter (page 95), I shall use, in a sense, a concept of the ethics of the body, by including a "physiology parallel" to Defensive Ethics, and by including physiology parallels to Creative Ethics.

To turn now to psychodynamics, we can say that a process very similar to body homeostasis occurs at the level of human behavior and feeling, at the level of emotional conflict. An adolescent boy of seventeen or eighteen may have the emotional drive to show he is a man, a very strong man, the strongest man, and the drive to prove it by sexual conquests and by fighting. The same adolescent may have the dynamic emotional drive to prove he is just a little boy. These forces often are in conflict. A swing in either direction may produce anxiety in the adolescent, and be followed by a swing in the other direction. Finally the two forces may come to an uneasy equilibrium, a temporary steady state, which is vulnerable to the stress of internal pressures, and vulnerable to the stress of external stimulation, of temptation. The accentuation of one force, either the pseudomasculine drive, or the pseudoweak-little-boy drive, may lead to an increase of the force acting in the opposite direction. Shortly I shall amplify this point, and carry the understanding of psychodynamics a step further by a discussion of two other human patterns, the wish to be independent, to be one's own boss, and the wish to be dependent, protected, and cared for.

The third kind of thinking, the recognition of emotional forces and their effects, can replace the use of static stereotypes and the use of good-guy bad-guy simple dichotomies, and may provide a way of understanding the "themes and variations," the fullness of human life. Also, the third type of thinking is the realistic approach, the pluralistic and multidimensional point of view, the approach of flexibility and combinations, an awareness of reactions and interactions.

Further, I want to add that this way of looking at life is more than the simple Hegelian formula which often is diagramed as a triangle or a pyramid, of thesis, antithesis, and synthesis. Thesis and antithesis are the two angles at the base of the triangle or the pyramid, and correspond somewhat to our description of the "Either-Or." The synthesis is diagramed as the top of the triangle or pyramid, and represents the attempt to go beyond and to bring together the thesis and antithesis.

The formulation which I use does begin with a Hegelian kind of pattern. But it becomes much more dynamic. The difference is highlighted by the fact that the dynamic approach is much better symbolized by a turning wheel or by the full circle turn of the hands of the clock, than by a stationary triangle or pyramid.

Now to point up the difference between this formulation and the Hegelian one, and to carry the understanding of dynamics a step forward, and further to indicate the richness and the fullness of the third kind of thinking, the dynamic approach, we turn to a discussion of the problem of independence and dependence. This is one of the most important equilibrating pendulum swings or circles in human life.

Earlier in this discussion it became clear that a "Life Is Simple" approach, of calling Tom Smith an independent guy, was not enough. A bipolar statement carried things at least a good step forward, recognizing Tom Smith's periods of dependence as well as his independence, and the inconsistency and contradictions in his behavior which are the result. But now we must say that this dichotomy also is not enough. We must think in terms of third alternatives, of interactions, of a process very similar to that of homeostasis.

Again we can start with a biologic fact. The human animal is the only species in which the young are dependent for a number of years on the older members of the group, for help, for food, for protection, for security. This period includes the first five years or so, in which many a child would die if no adults were there to help him stay alive. The period of dependence also includes many more years of childhood in which the individual is not yet ready to be on his own, to live independent of parents or other adults. This biologic species-pattern provides an extraordinary opportunity for the transmission of a cultural heritage. No other animal has such a long period of dependence nor such a rich inheritance to receive after it is born.

Apparently this early period leaves a profound impression in many ways. One is that the protracted experience of dependence is associated with many positive feelings of being cared for and protected. In this long period, the child's independence strivings inevitably are frustrated or blocked in varying degrees, by his small size, by his immaturity, or by the adults around him. He has fewer of the satisfactions of independence, and many more of dependence. The long period of relative dependence provides an experience of potential peace and comfort, of safety and security, of Nirvana, which often is idealized. Then it exerts a fascination throughout the individual's life.

Added to this is the fact that the period of dependence is the most vulnerable time for the child, during which destructive events can occur to which the child may respond in excessive ways. The destructive experiences and his own excessive responses may increase his need to be safe and secure, to be protected, to be fed, to be loved, to be cared for. The end result is that many human beings have a carry-over, a hang-up, in later life, of a strong and lasting drive for dependence and help. (See page 86: Using the shape and the numbers of a clock as a diagram, the dependent, help-seeking drives are visualized at 12 o'clock. At this point in the discussion, the big hand points to 12 o'clock, which is marked "dependence and passivity.")

But for many individuals, especially as they grow older, in childhood and after, a strong dependent drive is felt as if it were a noxious state. For many human beings, the urge to be dependent is shameful. (On the clock diagram, an arrow stretches in a curve from 12 o'clock to 3, to indicate the movement of the big hand in a clockwise direction.) Many a man would have his pride hurt deeply if he were to show, or even to recognize, his wishes to be cared for and protected, and would think of them as inferior, as stigmatizing him as a little boy. In other men, the dependent wishes arouse anxiety rather than shame, with the feeling that it is dangerous to be dependent on others, that this is a weak position, and that in such a position one can be attacked and damaged. (The big hand has moved to 3 o'clock, which is marked "anxiety and shame.")

And so, out of shame or out of fear, many a man denies totally that he has dependent wishes. He may become rabidly independent and self-sufficient, as a way of showing himself and the world that he is not a dependent little boy. (The big hand has followed the arrow from 3 to 6 o'clock, which is labeled "independence and aggressiveness.")

But independence, in turn, may be felt as noxious. In the eyes of many men, the attitude of great independence is dangerous.

CHART OF THE TURN OF THE WHEEL
OR THE HAND OF THE CLOCK

Relatively mature responses are indicated
within the circle; neurotic responses are
indicated outside the circle.

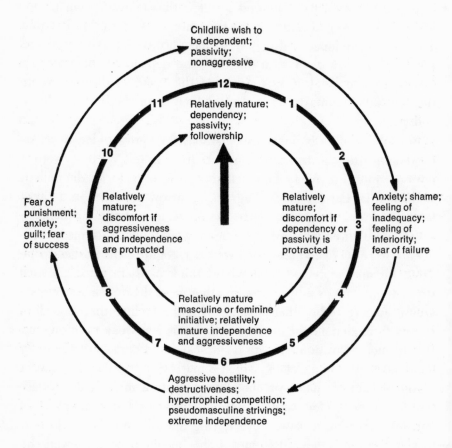

The diagram represents one of the frequent patterns of psychodynamics. Hostile competitive drives (6 o'clock) lead to guilt (9 o'clock), which lead to dependent or passive patterns (12 o'clock), which lead to shame (3 o'clock), which lead back again to independent and competitive drives (6 o'clock). The clockwise sequence continues, unless internal or external forces modify the pattern.

They may feel that independence is linked with strong hostile aggressiveness, that independence means too much dangerous competition, that it means giving up the chance of being helped, that it means being too much on one's own, of sticking out one's neck, perhaps hurting others or being hurt. (The big hand now is moving toward 9 o'clock, which is marked "fear of punishment, anxiety and guilt.")

Independence strivings, then, may lead to a flight in a direction away from independence, to an emphasis on dependence again. (The big hand has moved past 9 o'clock to 12, "dependence and passivity.") This is felt for a while as safe and secure, but again often leads to shame (3 o'clock) and so again to a period of independence (6 o'clock).

Such a full circle of the hand of the clock, repeated again and again, symbolizes the fact that dependence and independence are not merely a static pair of bipolar opposites, an either-or, but are closely related, each leading to the other, in a sequence that is understandable, a sort of "logic of the emotions." Such sequences could be diagramed as a repeated turning of a wheel, or as a pendulum swing or an upward or a downward spiral.

In some aspects of scientific work, far more sophisticated diagrams or mathematical models may be used. Eventually, such models may be appropriate for a precise and detailed study of psychiatry and of ethics. But at present the relatively simple model of the turning wheel or the rotating hand of the clock seems as sophisticated as it needs to be. Further, that diagram or model is obviously much more complex or sophisticated than would be a diagram for a stereotype or a diagram for a dichotomy, and so is acceptable enough for our current level of understanding of this aspect of psychodynamics.

The diagram is suitable for a discussion of homeostatic equilibria, and of many intrapsychic and interpersonal interactions. But when the physiologic process to be diagramed includes a shift in the whole homeostatic equilibrium to another level, the diagram must be modified, perhaps by having a second wheel. Similarly if in the psychodynamic process to be diagramed, there develops a new level or a new defense or a new resolution of the intrapsychic conflict, the diagram must be modified also. In the diagram on page 86, one way of indicating the new resolution is used. The relatively normal and mature version of the sequence in the logic of the emotions is shown inside the circle which marks the circumference of the clock.

Using the third type of thinking, and using the facts and concepts of psychodynamics such as those outlined above, we can try in the second half of this chapter to develop a dynamic, pluralistic approach to the field of ethics. In this, one basic concept will be Defensive Ethics.

Before we do so, however, there is another point of approach which will add strength to the foundation on which the concept of Defensive Ethics can rest. To make this point, we shall compare the content of this chapter, as given so far, with the content of the previous chapter, on "Survival and Ethics." This will provide us with a dramatic contrast, which in turn will suggest a new category for the definition of man, and will relate to the concept of Defensive Ethics.

In the previous chapter, the essence of the discussion centered around the patterns of survival in animals other than man. In those processes, all of the action seems to take place in the relation of one animal to other animals and to the rest of the external world. One animal competes with another, fights with him, lets him go. Or one animal kills another kind of animal for food. Or one animal helps another or is helped. Or animals get food from the world, or are in danger from the world. In each item the common denominator is the focus on the relation of an animal with the world *outside* itself, the world of other animals, of plants, and of the inanimate environment. And that chapter is typical of publications which report the studies of animals other than man.

In the present chapter, the discussion so far has concentrated on the human animal itself. The essence of the discussion in this chapter was *not* on events outside, but on events *inside* the human animal. (This chapter is typical of most publications which report the psychoanalytic studies of man.) In one instance, it was the conflict in *one* man, between his own dependence and his own independence. In a second, it was the contrast in Mr. Smith, between his own generosity and his own stinginess. In a third, it was the adolescent boy's conflict between his pseudomasculinity and his pseudo little-boy striving. In the fireman, it was the conflict within himself, between his own ethical principle of being brave and uncomplaining and his own ethical principle of wanting to prevent damage to himself and to remain alive and healthy for his own sake and that of his family.

This contrast in the emphasis in the two chapters can be stated more sharply. In the previous chapter the major emphasis was on the interaction of an infrahuman animal with the world *outside* that animal. In this chapter, the major emphasis has been on the relation with each other of the various forces which are *part of,* which are *inside* the human animal.

But we must add that these statements are not supposed to represent the total situation in man and in the other animals. These statements merely express the predominant emphasis in the understanding of the forces at work in infrahuman animals and contrast it with the predominant emphasis in the understanding of the forces at work in the human animal.

In each group, the reverse of the major stress can or must be true also. In addition to the infrahuman animal's obvious interactions with the world *outside,* there must be some conflicts of forces *within* the animal as well. But that process is difficult to demonstrate effectively when it exists, and so biologists tend to concentrate on the relation of an infrahuman animal with the forces *outside* him. In man, in addition to the pattern emphasized so far, of the interaction between the forces *inside* man, there exists also the highly important patterns of the interaction between the human animal and the forces *outside.* Each man interacts with other individuals singly and when they are in groups. And each man interacts with the patterns of his culture and with the various forces of his environment.

Even so, the primary emphasis, or at least one of the most essential emphases, when the human animal is considered, is on the forces *inside* him, the forces which are part of him, whereas the primary emphasis when the other animals are considered, is on their interaction with the forces *outside* them. Or condensed still further, we can say that man is the only animal known with certainty to have major conflicts of high importance between his own internal forces.

Not all of man's internal forces are in conflict. Some coexist in relative peace and harmony. But man's potential for conflict between the forces within himself may be one of the most important facts about man. And the resolution of such internal conflicts may be man's most important task. And still further, the resolution of man's internal conflicts may, in a way we shall discuss later, help to resolve man's conflicts with other men.

We come now to a brief delineation of man as a specific type of animal. In one point, the definition of man has changed in recent years. Man no longer can be defined as the only tool-making animal. Until the work of Jane Goodall it was thought that no other animal could make tools, even though many other animals can use as tools some of the objects they find around them. Jane Goodall has given convincing evidence that the chimpanzee not only uses as tools some objects which can be used unchanged, but also makes or prepares certain tools, one of which, the sponge, was mentioned in the previous chapter.

Therefore, part of the definition of man is that he is the animal which can make and use tools to a very much greater degree than any other animal. The difference is one of degree, not of kind.

It is appropriate at this point to list some of the differences, as usually given, between man and the other animals. One is man's upright, bipedal position which frees the upper extremities for jobs other than body support or locomotion. Another is a thumb which is more fully opposable to the other fingers, permitting more effective grasping or holding. The next difference is the greater size of the brain, especially the cortex, which correlates with a greater capacity to learn. A difference of high importance is the much greater capacity to make tools and to use them. Other items are man's much greater capacity to communicate with others of its own species, especially through language; the capacity to use symbols; the much longer period of dependency in infancy and in childhood; the greater capacity for fantasy. Of highest importance is the very much greater development of patterns of culture in man, and its transmission from one generation to the next not via the genes, but by social processes which occur after the birth of the next generation, through the impact of the older animals on the younger.

To these, we can add that "We are the only primates whose bodies are not richly covered by hair; whose infants are totally incapable of clinging to their mothers and nursing unassisted; whose favored mode of coitus is ventro-ventral; whose infantile attachments persist throughout life."[15]

My suggestion now is that there is still another point to be added to a definition of man. Man, apparently in contrast to the other animals, or to a much greater degree than other animals, is characterized by having within himself many internal, intraindividual, intrapsychic forces or processes, which often are contradictory and at times are in serious conflict.

In summary, then, the direct study of man reveals the primary importance of intrapsychic conflict. In addition, as indicated by the contrast between this chapter and the previous one, internal conflict is much more characteristic of man than of other animals.

Intrapsychic conflicts in man often are based on the fact that certain impulses or drives, e.g. the impulse to hurt others, are dangerous, or are regarded as dangerous by the individual himself, or were regarded as dangerous by others whose judgments the individual may have incorporated as part of his own set of standards. Such drives may evoke anxiety, guilt, and shame. Then, in response to the feeling of danger, and to the anxiety, guilt, or shame, the individual spontaneously develops defenses. Our shorthand phrase for these are "Defenses Against Internal Danger" or "Defenses

Against Anxiety." A simple example of such a defense would be a bout of extreme shyness and diffidence which occurs in a man of strong conscience, who has been having a sharp upsurge of impulses toward promiscuity about which he feels very guilty, and which he feels could endanger his wife's happiness, might damage his marriage or his children, and might damage the other women with whom he might be involved.

Such defenses against internal danger, which are part of intrapsychic conflict, stand in contrast to a second group of defenses, viz. "Defenses Against External Danger." An example would be the defense of flight from a fire, from a burning house. Another example of defense against external danger is the building of a barrier on the bank of a river which is rising steadily, after heavy rains, and might overflow its banks.

In human life, the defenses against internal or external danger may be concentrated solely on meeting the danger, or on defending against the anxiety, at times losing sight of other important considerations. At such times, the actual defense, while it lessens the original danger, may damage the individual himself, or damage others, and so we would not think of that defense as ethical. For example, a man's anxiety that he is nonmasculine may lead him to the defense of a repeated demonstration of his sexual prowess, of his ability to make sexual conquests, with no consideration of the interests of the partners, perhaps demeaning them in the process.

In an escape from an impending flood, an individual may concentrate totally on his own safety. If others are in danger also, a more suitable defensive response would include an attempt to help the others, and an expectation of being helped by them. Rephrasing this point, we can say that an individual's defenses may be patterned in such a way as to meet certain criteria of social or individual values, as well as being an effective way of coping with the danger. For these defenses, I suggest that we use the term "Defensive Ethics."

The ethical criteria used for such a definition can be simple. They are that (1) the defense being used by the individual does not cause unnecessary damage to others or to himself, even as the defense copes with the danger, and (2) the defense being used may in fact actually further the interests of others or of himself, even as the defense copes with the danger.

The term Defensive Ethics can have a wide coverage. In a murder trial, self-defense against an attack which actually endangered a man's life is regarded as being ethical and legal if the man can prove the truth of his plea. But the killing of another man because he may possibly be dangerous to oneself or to others is *not* regarded as legally justifiable or ethically defensible. Essentially there must be a "clear and present danger." Counterattacking or even killing another man when he is trying to kill oneself or others (if he can not be stopped in any other way) is regarded as legitimate and ethical.

A second example of Defensive Ethics is the procedure of placing in "isolation," in quarantine, an individual who has a dangerous contagious disease, if he is given good care during the period of quarantine, and is not exposed in the quarantine center to other dangerous contagious diseases.

The above examples are defensive ethical responses to external danger. The term Defensive Ethics may be used also to characterize a defense against internal danger, when the defense is in part ethical. For example, the loss of voice, which is called hysterical aphonia, in a boy who has "irresistible" urges to shout obscene words, usually is a defense against the internal danger posed by his surging impulses. The loss of voice has some ethical value; it protects his own interests as well as the interests of others. But it provides only a low-level solution in that it achieves the inhibition against saying prohibited words only by inhibiting the capacity to say any word, prohibited or not. A later more mature development would permit a "finer dissection," in which only a few words are selectively prohibited, and all others are permitted. This becomes a form of "selective inhibition" or "selective limit-setting," which is a more mature and realistic form of Defensive Ethics.

A fourth example of Defensive Ethics is the hysterical paralysis of the boy reported in the previous chapter, whose emergency ethical defense against his impulse to pummel or to strangle his baby sister consisted of being unable to move his arms. This provided an ethical defense in the sense of lessening his own guilt and anxiety, and in the sense of precluding any possible damage to the sister, if indeed there had been any real danger. But such a defense can also be regarded as primitive or inadequate in that it not only inhibited his impulses to hurt but also inhibited all movement of his arms, thereby blocking even those activities which would not have seemed dangerous to him.

The fifth example of Defensive Ethics is the adversary system in a court of law. This is a complex pattern of providing a legal and ethical defense against the danger of tyranny, or against the power of the strong over the weak.

The above examples of Defensive Ethics could be multiplied many times. But a lengthy exposition of the varieties of Defensive Ethics would be soporific and counterproductive. Instead, I shall try to present the central issues of Defensive Ethics in a schematic or tabular form (page 95), entitled "Defenses, Defensive Ethics, and Creative Ethics."

In this visual scheme, the first category is of defenses against external or internal danger, defenses which are not ethical in the sense in which we are using that term. The second category will be of defenses which can be regarded as partially ethical. The third category will be of defenses which clearly are ethical, defenses which without question can be called Defensive Ethics. The juxtaposition of these three categories in this schema indicates clearly the extraordinarily close relationship of many types of ethics with the patterns of defense against internal and external dangers, patterns which are so basic in human psychodynamics. The fourth category in this visual scheme is of Creative Ethics, which is not a form of Defensive Ethics, but is included to permit a fuller visual picture of the varieties of ethical patterns.

Several examples are given under each type. Some of the examples have been discussed previously; others will be discussed following the schema or in later chapters.

DEFENSES, DEFENSIVE ETHICS, AND CREATIVE ETHICS

I. *Defenses which are nonethical or anti-ethical*
   A. Violent, at times murderous attack by X on Y, as a defense against the fear (in this instance, essentially unnecessary) of being attacked by Y, who symbolizes those on whom X previously had projected his own unwanted destructive impulses.
   B. Other types of antisocial activity, e.g. sexual exhibitionism, which may be a defense against anxiety, but which can have a damaging impact on others and on the individual himself.
   C. Repeated demonstrations of sexual prowess, as a defense in a man, against the anxiety about being nonmasculine, without consideration of the interests of the partners.

II. *Defensive Ethics (Partial):* In which the defensive component predominates, and in which the ethical component is primitive or partial.
   A. *To external danger*
      1. Angry verbal attacks or body blows, by X on Y, who actually may be threatening but does not attack, or on Z, who seems to be threatening. The impulse may be to murder or to hurt the other seriously, but the behavior (although still excessive) is not severely destructive, i.e. is somewhat restrained.
      2. Infrahuman parallels: (a) The pecking order, which prevents unending struggles, between members of the group. (b) Species-specific patterns of ending individual fights, in which the winner permits the loser to leave. (c) In group living, patterns which govern the hostile interactions of its members, to prevent disruption of the group.
   B. *To internal danger*
      1. Hysterical paralysis, or other loss of function, of X, to prevent X attacking Y (and to make X less anxious), but which causes X to have a loss of activity important in other aspects of living.
      2. In response to primitive impulses, counterforces develop (strict primitive Superego), leading to severe repression, or to reversal into opposite, e.g. exhibitionism reversed into extreme modesty.

95

III. *Defensive Ethics*
  A. *To external danger*
    1. Self-defense against realistically dangerous attack.
    2. Defense (or protection) of the victim of a realistically dangerous attack.
    3. Quarantine of individual who has dangerous contagious illness.
    4. The adversary system in courts of law.
  B. *To internal danger*
    1. Parallel in physiology: Restoration of homeostatic equilibrium (e.g. of stable and safe body-temperature) when it is threatened by internal danger, e.g. by excessive internal production of heat, or by external danger, e.g. by extreme room temperature.
    2. Sublimation.
    3. Restriction of an action (not the fantasy) to an appropriate time, place, and person.
    4. Conscious renunciation of an action which is inappropriate under all or almost all circumstances, while permitting the thought or impulse.
    5. Conscious renunciation of the inappropriate inhibition of an activity which previously was not appropriate, but now is appropriate.
    6. Selective inhibition of certain words or actions, permitting others.
IV. *Creative Ethics*
  A. *Infrahuman parallels*
    Joint defenses against danger. Mutual help in obtaining food. Coordinated activity in hunting. Mutuality in sexual patterns. Parent-child linkages. Patterns governing social life and group activities.
  B. *Parallels in physiology*
    1. Homeostatic equilibrium provides stability by the adjustment of various processes with each other in an interplay of bodily forces, e.g. between heat production and heat loss.
    2. On the basis of a stable but dynamic homeostasis of the various body processes, other physiologic processes can occur, such as growth, development, and maturation.
  C. Golden Rule.
  D. Flexible combination of a selective limit-setting and a selective permissiveness, toward oneself and toward others.

E. Creative tension between opposites.
F. Partnership relations, which are at least partly postambivalent.
G. Dynamic, realistic, multifactorial, integrative activity of the Ego, in part replacing the rigidity and corruptibility of the Superego and primitive Ego functions. (See discussion of Superego functions in Chapter VIII.) Ego activity can be used not only defensively but also for growth and development.
H. Therapeutic alliance.
I. NON JOB alliance.
J. Cooperative work of scientists and of comparable groups throughout the world.
K. Certain types of family interactions, friendship, cultural patterns, religious and secular traditions.

The varieties and patterns of Creative Ethics will be discussed at many points in the last part of this book. In the remainder of this chapter, our aim will be toward a further understanding of Defensive Ethics. In this, we shall use a special way of clarifying the issues. We will choose one of the human conflicts which seem fairly universal, the conflict between exhibitionism and modesty. Then we shall examine some of the ways in which human beings try to resolve that specific conflict, to see which of the resolutions belong to the category of Defensive Ethics.

It seems that almost every child, and in a more hidden way, many an adult, has a strong drive to be exhibitionistic. This may be a drive toward sexual exhibitionism, of wanting to be seen naked or partly exposed, by another person, or it may be a drive toward social exhibitionism, of wanting one's qualities, such as skill (Look, Mom, no hands!) or intelligence or strength, to be seen by others. Inevitably, there are primitive counterforces against both sexual and social exhibitionism, counterforces which can be grouped together under the label of "modesty." The result is that almost everyone at some time is faced with an exhibitionism-modesty conflict.

The counterforces of modesty can be regarded as the first line of defense in childhood, and later against a surging exhibitionism. Such a defensive modesty does have some value for the individual and for others, and so can be regarded as a form of Defensive Ethics. But the strong counterforce of modesty developed early in childhood often is excessive, rigid, all-or-none, automatic, and unconscious, and so one hesitates to speak of it as more than partially ethical. In the following discussion, it will be clear that some of the resolutions of the exhibitionism-modesty conflict deserve the term ethical more than does the counterforce of modesty itself.

One interesting point, which relates to ethical issues in several ways, has to do with the parts of the body involved in exhibitionism. In some animals it has to do with the showing off of feathers or other brightly colored parts, in some species by the male, and in others by the female.

In the male human being the drive to be exhibitionistic is concentrated on the male genitalia or on his total size or muscle. In the female human being early in life there is some emphasis on female genitalia but more largely on a diffuse nakedness. Later in the life of the girl or woman, the emphasis focuses on breasts, legs, or other areas much more than on genitalia, and on the total body, its clothing or adornment. These facts are well known.

But two points are not so well known. The little boy often thinks he has much more to be exhibitionistic about, not knowing of the equally remarkable internal genitalia of the girl. And the little girl often thinks that the boy has had a great victory. Penis pride may develop in the boy and the penis envy in the girl, both of which can produce unfortunate results. Both of these can produce many important antiethical attitudes, for example, a man who demeans women as inferior, and a woman who undercuts men to prove the woman's superiority, or more generally, to prove her lack of inferiority.

There is a second point which is even less well known. It is that a large percentage of boys develop great envy of the woman's ability to carry a child within her, which seems far more important than his part in the process. Most men keep such envy deeply hidden from themselves. Women have a corresponding pride in that capacity, but it is "clouded o'er by discontent," by the hang-up on the penis envy.

This second point, of the boy's envy of child-bearing, may evoke disbelief in many of my readers. In this kind of emotion-packed issue, Coleridge's "willing suspension of disbelief" toward the author is not easily achieved, not nearly so easily as it is when one watches a play or an opera. So I want to remind you of two points. One is the couvade, a widespread practice in various cultures in which men have a ritual of imitating women who are in labor and after. The second point is the belief held by many students of prehistory that the first object of worship, at least in the areas that later were the sites of Western culture, the first deities, were female fertility figures.

It is important to add that in the conflict between exhibitionism and modesty, and in other internal conflicts as well, the pressure and counterpressure of two opposing forces provide only a part of the drama. There also is the fire and the passion of the deeply moving human emotions which are linked with the opposing drives. For example, exhibitionistic impulses produce strong feelings of excitement, of hope, and of pleasure. And they lead to strong feelings of fear and anxiety, to stronger feelings of guilt, and to even stronger feelings of shame. This parallels the fact that the central patterns in the great dramas, the great novels, and in the sacred books of the great religions, are the conflicts between various forces within the individuals, as well as the conflicts between the individuals, and the related emotions of delight and joy, of hope, fear, guilt, and shame.

Now for the exhibitionism-modesty conflict and its resolutions. The first to consider is the most distorted one, the resolution which occurs in some patients who are seriously sick, who in psychiatric terms are called psychotic. One of the central facts in a psychosis is a severe break with reality. Such a patient, in addition to whatever conflicts or other factors have caused his psychotic illness, may have sexual exhibitionistic impulses which he never has put into action. Even so he may begin to hear voices, hallucinations, which accuse him, falsely accuse him, of being a sexual exhibitionist, of having behaved in that fashion. Extensive study indicates that in all probability he did have exhibitionistic drives of which he was barely aware or totally unaware, with a strong counterforce against the drives, and potential feelings of guilt and shame.

He is sure that the voices come from outside himself. But the others in the room, his friends, family, physicians, and nurses, feel certain that no one other than the patient can hear the voices. The inference is that the voices must be part of the patient. In fact, when he tells them what he thinks the voices are saying, they are surprised, since no one in the room thinks he has behaved exhibitionistically, and no one other than the patient even knows that he ever has had exhibitionistic impulses. This reinforces the inference that the voices are a part of himself. One part of himself must be accusing himself of the unacceptable behavior. The defense against the feeling of guilt and shame is, in this instance, called the defense of projection, of hearing the accusations as coming from outside. This is one version of the adage that the guilty flee when no man pursueth. In fact, this situation is even more extreme, in that even a nonguilty man can feel guilty and accused when no man pursueth, and when no one actually accuses him.

The defense of projection can be regarded as having only a very limited ethical meaning or value to the individual or others. One can conjecture that the defense of attributing the impulse, and the sharp criticism of the impulse, to the outside world, may have played a role in lowering the pressure of the drive, and so helped the individual to avoid acting out his early impulses to sexual exhibitionism, which would have been unacceptable to him and to those to whom it would be directed. But even though the projection originally may have had some value, it now is linked with a severe distortion of reality. Also, when reality is seriously distorted, a reality-oriented ethics becomes impossible.

In fact, the defense of projection is included in this series of resolutions in order to underline the fact that some defenses may not become Defensive Ethics, but instead may lead in the opposite direction, to antiethical behavior. The projection of unwanted unethical impulses to the outside world, to individuals or groups outside, may start a disastrous chain of events. If the others, the strangers, are endowed with the qualities one would consider one's worst if one were to recognize them as one's own, the others become the incarnation of bad qualities, evil and dangerous.

We turn now to the second type of resolution of the exhibitionism-modesty conflict, the "resolution by neurotic symptom-formation." It is exemplified by the development of the symptom of hysteric convulsions. In this illness, the convulsions often are regarded incorrectly as symptoms of a physical disorder. In reality, they represent an attempted solution of an emotional conflict.

For example, one intensive study was of a girl in her late teens whose very strict modesty was struggling against her half-recognized impulse to be seductive by calling attention to parts of her body. Invariably in the past she had behaved and dressed in a very prim and sedate fashion. In the previous month she had developed an illness in which she had episodes of being "unconscious" and of having convulsions. Extensive studies showed no physical cause for the disorder. Observations of the patient as she had a convulsion indicated repeatedly to a number of doctors that the movements in the convulsions clearly would be regarded, in other circumstances, as seductive, uncovering, and suggestive. During a convulsion, the jerking movements of her trunk and legs caused parts of her body to be uncovered. But simultaneously the jerking movements of her arms and hands pulled her clothes back over the exposed parts of the body. Both sides of the conflict are evident, with almost diagrammatic clarity, in this type of resolution.

One can say that this patient had always regarded seductiveness as severely unethical and had repressed it severely. The conflict remained quiescent as long as her drive toward being seductive or exhibitionistic was at a low level. But under the impact of an increasing friendship with a man whom she found most attractive, she experienced a sharp upsurge of her sexual wishes, and the uneasy equilibrium, which had been based on a strong repression of her responsiveness and seductiveness, was disturbed.

It was clear that the rather sharp increase in her exhibitionistic and seductive wishes had brought her close to the point of overcoming her modesty. In response, her modesty, her Superego, mobilized its emergency defenses and a struggle ensued, which prevented the impulses from being expressed in her behavior with her friend, and from becoming conscious. The struggle had a compromise end-point, a sort of resolution, viz. the development of spells of unconsciousness and convulsions. In these, the exhibitionistic, seductive impulses had a partial victory, of achieving some indirect expression, of a moment of partial uncovering in the convulsive movements. But her modesty, her Superego, continued to have the predominant victory, of preventing her from actually behaving seductively or sexually when she was conscious or when she might be in a situation in which her Superego would regard uncovering behavior as unacceptable.

In a primitive sense, such a resolution is a form of Defensive Ethics. It lessened her anxiety and tension. It permitted some expression of both sides of the conflict. Also, this form of resolution has a kind of quarantine ethical value. The development of a somatic disorder may isolate the most intense portion of the conflict from the rest of the personality, which then can be relatively unaffected by the struggle.

But this type of defense, of neurotic symptom-formation, is one which ends in a form of illness. Of itself, it has little potential for growth. Of itself, it does not include a conscious reconsideration by this girl of her impulses and of her defense of modesty. However, it had the value, as a sickness, of precipitating her referral for psychiatric help, which had been considered previously.

In general, neurotic symptom-formation can be seen to be a form of Defensive Ethics of limited value. Hopefully, if life experiences become more favorable for the patient, if spontaneous change occurs, or if treatment is successful, the neurotic symptom-formation may be replaced by other forms of Defensive Ethics.

In the exhibitionism-modesty conflict, there are certain varieties of resolution which more clearly belong in the category of Defensive Ethics than do the examples given previously. One solution of the conflict is to limit the behavior (without necessarily limiting the thoughts about it) to a situation in which the circumstances are appropriate and acceptable. This principle is of limiting the behavior "to the correct time, place, and person."

To clarify this point, it is necessary to mention that a specific pattern of behavior may be unacceptable under certain circumstances, to the individual and to his culture, but under other circumstances, the same pattern of behavior may be acceptable to the same two judges, himself and the culture.

The behavior of phallic exhibitionism is seriously destructive under certain circumstances. When the place is public, when the other person, perhaps a small girl, is unwilling to have the experience and may be seriously frightened by it, the behavior is clearly unacceptable, both to the girl and to the community. It almost always is seriously unacceptable to the man himself, but he may repeat it time after time, until he unconsciously arranges to be caught and stopped.

But the same behavior, the uncovering, may be regarded as normal, as ethical, when it occurs as part of mature, or fairly mature, sexual activity, when it is private, and when the other is indifferent toward, or accepts, or welcomes, the man's activity. In an essential way, the difference lies not in the behavior itself, but in the time, the place, and the other person.

The difference lies also in its motivation. In part the motivation in the first instance is that the behavior seems to serve as momentary proof to the man of the frightening power of his masculinity. The need for such proof, at the time of his unacceptable behavior, had overpowered his recognition of its potentially unfavorable effect on the little girl and on himself. In contrast, in the second instance, in the correct time, place, and person, the motivation for the behavior is not essentially destructive, and the man is not indifferent to the interests of the other person.

Another resolution of the exhibitionism-modesty conflict is "sublimation." This also is a good example of Defensive Ethics. In this pattern, the essential point is that the primitive impulse of exhibitionism is not permitted direct expression but is expressed to some degree in a derivative way—in a personally and socially acceptable channel. Examples of sublimation are such patterns as giving a lecture, a college student's enjoyment of the public recognition of his having done a good job in a college course, a college student's wanting to be approved for winning a competition, or a college professor's enjoyment of the response to his giving a good lecture. The point becomes clear when one thinks of a lecture which is totally devoid of any wish of having it well received or of any wish for acceptance and approval. Such a lecture is likely to be dull and boring.

In this type of resolution, a sublimation, the essential point is that the unacceptable impulse is truly subordinated, and achieves its partial expression in the service of the acceptable activity. But when things are reversed—when the lecture is in the service of showing-off—the term sublimation would not be used.

The material of this chapter opens doors and raises questions in many directions. Inevitably some of the issues discussed here will be considered again. For example, the concept of Defensive Ethics will be used as a springboard for a discussion of the concept of Creative Ethics.

Also, there is a special linkage between parts of this chapter and the subsequent chapters. Some of the major problems of psychiatry and of ethics come into focus in the issue of free will versus determinism, and in the related issue of personal responsibility for one's behavior versus the irresistibility of one's impulses. These issues will be discussed later. But some material of high value for that discussion has already been considered. For example, when we considered the patterns of other animals in relation to, and in conflict with, the forces of the outside world, it must have seemed at times to many of us that the processes and forces confronting each animal are overwhelming or irresistible. When we considered the patterns of man, his conflicts with the forces outside him and the conflicts between the forces inside him, it must have seemed at times, to many of us, that the conflicts and forces confronting a man may be overwhelming or irresistible.

It was the same sort of response that led Freud to use the word "Id," the "it," for one group of forces within man, for what seem to be the impersonal forces "by which we are lived," such as drives toward exhibitionism, toward hostility, toward hurting others, and so on. But Freud recognized other sets of forces and named them. One is the "Superego," the set of forces which includes the conscience, the inner controls like modesty, and the drives which are the opponents of some of the powers of the Id.

Then there is a third group of forces which Freud called the "Ego." This is the executive, the coordinating, the adaptive, the problem-solving, the integrating, the controlling, the compromising set of forces in the personality, which works for the resolution of conflicts between the Id and the Superego, and for the resolution of conflicts between the individual and the external world. The functions of the Ego are all-important in providing a working base for the individual's self-development and for the process of therapy.

In the discussion of the Ego there will be an opportunity to consider the question of whether psychiatric experience has anything to contribute to such issues as the freedom of the will and psychologic determinism. Perhaps the concepts of free will and of determinism are bipolar, like some of the either-or contrasts which were mentioned in the first part of this chapter. We will explore the possibility that the third type of thinking, dynamic and realistic, might suggest some third alternatives, some workable and practical alternatives, to the polarized concepts of freedom of the will and of determinism.

5

The Therapeutic Alliance

IN the first part of this book I used the phrase "reader-author alliance." I expressed the hope that during its reading, there would be a number of moments in which the reader would realize that he and the author were working together in the process of understanding the issues raised, that the author and the reader had a joint investment of hard work in this book, and that both were using it for further understanding and for personal growth. If the reader did sense this joint effort, he would have an immediate experience of participating in a working alliance during the time in which he was becoming acquainted with the concept of a working alliance.

The reader-author alliance at times may be far more effective than the audience-lecturer alliance. But the audience-lecturer alliance at times is more obvious and more vivid than the reader-author alliance. The lecturer and the audience are in the same room and the interplay therefore is more dramatic.

Therefore at several points in the book I planned to focus on the interaction between the lecturer and the listeners which took place at comparable points in the lecture series. The reader, who has gone to innumerable lectures, we can be sure, can easily put himself in fantasy into the lecture situation. Then he can have some of the same experience by proxy, identifying with the listeners, putting himself in their shoes. And the reader can enjoy playing a double role, of being the reader of a book who at the same time can imagine for several pages that he is a member of the audience at a lecture given by the author.

To carry through on this plan, I shall phrase some of the material of this chapter as if I were giving the third lecture in the Weil series. The reader now can imagine himself in the lecture hall, and imagine my standing at the podium, trying to keep a large audience awake and listening.

He can hear me emphasize the fact that the discussion of a usually forbidden topic for the sake of truth and understanding does not mean that one must use the topic's forbidden words in the discussion. I do not use the four-letter words when I know that many of the audience would find the words unpleasant. It is essential at times, in the search for truth and understanding, to talk openly and clearly about subjects which at other times are regarded by the culture as forbidden in open discussion. The problematic topic is exempt from the cultural restriction because the search for truth and understanding has a much higher priority than does the restriction. The four-letter words are not essential in the search for truth and understanding, and so they are not exempt from the cultural restriction.

The reader can hear me say also that in the avoidance of four-letter words I need not avoid the kind of sexual joke or reference which is acceptable to the audience. (The key issue is the relation of the lecturer with the listeners.) A three-letter word like "sex" and a five-letter word like "sleep" will do the trick. Using these, I say I know that a number of persons who come to a lecture will fall asleep. In a group of fifty, there are times when no one falls asleep. More often several do. Snoring is rare. In a large group, of several hundred, there may be as many as ten or twenty asleep, at various times. In a group of fifty, my rule has been that when three are asleep at any one time I stop talking and then, in a very low voice, I whisper the word "sex." All three awaken, no matter how deeply asleep they have been and no matter how faint is my whispered word.

One of the pleasant experiences in life is the unexpected bonus that one receives occasionally when one behaves in an ethical fashion. When three have fallen asleep in a lecture and I awaken them gently by whispering the word "sex," there is often an unexpected bonus. Some of the others who had not fallen asleep but have blank facial expressions and seem to be far away suddenly begin to look interested, as if they realized that the speaker might have something to say in which they could be interested.

The unexpected bonus can be mentioned in a totally different context. One of the widespread breaks in ethical behavior occurs in libraries. Even people of high ethical standards seem to walk out of libraries with books that do not belong to them, or borrow books from a friend and forget to return them.

About ten years ago, I decided to do something about the gradual disappearance of my personal library. A notice was mailed to several dozen friends or suspects under the typed letterhead of "The Levine Memorial Library." The note announced that the executors of my estate were asking all those who had borrowed books from the Levine library to be so good as to return them anonymously. The combination of the impact, the humor, and the congenial awakening of guilt feelings without pointing the finger at any one individual had an amazing effect. Over fifty books which had been borrowed in the past twenty years or more were returned. The unexpected bonus was that a half-dozen books were sent to us which had never been borrowed from our home. They are in a special shelf in our library awaiting their rightful owners.

The joint fantasy of reader and author, of being in the lecture hall, permits the author to include some verses in this chapter. It is a lighthearted way of fostering the alliance between the reader and the author, as it did between the audience and the lecturer.

The jingle refers to the relation between lecturer and audience; it refers also to Homer's account of the use by Ulysses of Defensive Ethics, which makes the jingle most relevant at this point. It mentions the compact between Satan and Faust, which is a negative version of a two-way ethical working alliance, which makes the jingle not only relevant, but also an essential contribution to the ideas, to the substance of the chapter. These are compelling reasons, indeed, for the inclusion of a jingle!

The reader knows by now, of course, that at times the atmosphere of the lectures was informal and a number of interactions occurred between audience and lecturer which provided vivid examples of the more unconventional aspects of a working alliance. Some of the audience had heard me give lectures before. Many of them knew that I insist on a seventh-inning stretch at some point in a long lecture. In essence, the lecture-situation opened with a fair amount of congeniality, of relaxation, of a to-and-fro of feeling, a good degree of recognition of the needs of others, and a mutual respect.

The fantasy of being in the lecture hall now takes concrete form. It is shortly after the beginning of the third lecture. The reader, in his role as a member of the audience, hears me say to the audience that I had had several unexpected requests after the second lecture. Two of my friends had said they were disappointed that I had not included a rhyme or a word-play of the sort I had used in several meetings in the past. Another friend said he was surprised that I had not realized I had been asked to give the Weil Lectures because my jingles were amusing.

That did it, I said—not because I was insulted, but because it was such a great compliment. I took their comments, I declared, as a way of bypassing the conflict between my love of congenial nonsense and my love of sense and understanding. My friends had twisted my arm. My conscience was clear and the guilt, if any, was theirs. So, lapsing into rhythm, and once again into the present tense, I asked:

Dare I, who had professed
To be a dignified professor,
Yield to a temptation so far repressed
By every predecessor?

Dare I write a jingle, for this lectureship?
Should I listen, if Satan says, "Project-your-ship
Into space. Fly high with your verses and rhymes.
They're misdemeanors, not felonious crimes."

"Yes, Satan," I said, "You're right; you've sold me.
Like Faust, I'll do what you've told me.
But Satan, this will be two-way. You can't be averse
To having a compact. I'll be Faust in reverse.
Satan, you must sell me your soul,
And I'll teach you Psychiatry and the goal
Of Ethics. For you, a dramatic new role!"

So I yield to Satanic temptation.
I turn to mythology, an old avocation,
To use the story of the temptress Circe,
Who befriended Odysseus, when he came from the sea,
As Homer tells the story of the Odyssey.

Circe tempted me too, to have some fun,
To use her name for an atrocious pun.
As a punster, I hope for your groans.
Applause would mean failure; I want hisses and moans.

But also I ask for your mercy,
That gives me a rhyme for the difficult word Circe.
How perceptive she was, when she sized up Odysseus.
She knew he would think that the Sirens were delysseus.
She forewarned him, saying those girls are malysseus.

Then, fore-armed by his long-time-friend Circe,
Out of her jealousy, or out of her mercy,
He had himself tied to the mast of his boat.
He used Defensive Ethics, we surely must note.

The warning that saved him was Circe's.
He sailed past the Sirens. His temptation did cease.
Now, pun lovers, let's phrase it, this brought him surcease,
Surcease to his temptation.
No Circes, no more temptation.

We can call this a crisis resolution.
Sailing away, in Homer, is an ethical solution.

Temptation ceases, surceases, when past the Sirens we've gone,
Now, Satan, Circe, Sirens, all ye tempters, be gone.
This jingle, Madame and Sir, ceases. We too must sail on.

Enough for the fun of jingling, and the fantasy of being in the lecture hall. We must turn to the major job of this chapter, the discussion of the therapeutic alliance. There are a number of issues to clarify.

One is that in the process of writing a jingle, in fact in the process of writing a book, an important element is the enjoyment of words, the challenge posed by words, and the pleasure of mastering the challenge. Coping with words, and mastering them, is of prime importance in the clarity and effectiveness of writing. And coping with words, and mastering them, is of prime importance in ethics, as we shall see.

A lucky choice of a word may make a lecture or a chapter surge forward, make a concept or an emotion come alive and be meaningful. But at times words seem to have a life of their own, and are difficult to master. Words may go off at a tangent, and may modify ideas into meanings that were not intended.

Part of our job is to fight against being controlled by our language and our words. We must fight against having our ideas locked in by the words and by the meaning of words that have grown up in our culture over hundreds and thousands of years.

Words are of great value, as part of language, of communication, as providing symbols. But words are tricky. Most of our words developed in the days of past generations; they may embody old conditions and old ideas, and not represent the way things are today, or the concepts of today.

Further, words and their meanings are influenced by, are contaminated by, the mistakes, the strong feelings of others and of ourselves, in our childhood. Words may confuse, or distort, the development of a therapeutic alliance. So time after time, we must try to stop being controlled by words, look at life as it is, and be guided by the facts of life, in a therapeutic alliance and in other situations.

But it is not only words that force us to think in certain directions. The same may be true of our patterns of thinking and feeling. For example, many of us tend to think in extremes, and then to use words that represent extremes. When that happens, we may have locked ourselves into a situation in which we feel that we must respond with extremes.

This may be related primarily to the capacity of the human animal to fantasy, to imagine, to anticipate how things might be. If one expects to succeed, one may fantasy having a great success, saying the most intelligent, the cleverest things, being the most popular one at a party. If one expects to fail, one may fantasy being a smashing failure, being laughed at, humiliated. If one is afraid, often one fantasies great dangers ahead.

There are times when in reality great successes, great failures, extreme danger, extreme pleasure exist. One must not deny the existence of extremes or fail to perceive them when they occur. But if we want to be honest observers, and to get as much out of life as we can, we must accept one of the essential principles of science, that almost everything in life is quantitative as well as qualitative. There are quantities or degrees of things, as well as kinds or qualities of things. Success may vary from zero to 100 per cent. Failure may vary from zero to 100 per cent. Danger may vary from zero to 100 per cent, or perhaps since there is some danger in every situation and probably no situation ever is completely dangerous, we might say that danger varies from 5 per cent to 95 per cent.

This is most revelant to our discussion. Human defenses against internal or external dangers often are extreme, either because the danger against which they are defending occasionally in reality is extreme, or more often because the danger is incorrectly viewed as extreme. For example, the man discussed previously, who has the extreme defense of hearing voices accusing him of being a sexual exhibitionist, may have had a few such impulses (or a fair number of unconscious urges in that direction) but he reacts as if he were accusing himself of the extreme form of that pattern, of having actually committed the crime, behaved that way, many times.

We know that battered children exist, i.e. that in reality there is an extreme version of hostility of parents to children. But most hostility to children is much less than that, and the various kinds of hostile behavior to children and of hostile thoughts toward children must not be exaggerated and must not be regarded as extreme when they are not.

Another implication of the quantitative approach is that it opens the door to a correction of certain serious mistakes. For example, human beings often think that the punishment must fit the crime. So if a mild "crime" is regarded as extreme, the punishment expected is extreme. A parent who loses his temper and says some sharp words to a child may take that bit of behavior as an extreme hostility to the child, and feel exceedingly guilty. Instead of making the minor correction that is necessary, he may make a major correction, of trying to make restitution, for example by being subservient to the child, setting no limits, trying constantly to please the child. Such a correction obviously can be harmful.

In this situation, it was an internal danger, the impulse to hurt, that was regarded as extreme and led to a defense that was extreme. When the danger is external rather than internal, the process of Defensive Ethics may become entangled with thinking in extremes, in a similar way. For example, fighting off an attacker is fully justified. But the same aggressive fighting with one who merely has made a threat often is not justified.

There is another serious end-point in the pattern of regarding things as extreme when they are not. This pattern needs careful explanation. It starts with an impulse which is not extreme, but may initiate a sequence eventuating in destructive behavior which in reality is extreme. An example of this pattern occurs in some parents of battered children. The behavior of such parents in reality is extreme, yet they are not fiends or devils or the incarnation of evil, although as a psychiatrist I would recommend a firm stand with them plus appropriate treatment. My firmness with many of them may be greater than often is used.

But I know that often such a parent is immature and childlike. Often he has never developed beyond the point of wanting to cry and to complain and to be the center of attention. But also he often is deeply ashamed, as an adult, of his own wishes to cry and to be cared for, to be treated as a baby. Often such a parent has great contempt for that part of himself, hates that part of himself, and would like to kill that part of himself and get rid of it. When his own baby begins to cry and then will not stop, the parent beats the child, not only out of anger at the child's apparent refusal to obey, and not only out of a feeling of inadequacy in handling the child, and not only out of wanting to get rid of a rival for the baby role, but also because at that moment, his own child is behaving as the hated part of himself wants to behave much of the time. In part, the parent beats or batters the child as a way of beating the babylike part of himself.

The point most revelant to our discussion is that the sequence in such a parent may start with the fact that his own wish to be childlike may be only moderate, not extreme. But if his pride is very strong, it makes him regard the wish to be childlike as extreme, as extremely bad, extremely shameful. Then his counter-drive, his defense, is to get rid of that part of himself completely, in an extreme way. Finally, when his child keeps on crying, he identifies the child with that part of himself, and so may act in an extreme way to the child. There is a fair chance that if he could stop regarding his own wishes to be a child as so extremely shameful, he would not behave so extremely to the child. The inference is that even certain types of behavior which in reality are extreme may be lessened if there were a change in certain long-standing extreme attitudes toward oneself.

But even though the behavior of such parents is understandable and may be modifiable, one must use more than the simple principle that to understand is to forgive. The protection of the child must be paramount, along with the treatment, if it can be given, of the parent.

Further, some of the severe "moral" behavior used by parents toward young children may be unnecessarily extreme. Even a parent whose attitude toward a child is predominantly one of love and affection may be overly eager to have the child develop well, or to be perfect, or to make a good impression on others. The parent may take a misdemeanor by the child as being the first step to a major felony, even though 99 per cent of the time it will stay only a misdemeanor, or will be followed by another misdemeanor which also will not become a felony, even though the parent thinks it will.

He may treat each minor episode of sexual curiosity or exploration as inevitably the first step to becoming a sexual deviate, and each minor bit of independence or rebellion as the first step to a criminal career. When the parent handles it that way, he is using a battle axe instead of a fly swatter, he is using a moral principle of damnation rather than a minor correction or suggestion. That way he helps to lay the groundwork for the kind of extreme or rigid internal morality which is not very workable for the child in later years.

Erik Erikson's terminology for this is the morality of childhood, in contrast to the ideology of adolescence, and the ethics of maturity.[16] Perhaps this could be modified so that we would speak of the type of rigid internal morality just mentioned as being the unnecessarily extreme version of a necessary and workable Defensive Ethics in childhood. In turn, the various forms of Defensive Ethics, in childhood and in later life, stand in further contrast to the various forms of Creative Ethics, which start in childhood, develop further in adolescence, and develop still further later in life.

The discussion of words and attitudes which are extreme and may control one's thinking and behavior has a special relevance at this point in the discussion. Our focus has been on Defensive Ethics; it now will change gradually to an attempt to develop a concept of Creative Ethics. Defensive Ethics may go off the track because of extreme words, extreme feelings or attitudes. Also, the development of a Creative Ethics can be blocked by extreme words and extreme attitudes carried over from Defensive Ethics.

In fact, Creative Ethics in a number of ways must be based on concepts which give the highest honor, the place of highest importance, to words and attitudes which are not extreme. The concept of a good human relation, or of an alliance, a concept which is useful in describing one form of Creative Ethics, is difficult to use if one thinks of human relations only in terms of extremes.

To illustrate this point, we can refer to one of the concepts we use in developing the idea of a Creative Ethics. That concept usually is phrased as "the tension between opposites," or "the creative tension between opposites." But this phrase, good as it is, has a built-in problem in one of its words, the word "opposite." That word is one of the extreme words, and could block us if we used it without indicating that it is used only for sweet clarity's sake, or for the dramatic effect. It is a dramatic idea to think that there are two opposite ideas or patterns, that there can be a dramatic tension between them, and that out of that tension can come a new creation, a new integration. But the emphasis on the drama, the fact of the two forces being opposites, may slow the integrative process, make it less probable, simply because opposites seem to call for opposition, for struggle, for continuing conflict, rather than for working together. To improve the chance of the tension really being creative, we must put the emphasis on the fact that the tension is between forces that are not altogether opposites.

The Geneva Convention for the better treatment of prisoners of war had some value because it was based on the fact that even enemies at war did not show only opposite attitudes or opposing actions. They were opponents, but they still were in agreement in wanting to provide better conditions for their men captured by the other side.

The European Common Market had its resounding success by emphasizing the fact that countries which opposed each other in many ways, which had opposite interests in many ways, still were not totally opposite. A creative tension between countries which in good part were separate and antagonistic, but not at opposite extremes, could lead to a plan, an integration, of high value to all who joined.

The theory and practice of the rearing of the young of the human species, the process of child-raising, has been made much more confused and difficult than it need be by the use of extreme words and extreme attitudes, such as "breaking the child's stubborn will," or "setting the children free." The tension between such opposites or extremes is not usually resolved in a productive way. The resolution comes best by taking each extreme attitude or phrase several steps in the direction of being less extreme, and then seeing what can happen.

When we do this, in the field of the care of children, we see that there are two good and valuable patterns. The first is a selective permissiveness and approval. The second is a selective limit-setting and disapproval. It is not too difficult to work out a flexible combination of permissiveness and limit-setting for a child. But if permissiveness has become its own extreme, if the parent has become the doormat for the child, who is the master, if anything he does is approved and almost unlimited permissiveness or spoiling is the rule, a situation emerges which is no longer favorable for the child over the long run, in fact may be very unfavorable. And if limit-setting has become its own extreme, of destructive restriction and punishment, or a destructive forcing of the child to feel deeply guilty or deeply ashamed, that situation also no longer is favorable for the child over the long run, in fact may be very unfavorable.

It is true that the two processes in the less extreme pair, viz. selective permissiveness and realistic limit-setting, do point somewhat in different directions. But if they have not become extreme, they can be integrated into a way of being a parent or a teacher that is good or very good or excellent.

Most important, this integration can lay the groundwork for a more effective conscience in the child, for the development of his own standards for himself. He has a good chance of developing a conscience which uses both selective permissiveness and selective limit-setting. This kind of conscience can give valid and workable bits of advice when it appears as the "voice of conscience."

But it is exceedingly difficult, perhaps impossible, to integrate the two extremes, of severe spoiling and of destructive punishment. The pattern of unlimited permissiveness stimulates the child to feel all-powerful, and then to be disappointed by life, and at times demanding or alienated and resentful. The second pattern, of destructive punishment, tempts the child to feel excessively guilty and ashamed. The child's role in the development of these patterns is highly important also—it's not only the parent's approach that does the damage. With these patterns of child-raising, of opposite extremes, the child may later have two voices of conscience, one which tells him to get away with whatever he can, and the other which says he deserves terrible punishment for even thinking of having something that he wants.

This leads to the first of a series of suggestions for the development of a technology of ethics. This suggestion is that a kind of simple mathematics can be used as a technique for the further development of ethical principles and ethical behavior. (A much more advanced form of mathematics may eventually have value also.)

When there is a tension between opposites, and when the opposites clearly have been exaggerated or have been phrased as extremes, each one should be subjected to the simple arithmetic process of being divided by two, or by another number that reduces it to a size or a quantity or an intensity that seems more correct. Then one must find a good word for each diminished opposite. The next step is to put the two opposites together, and see if they join, if they integrate, see if the tension can become creative. Rephrasing this, a creative tension between opposites can appear more readily when the opposites are changed into contradictories, or contraries, or dissimilars, rather than opposites. The opposites now have a more positive magnetic pull toward each other.

The difference no longer is extreme and unworkable. The difference has become workable, a result parallel to that implied in the anecdote about a sharp argument between quarreling friends, about men versus women, in which the antagonists emphasized the great differences between men and women, the extreme ways in which they are opposites. Most of the comments stressed the hostile competition, the struggle, and the conflicting claims of great superiority of one or the other. Finally reality and logic prevailed. The notion of extreme opposites was converted into the reality of the noticeable differences. And the discussion of the differences, and of their positive potential, was ended by a pun. The Frenchman of the group rose to the occasion, not by his usual "Vive la France," but by a hearty "Vive la différence."

In a comparable way, severe rebellion and defiance can *not* be well integrated with extreme submission and complete obedience. The step to take is to divide each by two or more. This reduces the first, the severe defiance, to wishes to be independent, wishes to be heard and to play a role in directing one's own life. The next step is to reduce the second, the extreme dependence, to the attitude of wanting to be advised, to be supervised and helped, to learn what experienced people have to say. Then these two are not extreme and can be integrated into a most productive combination.

It is this type of resolution of the tension between opposites which seems to have taken place in America, in the evolution of its pluralistic society, in which there are two interacting patterns. One is the pattern of having a number of separate, distinct, productive, and creative groups and cultures, which are related and linked in many ways. The other pattern is of having an overall American culture in which all of the separate groups are involved.

At times the tension between the opposites could be phrased as the tension between the extreme drive toward assimilation and total integration and the other extreme drive toward separate ethnic identities and total separation, or as the tension between the extreme of complete unity and the extreme of complete diversity. Fortunately, the extremes do not remain as extremes. The pressure toward each extreme lessens and the end-point is the productive co-existence of contradictory tendencies.

In the future, in this tension between opposites, there can be a further decrease in each of the opposing extreme attitudes or principles. This in turn can lead to the further development of a pluralistic society, in which there is one overall culture which combines highly important components of each of the important subcultures, while each of the subcultures, or many of them, continue their own productive development.

This discussion of a simple arithmetic involved in the resolution of the creative tension between opposites can be used to clarify further the process of sublimation. Sublimation is one variety of Defensive Ethics. It can be used to provide one of the resolutions of the exhibitionism-modesty conflict, and of many other conflicts.

In the exhibitionism-modesty conflict, there can be no resolution of much value, if there is an extreme and persistent demand for the direct gratification of exhibitionistic impulses, or if modesty demands an extreme or complete suppression of exhibitionistic impulses. But the exhibitionism can make milder demands and be somewhat domesticated. And the modesty can be less extreme in its opposition. Then the exhibitionism may appear in minor or minimal form, or in a socially acceptable channel, such as lecturing or acting, of wanting recognition or approval for a job well done, or for winning in a competition.

In a sublimation, the impulse is gratified in a minimal or minor form, and is in the service of an acceptable goal, subordinated to that goal, such as becoming known and respected for one's achievements. That goal is in keeping with the standards of the individual himself, and sufficiently in keeping with the needs and standards of the culture, to make it be an acceptable resolution all around, and yet it makes use of the energy of a potentially unacceptable impulse.

The discussion of sublimation leads to a partial definition of ethical behavior, as behavior in which the interests of the individual, and the interests of the culture or the society are not regarded as contradictory or conflicting to an unworkable degree, are not regarded as adversaries locked in mortal combat. Rather they can be regarded as having somewhat different goals, or values, or as pressing in different directions. Inevitably this produces some tension or conflict. But the interests of the individual, and the interests of the culture or the society, often can be integrated successfully in a variety of acceptable or good solutions, which are both workable and creative. At times, there may be solutions in which the interests of one side, either of society or of the individual, are paramount, hopefully without damaging the interests of the other. Then there may be solutions which offer the most creative form of ethics, in which the interests of both the individual and of others and of society are all forwarded. This can be true of the therapeutic alliance and true also of other patterns.

So the first arithmetic process to use in ethics is to take two opposite or extreme statements or policies, then divide each by 2 or more. Then they can be put together, to see if they join forces in some way.

We come now to the therapeutic alliance itself. The concept of a creative tension between opposites could serve as a vivid description of the therapeutic alliance, to the degree that patient and psychiatrist might think of each other in oppositional terms. The suggestion that the phrase "tension between opposites" be replaced by the phrase "tension between contradictories or contraries" (thereby dividing by 2 the estimate of the opposition to be expected) would be a more accurate but a less dramatic description of the therapeutic alliance.

The existence of ambiguity in human life raises problems similar to those which are posed by the existence of opposites. But the problem of ambiguity, of possible double-meanings of one phenomenon, is different from the problem of opposites and so must be discussed separately.

One of the fundamental facts which emerged from the scientific work of Einstein, Nils Bohr, and others was that certain of the smallest "items" in the universe are to be regarded simultaneously as physical particles and as wave-lengths. This is presented as a most important concept even though it is ambiguous, almost shocking in its stark ambiguity. It suggests that ambiguity, as well as simplicity, is one of the basic facts of life.

The predominant emphasis, however, must remain on the fact that simplicity most often is of primary importance. Ambiguity usually means that the understanding is incomplete, because of a lack of facts, a lack of knowledge, or a lack of clarity or of understanding. Most of the time one must not rest content with ambiguity.

But the second emphasis, that at times ambiguity rather than simplicity is basic, can be of high value. There are situations in which ambiguity can be regarded as factual and valid, as a positive and productive state of affairs.

The discussion of ambiguity, like the discussion of the other topics touched on so far in this chapter, provides the groundwork for the discussion of the therapeutic alliance. It is noteworthy, for example, that there is a very valuable ambiguity in the therapeutic alliance. The psychiatrist is both participant and observer.

One of the basic functions of the psychiatrist is to participate in the process of therapy. He joins with the patient in trying to understand and to "treat" that part of the patient's personality which is causing trouble for the patient, and perhaps for others. But the psychiatrist must continue to function also as an observer, who must not be involved too closely in trying to help the patient to change, so that he can continue to make clear-headed objective observations, to use as a basis for the ongoing evaluations which are prerequisites for his further attempts to help.

The double role of participant and observer is essential in many of the important relations in life. It is a vivid example of the psychoanalytic concept of the multiple functions of the Ego, discussed most productively by Waelder.[17]

There are other aspects of the therapeutic alliance which can now be discussed. For this, I shall again use the plan of asking the reader to imagine that he is one of the audience at the lecture, so that in fantasy he can participate in the experience of the audience-lecturer alliance during this part of the discussion.

I shall shift to the present tense to help the reader have a more vivid fantasy of his being at the lecture. He can imagine hearing me say to the audience that I shall use a new approach to an understanding of the therapeutic alliance, which will have the desirable qualities of immediacy and relevance. I say that in the lectures something new has been born and has developed, in addition to the substance of the discussions: a relation, an interaction, has developed between the audience and the lecturer, as well as between members of the audience. This relation has nothing to do with treatment, of course, and so it is not a therapeutic relation, it is not a therapeutic alliance. But in the relation which grows between an audience and a speaker, or between a seminar group and the seminar chairman, there develops a pattern of interaction which has a number of points in common with many other positive interactions in life. So there may be many parallels between the interaction of lecturer with audience and the interaction of therapist with patient.

There are basic differences, of course, ways in which there is no parallel. For example, in the lecture situation, the relation is between a large group and myself. A therapeutic relation usually is between one patient and one therapist, or at the most, as in group psychotherapy, the relation between a group of five to ten individuals and one or perhaps two psychotherapists.

But there are, in fact, striking points of similarity between the relation between the lecturer and the audience, and the relation that exists between psychiatrist and patient. So in this discussion I will point up some of the similarities between the audience-lecturer alliance and the therapeutic alliance. And since I will be talking directly about you, the audience, and me, the discussion can be alive, relevant, evocative, and immediate.

The first point is that the relation, for almost everyone who comes to a lecture, is a voluntary one. I happen to know that a few of you come to the lecture because your college instructors, who are here also, urged you to come. I happen to know too that one student stayed away from the lecture because a teacher put pressure on him to come, and the student felt that his independence would be lessened if he came. Also, it is probable that several wives or husbands came to the lecture because the other of the pair insisted. But surely most of those who attend a lecture do so voluntarily.

Now for the parallel. In the therapeutic relation, there are times when it begins on a somewhat unwilling basis, which can lead to certain difficulties. But by and large psychotherapy is based on the fact that the individual comes voluntarily because of his feeling that psychotherapy has something to offer to him. In part, some patients surely must have some hesitation even when they come voluntarily, just as members of the audience may have hesitated to come to still another lecture.

After one comes to the first of a series of lectures, coming to the second lecture again is voluntary, and if one comes a number of times, there must be some feeling that it might be worth doing. The same is true of the appointments in psychotherapy, in the therapeutic relation.

A third point about the relation between this audience and this lecturer is that you may have sensed that I am strongly and sincerely interested in having you get something out of the lectures. I worked on this material with T.L.C., Tender Loving Care, partly out of my own interest, but also because I wanted it to be clear and effective for others. But you know that I am not so unrealistically dedicated to the cause of your development that I would be willing to spend many hours in strenuous preparation and in the work of giving these lectures without having something more in return. The fact is that I have received a great deal, such as an adequate fee, plus what I have learned during the preparation of the talks, plus the fact that the challenge of speaking before a receptive group has made me see some new points of interest even while I give the lectures and later when I modify them.

It is important to emphasize that I get something valuable out of giving the lectures. I do so realistically and not as an empty polite comment, because it is true, and because I want to point out that a similar process is true in the therapeutic relation. The psychiatrist should be paid appropriately for the time he spends with the patient, paid either by the patient or by the clinic or center. In addition, the psychiatrist's own body of knowledge and skill is enhanced by his experience as psychiatrist with each patient.

In the relation between you and me there is a marked concentration on your needs, but not merely in an empty, polite, pseudo-altruistic fashion, since that concentration is combined at the same moment with an adequate recognition of my own needs. It is not a one-way street. This pattern appears in the therapeutic relationship also. There is a tremendous concentration on the needs of the patient, but the needs of the psychiatrist are not ignored.

This fact, of attention to the needs of both, is of high importance. In the therapeutic relation, the fact that it is a two-way street helps the patient to accept the fact that another individual is concentrated on the attempt to help him. It becomes realistic and workable when the patient can see the professional aspects of the relation, in which the other is not trying to behave like a self-sacrificing, all-giving parent, focused only or overwhelmingly on the interests of a child.

Another point characteristic of the relation between you and me is that obviously I will not permit the temptations of Satan, nor of the Homeric figures, to interfere with my primary job. You know that I have enough self-awareness to recognize the temptation to be a Wise Elder Statesman and enough objectivity to renounce it. That means that I will not try to impose my ideas on you, out of an illusion of great wisdom, and that I will not talk down to you. In turn, I know that in spite of your temptation at times to fall asleep, you respond in part with a process similar to mine, of reciprocating to some degree by giving serious consideration to the facts I give and the inferences I make.

Still further, you know that in a real sense I regard this situation as one in which you and I are equal-equal. You know that I meant it when I said earlier that as far as I know most everyone in the room is capable, as I have been, of being a good member of a good team, and of being productive in various ways, if he wants to be, and if he works hard enough and long enough.

But you know and I know that I would not be standing on this podium if this were a totally equal-equal relation. Because of my work and the way in which I have worked, and because of the work of others, and because of the fact that your interests have been primarily in other directions, I do have something to say which you want to hear, and so you came to hear me. In this way the relation has a quality of inequality.

Comparably in the therapeutic relationship, there is a combination of an equal-equal relation with a degree of inequality, based on the training and experience and objectivity of the therapist. The psychiatrist must recognize the fact that through his training, and through his own individual work and experience, he can be a leader in the therapeutic situation to some degree, and that he has something valid to give. He and the patient basically have an equal-equal relation, but also the psychiatrist must be able, if necessary, to make a comment like this, with quiet confidence: "Look, brother, I am not trying to dominate, I am not trying to say I am better or stronger. I am saying that out of my experience there are some comments which I can make, about certain ways in which you are blocking yourself or others, or about certain mistaken ideas or misdirected feelings. I am not trying to punish you or to shame you. But I am saying that there is a trained person, myself, who wants what is best for you and for the others around you, and who urges you strongly to take another look and still another look at this or that part of your thinking or of your personality."

In my relation as lecturer to you as audience, I do not have the right or the authority to tell you what to think or what to say. I might be able to advise or to make a suggestion, if you asked me to do so. There is obviously an essentially equal-equal relation between us. The inequality between us is based primarily on the fact that I have spent a very long time being with patients and others (and of hearing residents-in-training talk about patients). And these patients actually tell me or the residents a very great deal about themselves, including their ethical problems, since patients are motivated by one of the strongest of all motives, the serious hope of lessening their pain or suffering.

Another parallel between the audience-lecturer relation and the therapeutic alliance can be phrased this way. In a previous section I mentioned that I, as lecturer, am willing to violate a taboo about talking about unacceptable things if it is necessary in our joint search for the truth. In the therapeutic relation, the parallel is that at times it is necessary for psychiatrist and patient to discuss matters which ordinarily are taboo.

But I said also that I paid attention to your needs in such a situation of frank talk. I indicated that I would not use four-letter words, since I knew that some of the audience would find them unacceptable, and using them was not necessary in our joint search for the truth. There is a parallel to this in the therapeutic relation, in that the psychiatrist is sensitive to the needs of the patient, and will not do something merely because he might want to do it, when it is out of keeping with the patient's real interests.

Another point in your relation with me is that the Weil lectures are in the setting of a specific tradition; there are certain rituals and traditions which have come to be associated with them. One is that the lectures are read rather than given extemporaneously, or rather are read with some spontaneous or extemporaneous additions or modifications. I would not have planned it that way, but I have come to recognize certain values in working intensively on such material in advance. It means that a lecturer using this plan will have given his topics a great deal of thought in the past, changed some of his ideas, and discarded some material which might be distracting. In fact, I have come to feel that this way of doing things is a good one, even though it has never been my first choice.

The parallel point in a therapeutic relation is that both the patient and the psychiatrist recognize that certain cultural patterns and traditions are implicit or explicit in the relation itself as well as in some of the experiences and fantasies which are discussed. Often this is a matter of practicalities. The psychiatrist has a number of other obligations and so he and the patient come to an agreement that the appointment starts at a particular time and is over at a particular time. If it did not, the psychiatrist's schedule would be in danger of becoming as chaotic as occasionally it is in the offices of doctors who do not use an appointment system. At the end of the appointment time, even though the psychiatrist or the patient may not want to stop the discussion, they do stop except under most unusual circumstances. Otherwise other patients would be short-changed in some fashion. This is traditional, and is part of the kind of limit-setting that is a built-in aspect of the therapeutic relation.

The reader no longer needs to fantasy that he is in the lecture hall, listening to me discuss the interaction between audience and myself. The reader's main emphasis will continue as before, to be on the substance of this book as he reads it, on its facts and its ideas, and his use of them in understanding the principles of ethics. Occasionally the reader can glance at the interplay in the partnership between reader and author.

The substance of our discussion turns now from the similarities between the therapeutic alliance and the relation between lecturer and audience to the essential differences between the therapeutic alliance and most other types of two-way working alliances. In the therapeutic relation, the patient comes primarily because he has pain or suffering or an awareness of there being something "wrong." Or he comes because friends or advisers whom he regards as honest and trustworthy have indicated to him that there is something that is wrong. Or he comes because he has a feeling of a lack of fulfillment of his own potential. Or he comes because a competent physician has told him that there are emotional factors of some importance in producing or perpetuating some physical disorder. From this, it is clear, then, that the motivation for coming for therapy is profoundly different in most ways from the motivation for reading a book or coming to a lecture.

A second point of difference is that it is understood in advance in the therapeutic relation that the patient will do his best to talk freely, to tell as much about himself as he can, will be willing to say whatever is part of his thinking or feeling. This does not mean that he will act out any of his suppressed or repressed desires, nor believe that anything goes. Rather he knows that an understanding of the complex web of the interplay of forces within a human being calls for self-observation by the patient of his thoughts and feelings and for the observation of them by the psychiatrist, and for a discussion of their observations. There is no dirty talk for the sake of dirty talk. The method does not recommend that the patient or the therapist lose their tempers, in fact does not recommend any type of putting of impulses into action. It is the discussion of the patient's thoughts and feelings without their expression in overt behavior, which is one of the unique characteristics of the therapeutic alliance, and which provides the road to understanding and to personal growth.

This description leads to my underlining one point, which may be of high importance in the development of a contemporary ethics. It is that the traffic light, the stop light in the human being, need not be placed at the point at which an unconscious impulse becomes a conscious thought. Human beings need not tell Satan to get behind them, need not keep their temptations hidden from themselves in the darkness of the Unconscious. Rather the stop light can be placed at the point at which the impulse or the conscious thought might be put into action. That is the point at which the individual should stop, look, and listen, so that he can have time to give some real consideration to the issue.

In certain instances he, or his Ego, the director of his traffic, may say that since he is no longer a child, a previously forbidden behavior may now be permitted by himself. But also he, or his Ego, at that stop light, may say that the previously forbidden behavior, such as driving his car one hundred miles an hour in traffic, still is forbidden. One of the basic issues in the therapeutic alliance is that in discussions of the patient's thoughts and feelings, a clear difference is made between two categories, one of impulse, thought or idea, in contrast with the other, of action or behavior.

To consider this further, as a more general issue of ethics, one might safely say to most human beings that they can give permission to themselves to have consciously in mind any impulse or thought or idea, as long as they can laugh at many of them, or can recognize that some of them are an awful waste of time even as thoughts or ideas. Then with the impulse in conscious awareness, the human being can take a second look, a clearer look, at the question of permitting the impulse to be put into action or behavior. He can see that some types of action or behavior which once were forbidden now are permitted, but that other types which once were permitted, such as a primary self-centeredness, are now not to be permitted, if he wants to have the greater value and the greater fun of the development of a good kind of partnership, or of a team, in human relations.

In the therapeutic relation there is a more permissive attitude toward having impulses, thoughts, or ideas than the patient usually thought possible. But also in the therapeutic relation, there is the pattern of urging the patient to have a profoundly skeptical attitude about the advisability of putting many of his impulses or ideas into action or behavior, unless they clearly have a favorable effect. And in some instances, the psychiatrist must have a strong and clear limit-setting attitude about the patient's putting certain impulses into overt behavior.

The therapeutic alliance then becomes an experience of partnership. The patient develops a workable degree of trust and confidence, not blind trust or blind mistrust. And in the setting of the growing trust between the patient and the therapist, there develop several patterns of importance. One is called the "transference," which in one typical form simply means that the patient begins to develop certain feelings, of anxiety, of liking, of disliking, of hostility, of jealousy, etc., toward the psychiatrist who seems in some fashion to be like one or more of the important figures in the past life of the patient. The goal then is to discuss such feelings openly and to see the way in which old patterns of feelings have been "transferred" to the therapist. This provides an immediate source of information about some of the important feelings of the past. The profound hope is that in the setting of the good partnership, the good relation, such feelings can be seen for what they are, and lead to further understanding of himself by the patient.

Also, since we will want to use the therapeutic alliance as a paradigm for other varieties of creative ethical alliances, we must mention that the patient is not the only one of the two who may have some illogical, inappropriate responses to the other person in the alliance. The psychiatrist also may have responses which in one typical form are comparable to "transference" responses of the patient. In the psychiatrist these responses are called "countertransferences."

This means that the psychiatrist must learn to look frequently and carefully at his own responses. This is not merely in conformity with the injunction of a great philosopher, to "know thyself." Rather it is a specific technical requirement of the day-by-day work of the psychiatrist. He has come to see that unless he scrutinizes himself, with the kind of stringency and respect he uses when he scrutinizes a patient, his work may suffer.

It is imperative to give a clear picture of the ways in which a therapeutic alliance can be less effective because of specific emotional responses on the part of one or of the other. Good human relations, alliances, are in general one of the most important, most productive varieties of ethical behavior. So it is imperative that we know some of the difficulties in having a good alliance, and of the ways of coping with such difficulties.

A typical case is this. One of our capable residents-in-training in psychiatry was treating a bright young college student who was about six or seven years younger than himself. The college student had severe but unnecessary guilt over having a better education than his father ever had or could have. His guilt had slowed him down in his college work and he had become an under-achiever.

Both the psychiatry resident and the student were intelligent and gifted. Both were eager to have good careers. Both were somewhat competitive, and both had a counterforce of wanting to be sure that their competitive feelings did not hurt others. The resident's problem was mild or minimal, while the student's conflict was fairly severe. But a psychiatrist or a psychiatry resident must not ignore his own patterns even though they are minimal.

The resident presented his work with this student at regular intervals in one of our Continuous Case Seminars. In several seminars, it was clear that the resident treating the student had a very good perception of what was going on, and perhaps had an unusual ability to see the student's strong urge to compete aggressively with his father, his guilt over that impulse, and the resulting impulse to lose in the competition. The resident saw the unfortunate pattern of resolution of the conflict, namely that the student was trying unconsciously to get no grades lower or higher than a C or a D.

The student flourished during several months of treatment with the resident, and his college work improved steadily. Then came a plateau in the treatment, in which no further improvement was taking place. At first, in the discussion, it seemed this might be related to the fact that the student's father had a period of illness, and the student had had a fantasy of having caused his father to worry so much that in some fashion he was responsible for the father's illness. But in the further discussion this formulation did not hold water.

Then the resident who was treating the student, and the six other residents and I, who make up the membership of the seminar, turned our attention to the feelings of the resident himself. It was not difficult to discover that when the patient, the student, began to make excellent progress in his college work, he had begun to talk, in his hours of therapy, of going to graduate school or perhaps especially of going to medical school. He had said that he then might want to consider training in psychiatry. With this, the resident had some feeling, which I shall give in exaggerated form to make the point, of saying to himself something like, "Hey, what is this business of making younger people stronger? All one does is to help these bright youngsters to be able to compete more successfully with people of my age."

The resident had been faintly aware of his response to the

patient's growing confidence. Of course, he had not said a word that would have been competitive toward the student, nor a word which would have made the student hesitate to go further in his own development. But it seemed now to the resident himself, and to the rest of us in the small group, that the resident may well have been slightly poker-faced during the interviews in which the student talked of his great progress. And when the student received an A on two successive semester papers, the resident may have been a trace less friendly, may have revealed a bit of his feelings in his facial expression. It was the understanding of all of us in the seminar that the resident may have been tempted faintly to express some of his competition, but only in facial expression and tone of voice.

I must add that this story had a happy ending. To preserve confidentiality, I can describe the resident as a professor of psychiatry, and the university student as a resident in the field of surgery.

This is a rough sketch of the therapeutic alliance, which can provide so many points for our thinking about ethics. Such an alliance is not easy to develop or to sustain, but it has been done successfully time after time. And as I see it, two points explain its success. One is that it is a partnership, of two people working together on the parts of the personality of one of them, which he wants to change.

The second is that a serious attempt to do an honest self-scrutiny is a built-in part of the process. The psychiatrist and the patient must look frankly at the patient's emotional problems, which interfere with his functioning. The psychiatrist knows also that he must look at himself, at the ways in which even minor or minimal problems can interfere at times with his own good functioning.

These two points, partnership and self-scrutiny, are vital for an ongoing consideration of ethics. They will be crucial in the discussion of the remaining topics, when we consider the generation gap, discuss the creative types of ethics, and consider the development of a technology of ethics.

Special Note to Reader from Author Re Chapter 6

Two extraordinarily gifted writers disagreed with my plan to include the following chapter in this book. One is Dr. Margaret Mead, the author of a shelf of books of the highest quality, many of them known throughout the contemporary world. She is Visiting Professor of Anthropology in this Department of Psychiatry in addition to her other professional appointments.

The second is Dr. Gustav Eckstein, the author of *The Body Has a Head*, and some fifteen other books, written in superb style. He is Professor Emeritus of Psychophysiology in this Department of Psychiatry in addition to his other Emeritus appointments.

In contrast, I have published only one previous book, plus chapters in some fifteen others. Yet I dare to disagree with the others in the decision to include this chapter. This disagreement of itself and its resolution provide a good example of one of the central theses of this work, viz. that disagreements and opposition can develop, that authentic disagreements can persist, and even so, in the setting of good human relations, of friendship, of a co-operative venture, of an alliance, the disagreements are nondestructive and perhaps very productive. Both the conflict and the alliance can contribute in essential ways, and the end-point often is a creative solution which includes elements of conflict and of resolution.

My friends say that this chapter is cut from the cloth of the technique of lectures and the discussion type of teaching, and therefore is not suitable for a book. The reader, they say, can and will go back over the material, and make his own tentative summaries; at least, it is a sign of respect for the reader to avoid doing it for him. In contrast, in a lecture or a teaching situation, the student may need more help.

In the heat of our correspondence about this book, Dr. Mead at one point said, "You needn't tell them what you're going to say, then tell it to them, then tell them you're saying it while you're saying it, then afterward tell them how you've just carried out your promise." The criticism was correct about various paragraphs in my writing of the previous drafts of the manuscript, and the guilty sentences have been eliminated.

But with regard to this chapter, my argument is that the material requires such a summary, whether it is given at a resting point in a series of lectures, or at a moment of quiet in a book. Therefore my decision has been to include the chapter, and to mention the fact of my friends' disagreement with me, to indicate that continuing differences of opinion are to be expected in life and are often most desirable and positive. They can be directly stimulating and productive for the reader.

There is a remote danger that the reader could be lost in such a shuffle, so, my comment to him is: "Please read this if you want. But since it appears as a separate chapter, it is easy to omit it and to go directly to the next chapter. I think it is helpful and won't violate your independence. But two experienced writers, Dr. Mead and Dr. Eckstein regard the chapter as a kind of foreign body. They suggest that you skip it, as being inconsistent with the respect shown you by the author in the rest of this book. Perhaps the best way of phrasing this is to say that several types of reader-author alliance can exist, and that you can play a part in deciding which type seems workable for you."

6

Midpoint Summary

ONE of the major goals of this book is the presentation in coherent form of a broad sampling of the ways in which psychiatry and related fields can contribute to the further development of ethical principles and ethical behavior. In such a presentation, some of the relevant facts and concepts, and their significance for ethics, can be presented briefly. But other facts and concepts call for a longer discussion and clarification, which may include notes and comments on a variety of related issues. At times the discussion must be freewheeling and broad-ranging, as a way of permitting the emergence of unexpected linkages and points of understanding.

When some of the discussion is extensive or freewheeling, it should include a specific sentence or paragraph in which the talk is focused or summarized. Then the reader can know what the author regards as the end-point of the freewheeling discussion. Therefore, at various points in this book, I included a summarizing sentence or two of my understanding of the topic under discussion. But in addition, it seemed to me that at this point it would be of value to cull out and put together some of the summarizing statements from the previous chapters, some extensively rephrased, with some new ones added.

This might provide a welcome change of pace in the reading, might clarify some points, and might provide an even more rounded communication from author to reader. It might meet the needs of the reader, who at the midpoint of this book, could make good use of a kind of summary of its first half.

So in this Midpoint Summary, the author presents a sampling of the facts and concepts presented so far, plus a number of statements which summarize the various areas of discussion in the first part of this work. The fact that they are presented in a series permits the reader to see their linkage and to have a clearer impression of the major thrust of the book.

These summary statements must not lead to a premature closure of any part of the discussion. The statements are succinct and condensed, but they are not exact or thorough or final. In a field like this, they must be open-ended and tentative.

1. The phrase, "Satan, get thee behind me" symbolizes a second-best technique, of putting temptations out of sight, in the darkness behind one (repressed into the hidden recesses of the mind). I suggest, instead, "Satan, get thee in front of me, so I can take a good look at you (i.e. at the temptations) and decide what's best for myself and for others."

2. The success of scientific discoveries and of applied science, as technology, leads to dangers which call for a comparable increase in man's scientific understanding of man, and an improvement of ethical principles and patterns of ethical behavior, to help him cope with the dangers.

3. The value of a multidisciplinary approach to ethics has become evident. Such an approach can use the contributions from biology, anthropology, psychodynamics, etc., as well as contributions from religious teaching and from the study of ethics by philosophers.

4. The pecking order (status order) in many animal species may be regarded as a Defensive Ethics, as a defense against continuing disruptive hostilities. But its existence is a disappointment to those who hope that biology would provide a basis for a democratic

or an egalitarian ethics. (Score one for pessimism!)

5. Social Darwinism was based on the idea that in the evolutionary process the survival of the fittest was achieved primarily through a ruthless hostility. Further, since man is an animal, the concept maintained that man was justified in his attempt to dominate or enslave weaker men or weaker groups, politically or economically, as part of the survival of the fittest. Scientific evidence in this century has undercut much of Social Darwinism and its negative implications for the future of man. (Score one for optimism!)

6. The predominant pessimism about man during the post-Darwinian period has been replaced by a cautious pessimism along with a cautious optimism. (No score.)

7. Biology stresses the fact that the stability of a species and the evolutionary change in a species both start with genetic transmission and genetic variations, followed by the process of natural selection in a struggle for survival. Survival may be achieved not only by competitive struggle, but also by patterns of cooperation and mutual help within the species. (A good serve!)

8. The well-developed systems of social organization among the higher animals may be prototypes of social organization in man and of his ethical behavior. (A good stroke!)

9. In many vertebrate animal species, living in their natural habitat, there are automatic interactions which stop severe fighting between members of the same species before one kills the other. Man may be almost the only vertebrate animal which as part of direct fighting regularly kills members of the same species. (An even better stroke, not necessarily a score for optimism, but negating some of the pessimism.)

10. Man's killing of man, man's inhumanity toward man, no longer can be regarded as the inevitable result of his biologic heritage. In good part, it may be cultural in origin, and related to the emotional complexities arising out of man's prolonged biologic period of dependency in early childhood. (It's a better game now, still very difficult, certainly more challenging, and perhaps more promising.)

11. "Either-Or" thinking (e.g. good guys versus bad guys) is too simple for a good novel, or for good theater, or for scientific understanding, or for ethics. This mode of thinking can be replaced by the kind of thinking which is characterized by the use of third alternatives and dynamic sequences, which includes the understanding of emotional conflict, of anxiety and defenses, and of resolutions, and by an awareness of the manysidedness of personality interactions.

12. One productive concept can be of a conflict of ethical systems within one individual, a conflict which can lead to a variety of resolutions. This can be phrased as a conflict between good and good, to supplement the usual concept of a conflict between good and evil (no matter what the definitions would be of good and of evil).

13. The chief emphasis, in the study of animals other than man, has been on their relations with forces *outside* them, that is, with other animals and with the forces of the environment. So the major problems of animals other than man seem to be found in their conflicts with the forces *outside* them.

14. In contrast, in the study of man, there must be two chief emphases. One emphasis is on the relation between the various forces *inside* man. The other emphasis is on man's relation with the forces *outside* himself. So the major problems of the human animal are found in the conflicts between the forces *inside* him, as well as in his conflicts with the forces *outside* himself.

15. Man is the only animal known with certainty to have major conflicts between his own internal forces. One example is man's conflict between his impulse to hurt or to destroy, and man's guilt and anxiety over those impulses. Another is the conflict between man's love and his hate.

16. Not all of man's internal forces are in conflict; some co-exist in relative peace and harmony. But man's potential for conflict between the forces within himself may be one of the most important characteristics of the human animal. Also, the resolution of his internal conflicts may be man's most important task. In part,

it is the central issue of ethics.

17. In the resolution of these conflicts, human beings develop many patterns of coping, many defenses. When the defenses are in keeping with the interests of the individual himself and at the same time do no damage to others, or even are in accord with the interests of others, they can be called "Defensive Ethics."

18. Also, an even more constructive type of ethical behavior, which is not essentially defensive, can be called "Creative Ethics." An example is the cooperative work of scientists throughout the world. Another is the mutual partnership between individuals, in productive work which has value for them and for a much larger group.

19. Ethical judgments, like scientific study, should be based, to some degree, on quantitative judgments as well as qualitative. A condemnation of oneself may be seriously incorrect unless a difference is made, in one's internal courtroom, between a felony and a misdemeanor.

20. Selective permissiveness and selective limit-setting can be integrated in child-raising. But the extreme version of each, unlimited permissiveness and destructive punishment, cannot be integrated productively.

21. "Contradictory voices of conscience," e.g. one of which tells one to try to get away with anything one wants to do, and the other which says one deserves contempt or severe criticism for even wishing for some minor pleasure or indulgence for oneself, often are based on child-raising which uses the extreme opposites of unlimited permissiveness and of destructive punishment.

22. "To understand all is to forgive all" is a very incomplete statement. In fact, in certain kinds of situations, psychiatrists may take a firmer approach than do most judges or law-enforcing agencies.

23. In the development of Creative Ethics and of effective ego-functioning, the use of the phrase "a creative tension between opposites" may be hampered by the word "opposites," which is part of the phrase. It is necessary, in spite of the word, to recognize

that opposites very often are not totally in opposition, but have vital interests in common. Examples are the development of the Geneva Convention about the treatment of war prisoners, and the creation of the European Common Market.

24. The concept of a productive relation, a two-way working alliance, can be one of the central patterns in a Creative Ethics.

25. Ambiguity in the patterns of an alliance may seem to provide a serious block to the development of an effective and productive alliance. But it need not block it. The fact that in many a good relation, the two parties ambiguously are basically equal-equal but also have certain inequalities, can be seen and accepted, and perhaps furthers the alliance.

26. The success of the therapeutic alliance seems the result largely of two of its characteristics. One is that it is a partnership. The second is that it is based on stringent self-scrutiny.

27. One pattern for Creative Ethics can be the development of many varieties of alliances, in which partnership and stringent self-scrutiny are built-in patterns.

7

The Conflict Between the Generations

A discussion of the conflict between the generations provides one of the most effective ways of demonstrating the impact of psychiatry on the further development of ethics. A number of facts, of concepts, and of insights from the field of psychiatry, and related fields, can be shown to have value, to have an impact on the understanding of the generation gap.[18] These patterns of understanding the generation gap then can be seen to have value in the further development of ethical principles and of ethical behavior.

For the first lead from the field of psychiatry, I shall use the story of the psychoanalytic society meeting in a nearby city, to which I referred briefly in the first chapter. The program chairman had invited me to be one of a panel of speakers at the meeting, a panel which was to consist of five elders of the tribe, each of whom had been in practice for thirty years or more. Each of us was asked to discuss the major trends of what we had learned in our work over the years. The invitation had referred to the length of our experience, and stressed how much we, the wise elders, could offer to the several younger generations now in practice.

The temptation was great to respond with pleasure to his politeness, to his optimistic hope, and to regard it as meaning that he
was a very perceptive person. The temptation was to accept the
implication that age and length of experience alone means that
one has much to say, or to teach, to the younger generation. It is a
marvelous fantasy, when one is in the fifties or sixties, to think that
omniscience now is inevitable.

This is the kind of temptation which must be faced by most of
us who are members of the older generation. In such an emergency,
the best prescription is to take a skeptical but benevolent self-
directed look inward. It takes only a quick look to show a man of
the older generation that although he may have some real assets,
they have clear limits. And he knows that in reality, age and experience at times may have led only to a large dark pile of incorrect observations and inferences. He knows also that years of work
and experience at times may lead in part to an increase in confusion, as the result of the accumulation of a larger number of
unclear observations.

But he knows too that in reality there are times when an older
man has some wisdom, or at least some good sense to pass on, and
that this evaluation need not be wishful thinking altogether. The
older man must look at the facts. He must try not to overevaluate
nor to underevaluate what he has to say to the younger generation.

Going further with this, it seems true that at all ages, there are
realities which may be exaggerated or distorted. During the first
third of our lives, the reality is that in certain ways we are relatively weak and dependent, very much so at first, then less so later
on. During this early period, one of our major problems is to avoid
some of our distorted or excessive reactions to our relative weakness and dependence. In the first third of one's life, one is a child,
then an adolescent, then a young man or woman. During that
period, one is a learner, a student, a beginner, one over whom
there are authorities. All of this often leads to feelings about oneself which are exaggerated or excessive or distorted, such as the
feeling of being totally weak and helpless, the feeling of needing

143

to be completely dependent and cared for. Strong feelings of weakness and helplessness lead to excessive feelings of inferiority and shame. These in turn may lead to intense anger and hostility over feeling so weak or so dependent, or to reactions of great impatience, of tremendous ambition and destructive competitiveness.

But as we keep going and working and developing, there is a remarkable change in our roles and in our problems. We become, in reality, more independent and much stronger in many ways. This begins at some point in the first third of our lives, and reaches full growth in the second third of our lives, say from twenty-five to fifty, and often increases still further in the last third. Usually, in the second third, we have come to assume a position of some leadership or authority, of being a parent, an older brother or sister, an adviser, a teacher, in some ways a leader. When this happens, one of our major problems is to deal with the temptation to distort this new status, and to have excessive or exaggerated or distorted feelings about this new role in life. For example, we may be tempted to have exaggerated attitudes of pride, or of grandeur, to feel Olympian, to have exaggerated feelings of achievement, to have impulses to dominate or to control, and then to have excessive feelings of guilt over being stronger, or feelings of guilt over our success.

During this period of strength and of leadership, especially when one is past forty or fifty, but often earlier, there is a danger that others will ask not only for some help, but for words of wisdom, for authoritarian answers. Then one may be tempted to have an unrealistic estimate of one's knowledge and experience, to talk with *ipse dixit* authority, and to have fantasies of omnipotence and omniscience.

It is of value to look further at the position of having some degree of authority or power or success, e.g. when one is in the position of being a teacher of students. At first, for most of us, when we speak from that eminence, no one listens! But as one comes to the five-year, the fifteen-year, or the thirty-year anniversary as a teacher, a different situation begins to evolve. If one knows one's job even fairly well, there will be times when residents or others will think of one as an oracle, as one who is able to speak the last word. This provides a marvelous temptation—which, Satan, must be resisted.

Then comes a more difficult job. One must be prepared to be regarded at times by the younger generation as not living up to their high expectations, as having to be protected by the younger generation because competing oracles have appeared on the scene. For example, in a good group of residents-in-training in psychiatry there often are many who are quick and perceptive, who have ideas which are unusually good. But often they hesitate about speaking out, for fear their ideas will be better than the ideas of the chief, of the one leading the seminar. A number of times during seminars I have seen a resident's face light up, obviously with understanding, and then his expression changes quickly to one more suitable for a game of poker. With this kind of data, plus a fair amount of looking at myself, I came to realize that something in me may have contributed in those instances to a resident's being afraid to express his own ideas. Essentially his fear was that the expression of his own good ideas would be competitive and destructive, would undercut the authority of the seminar leader. He seemed to feel that he must not speak out until I had reached a greater understanding on my own. Then he could make his comment without being afraid that it would be a blow to me, to my pride.

Finally, I devised a pattern which seems to be working. When I see a resident show the typical sequence, an expression of understanding followed by a poker face, I interrupt the seminar to say that I know that at least half of the group some day will be better psychiatrists than I am, and that some of them even now may understand some patients more quickly than I do. I say that they need not be afraid to speak up, that they know that I am a tough old so-and-so, who will not be hurt if they have good ideas, and that I will beat them the next night at table tennis if necessary.

Also, I say to them that the more good ideas our residents have and express, the more they may stimulate me or others of the faculty to have good ideas. And even more emphatically, I say that it is not surprising if at times they see things quickly and well, perhaps more so than I do. That happens, I insist, not because they basically are better or stronger than I am, but because they now are having so much better training than I had when I was a resident.

For my paper in the panel of elders, in the psychoanalytic meeting, I used the title, "The Myth of the Wise Elder Statesman." The point of view implicit in such a title has obvious relevance to the discussion of the generation conflict. The gist of the paper was that members of the older generation, out of experience and hard work, often do have important things to say, but not always. They must look at themselves, and at their temptation to make myths about themselves, and then be as honest as they can.

I began to insist also that members of the younger generation look at themselves, and at the fact that wishful thinking may occur at all ages, in all generations. Members of the older generation often have a "Myth of the Wisdom of the Older Generation," and members of the younger generation often have a "Myth of the Superiority of Fresh Blood and New Ideas." This type of wishful thinking is observed in psychiatric studies to be widespread, to be found in varying amounts in most human beings.

The impact of such wishful thinking may be reduced at times by a process of self-scrutiny. Therefore, it is imperative to express the profound conviction that in the conflict between the generations, the first step, the basic necessity, is for each one, or each group, to do a job of stringent but benevolent self-scrutiny.

Please note that my primary recommendation is *not* that one group start by scrutinizing the other group, or that the second group start by scrutinizing the first. That is being done all of the time, and if it is done correctly, and factually, without distortion, and not as an attack, it has value.

But stringent, honest, self-respecting self-scrutiny—that is not done, or not done enough. And yet it is one of the most valuable processes in life, which works well in many situations of high importance.

The next set of facts and concepts from the field of psychiatry, relevant to the conflict between the generations, can be presented with the mystery story title of "The Case of the Impossible Patient." The setting of the story is our low-fee psychiatric clinic which serves a wide variety of patients and agencies. A good part of the treatment of these patients is done by our residents, whose work is closely supervised by the faculty. The residents are medical school graduates now in their years of training in psychiatry. A basic part of their learning occurs in the process of intensive supervision by the psychiatry faculty of their work with individual patients.

One aspect of the supervisory process is an occasional discussion with the resident of the overall status of his caseload, i.e. the group of patients he is treating under supervision. For example, it is important that each resident have a varied caseload, so that he will have experience with a large variety of patients and problems. And over the years, I have come to suggest, to urge, even to insist, that each resident should always include in his current group of patients one or two of the kind which can be called "impossible cases."

To clarify that phrase, I must mention the fact that each resident (in psychiatry and in other fields) must learn the facts and the principles of his profession, and that he must base that learning largely on his own direct experience with patients. Out of his extensive and intensive experience, and out of observing the work of his contemporaries, he usually comes to the conclusion that a fairly large part of the body of working knowledge and techniques in his new field is sound and reliable. He comes to recognize the validity of many of the ideas of previous generations, ideas which were developed out of many hours of hard work, of hard thinking, of sweat, blood, and tears.

But we of the older generation know that conditions change, that the culture and the subcultures change, and that some of the problems of patients can change. We know that current residents-in-training are slightly different from the residents of previous generations. So we urge residents not only to make use of the work of the past, but also to test the validity of past conclusions, and to develop new patterns if necessary. As an example and as a symbol of this type of independence, we urge each resident to take on a patient occasionally who has a problem which usually is regarded as *impossible* to treat, as being out-of-line with the current concepts of treatability which are based on the work of previous generations.

An example of the impossible case is this. For generations, it seemed clear that enforced psychotherapy, i.e. treatment which is carried out under duress, in which a patient seems to have little motivation for the process of therapy, does not work out well. Specifically, a judge may say to a man who has been found guilty of gambling with his company's money that he has the choice either of going to the penitentiary or of having treatment in our outpatient psychiatric clinic, for which he is eligible since he now has little or no money. Over the years, our experience was that the man would choose the clinic rather than the penitentiary. But then he would regard the treatment as a process about which he was politely cooperative but in which he would be uninvolved. Therefore, years ago we asked the judges not to use this pattern of referral.

Some years later, I began to emphasize, even more than before, the value of individual and group self-scrutiny and self-criticism. I mentioned in seminars the value of trying to treat various kinds of "impossible cases." Several of the judges were told about my comments. In court, they gave several men the choice of going to our clinic or to the penitentiary. After our diagnostic studies, we decided to take in treatment several of these men—"impossible cases"—as a challenge. We found, perhaps because some component in our own attitudes had changed, that occasionally under certain conditions, such patients can get involved in treatment and can make good progress.

To make this more vivid, a more real experience for the reader, I shall describe what happened with one of these patients, who had been referred by a judge, and about whom there was a discussion, early in treatment, of the pattern of the referral, of his having been offered the choice of coming to the clinic or of going to the penitentiary. The patient followed this by giving vivid accounts of several episodes in his childhood, which showed, he said, that he had developed the point of view that it was demeaning, a sign of serious weakness, ever to ask anyone for help. For example, he never asked for and never got the help he needed in school work, until he was forced to stay after school for special tutoring. Also, in high school, he was regarded as a very good baseball player, but in his junior year his batting average slumped and stayed low, and he was about to be dropped from the team. He knew there was something wrong with his way of batting, which he could not bring into focus himself, but again he would not ask for help. Then the coach insisted on the two of them having several practice sessions together. During the practice, the coach persuaded him to use a new stance in batting, with very good results.

We took his recounting of those memories as a kind of signal to us that he knew he needed help, and that he was glad he was being forced, in a way, to have it. We took it as meaning that we should insist on full cooperation from him. In such an instance, the treatment still can not be easy, but a door to change had been opened by the judge forcing him, in effect, to have treatment. In fact, this patient, like some of the other impossible cases, has done well.

This pattern, of our saying that a resident always must have one or two impossible cases, is relevant to our understanding of the conflict between the generations. It means that both the older generation, the psychiatry faculty, and the younger generation, the psychiatry residents, in a program which tries to do a decent job, must recognize whatever sound values there are in the past achievements of many generations. But also they must have an open-mindedness to change, whether the change is suggested by the current older generations or by the younger generation. This is not out of righteousness, nor out of a wish to avoid a generation conflict, but out of the fact that all treatment methods and policies must be under constant scrutiny, for the sake of the well-being of our patients.

This example can be used to call attention to the fact that the conflict between the generations usually is visualized as a two-way street, as a two-sided situation. It is necessary now to see that some potential conflicts between the generations, e.g. between a faculty supervisor and a resident-in-training, must be visualized as three-sided, as a triangle. The three sides are the resident, the supervisor, and the patient. In this situation, the interests of all three sides are to be considered, but the interests of the patient must be pre-dominant.

Under such circumstances, the relation between the other two sides, the two generations, the resident and the supervisor, can be seen in a new perspective. The overriding interests of the patient, the third side of the triangle, makes it urgent that both of the others be realistic, they must see the value of using tested and proved procedures, and they must realize the high value of experience. This approach, these values, always have been the battle cry of the older generation. But also the overriding interests of the patient make it urgent that both generations see also the value of new ideas and of change. This has been the battle cry of the younger generation.

The Case of the Impossible Patient indicates, then, that a new and valuable perspective can be achieved by looking at the generation conflict when it occurs in a triangular setting as well as when it occurs simply in a one-to-one pattern. Then one can see that the values and the battle cries of both generations have a very great deal to offer.

There are other experiences also, in psychiatry, which give us leads about the generation conflict. For example, our work demands that we look carefully at any conflicts which develop or could develop between patient and psychiatrist. A patient may come to resent or to distrust the psychiatrist. And a psychiatrist may be irritated by the fact that a patient may not be impressed by the psychiatrist's understanding and skill, or may not appreciate his attempt to help.

We have come to recognize also that in spite of the conflicts which develop between patient and psychiatrist, there often develops a fairly good working relation between them, a therapeutic alliance, an alliance or a partnership for treatment. This alliance permits the work to go forward in spite of areas of conflict. In a way, the therapeutic alliance is the most important fact of life in the joint work of patient and psychiatrist. It can be nurtured and developed, as a vital condition for cure, for health, and for independence.

In brief, the potential gaps and conflicts between patient and psychiatrist are resolved, in the therapeutic alliance, by the patterns of partnership and of stringent self-scrutiny. This leads directly to a suggestion which may prove valid and valuable in the general field of ethical principles and ethical behavior. If the patterns of partnership, of alliance, and of self-scrutiny work well in the therapeutic alliance, they may be of high value also in dealing with a comparable issue, with the conflicts between the generations, and they may prove to be of value in the gaps and conflicts in other human relations as well.

The same suggestion can be derived from our experience with another kind of human relation which has been closely studied in psychiatry. This is the process of supervision. Even when we do not concentrate on the triangle in supervision, of patient, resident, and supervisor, and instead look carefully at supervision as a two-way process, we find that the process of supervision throws a flood of light on the generation conflict. In supervision, a younger, less experienced person, the resident, discusses his work with a more experienced person, the supervisor. Here, too, there are potential conflicts, since the two, the resident and the supervisor, are human beings. Each of them has certain strong impulses, perhaps too strong, e.g. to dominate or to submit, or to make an impression, or to be agreeable and accepting, or to rebel.

In the process of supervision and its problems, we find that if a supervisor expects his comments to be taken as gospel, he may be slightly arrogant in his approach to the resident, who then may resent being depreciated, and be tempted to enjoy catching the supervisor in a mistake. Therefore, in the process of supervision, a stringent self-scrutiny, as well as a feeling of partnership and of a two-way working alliance, are essential in preventing or overcoming a gap or conflict. Again the suggestion seems valid that stringent self-scrutiny, and a feeling of partnership, in a two-way working alliance, could be important in the resolution of a variety of interpersonal conflicts, and so can be regarded as ethical processes to be tried in many situations.

We turn now to an attempt to get beyond one of the great hurdles in understanding the conflict between the generations. Often the two generations seem to be unable to communicate, in part because each generation has a different understanding of the very starting point of their relation. Each of the two generations may have a different answer to the question of whether the two generations are basically equal or basically unequal in their relation to each other. One generation may think its own generation is, or should be regarded as, superior. Or one generation may be angry about the other generation's thinking itself superior, instead of recognizing the equality between the two.

The basically correct answer seems to be that the two generations are essentially equal and also that the two generations are unequal in certain ways.[19] The relation seems to be of equality and of inequality simultaneously. Much of the confusion in the present generation gap may arise from the fact that ambiguity, a double meaning, is one of the essential points in the relation between generations.

In each of the relations we have discussed so far in this book— in the relation between psychiatrist and patient, between supervisor and resident, between older adult and younger adult—there is an ambiguity, or an apparent ambiguity, something which seems to have a double meaning, which seems to be a contradiction that could only lead to confusion. The ambiguity resides in the fact that in each of these situations, the relation is one of equality and also one of inequality.

Of course, in certain cases the potential equality has been badly damaged or seriously prevented, by limitations in the chromosomal inheritance, or by seriously destructive experience in childhood, etc. But in most situations of generation conflict, and similar conflicts, the two are fairly equal-equal, or close to it, in ability, in potential strength, in rights, and in responsibility. But at the same moment, in each of these relations, there are a number of inequalities, not those due to chromosomal disorder or to destructive experience, but to universal human differences related to age, experience, etc. The older person or group, the psychiatrist, the supervisor, and the parents have a greater experience, a greater awareness of some of the facts of life and its opportunities and dangers. Often they have a slightly greater maturity, as well as the legal or professional or tribal responsibilities of guidance and help. But the others, the younger adults who are the relatively mature offspring of the older generation, or the graduate students, or the patients, have a number of qualities which are greater than those of the older adults. The younger adults often have a greater energy and enthusiasm, perhaps a more acute awareness of current developments, certainly a greater desire to learn, even though they deny it, and perhaps a greater ability to focus on the problems of the future.

In each of these relations, there is equality and inequality. Each relation is ambiguous. We hate ambiguity. We love simplicity. But at times we must learn to live with ambiguity. In fact, in certain ways, it provides an opening for favorable developments. For example, a husband and wife are equal-equal in many ways but very different in other ways, and out of that difference arises some of their happiest moments. A football player who throws a forward pass, and the offensive linesman who protects him, are both extremely valuable, equal-equal, but they have different body sizes and shapes, and different skills which can work together for great success.

The recognition of ambiguity in the relation between the generations is an honest appraisal of the way it is. It provides a solid basis for the two generations, or the two of another pair, to work together and to make something positive out of the relation. In fact, out of this ambiguity in the work of psychiatrist and patient, as well as in the work of supervisor and resident, as well as in the relation between older and younger adults, there can develop a creative interdependence, a new integration. Building on the ambiguity, the two generations can share in working toward the future, can work toward a greater joint responsibility, can develop a partnership which for a while longer consists of senior and junior members, which then becomes a partnership in which neither is senior or junior, and which finally becomes a partnership in which erstwhile seniors are juniors, and erstwhile juniors are seniors.

The next lead for the understanding of the generation gap, and of ethical principles more generally, comes from psychiatry, stimulated by a new set of facts in the field of anthropology. Our discussion of this lead starts with the fact that in our Cincinnati program, we have developed a new session, the NON-JOB Seminar. (The Job in the seminar title refers to the Old Testament figure of Job; it has no relation to the word "job," as meaning task or work to do.)

Our experience with this new seminar provides further material relevant to the conflict between the generations. It is a special breed of seminar, focusing on certain conflicts between our residents-in-training in psychiatry, most of whom are under thirty, and myself. A part of me is still much younger than thirty, in my love of lighthearted jingles and my dedication to the game of table tennis, but most of me is much over thirty.

Our discussion of the new seminar will have much more meaning and relevance if I mention some features of the setting in which it developed. Over the years, I have been deeply interested and involved in the process of the training of residents in psychiatry. As a result, the relation between the residents and myself has been a rather good one. But until recently the relation between us had to do primarily with our joint interest in their training, plus a joint interest in table tennis and some other games.

Then several years ago, a half-dozen issues and problems came to the boiling point. These were primarily administrative, involving policy decisions and implementation, interactions with workers of other disciplines, problems in the relations with faculty and administrative personnel, and issues of stipends and service rotations. In response to the immediate need for joint discussion of the issues, the pattern developed of the residents and myself having an additional series of regular seminars, not to discuss diagnosis and treatment, but to discuss administrative and departmental issues and conflicts.

During this period, I had been reading extensively in fields related to psychiatry. In this, one of the most stimulating experiences was provided by the book *Oedipus and Job in West African Religion*, written by the British anthropologist, Meyer Fortes.

Fortes demonstrates that in the religious beliefs and mythology of a number of West African cultures there are figures which correspond to Oedipus in the Hellenistic tradition and others which correspond to Job in the Old Testament. Fortes uses these two patterns as contrasting paradigms, not only in the field of religious belief and ritual, but also in discussing the relation of the growing child with the authority of the parents, and the relation of the individual with the authority and customs of the social organization. Fortes says, "They, Oedipus and Job, epitomize, poignantly and dramatically, two religious and ethical conceptions that seem to be mutually opposed in some respects but complementary in others." [20]

Fortes presents the detail of these patterns and beliefs as they appear in the tribes studied by himself and others, the rituals involved, etc. In this discussion, Fortes makes several general comments about the family and social sources of Oedipal and Jobian attitudes which are of high relevance to our discussion, such as: "Custom defines sons as their fathers' eventual supplanters but puts them in their fathers' absolute power." "Paternal authority, however conscientiously and benevolently exercised . . . . inevitably gives rise to suppressed hostility and opposition in sons." After discussing the central role of descent and kinship in the life of the individual, Fortes says, "But there is another pole of existence for him. There is the fact of his individuality." [21]

In his evaluation of these two patterns as they appear in the conflict between the generations, Fortes gives higher value to the Jobian principle than to the Oedipal principle. The Jobian pattern, he says, "recognizes the paramountcy of the moral norms emanating from society as a whole over the dangerous egotism of childhood." But at other points he says that Oedipal concepts "recognize forces in social and personal development that cannot be changed or regulated by society." [22]

My own experience and that of others would lead us to put more value on the Oedipal pattern and its derivatives than does Fortes. I would place greater emphasis than he does on the productive potential as well as the danger of the aggressive competitive impulses of childhood. Therefore the following notes on Oedipus and Job differ somewhat from those of Fortes. But it is deeply influenced by his material and especially by his Oedipus-Job contrast which seems so valuable in clarifying the issues of the conflict between the generations.

The figure of Oedipus is of one who acts out, in minor or major ways, certain impulses which may be universal, or at least very frequent. He seems driven to have the forbidden, to be independent and nonconformist, to break the laws, to defy his fate, or to rebel against the authority of the gods. In other ways he may be conformist and law-abiding.

The figure of Job also is of one who acts out in minor or major ways certain impulses which may be universal, or at least very frequent. He seems deeply accepting of authority, driven predominantly to obey the customs and the laws. He believes the Deity will reward goodness and punish evil. When he is convinced of his innocence and yet must suffer, he insists that the Deity should follow the expected pattern, should praise Job for his goodness, and not make him suffer. But eventually Job accepts as inevitable the fact that the Deity may fulfill Job's expectation or not do so. And at that point, he bows to the inevitable, because he is certain of the wisdom and the essential goodness of the authority, the Deity.

In the Hellenistic tradition, Oedipus was not the only figure who emphasized rebellion and defiance. The Greek word "hubris," which may be translated as arrogance or overweening pride, expressed a dominant quality of many of the figures of Greek mythology, and represented one of the patterns of the culture, of aggressive independence, of striving to be as strong as a god. The defiance often was linked with severe punishment, such as a god-inflicted curse which was to persist for generations. There are patterns of obedience and submission in the Greek tradition, but the greater emphasis seems to be on the value of independence, and on the defiance of what seems to be unfair authority, an unjust Fate.

Somewhat in contrast, in the Judeo-Christian tradition, the emphasis is on the value system of obedience to Deity and to law, and the need for an acceptance which glorifies the authority. (Job was more contentious and argumentative with the Deity than were many other biblical figures.) In the Old Testament and in the New Testament, there are many clearly rebellious figures such as Adam and Eve, but the predominant emphasis is on the observance of the law, and on regarding the power and the wisdom of the Deity as preeminent.

Both Oedipus and Job are complex figures, not merely stereotypes nor merely bipolar; like the Hellenistic and Judeo-Christian cultures they are complex and many-sided. But Oedipus and Job each have dominant patterns which differ from those of the other, and their names can be used to symbolize an essential issue in our consideration of human responses and of ethical patterns.

We can avoid making the contrast into a pair of opposites or extremes, and still make productive use of the fact, based on many observations, that there are two central patterns, among many others, in the relation between man and Deity, in the relation between child and parent, in the relation between a member of a group and the group norms or its leaders, and perhaps between a younger adult generation and an older generation. These can be phrased as two types of response to the task which faces each child as it develops from infancy to maturity, and to membership in the tribe or culture. In that process, the younger generation at first is young and weak, then goes through various stages of its own development as it learns the ways of the tribe or the culture, and eventually becomes a participant and perhaps a leader.

In the first of the two patterns, the one symbolized by Oedipus, the stress is on rebellion and on defiance of authority or defiance of the patterns of the group. At various periods, the young one gives priority emphatically to his individual needs, to his independence. But eventually, in many instances, perhaps after a stormy period, he becomes in most ways a member of the culture, perhaps as a conformist, perhaps as an individualist. Occasionally he remains primarily independent.

In the second of the two patterns, symbolized by Job, the young one accepts in most ways the patterns of the group, and behaves in conformity with them. He may be competitive or rebellious at times, and may voice his criticism of the injustice that limits him or causes him to suffer. And in various ways he may be independent in his thinking and feeling. But in this second pattern, there is a much greater emphasis on group values, and on an identification with the authority of the group or of its leaders.

Each pattern may be exaggerated into an unworkable or destructive caricature of itself. The Oedipal drive toward independence and individualization, of wanting to be as powerful as any of the authorities or to supplant or to surpass them, of wanting to be free of group standards, may be exaggerated into a severely rebellious unworkable defiance. Also the Jobian drive toward dependence and group participation, of acceptance of the authority of the leader and an identification with the group values, may become its own caricature, of an extremely submissive attitude.

It must be emphasized that both approaches have many positives. The Oedipus pattern seems to be linked with a persistent need to know what the gods can know, to understand what is happening in the world, to try to do or to see what was reserved for the gods or was forbidden to man. This can be linked with the extraordinary development of philosophy, mathematics, the sciences, and the arts, in the "glory that was Greece." And the Job pattern, with its great emphasis on the benevolence, the righteousness, and the wisdom of the authority, can be linked with many of the enormously important values in the Judeo-Christian tradition.

In my own work I found the Oedipus-Job contrast to be even more productive than some of the other important dichotomies which previously had been proposed. One was the Apollonian-Dionysian contrast of Nietzsche. Another was the extrovert-introvert dichotomy of Jung.

But I must sound a warning. There are dangers in even the best of contrasts or dichotomies. Any dichotomy tempts one to use the either-or approach. So if we use the Oedipus-Job contrast, it always must be with a full awareness that contrasts are valuable primarily to foster clear thinking, but in reality represent emphases or high points in a pluralistic and dynamic set of patterns.

The reading of the Fortes book happened to come at the time when the residents and I were developing the new seminar, in which they and I were to talk not about diagnosis and treatment, but about the relation between the generations, between them and me, about their relation with other faculty and with administration, and with other disciplines. So, when we were thinking about a name for the new seminar, I suggested, in a halfway teasing fashion, that the title be "The Neither Oedipus Nor Job Seminar." This quickly became shortened to the NON-JOB Seminar, with the N-O-N in the NON-JOB title referring to the first letters of the words, Neither Oedipus Nor.

The title often seems a bit amusing. It is reminiscent of the non-heroes or antiheroes of recent literature. But the title has been of high value. It helped to set the tone for the ongoing discussions, a tone which is much more difficult to achieve in a discussion of the problems which exist between the discussants themselves than it is to achieve in a discussion of the diagnosis and treatment of a third party, a patient. In the new seminar, the situation no longer is the triangle of residents, faculty, and patient, but is a dyad, of two sides, of residents and faculty. The stabilizing effect of the primacy of the interests of the patient no longer is present, and in its place there developed the NON-JOB conceptual framework, as the stabilizing force in the interaction.

The name of the seminar is a constant reminder of several crucial facts in that conceptual framework. The "Neither Oedipus" portion of the title means that the residents will attempt to behave toward me, or to learn to behave toward me, in a way that will be relatively free of the untamed Oedipal drive to replace me, to kill or defeat a father or a father figure, or to be persistently rebellious or nonconformist. Concurrently the "Neither Oedipus" portion of the title means that I, as the party of the second part, will constantly try *not* to behave in an untamed way, like a force of Destiny, or like one of the gods against whom Oedipus and others felt it their obligation to rebel. I was to learn *not* to act as if I were a powerful figure of Fate, *not* to act as if I were one of the gods of the Pantheon, who could be threatened by the independence of men and women, and who could throw thunderbolts or curses at men.

At the same time, the "NON-JOB" portion of the title means that in this seminar, the residents were *not* expected to be submissive and obedient if and when I had done something they did not understand, *not* expected to accept the power of my presence, or my leadership without question. And at the same time I was expected to avoid the temptation to behave as if I were Jehovah, as if at times I could be above all agreements and laws, as if I could be so trustworthy and righteous that what I did would deserve unquestioning acceptance and obedience.

It has been a very good learning process for the parties of both parts, for many of us. We have learned that it is possible to behave with a much greater degree of partnership than before, and to have many a productive dialog and meaningful encounter. And we have learned that in this kind of NON-JOB relationship, there still are rules. This is not a group in which anything goes, in which the residents insult me or I insult them. This is not a situation in which they try to expose my weaknesses. Nor do I say that their behavior is childish or neurotic.

The seminar has a combination of permissiveness toward honest expression of opinion, of permissiveness toward the kind of criticism of others which is in fact acceptable in such a relationship, plus a set of understood limits which excludes the acting out of hostility. The old concept of abreaction, of the release into action of previously dammed-up expressions of emotion, has no place in the conceptualization of this seminar. Inevitably a healthy limit-setting is present from the beginning. There is no attempt to make the party of the other part feel guilty or ashamed. There is no use of the technique of threats or punishment.

One element of the process of the seminar is the development of mutual understanding, the correction of misunderstandings, and often some compromises and new approaches. Even more, it becomes evident that out of the interchanges and interactions in which there is a sincere attempt to clarify differences and to find bridges, linkages, areas of agreement, and better patterns of relation, there develops something new, a new kind of partnership, an alliance. Or more correctly phrased, the alliance which previously had been present in the seminars on diagnosis and treatment now in good part is present in the NON-JOB Seminars, as an alliance with regard to administrative and organizational matters.

But one can never expect completeness or fullness or perfection in this sort of development. Even after several years of such a seminar, it remains clear that in certain ways some of the group are somewhat skeptical about my patterns of administration, perhaps even about my honesty or integrity. And it remains clear that I have some degree of skepticism about certain patterns of some of the residents. But this seems inevitable and healthy. If it were not so, we should be skeptical about the whole process, be concerned that it might be merely like a soothing salve on an irritated skin, or that it might be merely a pattern of sweetness and light which conceals the problems which had led to the bitter taste or to the dark shadows.

At this stage in the description of the NON-JOB Seminar, it is imperative that I be blunt about one point. There is a danger that my phrasing of this approach can give the impression that in such NON-JOB Seminars there is a predominance of warmth and affection and congeniality. Such feelings occur, but so do uncongenial and angry emotions. There is a great deal of frankness and openness. Insults are not part of the pattern, but a frank statement can be made by one about what seems to be mistaken logic on the part of the other, or what seems to be an attempt on the part of one to dominate the other. In good working relations in general, sharpness can occur with some frequency, if the other person or persons can take it, and if the chief motivation for the sharpness is to make progress in the discussion of the problem at hand or in the relation, rather than the chief motivation being the wish to make a point, or of winning in the game of one-up-manship.

The NON-JOB Seminar can be contrasted with two other patterns. It differs from sensitivity training groups, encounter groups, and related procedures in that the NON-JOB places strong emphasis on Ego patterns. It emphasizes limits as well as permissiveness. Second, the NON-JOB differs from the debating process, and from the adversary system in a court of law. In the adversary system, each side does try to win points, does try to undercut the other, does try to take advantage of slips by the other. Such an essentially hostile, or potentially hostile, interchange, if it is to work well, requires that there be an impartial judge or jury. The NON-JOB Seminar, since it is not primarily an attempt to win out over the other side, does not require a judge or jury.

But this is not to underestimate the value of the adversary system in the history of mankind. As long as there are individuals who are tyrants, as long as there are some who are strongly motivated to take advantage of others, as long as serious accusations are made by one person against another, or by those in authority, there must exist a system in which the individual can defend himself, and can have the guidance and help of someone who knows the law and is skillful in planning a defense against attack. There must be a forum in which the accused can face his accuser. There must be a situation in which those who are less powerful can make use of a preformed pattern in which they can defend themselves against those who are more powerful.

In spite of its great deficiencies, the adversary system has an important place in our civilization. It can be regarded as a form of Defensive Ethics, as a system in which an individual can defend himself against unfair attack, one in which there is a goal of fair play and justice and the protection of all individuals under the law. In this system, the goal is to have a government of laws more than of men.

But the adversary system's deficiencies, its emphasis on the struggle, on the attack and counterattack, means that in many situations, when there is criticism or attack but also a basic mutuality of purpose, the adversary system is not good enough. Another pattern is needed, such as the NON-JOB, one which does not emphasize a defensive ethics, the process of attack and defense against attack, or a counterattack against attack. Rather, in good part, the NON-JOB pattern is beyond the adversary system.

The NON-JOB approach is in line with the widespread biologic pattern of cooperation and mutual help, which is one of the two major categories of techniques of biologic survival. The other widespread biologic pattern, of competition and struggle, is the other major category of techniques of biologic survival. If one tries to phrase these two patterns of behavior in terms of ethics rather than in terms of survival, one can say that in individual human beings and in groups of human beings there are at least two basic patterns of ethics. One is a Defensive Ethics, the attempt to prevent struggle and conflicts and hostility (which are related to one pattern of survival) from becoming disruptive or lethal. The second is a Creative Ethics, the development of patterns of joint effort (which are related to the other pattern of survival) in which many positive creative developments can occur. The NON-JOB in this frame of reference is part of the second type of ethics.

Inevitably, my conviction of the value of this approach leads me to suggest that various groups explore the ways in which the NON-JOB pattern can be used, as a technique which is profoundly ethical, and which may have great practical value. The NON-JOB seems most suitable for an interaction between some younger adults and some older adults, as we have used it. It may be useful in other age groups also, and in other situations, but perhaps with modifications. For example, with adolescents, it often would be necessary to modify the pattern in the direction of having the older generation use a greater amount of leadership. This is so, because in adolescence (and to some degree afterward) there are many feelings of uncertainty, many fluctuations, and many a fast turn of the wheel of personal dynamics. Many human beings, perhaps particularly in the period of adolescence, have strong needs to have limits be set, even though they express strong rebellious attitudes. Many adolescents want parents to express their affection and love and helpfulness by saying "No" when it is needed, as well as by saying "Yes" at other times.

There is much more to be said about the conflict between the generations. But most of it is based on sociologic and anthropologic understanding, and so it should be said by those who are in disciplines other than psychiatry. I shall limit myself to some comments on the use of violence.

Obviously there are many times in which an emphasis on partnership and on self-scrutiny cannot work. At times it is necessary to use physical force to defend oneself or to protect another person. For example, if one sees a stronger person, or an armed person, attacking another, one must try to stop the attack, either by calling the police, or if necessary, by a direct defense of the one being mistreated and using whatever means are at hand.

Or, let us suppose that one is a doctor taking care of a patient who has heart trouble. Suppose, further, that the physiologic state of the patient begins to decompensate. The oxygen supply of the brain becomes lower than is required for good function, and waste products of the metabolism of the brain are not washed away because of the weakened circulation of blood. This is a situation in which the patient may develop a cardiac delirium.

In the delirium he may be sufficiently confused so that he thinks he is at home rather than in the hospital. He does not recall that he is sick, and begins to look for his clothes, to get dressed, and to leave. The physical activity involved in this behavior could lead to his death or to a severe exacerbation of his illness. Under such circumstances, the ethical responsibility of the doctors and of the nurses is to deprive him of his civil rights for the time being, and to force him to stay. Physical restriction may be necessary for a short time. Hopefully, this would not be the kind of physical force that would evoke a struggle. Most of the temporary restraint can be achieved by the use of adequate medication.

Then, since the patient is being forced to stay in the hospital, i.e. to do something which he says he does not want to do, it is imperative that the family (and at times his lawyer) be asked to come to the hospital, to join in the decisions which must be made. Also if the patient must be forced to stay in the hospital against his wishes for a longer period of time, legal action often is called for, so that the decision to deprive him temporarily of his rights, for his own sake, can be made by a legally constituted authority, by a judge who would have the right to appoint his own experts to determine the patient's condition. But along with such measures, there must be expert nursing and medical care, in which a NON-JOB partnership with the patient may contribute more to a good result than does the use of physical force or medication.

This example, of the procedures used with a delirious cardiac patient, indicates that surely there exist a number of situations in which a sincerely accepted ethical responsibility requires the use of physical control of one individual over another, which may require even a physical struggle to achieve the control. But this ethical pattern raises serious dangers of misuse. Consequently the recommendation must be that any one who takes such a responsibility must repeatedly use the process of stringent self-scrutiny, and must share the responsibility with other responsible individuals, such as family, friends, and legal authority.

In this example, we referred to the protection of the patient In other situations, the protection of others and of society must be regarded as paramount.

I recognize the danger of the concept that force occasionally must be a part of the process of defensive or protective ethics and could be used as an argument to justify violence as a primary or essential or inevitable component in the relation between the generations. This would be a mistake, but the risk of that mistake should not block our recognition of the fact that, as a part of defensive or protective ethics, the use of force can be necessary occasionally by the younger or by the older generation. For example, if a boy of fifteen or sixteen sees his father or his uncle be physically cruel to his sister or to his mother or to his younger brother, the boy has an obligation to do his best to stop the aggressor, even by force. Similarly if a father or mother sees that an adolescent is about to take a drug which in reality, not merely by legal definition or regulation, may do serious harm, the parent's ethical responsibility is to take away the drug, by force if necessary. But I would emphasize the fact that the son or nephew in the first instance, and the parent in the second instance, must do his best to see to it that the use of physical strength is only an emergency episode in an otherwise good working relation.

From the perspective of psychiatry, I see physical force, even violence as an occasional part of Defensive Ethics. But I see nothing in the field of psychiatry that would justify violence as a basic or necessary ingredient in the development of a workable relation, of a Creative Ethics. Perhaps in certain cultures or social systems, a quota of violence is necessary as a step that precedes the development of a conjoint positive relation; this is a question which cannot be answered on the basis of psychiatric evidence, as far as I can see.

In general we can see fairly clearly what the pattern can be, what the Creative Ethics can be, in a therapeutic alliance, in a supervision alliance, in a NON-JOB Seminar, and in a NON-JOB approach to the conflict between the generations. In each, there are prominent elements of stringent self-scrutiny, of mutuality, cooperation and partnership, and of the avoidance of excessive rebellion, compliance, or domination. There can be a tolerance and an acceptance of the inevitable ambiguity of equality and inequality in many human relations. There can be a sincere attempt to develop a new and productive relationship. And in a Creative Ethics there may be short periods in which techniques of control or the use of physical force is necessary, safeguarded by the speedy participation of the family and of the law.

This approach, of Creative Ethics, seems the most effective, the most promising, in many situations. But at times it will not work.

When there is dogmatic cruel leadership, or a destructively aggressive takeover, or destructive revolutionary activity, or destructive dictatorial authority, or the continuing use of force which throttles opposition or individuality, or a serious misuse of power, when any of these exist in reality, the situation becomes a different kettle of fish, requiring, for a time, other considerations and other behavior than that of Creative Ethics. Instead, the patterns used may be of Defensive Ethics, including even the use of defensive violence, if it is an urgent overriding necessity. But it must be done with as much honesty, as much stringent self-scrutiny, as one can mobilize. And such a decision should be based on a consensus of opinion of others whose stability one can trust.

It seems true that so far in human history, man's approach to life, to other human beings, and to himself has been based to an extraordinary degree on a competitive struggle, on the use of force, on a destructive offense and defense, on fighting and killing, on severe punishment, and on self-punishment. It seems true that in human life there are many opportunities to emphasize another approach, of the use of a positive and creative alliance, of various forms of Creative Ethics combined with various forms of Defensive Ethics.

The recognition of the value of this approach may be increased in the future as a by-product of the recognition by biologists of the widespread occurrence in animal life of an extraordinary emphasis on cooperation for survival and on social organization, as well as on competition and struggle. Also the cogency of this approach is underlined by the fact that in man all known cultures have extensive patterns of social organization and group living. Further, the logic of this approach is underlined by the fact that in man, in almost every known culture, there is a prohibition of some forms of in-group killing and of some other forms of in-group destructive behavior. For example, in all known cultures, there is a prohibition of some forms of incest, perhaps as a cultural delimitation of behavior which can be destructive, can damage others or disrupt the group.

Further, the cogency of this approach is increased by the fact that certain alliances, such as the European Common Market, have been more effective than was predicted. And in human relations such as the therapeutic alliance, the difficult role of partnership and the difficult process of self-scrutiny have led to surprising improvements.

To shift still further from the conflict between the generations to destructive conflicts in general, one can say that from the available facts the conclusion may be that human beings some day will learn that violence often is second-best, often is self-punitive and self-defeating. We may learn that interdependent alliances and integrations can be effective as practical measures. Changes in transportation and in communication may facilitate the process of regarding all humanity as members of the same species. Techniques may emerge that are solid and workable for the lessening of destructive hostility and for the building of a civilization which to a much greater degree is based on joint interests and mutual relations, which can be beyond the adversary system, and to a greater degree deserve Freud's term of being postambivalent.

Finally, there is a widespread recognition of the fact that for the first time in history there is a force—not superhuman but a force in human hands—the power of nuclear weapons, which is capable of destroying or of decimating the human race. This may stimulate the emergence in man of some form of the pattern found in most other animal species, of an effective avoidance of the killing of animals by members of the same species. The stalemate of nuclear power has given us borrowed time. It may give time enough for the emergence of a defense against man's killing of man, which in man may prove to be a cultural defense against a destructiveness which is cultural in origin. And one pathway toward such a defense may be the combination of a further development of Defensive Ethics, along with the development of new types of integration, new kinds of alliance, new forms of Creative Ethics.

8

Id, Ego, and Superego

Ⅰ F one looks at the substance of the previous chapters from the perspective of man's attempt to cope with the world, one can say that two major emphases have emerged, which seem to be in sharp contrast. The first is that man is really up against it, in this his life. Man is confronted by many powerful forces, both outside and inside himself. And these forces often seem impersonal and overwhelming.

The second is that man has done an amazing job, responding in many ways with strength and flexibility. He has tried hard to cope with, and to master, the forces which threaten him. He succeeds in some ways, and fails in others.

This contrast between the forces acting on man, and man's active responses, can be understood more fully in the setting of a similar interplay in the lives of all animals. The starting point is the DNA code, the set of genetic messages in the chromosomes which go from one generation to the next, spelling out the basic biologic inheritance. There is a specific pattern of messages for each species, which is a powerful factor, indeed, in the life of any member of the species.

But also there are many individual variations in heredity, in the genetic endowment. These variations, mutations, appear constantly in any animal population, in what George Wald, the biologist, calls the mistakes in the messages in the genetic code.

The beginning of the life of an individual animal, therefore, can be regarded as a "passive" process from the standpoint of the animal to be born, since the individual animal does not play an active part in receiving the chromosome stability of the species or in receiving the chromosome variations in itself. Then, after it is born, the animal is passive in another sense, in that its life is deeply influenced by the conditions of its environment and by the impact of other animals. The interplay of these three—genetic endowment, environmental circumstances, and the impact of other animals— are the forces which in good part shape the life of the animal.

But there is activity as well as passivity in the picture. The young animal begins to be an active participant in the process. It plays a role in its own individual survival, by its active responses to the environment, within the range permitted by its genetic endowment and by the residuals of the influence of its earlier experience.

The members of each species play an active role in the destiny of the species. They adapt and adjust and change. They must do so to survive. The species' struggle for survival, both by competition and by cooperation, is an active process, of interaction, of change, and of growth. In the individual animal, the alertness to danger, speed of response, coping with the environment, patterns of adaptation and adjustment to other animals and to external conditions— all of these are active processes, which differentiate living organisms from nonliving objects, from the passivity of a grain of sand.

To this degree at least, life, for infrahuman animals, is not only a passive submission to the forces of the environment, to the availability of food and water, to the animate and inanimate dangers. Each species of animal has specific patterns of coping actively with, or of mastering the problems of, life, or of trying to do so.

Then when we turn to the human animal, we see that in man there is a comparable struggle between powerful external (and internal) forces and his own powerful attempts to defend himself, to cope and to master. First, man must cope with most of the forces confronting the other animals. In addition, man, in contrast to most of the other vertebrate animals, must face the danger of being killed by others of his own species. His development of conceptual thinking, of language, of fantasy, and of projection means that men may regard men in a nearby valley as if they were members of another species, and so may kill and be killed. Third, and at times most important, man must cope with a large variety of forces within himself, which often are in conflict.

These internal forces in man, when they are seen clearly, in the course of psychiatric diagnostic studies, may give the impression that they are so powerful and so impersonal, like the forces in the world outside, that they can determine the course of our lives. So Freud used the impersonal pronoun, the Id, the "it," to epitomize their impersonality. The Id forces in the human being are the basic biologic and psychologic drives toward gratification, toward behavior of one sort or another. They are the untamed or partly tamed drives, which basically need not be destructive, but in their original form are destructive but with the potential for valuable development. In general they are the internal forces by which we seem to be lived, in Freud's description, emphasizing their power. They include the insistent, persistent, and repetitive basic impulses or drives (at times called instincts) which may be sexual, aggressive, self-aggrandizing, competitive, destructive, hostile, etc.

In the development of an ethics which is sound biologically and psychodynamically, it is imperative to emphasize the existence and the strength of the forces we call the Id. In their untamed, unmodified form, these internal forces often are antagonistic to the interests of others, as well as to the intelligent self-interest of the individual himself. And these forces may actually be irresistible in good part at times, or may seem to be. To some degree they are not under man's own control. Some of them are unconscious, are not even known to man, even at the moment they exert their great pressure.

In the development of a workable ethics, two points must be made about the Id forces. One is to emphasize the fact that the forces of the Id, in their unchanged or primitive form, often are unacceptable to the individual himself and to others. Second, an emphasis on the demanding, persistent, surging forces of the Id can help us debunk the unworkable notion that a human being can simply be given a set of rules and be expected to behave fully in accordance with those rules, or that he is free to do so, free of the forces within him which fight strongly against his behaving in obedience to the rules.

Historically, the first group of psychoanalytic studies, by Freud and others, focused primarily on the Id, the deep and hidden forces, the drives. Then came the second period, in the 1920s and 1930s, in which the studies focused more directly on the internal standard-setting forces which together are called the Superego. This term includes the forces usually called the conscious, which is the conscious part of the Superego, plus the unconscious portion of the Superego, i.e. the more deeply embedded unconscious portion of the internal standard-setting forces. To link these terms with the material in Chapter IV, we can say that modesty was the Superego force and exhibitionism the Id force, in the conflict between the two, which was discussed entensively in describing the varieties of resolution of conflict, the Defensive Ethics of sublimation, and the Defensive Ethics of restriction of overt behavior to a suitable time, place, and person.

One of the extraordinary discoveries of psychoanalytic research, during the second period when the focus was on the Superego, was that it is a mistake to conceptualize the conscience, the Super-ego, as exerting its influence by a single voice of conscience which will give the right answer, which represents the voice of morality or of reason. The conscience has several voices. And even more important, a good part of the Superego can not speak, has no audible voice, is unconscious, is unknown to the individual, but nevertheless is acting with great force and impact. In fact, the unconscious portion of the conscience, which often is archaic or outmoded, is one of the strongest forces in human life.

For example, many a woman wants to have a good sexual relation with her husband, but she is unable to do so because a hidden,
deeply forgotten part of her personality had accepted totally and
forever the doctrine that sex is dirty and forbidden. And many a
man recognizes, in terms of his contemporary conscience, that marriage essentially is an equal-equal relation, but he behaves at times
as if there were a part of his conscience which says, "Thou shalt
never permit a woman to be thy equal or thy partner." In his
childhood he may have seen that attitude used by an adult with
whom he identified strongly, and so he came to think that this was
the way life should be. Or perhaps the principle he uses is his
own distorted version of a less extreme pattern which he had
seen in his childhood.

During this second period of the history of psychoanalysis, in
which the pathways of the Superego were charted, there were many
direct observations of the ways in which the Superego could be
corrupted. It has been known since time immemorial that a man
can be corrupted by power, by weakness, by money, by pride, by
sexual temptation, corrupted to the point of violating his own
standards, his promises, and his loyalty, and then of justifying or
rationalizing the change. The new finding was that suffering, perhaps even more than power or money or sex or other temptations,
is the corrupting force. It may be suffering produced by conditions
outside the man himself but which unconsciously he uses in the
process of being corrupted. Or the suffering may unconsciously be
imposed by the individual on himself, and then used as the agent
of corruption.

A study of one man, Mr. X, who had this Superego pattern,
showed that he had deep and persistent impulses to compete
destructively with other boys and then with men. But he did not
put these impulses, strong as they were, into action. Even so, he
felt as guilty as if he had actually behaved destructively toward
others, as if one must feel just as guilty over bad impulses as over
bad actions. He had not acted or spoken destructively toward

others, but his guilt over his impulses to do so was severe and harsh and unremitting.

Gradually the feelings of guilt seemed to dominate his emotional life. And feeling pervasively guilty, he seemed to be trying to do penance, to seek absolution, by becoming extremely gentle and passive and subservient to other men, frequently demeaning himself unnecessarily. It was as if he were trying to prove that he had no trace of hostility to others, that he was just a "sweet guy," who would "never hurt a fly."

But then his subservient, self-demeaning behavior began to hurt his pride. He began to feel ashamed of himself, was convinced that he was a failure, unable to hold his own with others. He was chronically somewhat depressed. Over a long period of time, he behaved as if he actually were guilty of destructive behavior, and punished himself by feeling worthless, inferior, and deficient, and then behaved as if he actually was incompetent and deficient. He continued to work and to live an average life in many ways, but just beneath the surface, he was in a state of real and fairly constant suffering.

Then after several years of this pattern, of suffering, depression, guilt, self-depreciation, and shame, he began for the first time in his life to be openly hostile in his behavior toward other men, mildly but repeatedly. He was sarcastic and depreciating toward them, and about them. Finally, he began to lie about other men, merely small lies of little consequence. But in two instances, he told enough small lies, distorted facts enough and for a long enough time, to do real damage to the business career of one friend and to the professional career of a second. Mr. X, who for years had been overly gentle with others, even subservient, never openly competitive or hostile, deeply self-critical, and suffering rather severely, now became capable of lying destructively about others.

In a sense, over the years, he had built a bank account of suffering, of self-imposed martyrdom. And suffering is an extraordinary currency when it is banked, at compound interest. It may permit an individual to feel severely mistreated by life, to feel that he had suffered so long that he now could feel free to make others suffer as well, ignoring his own conscience in the process. In this sense, suffering, at first imposed by a guilty conscience, is used unconsciously to corrupt the conscience. Speaking metaphorically, we can rephrase this sequence and say that the conscience is deeply impressed by the severe suffering. It is convinced that the guilt was washed away by the atonement of suffering. The work of the conscience seems finished, and it becomes drowsy. It pays no attention, then, to the fact that the original hostile impulses have reappeared and have led to hostile actions, to destructive behavior.

Another metaphor which can be used for this pattern is to say that the conscience, in its functioning as a border guard, at the border between impulse and action, is given the bribe of severe and long suffering, to close its eyes and ears to the fact that impulses toward hostile behavior no longer are merely impulses, and that behavior which is destructive, the lying about other men, is actually taking place. The "bribery of the Superego," of the conscience, is a famous phrase in psychoanalysis.

There are dangers, then, of serious distortion in the functioning of the human conscience, dangers which may arise from unconscious dynamic patterns. Therefore, the old prescription in the field of ethics, to "let your conscience be your guide," may not be good enough. The new prescription can be, "Let your conscience be your guide, but only if you, as a self-respecting man or woman of conscience, have been skeptical enough, and used a stringent self-scrutiny often enough, about your conscience."

In the historical sequence of psychoanalytic studies, the primary emphasis shifted gradually from the studies of Id and Superego, to the study of the third group of internal forces, those of the Ego. The work of Anna Freud and a large number of psychoanalysts and other workers has given a firm basis for the understanding of the forces of the Ego, for an Ego-psychology.

The Ego comprises the set of forces which can be defined as

having the basic job of doing something about the various forces and conflicts within the human being. The Ego is a kind of mediator, a conciliation service, one which says "Hey there, boys, stop fighting and we'll find a way to deal with all this."

These three, the Id, the Superego, and the Ego are not three little men inside the skull, fighting for control and domination, although at times the metaphoric or anthropomorphic use of these three words makes it sound that way. The three terms are essentially shorthand words for three overlapping and interacting groups of forces, at a number of levels.

The Ego is the set of forces which tries to cope with internal conflicts. It is the executive, coordinating, adaptive, problem-solving, integrating, controlling, and compromising set of forces in the personality. Also it works toward the resolution of conflicts between the individual and the external world. To a large degree, the Ego is realistic and pluralistic. It has many of the attributes which were described earlier as comprising the third kind of thinking.

This description of the human animal, then, includes three sets of internal forces. One is the profoundly strong, rather impersonal forces of the Id. The second is the Superego. The third is the group of forces, the Ego, which attempts to use reason, reality, adaptation, integration, and resolution as its principles.

Such phrases as the impersonal forces of the Id, the rigid unconscious portions of the Superego, and the integrative functions of the Ego lead inevitably to the question of whether this picture of man throws light on the age-old problem of freedom of the will and of psychic determinism. Involved in such considerations also are several very practical questions. One is the issue of man's responsibility for his own behavior. Can human beings control their primary drives or their disturbed feelings, thinking, or behavior, if only they would try to do so, or, on the contrary, are these irresistible?

To find the road toward some partial answers, I turn back to clinical experience, an experience with a common procedure, the use of a thermometer to take one's temperature.

Taking the temperature by mouth usually is accurate enough. But there are times when mouth temperature-taking is impossible or inaccurate. The second method, arm-pit temperature-taking, is unreliable. Therefore when an accurate knowledge of the body temperature is essential, to see what direction an illness is going or what the patient's response to medication has been, rectal temperature-taking may become an urgent necessity. But many a patient objects to a rectal thermometer. A small number object very strongly, and a few resist most strenuously.

Strong objections to rectal temperature-taking occur chiefly under two conditions. In one, the emotional forces within the individual are very strong indeed. Such a patient often has enormous anxiety about the apertures of the body, with the exception, usually, of the mouth. If something is to go into an aperture, it may be regarded as very dangerous, as getting past the defenses into the body. Occasionally rectal temperature-taking may be visualized by a woman as symbolizing a rape, or as a dangerous rectal intercourse, or visualized by a man as a dangerous homosexual experience. In a very rare circumstance, the prospect of rectal temperature-taking may evoke so much anxiety that it no longer can be called anxiety, but rather is a panic state in which the patient may be seriously out of control. Such a panic usually lasts for a few hours or a few days.

The other strong objection to rectal temperature-taking is based on a different sequence. This is one which can be called the hysteric dramatization of anxiety about an experience which is regarded as very unpleasant rather than as an overwhelming danger. The second type of patient feels a moderate degree of anxiety and strong resentment, and then unconsciously uses the technique of dramatizing the anxiety and the danger, so that it begins to feel unbearable. But in such an instance the actual experience of having the temperature taken by rectum is disturbing only to a moderate or minor degree. When those in charge are firm, are not controlled by the dramatic response, the temperature-taking usually proceeds fairly easily, and the patient feels relieved when it is over.

This contrasting pair of responses are distilled from a large mass of experience, which helps to give a working answer, not an ultimate answer, to questions of free will and determinism. More correctly phrased, such contrasts provide part of the answer to the question of whether the internal forces in human life are irresistible or resistible, either by the individual himself or by those around him. In the first type of response, described as a panic about the penetration of an aperture of the body, the forces involved in some cases are *not* controllable by the individual's Ego. In the second example, of the dramatization of an unpleasant experience, the forces almost always *are* controllable by the Ego.

We turn now to a second pair of contrasting reactions. This has to do with fear of horses. The first example of the pair is epitomized by the reaction of a man who likes horses and rides frequently, who one day goes horseback riding and is thrown from the horse and sustains slight bruises. He is shaken up, and becomes anxious. He may say that he never again will ride a horse. The best bit of friendship one can show him is to insist on his getting on the horse immediately (or perhaps on another horse). Hopefully, this will happen before his anxiety about horseback riding or about horses can be intensified by his repeated retrospective anxiety about being thrown from the horse. If he begins to ride again without delay, the memory of the fall and his emotions are counterbalanced by the actual living experience of riding on a horse again without being thrown.

The second example in this contrasting pair is the panic reaction of a man who for years has had a severe phobia of horses, who from childhood regarded a horse as a very dangerous biting or trampling animal, and who in his deeper unconscious may regard a horse as a threatening instrument of punishment for all of his past misbehavior or guilty impulses. If he now is forced to get on a horse, he may develop a severe panic and go into a period of decompensation, of uncontrolled, largely uncoordinated behavior. With this man, such a procedure, unless it is preceded by an effective period of treatment, is clearly dangerous. One must say *primum non nocere*, i.e. insist that the first principle is to do no harm—or in slang, to say that when you are dealing with forces like these, you are not playing with marbles.

To summarize this contrast, the first man, who enjoys horseback riding, and then is thrown from a horse, often is able to control the forces which are stirred by the experience. These forces are not irresistible, and he can handle the situation, perhaps with some urging from his friends. On the contrary, the second man, who has a long-standing severe phobia of horses, can not control the forces unleashed within him when he is forced to get on a horse. With the forces out of control, the next step may be a panic, which also he is unable to control.

This contrast leads to the same end-point as did the other contrast, of the two patterns underlying strong objections to rectal thermometers. In each pair, one set of forces usually is not controllable by the Ego, but the other set of forces usually is controllable by the Ego.

This must be phrased in more quantitative terms. Ego strength differs in various individuals, along a continuum, from weak to strong. Also the Ego in each individual may be strong in some ways, but less strong, or weak, in other ways.

Similarly the Id forces may vary in strength, in intensity, and in duration. Id forces in various individuals can be visualized as being on a continuum, from weak to strong. Also, in one individual each of the various drives comprising the Id may be strong or moderate or weak.

The outcome at any time depends on the interaction between the Ego, in its different kinds and degrees of strength, and the relevant active, surging, erupting Id forces, in their differing kinds and degrees of strength. In this interaction, this struggle, it is clear that the Ego, the executive, integrating set of forces of the human being, at times can cope with, can master, some of the drives, the surging, untamed Id forces of the personality, but at other times the Ego can not cope with or master some of the Id forces. This formulation seems to permit a tentative working answer to the basic questions of responsibility, irresistibility and the like.

To answer the questions in the terms in which they are asked, we first must try to equate several phrases from two different frames of reference. We can equate the Ego's successful coping with Id forces with the "acceptance of responsibility." We can equate the Ego's failure to cope adequately with Id impulses, with "irresistibility of impulses."

Therefore we can say that at times the human being can accept the responsibility of coping with his impulses, and at other times the impulses seem irresistible. Further, the outcome varies, in the struggle between Ego and Id, depending on the strength of the forces involved in the struggle. Therefore when we use the other frame of reference (responsibility and irresistibility) we can say that the degree of successful acceptance of responsibility will vary and the degree of irresistibility of the impulses will vary, depending on the strength of the forces involved.

Often one can not predict in advance if the Ego will win in the struggle. But since it may win, and since its winning has high value, one must give it every chance to win. Using the other frame of reference, one can say that the attempt to accept responsibility often may succeed, and so is worth the effort.

We come, then, to a fairly workable end-point, when our discussion is limited to a consideration of the interaction, in their present form, of the three major sets of forces, the Id, Superego, and Ego. The workable end-point is that the Ego can function strongly enough at times to accept the responsibility for inner control, but the forces of Id and Superego at times are irresistible. At times, the Ego has the "freedom" to be responsible and to avoid being controlled by irresistible forces.

But that end-point, workable though it is, has neglected one factor which must be considered, as we turn now to a consideration of the problem of freedom of the will and determinism. The Ego, which is the agent of one's current responsibility in dealing with surging inner forces, can be said to be able very often to protect the human being from having his behavior, his activity, "determined" or dominated by the forces of the Id or Superego. The Ego provides a certain degree of freedom from control by other forces. But the neglected point which must now be considered is that the Ego itself may be considered the end product of past experiences, of past developmental forces. These can be said to determine whether the Ego will respond with weakness or with strength, and to determine the way in which the Ego will respond to specific dangers and challenges. The Ego in part is influenced by the inheritance of specific genes, with that influence being modified extensively by the impact of the environment on the Ego in its development. Undoubtedly the current functioning of the Ego is in part determined by a very complex series of causal interactions in the past. These past interactions in part determine the current capacity of the Ego to cope with the forces of the Id and of the Superego.

At first glance, this set of facts seems to point toward the conclusion that a full-scale determinism, in the usual sense, is the most tenable answer, and that any degree of freedom is an illusion. But a further consideration of the facts calls for a third alternative, viz. that "determinism" and "freedom" must be redefined.[23] The Ego surely is deeply influenced by past experience and other determinants, but it is true also that at each step in the past the developing Ego participated in the experience, responded actively to the environment and to the experiences which were shaping it. Gradually the Ego was being shaped by the environment, by its experiences, and by its own maturation. Gradually the Ego was developing, in some degree, its own autonomy. And gradually the Ego came to include patterns of flexibility, plasticity, variability, strategy, decision-making, and choice. The Ego, shaped and determined in part by its own past experience, but also developing its own strengths, now is capable of struggling in a flexible, many-sided way with the other forces of the personality.

To underline further the need for a redefinition of determinism, we can add that the further development of an understanding of

Ego strength, of the integrative activity of the Ego, must not be blocked by an overly simple definition of causation or determinism. A contemporary definition must be far more complex than simple, more multiple than single, it must be multidimensional rather than linear, more dynamic than static. In the same way the study of the integrative activity of the cortex of the brain required explanations far different from the explanations of simple reflexes.

Brain activity includes a range of integrative patterns, e.g. the capacity to inhibit specific patterns and to reinforce others. Similarly the understanding of the functions of the Ego must include not only the facts that its functioning is the result in many ways of past events and causes, and that many of its responses seem automatic and predetermined, but also the fact that, in its development, the Ego has developed a range of flexible choices and decisions and a variety of methods of coping and of integration.

At times, the Ego does seem to be altogether determined by its past and by the rigidity of its current structure. At other times it seems to have the strength to choose from among an extraordinary range of choices. Then it gives the impression of full freedom in decision-making. That impression, of full "freedom of the will," is certainly an illusion, but the existence of a range of choices and decisions seems clear.

The inference seems inevitable that in the process of evolution Ego functions which were integrative and flexible would have great survival value. It seems highly probable that Ego functions developed which provided a more effective way of coping with internal and external problems, Ego functions we must call choice, decision-making, central direction, integration, adaptation, and coordination. These Ego functions are autonomous and flexible enough in their current functioning to meet new threats, new dangers, and new opportunities with a varied repertory of defenses, of methods of coping and control, at times in an original or creative way. At other times the Ego functions can not do the job, may fail, or succeed only in part. The shorthand phrase, a "partial Ego control" or a "limited Ego control," is a useful way of summarizing this fairly complex situation.

There are other factors to be considered in the understanding of Ego control, and its success or failure. We may contrast two types of situations in which Ego control fails. In one type, the forces opposing the Ego are too great to be controlled by the Ego. An example is a homosexual panic, discussed above. In the other type, the forces opposed to the Ego have not increased in strength but the strength of the Ego itself has been diminished. An example is the weakening of the Ego which occurs when the cortex of the brain is saturated with enough alcohol to lower its capacity to function. In both instances, the Ego may lose its control over Id or Superego forces.

During a state of alcoholic intoxication, the integrative activity of the Ego is lessened, and the individual may behave in a hostile way which ordinarily is unacceptable to himself. Or he may make a suicidal attempt based on primitive Superego self-punishment, of trying to kill himself because he feels guilty over a fantasy he regards as being as evil as the behavior would be. Ordinarily the Ego keeps such primitive self-punishment patterns under control. But when the Ego is in part put out of action by alcohol, the primitive self-punishment pattern rears its ugly head.

The comment about the lessening of Ego strength when the brain is saturated with alcohol calls for a further comment about the role of somatic factors in personality functioning in general, and specifically in ethical and anti-ethical behavior. The role of the genetic stability of the species and the genetic variations in individuals has been mentioned. In addition, disorders of brain function obviously are of major importance in producing disorders of personality function in general. One example among many is the fact that a child who has a certain type of brain infection, encephalitis, later may show a postencephalitic type of aggressive activity which can interfere seriously with the interests of others and of himself. In this, the child's Ego is not strong enough to control the neurologically based aggressive hyperactivity.

Similarly an endocrine-based overactivity, as in hyperthyroidism, may endanger the interests of others and of the individual himself. At times, the drive toward such overactivity may be too strong for the ethical firm limit-setting functions of the Ego.

Further, somatic illness of various types, as for example chronic heart disease, may produce anxiety, which in turn leads, for the sake of a feeling of security, to a regression to earlier levels of personality development, to an increase in a childlike dependency. In such a regression to childlike patterns, the individual may behave in an excessively demanding fashion at variance with the ethical behavior of his usual level of maturity.

These are merely a sampling of the somatic impact on human functioning, on ethical behavior. In psychiatric work with patients, such physical factors are of high importance.[24]

We return now to the issues of responsibility, of the irresistibility of impulses, and of the clinical experience bearing on these issues. Many a patient who acts on the basis of psychotic delusions and hallucinations finds it impossible to correct his hallucinations or delusions or to avoid acting in accordance with them. And an individual who has a severe hand-washing compulsion might become panicky, and even briefly psychotic, if someone by force prevented his washing his hands over a period of time. In both cases, the anti-Ego forces predominate over Ego forces.

But many of us have known individuals who insisted that certain patterns were irresistible, who apparently were unable to control some of their behavior, but then were surprised to find that they are able to do so under certain circumstances. For example, during wartime or in a civil crisis, many men and women have been able to force themselves to work more effectively and productively than they believed was possible.

Another example is of a father who was sure that he could *not* resist one of his patterns, even though he was contrite and apologetic. His pattern was of repeatedly undermining his son's concept of himself, as one who was able gradually on his own to develop a more adequate strength. Whenever the father saw that the son was not solving a problem instantaneously, the father quickly took over, came to the son's "rescue," and solved the problem. After each episode, the father was self-critical, but was argumentatively certain that he could not change his own pattern, that it was irresistible. Arrangements were made, however, for interviews with a psychiatrist whom the father regarded as strong and reliable, and as dedicated to the father's real interests as well as the son's. The major pattern of the interviews evolved quickly into one in which the psychiatrist teased the father about his great pride in the irresistibility of his impulses. The psychiatrist sharply and strongly insisted that the father must show his real strength by resisting the temptation to be the son's savior, and that the father instead should stimulate the son to develop his own strength, which the father would enjoy also, by proxy. The father responded rather quickly and surprised himself and the psychiatrist by his own ability to use better techniques, and to persist in using them.

Another example is that, with some frequency, even a moderately heavy cigarette smoker may find that he had underestimated his ability to stop smoking and to continue without cigarettes.

These can be given dramatic emphasis by the story of what happened some fifty years ago when a group of very disturbed psychotic patients in a hospital in Switzerland were by mistake given axes and sent into the forest to chop down trees. The story is that, on the previous day, the hospital had prepared two lists of names of patients. One was a list of those who had volunteered to work in the woods, to cut down several trees, to prepare wood for the hospital fireplaces. These were patients who had made a good or an approximate recovery and were about to be discharged from the hospital.

The second list was of patients who were to be given an improved variety of medication, which might lessen or ameliorate their seriously disturbed thinking and behavior. These patients were typical of those who, in the days before the advent of contemporary treatment, were overactive, at times violent, breaking furniture, defending themselves against attacks by enemies in their delusional systems.

The two lists of patients were reversed, by some mistake. The disturbed patients, who were supposed to be given the new medicine, instead were taken into the forest under the supervision of one attendant. They went fairly peacefully, with an occasional noisy outburst, carrying the kind of axes they often had used earlier in their lives. They did a fairly good job of chopping down an adequate number of trees, and of cutting the wood into usable lengths, with only occasional responses to individual hallucinations. They brought the wood back to the hospital, put it in a shed, went back to their own area of the hospital, and after a while again became seriously disturbed.

Comparable but less dramatic experiences have led psychiatrists to conclude that the behavior in the disorder called paranoid schizophrenia is not totally uncontrollable, as previously had been thought. Many changes in the hospital management of psychotic patients have been made. Many such patients now do better in a less restricted environment. It is clear that under certain specific circumstances, such as the doing of a routine task of the kind which the patients had done many times before the sickness began, in which delusional enemies are much less involved, there can be a pattern of response in which the Ego of the individual is able to avoid or to control the kind of behavior which he can not control at other times.

Such an episode as in the Swiss hospital and other comparable but less dramatic episodes helped to challenge the idea that most psychotic patients were out of control most of the time. But it would be folly to believe that it would be correct, most of the time, to give an axe, a dangerous weapon, to psychotic patients. Occasionally the danger would be very real.

It may be risky to use such a story in this book. It may overshoot the mark because it is dramatic and because everyone loves to undercut an authority or a specialist. The idea of dangerous patients being given axes and their behaving rather well gives us some feeling of being able to say, "So, expert specialist, see how wrong you are." The story produces some of the pleasure that might go with a boy's throwing a snowball that knocks the hat off the head of the important or self-righteous or pretentious man. The Swiss story might give the false impression that all unacceptable patterns can be controlled, if only we try hard enough. The story must not be used to justify the doctrine that self-control is so powerful or so effective that it can be the basis of all ethics. There are stories which just as dramatically would demonstrate the opposite.

The generalization which seems most valid, most soundly based on facts and therefore most useful as a part of ethics, goes as follows. Each human being has a strong obligation to himself and to those whose interests have or should have high priority in his own feeling and thinking, to use as much Ego control as he possibly can mobilize whenever it is necessary. This would apply especially when he is behaving in a way, or is tempted to behave in a way which he himself thinks might be a mistake or which is considered a mistake by one or by several whom he has come to know he can trust.

This is a crucial issue and so I would like to rephrase the generalization just given. The most workable summary of the facts, as we know them, is that an individual has a high degree of responsibility for his own life, for his own behavior, for having and using an intelligent self-interest and attention to the interests of others, to the extent that he can mobilize his Ego forces, his Ego strengths, to carry through on that responsibility. He has an obligation to himself and to others to make a persistent effort, with as much honesty and integrity as he can mobilize, to do as good a job as he can.

Put in terms of negatives, one can say that human beings can not control all temptations and unwanted patterns. But human beings are not merely at the mercy of such forces. At times, under certain circumstances, human beings have an amazing capacity to perform in a way which they believed they never could do. At other times, they have an amazing capacity to fail in attempts in which they expected to succeed.

To give specific answers to specific questions about the when, how, and why of internal control or loss of control would require much more discussion than is possible in this book. My comments are not intended to answer specific questions but to serve as a guideline for further discussion, and to indicate that some past generalizations are contrary to the facts. For further discussion, the best brief starting point can be the suggestion that one ethical guideline is "the use of as much ego-control as one can mobilize."

The material of this chapter so far has had one primary focus: the description and clarification of the internal drama of human life, especially the struggle between Id and Ego. But gradually the story began to sound like the struggle between good and evil, or between a good and legitimate government and the evil dastardly rebels. Now that the point has been made that the Ego can do a moderately good job a fair part of the time, in keeping order, we must add, metaphorically again, that the Ego, the government, has some agencies which are staffed by illogical bureaucrats, who might control or suppress some good ideas because they are unfamiliar. The Ego, like the rest of the person, begins its development early in life, and some of the childhood Ego patterns persist into adult life. At times the Ego behaves in a childlike fashion. In fact, some of the controls or the defenses used by the Ego are seriously unacceptable to the later more mature parts of the Ego.

Also the Id is not just evil, not simply a disruptive set of forces, not merely a threat to stability and order. The unmodified sexual impulses of the Id often are unduly aggressive, and may not be very discriminating. But they are not simply a set of unacceptable impulses which must be repressed or controlled. In fact, many of the basic Id impulses essentially are of high value in many ways, impulses such as competition, independence, dependence, hunger for food and for love, and many others. Id impulses often are not domesticated nor house-broken, not trained nor peaceful, but at times they can be modified, they can be domesticated. In fact, much of the Id is quite likable, if we anthropomorphize for the fun of the phrase.

This evaluation of the Id forces must not be phrased in terms of sweetness and light. Much of the Id is not acceptable, to the individual, or to the group. Murderous impulses, cannibalistic urges, smearing and soiling attitudes, narcissistic patterns, all are there, and more.

From this closer look at the Id forces, one can see that the job of the Ego is not only one of control. It functions also as a guard at the border, or as a customs officer, to separate the permitted from the unpermitted, often using the standards set by the Superego, the conscience. At times, the job of the Ego is largely one of permissiveness, of saying that of course what the Id wants can be arranged *now*, without harm to anyone, even though it was not feasible ten or twenty years ago.

And often the job of the Ego is to be a guide and mentor. It often must talk to the Id as a reliable friend would talk, saying, "Yes, brother, that impulse, that behavior is O.K., but only if it's in the right place, at the right time, and with the right person," with the word "right" being defined according to the criteria of biology, of the culture, and of the individual himself.

The Ego must be selective in its response to the Id. And to be selective, it first must have some degree of power to control, to inhibit some of the Id forces. Therefore the major thrust of this chapter has been to establish the fact that the Ego has the strength, fairly often, to cope to some degree with, and to master to some degree, those Id forces which are unacceptable.

With this fact established, it seems valid to expect good Ego functioning to occur also in an ethics which is not totally based on control. If the Ego can be moderately "confident" of its strength to control or to inhibit Id impulses if necessary, and to prevent being overwhelmed by Id forces, it would seem highly probable that the Ego could develop a selective function, which would appear as a selective limit-setting and a selective permissiveness. If this were the sequence, it would follow that a related Ego function would develop, of the ego guiding some Id impulses toward gratifications which are not destructive.

An ethics which would be based almost entirely on the doctrine of self-control, guided by general rules, would have some solid basis in the fact that the Ego is fairly strong. Such an ethics, therefore, has certain values. But the more or less opposite type of ethics, based on the doctrine of the expression and development of individual wishes and needs, also has a sound basis in the strength of the Id drives and in the potentially high quality of many of the drives. Therefore this type of ethics also has certain values.

But both types of ethics have great shortcomings. An ethics of self-control can become rigidly and excessively restrictive. An ethics of full-expression and self-realization can become severely disruptive.

In the light of psychiatric knowledge, one can say that neither of these two approaches must be regarded as *inevitable*. Also, neither of these approaches must be regarded as *impossible* in the light of psychiatric studies. The study of human psychodynamics indicates that both types of patterns can occur and that both have value. So I urge an ethics which combines the two, and in which the doctrine of self-control is replaced by the policy of selective limit-setting, and the doctrine of the expression and gratification of one's needs is replaced by the policy of a selective permissiveness toward one's needs. This ethics can be phrased as the use of a "flexible combination (or integration) of a selective limit-setting toward oneself with a selective permissiveness toward oneself." In this pattern of ethics, each individual would be expected to use toward himself and his own drives or temptations, the same combination of selective permissiveness and selective limit-setting which he would be expected to use toward others. Then, in the most difficult kind of situation which arises in this kind of ethics, when strong destructive impulses or patterns surge upward and seem to be irresistible, the individual must use a very severe limit-setting toward such impulses, must use as much Ego control as he can mobilize, and must take as much responsibility as he can.

One of the most interesting questions is whether, using this approach of selective permissiveness plus selective limit-setting, there are principles which would have fairly universal validity. There may be. For example, one might state that killing a member of the same species is ethically forbidden, unless that person is violating ethical principles of the highest importance and unless he cannot be stopped without taking the chance of killing him.

There is another principle which can be proposed tentatively as generally acceptable. It is that one should regard as valid a prohibition which appears in all known cultures, or in most of them, unless there is evidence that the prohibition is clearly destructive or mistaken in one's own culture. An example is that in all known cultures, incest, of some type or types, is forbidden.

Then there may be ethical principles which are not universal but can be generalized as applying under certain types of situations and circumstances and not under other types. For example, in many a human being most of the time, and in many another a fair amount of the time, there is a very strong drive to be dependent, to be cared for, to receive. In its strong and dominant form, such a drive is potentially limiting and destructive, to others as well as to the individual's own enlightened self-interest. In such instances, it is necessary to express and to use the conventional principles that "it is more blessed to give than to receive." But in many a human being most of the time, and in many another some of the time, there is a strong drive to be independent, to take care of others, and to give. When the drive to give becomes extremely strong, it may exclude any form of receiving. The drive to give can become so pervasive and so destructive, to others as well as to the giver, that it becomes urgent to express and to use the unconventional principle that it is much "more blessed to receive than to give."

There are other situations in which the ethical decision-making process can or must make little use either of overall or universal principles or of principles which apply to certain types of situations. Then decisions must be made primarily on the basis of considering the individual himself and his individual situation.[25]

Such a spectrum or continuum of decision-making in ethics has a parallel in medical practice. In medicine, the spectrum extends from the use of general principles to the individualization of each situation. At one end of the continuum there are medical principles which apply to all situations, apply in general. One is the principle of *primum non nocere,* of first making sure that one does not do harm. A second principle is the assumption that just about all patients place a high value on life and on health, and on the struggle against death and disease and suffering. A third principle is that much time can be saved, and more patients can be treated, if one can set up reliable routines of treatment and schedules for the dosage of medications.

In the middle two-thirds of the continuum, there are medical principles which apply to some groups or types. For example, rest in bed should be fairly prolonged in some patients with certain types of illness. But it must be as brief as possible in elderly individuals who might develop pneumonia if they are in the horizontal position most of the time.

As one visualizes the continuum of medical principles, at the left-hand one-sixth there is the area which comprises those general principles which seem to apply to all medical situations. In the right-hand one-sixth is the area of individualization. In this area, the individual situation in each medical situation is given major emphasis. General principles and especially routines are given little attention. It is well known that, to some degree, personal attitudes and individual problems and variations may affect the course of many an illness, and so at this end of the spectrum individualization is the predominant goal.

Several comments are in order at this point, about the approach to the problems of ethics used in this chapter, which makes extensive use of psychoanalytic findings with regard to Id, Superego, and especially of Ego. This approach, which considers extensively all three groups of psychodynamic function, can be called the realistic, pluralistic, dynamic approach to ethics. Using the developmental concepts of psychoanalysis, it emphasizes the ongoing development of ethical principles and behavior. Also, this approach, emphasizing the integrative activity of the Ego, underlines the fact that each individual is deeply involved in developing his own ethics as well as in having an ethics passed on to him by the previous generation, by his religious group, or by his culture.

9

Creative Ethics

T HE Golden Rule, one of the most highly regarded of man's ethical principles, provides us with an appropriate topic to open our discussion of Creative Ethics. Also, from the point of view of the reader-author alliance, the Golden Rule could be expected to be an ideal starting point. Most of my readers have a warm and comfortable glow when they think of the Golden Rule. It is non-strenuous, easy to understand. And it seems not to be controversial. In fact, I expected to discuss the Golden Rule fairly briefly and then go more deeply into a discussion of other patterns of Creative Ethics.

But in the process of rewriting this section of the book, I saw that the Golden Rule discussion in this chapter was rocky and un-even, and I realized that I must revise and rewrite it more exten-sively than I expected. In that process, I saw that I had never looked closely enough at the Golden Rule. I could not escape the obligation to focus more fully on the Golden Rule itself and on my reasons for not having done so in the past.

This process may test the strength of the reader-author alliance. My discussion of the Golden Rule will have to be rather critical in some ways, which may lessen the reader's congeniality and fellow-feeling with me. But I can rely on the fact that the author and the reader have developed some mutual trust by this point. You know that I would not want to introduce an unnecessary difficulty in your reading of this book. And I know that since you have read this far, you will not be stopped by this issue. In fact, you may be intrigued by the fact that I have found problems in the Golden Rule.

The Golden Rule is that one should *do* unto others as one would have others *do* to oneself, or that one should *not do* unto others as one would *not* have others *do* unto oneself. At times in the past, the Rule seemed too pat to many of us. But it seemed sound and solid enough, often hard to achieve in life, but one of the magnificient statements of man's thinking and feeling.

In the process of reviewing the original version of this section, I saw that I had not been skeptical enough about the Golden Rule. I recalled that over the years I had been skeptical about some aspects of the process of empathy, which I knew was closely related to the Golden Rule, but I had not taken the next step of being skeptical about the Rule itself. My belated self-scrutiny indicated that I had hesitated because the Golden Rule at times has been described as the cornerstone of our civilization. I must have felt intimidated by what seemed to be the universal approval of the Rule.

So in the revision, I made up for lost time. It became clear that in several ways, the Rule has serious deficiencies. My comments may be reminiscent of the witty criticisms of the Rule by George Bernard Shaw. And they resemble, in part, the comments in an excellent chapter by Erik Erikson on the Golden Rule in his book, *Insight and Responsibility.*

In the Golden Rule variety of ethics, the central process is of thinking and feeling about the other as if he were oneself. In this process one says to oneself, "How would I feel if I were in his shoes, and would be doing that to myself?" or "How would I feel, if the situation were reversed, if he or someone else were to behave that way to me?" If one sees that the action one is doing to the other, or might do, is unwelcome to oneself as one thinks of oneself in the shoes of the other, then one's behavior must be regarded as unwelcome to the other.

This is an example of the basic process of empathy, of momentarily identifying with the other and of looking at one's feelings at that moment. The assumption is that he and I, as two human beings, are alike, and so by looking at one's feelings after identifying with the other, one can know how the other must feel.

The Golden Rule can be understood more fully if one recognizes that is is a condensation of two different recommendations. It can be regarded as the statement that a basic goal of human relations, a valid ethical policy, is that every human being should try to be sensitive to the feelings and wishes of others, and should behave toward others in terms of the others' feelings and wishes. Second, the Golden Rule indicates the method to be used in trying to achieve the goal of behaving with sensitivity to the needs of others, viz. by empathy, identification, putting oneself in the place of the other, and so using oneself to determine or to gauge how the other must feel.

The need to be sensitive to the wishes and feelings of others and to behave toward them with such sensitivity seems to be a solid and dependable recommendation. It would be of high importance to find reliable methods of achieving that goal of sensitivity to the needs of others. But the method of empathy, as it would be used in the Golden Rule, has shortcomings in spite of its great values. It makes one's own feelings the criterion, makes oneself the judge. Yet we know that one may not be altogether reliable in judging the feelings of others when the process being observed involves oneself as well as the other.

As an example of the difficulty, I shall quote part of the study of a man who made a number of mistakes in the use of the Golden Rule. This man preferred to avoid frank talk. Whenever even a slightly sensitive topic appeared in a conversation in which the customary fairly easy-going and frank talk might include some mild criticism of one person by another, he kept quiet or left the room.

In several discussions in the past, he had told me that he felt extremely vulnerable if someone expressed even a slight criticism of him. He was afraid, he told me, that mild criticism could open a floodgate, would lead to devastating criticism. And, according to the Golden Rule, since he would not want even a mild criticism of himself, he had to avoid even a mild criticism of others, or even hearing a faint criticism of others. Such a conclusion is a mistake in human relations, since his mild criticism of others might have been acceptable and perhaps of value to them, and since his avoidance of mildly critical remarks made his conversation somewhat restricted, even boring, and tended to stultify his relations with others.

From past discussions I knew also that this man's son had come to learn that a limited amount of frank talk was of real value in his own life. The father had difficulty in believing that the son really preferred frank talk, since he himself so strongly did not. The endpoint was that the father never talked frankly to his son, since he would never have wanted his son to talk frankly to him. His son had come to regard a conversation with his father as stilted and cautious.

At another point, the father advised his son, who liked frank talk, never to talk openly with the son's boss, who had said he liked frank talk, too. In both instances, in the father's way of talking to the son, and in the father's advice to the son about his style of communication with his boss, the father's use of the Golden Rule was unfortunate, since he was using as a standard his own exaggerated pattern of feeling about mild criticism.

It is important to emphasize that the Golden Rule works well enough much of the time, since human beings have so much in common that identification and empathy often provide us with the right answer. The Colonel's Lady and Judy O'Grady are sisters under the skin. Blacks and whites, Jews and non-Jews, men and women, those over thirty and those under thirty, are alike in the essential humanity of human beings, and alike in the basic patterns of intrapsychic and interpersonal processes. Therefore the use of the Golden Rule often leads to correct conclusions, e.g. that one should not kill the other, since one can assume that the other does not want to be killed, just as one does not want to be killed oneself. Most others are like oneself in so many ways that the Golden Rule can be a good guide much of the time.

But, as we indicated above, there are times the Golden Rule does not work well. In some ways individual human beings differ. Others may *not* want done to them what one wants to have done to oneself. And others may want to have done to them what one does *not* want done to oneself. So at times the Golden Rule must be checked against the realities, against the actual patterns of other individuals.

In many instances, all that is necessary is to stop, look, and listen for a few moments to what the other says and does. Or if the issue is important, one must spend some minutes or more in getting to know the other as an individual, as one who may be different from oneself. One must do a few minutes of self-scrutiny and if necessary then say to oneself that "The world is not built in my image, or in the image of my family." One can come to have some impression of the other as he is, his similarities to oneself, and his differences, and then respect his sensitive spots even though they are not the same as one's own.

An even more important deficiency of the Golden Rule arises from the existence, the frequency, and the importance, of ambivalence in human beings, and in this instance, in the one who is trying to use the Rule. For example, in our culture many a man is ambivalent both about giving and about receiving. He wants to be a strong and powerful giver, generous toward his family and friends. His giving may make him feel self-respecting, loving, proud, and strong. But also he may develop some hesitation about his generous giving, and develop a fear that he will "run dry" (as many a man fears about his semen) and then have nothing to give.

In Western culture, the same man usually wants also to be a receiver. Receiving makes him feel wanted and accepted and loved. But also when he receives, he may feel ashamed, as if he were a boy being cared for by a stronger person. Often, at the moment he receives, he feels safe and protected, but a few moments later, he may feel ashamed and weak over having wanted to be a receiver, over feeling like a little boy.

So when he wants to be giving to others, and tries to use the Golden Rule, and to imagine how the other would feel when he receives, he may get a number of answers, some of them confusing and contradictory. For example, the answer could be "yes," that he should give to the other, since there is a part of himself that wants to receive and like it, and so he can assume that the other wants to receive also. But he knows also that often he hates to receive, because of the feeling that when he is on the receiving end it is demeaning, like being a little boy. From this he might assume that the other also would feel demeaned when he receives. Therefore out of this part of the first man's ambivalence, the Golden Rule answer would be "No," that he should not give to the other. So, following the Rule, he now has two contradictory answers.

Faced with this problem, of ambivalence giving two contradictory answers when the Golden Rule is used, we must broaden our conception of the use of the Rule. First, we must reiterate that an ethics governed in good part by the Golden Rule can be rather good, even without an awareness of the issues raised by ambivalence. Certainly a fairly simple and direct use of the Rule represents an enormous advance over human relations not based on that Rule. But for an even better ethics, it is imperative to know that ambivalence exists, and that one must work toward a solution based on a reliable pattern of self-scrutiny. One has an obligation to look at oneself enough to say, "I'd better be careful at times about judging others in terms of myself. I know that I'm ambivalent about several things. For example, I want to be strong and I want to be weak. Perhaps the other person also has both of these wishes, but in a different ratio, or in a different pattern." So in part one must say that the other person must be a judge also, in addition to oneself as judge, in the use of the Golden Rule. With this comment we come close to saying again that the pattern of self-respect and of respect for the other, and of sensitivity to the needs of others, as it occurs in an alliance, must be given high priority in the development of ethics.

So the Golden Rule pattern in Creative Ethics, when it is regarded with high respect and also with skepticism, has great value but also potential deficiencies, so that it must be cross-checked at times by other forms of Creative Ethics. In a relatively minor situation, one needs only take a quick look at the other, to see what he really may be like, and then take a quick skeptical look inward, at the reliability of one's own impressions. In a more important situation there are two comparable steps to take before relying on the Golden Rule. One is the development of a good human relation, in which one comes to know the ways in which the other person is dissimilar as well as similar to oneself. The second step is the development in oneself of a pattern of an honest self-scrutiny, especially to see if one is ambivalent enough to have it affect one's clear thinking about what to do and what not to do, in relation to other human beings.

The Golden Rule may be in part a sophisticated derivative of Defensive Ethics, starting with the talion law, viz. that the punishment must exactly fit the crime, an eye for an eye, a tooth for a tooth. Starting with the talion law, one could in imagination measure the impact on another of what one does or might do, by imagining oneself being punished for doing it, by having the punishment fit the crime. The talion law impact on oneself would be identical with one's impact on the other. Then as next step, the Rule would shorten the process, by the imaginative feeling of identification, instead of imagining the action and the punishment. It would become an "as if" or fantasy situation, of having to imagine oneself in the other's shoes and to imagine how one then would feel.

More probably, the Golden Rule is a form of Creative Ethics. It seems closely related to the overall biologic pattern of mutual help and social organization. Then the primary pattern of the Rule would be the drive to do certain things to others, or to avoid doing certain things to others, in order to foster or strengthen or stabilize the pattern of mutual help, of friendship, of positive interaction.

It represents an attempt to develop a technique in which human interactions are facilitated by a sensitivity to the needs of others. It introduces, although in a rather simplistic fashion, the important principle of empathy, of the understanding of the other person through the process of momentary identification followed by the process of self-scrutiny.

Certainly the Golden Rule represented a major step forward in human civilization. Our respect for it obligates us to suggest improvements in the Rule and in its use, now and in the future.

We turn now to a further consideration of Creative Ethics. In this chapter, we need not delineate the major patterns of Creative Ethics. That has been done at various points in the previous chapters. Whenever a discussion of a pattern of Creative Ethics seemed germane to the focus of the book at that time, the pattern was discussed. It would have been out of keeping with the reader-author alliance had I withheld the discussion of an item that was clearly relevant and essential at that point, in order to include it in this chapter, in which it would have had its more conventional place. The end-point is that most of what needs to be said about Creative Ethics has already been included in previous chapters.

We are free, therefore, to discuss the phenomena of Creative Ethics in several new ways. One is to turn to the field of athletics, of sports, and to note how essential the principles of ethics are in the various sports, as rules, or as accepted patterns of behavior, as standards which are observed, and, of course, often not observed. The contrast of Defensive Ethics and Creative Ethics is especially clear in sports. This makes a discussion of ethical behavior in athletics most relevant to our attempt to give greater clarity and definition to the field of Creative Ethics. By contrasting the two types of ethics as they appear in athletics, the general differentiation of Creative Ethics from Defensive Ethics becomes more clear.

There are many patterns of Defensive Ethics in various athletic games. Examples are of "fair play," of not cheating, of playing the game by the rules, of being a good loser, of being a good winner. These ethical attitudes occur in athletics, as they do in life in general, as part of the defensive ethical need to control or to modify the contestant's own aggressive competitive destructive impulses. For example, in competitive sports, each person in a two-person sport, and each team in a team sport, is expected to use a legitimate Defensive Ethics, and not a nonethical defense, against the legitimate aggressiveness of the other, or even when the behavior of the opponent goes beyond legitimate aggressiveness.

Also each person in a two-person game, and each individual of each team, must use a Defensive Ethics against his own spontaneous impulses to cheat, to break the rules, to damage the opponent or the other team, impulses which may appear within himself before the other is aggressive, legitimately or not. These are the competitive destructive impulses which appear within the individual, derivatives of his own past experience and present internal problems, and not simply in response to patterns initiated by the other person or team.

The referee or umpire is part of a different Defensive Ethical System. He must use and interpret the rules as a system of limit-setting and restrictions, to prevent both sides from going beyond legitimate aggressiveness.

From a slightly different angle, one can say that there are three types of Defensive Ethics in athletics. One is the intrapsychic, the conscience of the individual player, his intrapsychic defenses against his intrapsychic temptations to break the rules, to hurt the opponent, or to violate his own standards. The second area is the interpersonal, the ethical defenses of each player against the aggressiveness of the opponent. The third area can be called the social, viz. the external or social control provided by the rules and by the activity of the referee, to prevent or limit the damage or the cheating.

In all types of Defensive Ethics in sports, there is the understanding that certain forms of aggressiveness are permitted and some are not. This requires the development of a Defensive Ethics which can differentiate between two similar patterns, two similar types of behavior. This permits each individual to become a strong but fair competitor, to use his assets and his skill in the competition but within the framework of a mutually accepted set of rules and patterns. In ethical behavior in general, the capacity to differentiate between similar patterns is of high importance, e.g. the difference between realistic guilt and neurotic guilt, the difference between a legitimate leadership and an attempt to dominate.

Various forms of Creative Ethics are very much in evidence in team sports. Sports provide examples of Creative Ethics that are vivid and clear. In team play, the members of a team often develop a remarkable degree of mutual helpfulness, of partnership, of team spirit, of mutual respect, of complex, smooth-working interactions, of an alliance, of being beyond the adversary system. Experienced athletes, coaches, and observers often regard the "morale" of the team, the mutual help, the capacity to subordinate individual interests to the interests of the team, as being of crucial importance in determining the success of the team.

A team which is having problems often does a much better job when the players have done some self-scrutiny, i.e. have had some productive discussion, and have come to see their own mistakes. But often, self-scrutiny is a pattern to which the players are not accustomed. That part of the job may have to be done by the coach. The showing of movies of the previous games often is a powerful stimulus to self-scrutiny, as well as to the scrutiny of others.

The phenomena of Creative Ethics in the field of sports can be seen most vividly in team games, in the relation of members of a team to each other and to the team as such. But also, especially in a two-person game, a relationship may develop between opponents which can be regarded as another form of Creative Ethics.

In this, two opponents, e.g. in the game of tennis, may enjoy playing each other, win or lose. Of course this pattern may be merely the way in which two human beings, the opponents, are making the best of their both having a pattern of serious self-restriction. The essence of this self-restriction is that both of the opponents have an inhibition not only of unfair competitiveness but also of fair competitiveness. In this neurotic version of the pattern, the two opponents need to avoid competition in any form, and so make the best of the situation, emphasizing the pleasure of playing, and ignoring or denying the drives toward active or hyperactive competition. When the pattern of preferring a noncompetitive game represents an unnecessary defense against even the acceptable form of competitiveness, it should not be regarded as a form of Creative Ethics.

It is clear that there are situations in which each of the two opponents wants to win and has not inhibited his legitimate competitiveness, but in addition each enjoys playing the other, win or lose. The skill of the one may stimulate the second to play at a better level, which he enjoys more thoroughly. He may also know that the first will devise new strategies of offense for which he can develop new strategies of defense. Each enjoys the process of the interaction, the friendly struggle, the increase in skill, the pleasure in stimulating the other to more skillful responses. Perhaps this deserves a new title, "Creative Competition," as a variety of Creative Ethics. The contrast is with "Fair Play Competition" or "Regulated Competition," highly respected, also, a form of Defensive Ethics.

Creative Ethics, then, can be of two varieties in sports. One is the creative ethical interplay between members of the same team. The other is the creative interplay which can develop between opponents, who find that some forms of competitive activity can include mutually valuable patterns in which both grow and develop in the process.

It is of high interest that in athletics, a human activity in which the forms of ethics are highly developed, there exist several varieties of well-developed Defensive Ethics and several varieties of well-developed Creative Ethics. It is noteworthy that in athletics there exist both Creative Ethics and Defensive Ethics, rather than only one variety without the other. Using athletics as an analogy, one may speculate that both types are needed in many complex fields of human activity. Perhaps in the potentially destructive conflicts between the groups of mankind, the goal of ethics should not be simply an improvement in Defensive Ethics, nor simply an improvement in Creative Ethics. Perhaps the goal should be of a greater development of both Defensive Ethics and Creative Ethics. Perhaps in man's struggles toward the avoidance of war and of other disasters, man must work toward a greater suitability, a greater honesty, a greater nonprovocativeness of his Defensive Ethics. Concurrently man must work toward a further development of the current productive types of Creative Ethics, and, hopefully, develop new ones.

Now let us look at two aggregates of words and phrases. The first list includes many of the nouns, the verbs, and the terms which are used frequently in descriptions or discussions or definitions in the broad field of Creative Ethics. This will be followed by a second list which includes many of the words and phrases which are used as the titles or the names of the specific processes and principles which are forms of Creative Ethics. Together, the two lists give a condensed impression of the field of Creative Ethics. Together, they make the area of Creative Ethics visible in sharper perspective.

The words and phrases in the first list, those that appear in discussions of the field of Creative Ethics, are:

Mutual help
Mutuality of interests
Mutual respect
Friendship and partnership
Beyond the adversary system
Postambivalent attitudes
Group patterns
Furthering the joint interests of the individual and of the group
Positive and creative interchanges or interactions
The avoidance of unproductive domination, submission, or rebellion
Empathy
Sufficient observation of others to prevent mistakes
Sensitivity to the needs of others as well as of oneself
Long-term values
Good human relations
Interdependence

Capacity to see beyond the surface defensiveness of others
Flexible choice of appropriate values
Realistic trust
Respect for the other
Self-respect
Loyalty
Affection and love
The appearance of a new integration
Attempts to develop a new and productive relation
The ambiguity of equality and inequality
Realistic cooperation
Intelligent self-interest
The capacity to differentiate between similar phenomena, one of which is often destructive and the other is rarely destructive, e.g. between pride and self-respect, and between self-depreciation and relatively mature modesty.

The second list includes many of the patterns of processes or principles which are forms of Creative Ethics:

The Golden Rule
The therapeutic alliance
The NON-JOB Seminar approach
In general, the two-way working alliance
The creative use of the tension between opposites or contradictories
The creative dialogue
The preference for the reality principle over the pleasure principle except when the pleasure principle does not block the ongoing use of the reality principle
The realistic consideration of the interests both of the individual and of the society
The flexible combination of selective limit-setting and selective permissiveness toward oneself
The flexible combination of selective limit-setting and selective permissiveness toward others
The patterns of relatively mature ego-function which are integrative and selective in dealing with conflicting forces in the personality
A leadership which permits, stimulates, and fosters the growth in strength of the others of the group
The pattern of a relatively mature ego which is able to take the initiative at times and is able to be responsive to the initiative of others at times, in interpersonal and group interactions.

Looking toward the future, we must stress the fact that the further development of Creative Ethics will include an ongoing search for patterns of living which forward the interests of one individual and at the same time forward the interests of other individuals and of the group. We need not wait for the future, or for the millennium, for many examples of this pattern. A scientific discovery may enhance the life, the career, the prestige, and the self-respect of the discoverer, and simultaneously may alleviate the suffering and promote the interests of all mankind. A good teacher or a good parent can do a very good job for members of the next generation, and simultaneously get great personal satisfaction out of the process, in spite of the many rough spots along the road. And there are many types of human helpfulness, in the professions and in personal life, which are based on respect for others and for oneself, which increase the individual's own self-respect, and which foster the well-being of all concerned.

10

The Technology of Ethics

T O an extraordinary degree, the world is being transformed by the recent and the ongoing developments in science and in technology. These changes are crucial in the understanding of contemporary man and of his ethics.

In the first chapter of this book, some of the exceedingly valuable advances and some of the great dangers in science and in technology were discussed. The emphasis was on the challenges these changes involve, the challenge to mankind to cope with the dangers and to make productive use of the advances.

In this chapter, we will focus on another aspect of science and technology, viz. on the close relationship between the two. That relationship is of high significance in our attempt to find pathways for new developments in ethical principles and ethical behavior.

The dynamic interplay of science and technology is active in both directions. In one direction, technology contributes to science. A new tool or technique, such as the electron microscope or radioisotope methods in research, leads to new developments in science. In the other direction, new discoveries in science lead to new techniques, new methods and processes which can be used in the development of new industries, new types of medication, new agricultural processes, etc.

This very close relationship between science and technology has been true for the past hundred years or so. But it was not always so. Through most of man's history, the techniques of planting and harvesting, of domesticating animals and caring for them, of making pottery, baskets and tools, were not based on the kind of systematic study or research which is basic for the development of the sciences. The techniques of living, of daily activity, of hunting, of farming, of building, and of the arts and crafts, were the product of direct experience, of learning each art or each process or technique. Even without a science of animal biology, a shepherd provided good care for his flock, although within fairly narrow limits.

Several centuries ago, scientific work began to influence the techniques of everyday living. In the past century the impact of the sciences on practical affairs has been extraordinary. In *A Runaway World?*, the recently published Reith lectures, Edmund Leach, the British anthropologist, says that with present science and technology we are like gods, but afraid to use our power to plan the future of mankind. This thesis and similar ideas proposed by others need thorough discussion in another context.

At the moment, we need only say that in many countries the techniques of raising food, both plant and animal, are based on genetics, on biochemistry, and on the scientific discoveries which had led to the development of agricultural machinery. Scientific research produced great changes in industrial processes. Totally new industries have appeared. As one example, research in chemistry led to the technology of the use of plastics, of synthetic fibers, and a host of new medicines. Enormous changes in communication and transportation are based on techniques derived from various sciences. The list could be very long indeed.

But that story is well-known, and need not be elaborated further. To many, it seems like an unpleasant, ugly story, leading only to pollution and the degradation of the environment. This is one part of the story, and is correctable by a combination of further research and its application to the guilty processes, by an ongoing social self-scrutiny and self-criticism, and by political action.

The crucial point for this discussion is that in the science-technology linkage, we are talking of a sequence which works, and is enormously productive. Sometimes the end-point is extremely dangerous, such as the techniques of nuclear warfare. But that must not becloud our recognition of the fact that the combination of science plus technology is one of the most effective combinations ever known. In fact, it has worked so well in so many fields that we now must try it in the field of ethics, but carefully.

This can be phrased in terms of Id and Ego, to help make an essential point. We can say that many of the technologic advances developed so far have enriched the potential for the productive satisfaction and realistic fulfillment of some of the Id forces and for the strengthening of some of the mature forms of the Ego forces. Techniques are now available and more will be, which may satisfy many Id and Ego needs, e.g. for food, health, shelter, communication and interaction with others, relative safety plus freedom to explore, productive and creative work, pleasure, gratification and leisure, hopefully for everyone, if the world population increase slows down, and if human interactions become more realistic and nondestructive.

But the new technology also has the potential of being used destructively by the primitive portions of man's Id and his Ego, and by the corruptible parts of his Superego, e.g. in warfare, in killing other men, in cruelty to other individuals and to other groups, in the pollution of air and water, and in many other ways. A new technology of ethics, and of human relations, is needed urgently to counterbalance the dangers of the destructive use of the other new technology.

There are valid reasons for having a skeptical attitude about each point in the attempt to add to the techniques of ethics. Self-criticism and criticism by others, of each step suggested, is essential in this difficult field. But some of the points of skepticism must in turn be debunked. One is that such changes in man and his ethics would contradict the fact or the dogma that human nature can not be changed. Human nature can be changed, at least in certain ways. Human nature is in good part an expression of the culture, and changes in a culture can change human behavior.

One very serious contemporary danger lies in the proposals to change human nature by manipulating the chromosomes, by electric stimulation of the brain, and in other ways. This trend may be one of our enemies in the future.

My proposal is a different one. It is that human nature should be changed by using techniques which will foster the further development of individual freedom and its values, and the further development of the culture and its values, and to foster also the ethical combination of the values of the individual and of the culture. Obviously these are the goals of the process, but also they are the means to be used in the process. One example in which such a process already is underway is the Manus group in New Guinea, studied by Margaret Mead over the past forty years. Many of the individuals of that culture have moved from being Stone Age men and women to men and women of the twentieth century, in a short period of time.

We must try to develop a technology of ethics, but we must be persistently critical and self-critical of the attempts to do so. The science of man is different in some ways from the physical sciences, and from many of the other sciences. Our scientific knowledge of man as man, in biology, anthropology, and psychodynamic psychology, is well developed in some areas but not in others.

Therefore two developments should be fostered. One is to attempt actively to develop new techniques of ethics from what we know now. Concurrently, further studies of man—our scientific and humanistic knowledge of man—from which we later can derive further steps in the technology of ethics, must increase rapidly as well.

We turn now to the question of whether our current knowledge of man suggests specific techniques for the further development of ethical principles and ethical behavior, or indicates in what direction such attempts might be made in the future. This chapter on the technology of ethics will be divided into a series of sections.

Each section will present one item or pattern which seems to provide an opening toward a new technology of ethics. The division of the overall topic into segments (separated by a line across the page) can help us to avoid the fatigue which might result if out of my intense interest I slipped into a long or elaborate discussion of one or two of the items or patterns of technology.

The *first suggestion* is that we can turn to the field of mathematics for leads for the development of a technology of ethics. In fact, in the chapter on the Therapeutic Alliance, I suggested (p. 118) that we might begin to look for simple arithmetical techniques to improve some of our statements or descriptions of ethical principles or processes, or to develop new ones. In that chapter, I limited the arithmetic to simple division, and with the simple number 2. I suggested, for example, that we could eliminate certain hurdles in our thinking about ethics if first we divided by two the force of each of the two "opposites" when we use the concept of the creative tension between opposites, as an ethical process.

That suggestion of the use of a simple arithmetical process in thinking about ethics leads to a suggestion of another way in which mathematics can be used in the development of techniques of ethics. Again this is a simple process, but it has some resemblance to the "theory of sets" in a more advanced field of mathematics. To clarify the basis for this second mathematical suggestion, I must rephrase the first suggestion. That process starts with the recognition of the existence in life of many sets, or pairs of opposites, or of contradictories, which at times may seem to make a situation unworkable or to block our thinking. At other times, however, these sets or pairs of opposites may lead to a very productive process, if they are reformulated as providing a challenging and creative tension between opposites (or after being divided by two) between contraries or contradictories.

In that pattern, the existence of opposites (e.g. extreme punishment versus extreme permissiveness in the education of children) was transformed from a negative situation to a positive one by dividing each extreme by two, to permit a creative tension and resolution. In the suggestion being made now, our starting point is that in certain situations there are no opposites and therefore no creative tension and resolution. I suggest therefore that, in such a situation, we formulate an opposite and carry through the process as before. (In the mathematical theory of sets, the first step is to establish a set of conditions which may be nonexistent, to see where it leads.)

I suggest that, as an example of the use of this technique, we start with one of the good maxims, or statements of ethics. It need not be an extreme. It should be one for which an opposite or contradictory maxim is not easily found, or only minor versions of an opposite. In such a situation, there has been no apparent tension between opposite maxims or rules. I suggest that we devise an opposite or contradictory maxim, put the two together, and fantasy the result.

For our example, we start with one of the Ten Commandments, which is the injunction to Honor One's Father and Mother. Surely this is a most acceptable pattern of behavior, although parents who actually batter their children, or in other ways behave destructively, would have difficulty in expecting honor without other reactions as well. Without question this Commandment stands as a statement of a highly desirable ethics.

The next step in this second mathematical sequence is to fantasy an opposite maxim. One can not base the opposite maxim on reversing the verb since then one would have a maxim advising one to dishonor one's parents. In this example, one must reverse the generations in the original Commandment or reverse the subject and object of the sentence. Then the injunction would be that the first generation should honor the second generation. Parents must honor their children. Much of the work in the field of psychiatry indicates that a further development of respect and trust for the next generation, an empathic fellow-feeling in older adults for children and younger adults, would be of the highest value.

The final step in this sequence is to put the two maxims together, viz. the original one and the one produced by the reversal. Then one can see if a creative tension, and an integration, will appear. In the instance of Honor Thy Parents, and Honor Thy Children, the value of integrating the two is clear. One of the most important steps forward could be a strong ethical statement of the high value of a joint working together, of parents and children, in a mutually respecting and honoring relation.

Another example of the use of this simple mathematics has to do with Occam's Law, the Law of Parsimony, which is widely used by philosophers and scientists. It states that if one has two available explanations for some data, one always should choose the simpler explanation, if both explanations seem to cover the available facts. This law sounds reasonable, and in a way, most ethical.

But this law often has been profoundly restricting in the development of human thought. It is a superb example of the way in which language controls our behavior and distorts our principles. The phrase "seems to cover the available facts" permits a kind of personalized judgment in which human emotions can be involved inappropriately. For example, according to the Law of Parsimony, dreams were easily explained in terms of some type of stimulation or activity of some part of the brain during sleep, producing fragments of memories or fantasies in a kind of senseless mixture. For a time that summary seemed to cover all of the available facts. But it also was used as an argument against new facts which began to appear, in addition to some which had been ignored previously. If the Law of Parsimony had been followed as rigidly as often happens, Freud could not have developed his ongoing interest in dreams. The understanding of dreams, one of the most important sources of information about the hidden phenomena of human life, one of the sources of our basic knowledge of the conflict between the forces within men, would have been much more limited than it is today, if Occam's Law had prevailed at that point. And our knowledge of some of the varieties of ethical behavior and ethical principles would be more limited.

So with regard to Occam's Law, my suggestion is that it should be regarded as a stereotyped way of thinking, even if it is not phrased as a stereotype. But it still is a good rule, and so I suggest that we should try to reverse it, and so have an opposite rule which mockingly we might call Moccam's Law. We could call it the Law of Extravagance, instead of Parsimony. Then, in one's work, if one has two generalizations which seem to cover all of the facts, with one generalization much simpler than the other, one might be tempted to obey Occam's Law and to accept the simpler because it is simpler. But one would also have a benevolent skepticism toward the simpler generalization and be tempted also to think that the more extravagant generalization is preferable, and so obey Moccam's Law. This second approach would stimulate one who is working in any field to take time out occasionally to let his imagination soar, to let himself formulate novel explanations. Of course, each parsimonious generalization, and each extravagant generalization, must stand the test of time, of further data or discoveries.

Then, using the suggested process again, we would see if the two would integrate. We could try to formulate an Occam-Moccam Law, which would say that in some instances the Law of Parsimony seems more appropriate and that in other instances an open-ended law seems more appropriate. Or as we tried to fit the two together, we might see that the whole issue of parsimony and extravagance in scientific generalizations is a residual from an earlier stage of science.

A justified confidence in the scientific method and its achievements means that it no longer is necessary to ignore the unresolved, uncertain, or incomplete portions of a topic for the sake of brevity or simplicity. Brevity may still be the soul of wit. But brevity or parsimony in scientific conclusions or statements must be regarded as pleasant but not essential.

The *first* suggestion, then, for a technology of ethics, is to use simple (and some day more complex forms of) mathematics to develop new techniques of ethics.

My *second* suggestion in the development of new techniques can start enjoyably with a reference to puns and jingles. This will lighten the discussion. But more important is the fact that puns and jingles can have a serious purpose, in addition to the frothy purpose of having fun, and some moments of relaxation in a serious hour or day.

The serious purpose of this type of word-play has to do with certain facts about thinking and work. Intensive and extensive thinking, working on data, trying to interpret and understand the facts, in general the process of logical critical thinking, is of central importance in our coping with the world and with ourselves. The second fact is that such a pattern of thinking and work carries with it the danger of becoming rigid, too focused, and compulsive. And there are moments when it becomes a dead-end street. The same thing may happen in the growth of a science, in which one route at first is very productive and then becomes repetitious. And the same may happen in one of the arts, in which a productive new turn is followed by good development, and then merely by repetition or elaboration.

An example of the way out, of what works at that point, is the story of Kekule,[26] who, when he was blocked in his thinking about the linkage of carbon atoms in certain compounds, fell asleep and had a dream of a snake with its tail in its mouth. This figure in the dream led him, half-awake, to the concept of the six carbon atoms in a circular or hexagonal type of linkage. This led to the well-known formula of the benzene ring of six carbon atoms as the foundation of organic chemistry.

Dreams and daydreams have been used to get beyond a block, out of a rut. Alcohol has been used and misused. And LSD is regarded as the answer by some misguided souls. Doodling, distraction, leisure, relaxation, a change of pace, music and other arts are some of the patterns which may help at such a point.

It is relevant that Jonas Mekas, one of the best of the *avant garde* underground movie producers, teasingly said in a meeting several years ago in Cincinnati that the use of drugs no longer is *avant garde*, since it has been in the newspapers for years now and so is passé. He stated that there was no need to use drugs in trying to be creative. His method of being creative, and of being up to date, he said, is to open his eyes and ears, and to keep them open, and to open them wider, and to broaden his consciousness without any drugs, and then to work, as artists always have worked, all day or all night if necessary, being imaginative, spontaneous, and self-critical.

Put in terms of our knowledge of psychodynamics, we can say that the use of logic and intellect, the secondary mental processes, which ordinarily are so effective, at times becomes rigid and restrictive. Then somehow the individual must find a way of getting out of the intellectual rut, into a way of becoming imaginative, of getting in touch with a part of the human mind which Freud called the primary mental process, the process which is more primitive, more symbolic, and more free-flowing, and which produces unexpected linkages of ideas or of emotions.

When I find my thinking is blocked, I take off a few minutes, and try to write a jingle. The nonsense, the playing with words, the unexpected linkages, seem especially suited for this job. For me this is the quickest way to get out of a rut of thinking, of being blocked in finding a solution. It has worked many times.[27]

I do not suggest that others become punsters or rhymesters, unless that is the best way for them, as well as for me, to get to the primary process. I suggest only that others recognize that logical straight thinking has its limits, and that others try to develop techniques for themselves to get beyond a block, to use when they are needed, for short periods of time. Of course, the use of logic and reason remains the most reliable method 95 per cent of the time.

Logical thinking is usually the most effective process when one attempts to evaluate and develop ethical principles and ethical behavior in general, as well as when one tries to think about the ethics of a specific immediate situation. But in this area, also, logical thinking can get into a rut, and be unproductive. Then some other technique should be used, perhaps one which dips into primary process thinking.

This, then, is the *second* technique I suggest for the further development of ethical principles and behavior, in specific situations, and in general for the emergence of original or new or creative ideas in the field of ethics. We use what we know of primary process thinking to devise effective techniques, which are not destructive as drugs may be, to by-pass the ruts and blocks in logical thinking, in the field of ethics as in other fields.

As an example, I can choose an actual point in my own thinking which was facilitated by the use of this type of word-play. The thinking had to do with the attempt to derive a point of ethics from certain experience and data collected some years ago. At that time I was involved in research on gastrointestinal disorders. In that study, it became evident that certain patients had caricatured the ethical ideas of their parents.

As I recalled that data recently, it suggested a new technique in the development of ethics. I wanted to discuss the point in this book on the impact of psychiatry on ethics. But the idea remained unclear and fuzzy. Each time, I tried harder, and the discussion turned into a fifteen-page essay, much too long to be effective, and even then not altogether clear.

So I turned to an old reliable friend, my pattern of trying to jingle and to play with words. I wrote and rewrote a jingle. That technique helped me to find a way of phrasing fairly clearly an important point about ethical behavior.

An ethical principle which has been used effectively many times, and which has stood the test of time, the test of stringent self-scrutiny and of critical discussion with others, may suddenly seem to collapse when it is used again in a discussion with another person whom one is trying to help, a child or another adult. When that happens one possibility to consider seriously is that the ethical principle had a previously unsuspected and undetected weak point in its foundation. This should be checked carefully. But there is an alternative possibility. The principle used in the past may still be sound and solid, and not collapsed. The explanation may be that a sound principle had been caricatured by the other person without the one using it being aware of the fact that it had been caricatured. A slight caricature may resemble the original rather closely and yet have a very different meaning. And the caricature of an ethical principle can easily collapse of its own weight, as obviously incorrect. But if the difference between the principle itself and its caricature is recognized, the principle itself does not collapse.

More briefly stated, an ethical principle can be caricatured or exaggerated, even to the point of making the original principle seem nonsensical or ineffectual.

This leads to the *third* suggestion for a technology of ethics. It is to take a critical inventory occasionally of one's own ethical ideas. One can look at one's own principles, to see if one of them is overstated, is overblown, is a caricature of a principle that is important. One may have caricatured one of one's own principles without noticing it, just as one may not notice a caricature of a principle by another.

Now to give the jingle, which now represents two points in the development of the technology of ethics. First, this sort of jingling may be a substitute for whiskey, gin, and LSD. In other words, it is a sample of the technique of finding a workable, nondamaging way of getting in touch with the wellsprings of human imagination and creativeness, which must be available for the further development of ethics. This time the jingle helped me to clarify my thinking about the problem of the caricature of ethical principles, and so the jingle represents also the principle of the ongoing struggle against the caricature of ethics. The jingle represents the need to be on the alert for the caricature of ethical principles by others and by oneself.

The jingle is this:

"It is more blessed to give
Than it is to receive."
Most of us think that's a good way to live.
It's an idea that we learned to believe.
It's a maxim that is ethical,
Helps a child to get beyond the unethical
Overdone grabbing stage, which is omnipresent,
In which his life is happy and pleasant
Only if he can expect another present.

In that stage, the idea of being giving,
Which is a spontaneous part of loving and of living,
Gets covered and smothered, in us, her, him, me,
By the persistent drive to say "Gimme."

So to help, it's taught that "it's more blessed to give
Than it is to receive."
Some seem to take this very, very seriously,
And later say to the world, imperiously,
"I'm a giver; I'm always a giver
If I were to receive, I'd get a shiver
Of feeling that I'm only a child.
That would make me wild.
I'm very big and strong,
Please don't get me wrong.
Everyone can see I'm strong, since I give.
That's the only way one should live."

But most of us know now, that's only a halfway to live,
When one never receives, and always must give.
It's a pity to caricature life, to deceive
Oneself, to come really to believe
That it's weak or is bad to receive.

So we must devise another maxim,
I almost said another axiom,
That "it's blessed to receive, as well
As to give." Even a body cell
Must receive. So life is for living,
Life is not merely for giving.

The *fourth* approach toward a new technology of ethics is this. The growth of the field of psychodynamics, which in good part can be regarded as a science, has led to the development of an application of its knowledge in a technology of psychotherapy, which is a process of treatment. The question asked in this fourth approach is whether psychodynamics as a science might lead also to a second application, to a second set of techniques, this time to techniques in the field of ethics.

Further, if that seems feasible, if two sets of techniques can be developed from the one science of psychodynamics, there is a short-cut we might try out, with all due caution and self-criticism. If two sets of techniques are developed from the same science, they may resemble each other, be similar in some ways. We might hope for a correlation between the two sets of techniques, even hope that some of the specific techniques of psychotherapy which now exist might be modified slightly and then found to be useful also as techniques in the field of ethics.

To try this out, I will start with a rather small point. In psychotherapy, it is clear that only rarely can things go rapidly. Psychotherapy is the many-sided set of techniques which are used in the attempt to cure or alleviate signs or symptoms of certain kinds of illness, to lessen maladjustment, to lessen problems in human relations, and more positively phrased, to increase the individual's strengths and health and effectiveness. In psychotherapy, it is only rarely that the psychotherapist and the patient, in their alliance, can effect a change quickly or rapidly. Innumerable efforts have been, and are being, made to shorten the process. But none so far makes it really short.

Only twice in forty years of work in psychiatry have I been successful in curing a serious and persistent symptom in two hours. I shall talk about one of the two times, and again I can say that this story as I give it preserves confidentiality. This happening occurred during one of the several periods of time in which, after my training, I did further graduate work and research in another part of the world. As part of a research program, I saw some patients in a project which was cross-checking several areas of the Kinsey report on the Sexual Life of the Human Male.

One married man of sixty-five was referred to me who had been totally impotent for about thirty-five years. In the first hour, we discussed his history, and planned a number of studies of his physical health. Also, in a fairly intensive interview, I learned something of his emotional life in general. In the second hour, he began by saying, "This is marvelous. I was seen by Freud. He failed. I was seen by Jung and Adler. They both failed. I was seen by Ernest Jones, Adolf Meyer, and Franz Alexander. All great men. They all failed. Now I'm seen by you. I'm sure that you won't fail."

I laughed, but it did not offend him. And I said, "You surely put me in very good company. But maybe, maybe, beneath the nice things you just said about me, you really might expect me to fail also, as they did. You know that several of them were my teachers, and you might think that most of what I know I learned from them, from these men who were failures with you. I have a hunch that you feel that when I fail, you will have another scalp at your belt, another man you have beaten at his own game." This was followed by a fairly hectic discussion.

The next day his wife called me to say that they both wanted me to know that I had performed a miracle. I agreed that I had helped. But I knew some of the facts about their lives and knew that their thinking of me as doing miracles was almost as unproductive over the long run as was his thinking of psychiatrists as skillful men whom he could defeat, as antagonists worthy of his steel. In fact, these attitudes are two sides of the same coin, two halves of the same rolling wheel, which turns from the fantasy that the authority has extreme power or potency to the anticipation that the authority will fail or be impotent. So I insisted, with full conviction and strong emphasis, that it was true that I was an important person at that point in their lives, but that more than ninety per cent of the credit in reality, in absolute truth, was theirs. Five years later, the group sponsoring the research wrote me that their follow-up showed that the change had persisted, with some fluctuations.

I wish I could say that this sort of response is a frequent occurrence in a brief treatment. Some day in the future it may be. But now it is not. Psychotherapy takes time.

Now as to ethics. Perhaps the reader can recall past conversations in his life in which others talked about how quickly they have helped others with ethical problems, or how they have set others on the right ethical path by a brief "talking to," by a few words of wisdom, by giving them some advice, by laying down the law, by setting them straight on something. I have my doubts. My suggestion is that helping someone about ethics, like helping someone in psychotherapy, almost never can be done quickly.

I would put down as the first principle of the everyday practice of ethics, of the technology of ethics, that it takes time. It takes time to help improve the ethical principles or the ethical standards of another person, and it takes time to improve, in a lasting way, one's own ethical principles and ethical behavior. I am not talking about frightening or overwhelming someone into ethical behavior for a moment, or an hour, or a day. That is easy. I am talking about a real change. That is not easy or quick.

This could be elaborated extensively. But Satan, Circe, and all Sirens, and all of my own temptations to give a whole book in one chapter, be gone. We too must go on.

It may be productive to comb the field of psychotherapy to see which techniques, general or specific, have direct relevance to the techniques for the improvement of ethical principles or standards. Some will not apply. But some will. I shall mention one other.

Most of the specific techniques of psychotherapy seem to depend on having a workable therapeutic alliance, which has been discussed at various points in this series. In a comparable way, the process of one person helping another in the further development of his ethics conceivably may depend on their having developed a two-way working alliance somewhat similar to the therapeutic alliance. We can call it *The Ethicogenic Alliance*.[28]

We turn now from our scrutiny of the techniques of psychotherapy to a further scrutiny of the mother-lode of the science of psychodynamics, from which the techniques of psychotherapy have been developed. This can be phrased as the *fifth* pattern for the development of a technology of ethics. This approach is to search the field of psychodynamics itself, and the related disciplines, such as anthropology, history, jurisprudence, and social psychology, to look for areas which have not been applied in devising techniques of psychotherapy, but which conceivably could be applied in devising techniques for the further development of ethics.

My own study of psychodynamics and of human relations leads me to make the following comments. All indications point to the fact that the human animal, at this stage of its development, needs both an internal and an external set of standards. We need both a good conscience internally, and a good set of laws or customs or socially accepted patterns of behavior, externally.

Laws alone may be extraordinarily poor guides to ethical behavior, such as the German laws in the 1930s and early 1940s, obedience to which led to the destruction of millions of human beings. Customs of enslaving groups of other human beings, and laws which codified the institution of slavery, also are very poor guides to ethical behavior. Further, the conscience alone may also be a poor guide to ethical behavior, since the conscience speaks with contradictory voices at times, and since a major part of the conscience, the Superego, is unconscious and primitive.

It would be a major mistake, however, to comment only in negative terms either about conscience or about laws and customs. Much of the time the voice of conscience is reliable, to a good degree, and can become more so. And much of the time a good part of the laws and customs are workable and valid and relevant, or can be changed by general agreement.

But it is a mistake to say, as some surgeons have said, that we do not need a multidisciplinary discussion of the ethical problems in organ transplantation, since the surgeon can rely simply on his own conscience. The conscience is not altogether reliable, in anyone, all the time.

Also we must look at the other type of problem, of what one should do in a specific situation when most others are convinced that a group decision or a law inevitably is more reliable than anyone's conscience, and yet one is convinced that one's conscience is more correct than the voice of the group, or is more correct than certain rules or customs. Just as conscience is not always reliable, so laws and customs are not altogether reliable, and at times one must follow one's own conscience. There are times when each of us must take this stance. Certainly it seems likely that no man or woman of integrity in the last third of his or her life could have lived that long without seriously jeopardizing his career a half-dozen times, without being unpopular many times, and without being in physical danger at times.

The process of sticking to one's guns, to one's conscience decisions, can be a tricky business. I have seen many individuals make serious issues of conscience of unimportant or incorrect points, which they regretted later. This has been my experience several times also. So on this point I have developed one rule for myself. If the issue at hand seems to me, but not to others, an important issue of conscience, I try to find at least two very reliable persons who think as I do. An amusing example is that when I brought one such issue to a vote in a board-of-directors meeting of a national organization, I knew I probably would be voted down, fourteen to one. I hesitated to stand alone until I found that two former members of that board felt as strongly as I did about the issue and were in agreement with my stand. The vote itself was fourteen to one.

So, *fifth* suggestion: Search the field of psychodynamics and related fields, such as the studies of the conscience, for new techniques of ethical understanding and behavior. From such areas of study, my specific suggestion for a new technique, is that (a) one should examine critically one's own multiple voices of conscience; (b) with the aid of a free press and information as valid as one can find, one should examine critically the contradictory or dubious laws, customs, policies, and commands; and also (c) one should compare one's conscience with the external standards and test one against the other. In brief, this suggestion calls for the creative development of techniques for the cross-checking of internal and external set of standards.

The *sixth* variety of techniques for the development of ethics can be phrased quite simply, that one must check one's favorite aphorisms or maxims against the facts. Some of them will be found to be inappropriate, perhaps seriously wrong. For example, one often hears the maxim that "offense is the best defense" when an individual tries to explain his aggressive behavior in a discussion or a disagreement, even though it occurred in a meeting in which the focus was on the working out of a problem which was mutually important, by productive discussion.

If that is one of your maxims, check it against the available facts. It may be a good maxim in military conflict, or in revolutionary movements, or in counterrevolutionary activity. In a debate, or in a hostile argument in which the goal is to win out over the other, or to become the dominant figure, it may be good strategy to attack, to take offensive action before one is attacked. In a sport, an athletic contest, aggressiveness is good, but is limited by the rules and by the referee. Within those limits, an attacking aggressiveness has some value. In the game of sharp-edged badinage, in which everyone expects to give and to receive verbal body blows, offense as defense is the name of the game.

In good human relations, however, there are several important reasons for rejecting the policy of regarding offense as the best defense. One is that it is a frequent observation that a human relationship characterized primarily by this pattern, of attack by A and defense by B, followed by an attack by B (with the intent of having it serve as a defense against another attack by A), which then leads to a defense by A, is an extraordinarily risky style of relationship, which usually is not workable. Perhaps the attack as defense relation is workable, e.g. in a marriage or in a business partnership, primarily when one of the pair is strongly sadistic and the other, fitting like a lock to a key, is strongly masochistic, or when the two take turns at the wheel.

The "attack as a defense" pattern also may work in a human relation if the pattern is only a sideshow, i.e. if the central pattern is much more largely one of teamwork. In general, the "attack as a defense" pattern often is present in human relations; if it is mild and congenial and peripheral, it can be stimulating without being destructive.

Most often, that pattern is not to be taken lightly in a potentially good relation. If one individual feels the need to be defensive, and uses a fairly aggressive attack as the best method of defense, he not only has defended himself but also he has offended the other. In general, he has run the risk of accentuating or increasing the attack-defense part of the relation, which might not have been so prominent otherwise. In fact, in human relations which have high potential value, offense may be the worst pattern to use. But the alternative need not be a flabby approach. A valid and workable sublimation of offense-as-defense, in a good relation, is the pattern of being firm, sharp, and limit-setting, e.g. when the other is testing the limits, or when the other is trying to dominate.

The *seventh* variety of techniques for the development of ethics is to use athletics, sports, or other games as a source of maxims or analogies or principles, to replace obsolescent phrases in ethics. The widespread participation in sports, plus the even more widespread attendance at spectator sports, makes the use of game-phrases as ethical maxims seem immediate and contemporary, a slice of life, not merely a distant goal.

Also, most sports are not regarded as the activities of weaklings. Phrases from sports are not regarded as urging the stance of purity or sweetness. One of the great tragedies is that ethical principles often are construed as placing great stress on the value of weakness or subservience or automatic obedience or passivity. For most boys and girls, the phrase of being a good boy or being a good girl is regarded as the equivalent of being a weakling. Ethical phrases derived from the field of athletics are much less likely to be contaminated in that way.

Many authors in the past have used athletics as a source of ethical phrases. The concept of fair play, the concept of the Marquis of Queensbury rules providing an analogy in fields other than boxing, and the learning of courage and leadership on the playing fields of Eton have been mentioned time and again.

To these, we can add that the concept of perfectionism can be replaced by the concept of a good batting average in which no one expects even a great slugger to make a hit each time at bat. But often such a comment which implies the replacement of perfectionism as an ethical standard arouses concern that a debunking of the standard of perfectionism would lead to carelessness, to "laziness," to an absence of a pressure to do well. But everyone knows that a great slugger who uses the standard of a high batting average rather than of perfectionism, and who knows that no one can bat 1,000, still does not take life easy. Far from it. The slugger works hard to keep his batting average as good as it is or to improve it.

As another example from the field of sports, we can use the fairway in golf, with the rough on one side and the rough on the other, as the basis for a concept of an ethical fairway in life, to symbolize several facts, e.g. that the ethical fairway is broad, not a thin line on which it is too difficult to stay, and that it is broad enough for individual variations, not merely for a restricted narrow compliance. Further, the fairway concept symbolizes the fact that one can get off the ethical fairway in at least two kinds of rough. For example, in driving along one of the ethical fairways in life, viz. of showing consideration for the needs and the feelings of others, one can get into the rough on the one side of being careless about the needs of others, and perhaps of hurting others. But also one can get into the rough on the other side, of being overly considerate of others, of acting as if the others were fragile and thereby slightly inferior, as if they were unable to take life as it is. This, too, can hurt them.

Throughout this book, there has been an emphasis on the value of a stringent, honest self-scrutiny in preventing mistakes and in improving one's effectiveness. Without hesitation, we can list the process of *self-scrutiny* as the *eighth* suggestion for a technique for the improvement of one's ethical standards and ethical behavior.

Self-scrutiny may not be sufficient at times, and so there must be developed, as a technique for the improvement of one's ethical behavior, some form of occasional supervision by a reliable person. For example, a mother's handling of a child can be supervised, at her own request, by a well-trained, understanding pediatrician. The *ninth* suggestion then, for a technology of ethics, is to develop a pattern of the *supervision of ethical behavior*.

Still further, I urge, as the *tenth* suggestion, the further development of what may become one of the most important technologic innovations in the field of ethics, the use of *peer supervision*. These three processes, self-scrutiny, supervision, and peer supervision, will be discussed as a continuum.

First, we must focus again on the technique of self-scrutiny. It should be stringent but affectionate. The need for self-scrutiny is based on the fact that in loaded questions, e.g. in issues of Defensive Ethics and of Creative Ethics, one must be on the lookout for the impact of one's own personal patterns and that of others on the issues at hand, on the decisions to be made. For example, in developing my own understanding of the conflict between the generations, the most important step was to see in myself the danger of having a Myth of the Wise Elder Statesman. Also, self-scrutiny is essential in doing supervision and in being supervised, in graduate training, as indicated in the discussion of supervision in the early chapter "The Conflict Between the Generations." Self-scrutiny is the essential matrix of the NON-JOB, the Neither-Oedipus-Nor-Job approach to life.

Further, no one can expect that all of his potentially destructive and distorting patterns can be settled forever by one period of self-scrutiny or by one act of renunciation. One must work on oneself time after time. Eternal vigilance has been called the price of freedom. We can add that *eternal internal vigilance is the price of internal freedom.*

From the discussion of self-scrutiny, we turn to the process of peer supervision. Some years ago I proposed this technique for psychiatrists after their training was over. I suggested that they should form small self-selected groups of four or five individuals who like each other and feel they can trust each other. In rotation, one evening a month or so they present to each other their work with patients, preserving confidentiality. In each meeting, the presenter gives special emphasis to his own responses, his feelings, his patterns of work, especially in difficult cases. The others give their impression of the presenter's approach and his responses.

Some of their comments are directly helpful. And a most important effect is to stimulate an increase in the presenter's self-scrutiny. In peer supervision, each one is a supervisor of the work of all of the others, which means that each one is being supervised by all of the others of the group.

One of the important factors in peer supervision is that it has many of the qualities of individual supervision but avoids some of the temptation to be dependent that might be stimulated by a plan to initiate again the process of individual supervision, which was used extensively during the psychiatrist's original period of training.

My suggestion now is that in the further development of ethics, small self-selected groups, of lawyers, of judges, of teachers, of clergy, of graduate students, of mothers, of fathers, and of others, should develop the process of peer supervision. Group meetings could occur once a month or so. At such meetings, one member of the group would be the "presenter," would talk about a current problem of the sort all of the group must deal with, then discuss his own way of dealing with it. The others would comment, might suggest other ways of dealing with the situation, or express their agreement. Each month, there would be a different "presenter," until each one has "presented," and then start over again.

If there is a fair degree of honesty, a wish to help and to be helped, and a wish to learn, everyone can give and everyone can gain. Such a peer supervision group is a profoundly important technique of ethics, a mutual-assistance pact in which everyone can gain.

Peer supervision and self-scrutiny in general is motivated by the need to improve one's understanding and skill. Peer supervision of a group of high school teachers would focus on the process of teaching in a high school. But understanding and skill often involve ethical decisions, and so self-scrutiny and supervision and peer supervision often involve a scrutiny of ethical attitudes. Further, self-scrutiny and supervision can be planned to focus primarily on the ethical aspects of one's work and on one's relations with individuals outside the peer supervision group.

Perhaps some peer supervision groups should plan to have, at the beginning, an experienced person who would act as a sort of seminar leader or a supervisor, and then eventually have the "seminar leader" come in only when he seems needed.

Also some groups may focus on a problem or an issue rather than be limited to a group of individuals of the same category. For example, a peer supervision group might consist of two teachers, two principles, and two professors in a college of education, focusing not only on the problems of improving the quality of secondary-school education but also on the ways each presenter handles his problems, with the comments of others focusing on his patterns of work and his responses to various situations.

One of the difficulties with regard to peer supervision is that usually one can find a group of four or five who will agree with oneself on most topics or will agree on the special topic or area which will be central in the meetings. Consequently one must be careful, if one is organizing a peer supervision group, to avoid choosing only those whom one knows in advance would be willing to go along with most or all of one's ideas. At the same time, one should hesitate to be in a peer supervision group with someone who disagrees with almost everything that one says or does.

The technique of peer supervision is not the primary pattern to use when the job is to make up one's mind about controversial issues. Other processes are more effective in reaching that goal. Peer supervision is more suitable for gaining some perspective on one's style of behavior, on the style of responses one uses frequently, and which often are not clearly recognized by oneself. Peer supervision is suitable for a discussion of the ways in which others act or work or behave in a fashion different from one's own.

For coming to a decision on realistically controversial issues, the ethical approach probably would be along other lines. It would emphasize the process of becoming well-informed. The independence of the press and other media is highly relevant to this kind of ethics. In some critical issues, a most important technique is of going to source material for information. The process of becoming acquainted with the critical evaluations of controversial topics by well-informed and objective writers or speakers is a part of good ethics.

Controversial material need not be excluded from a peer supervision discussion, but the purpose of peer supervision is not to arrive at a position on local or national affairs but to discuss one's own and each others' patterns of approach to common problems. But after one is well-informed, a peer-supervision group focused on the way each member of a small group responds to the same body of available information could be of great value. Also a peer supervision group of those who are especially well-informed, e.g. foreign correspondents, could be most useful to them. This would be done in private, not on TV.

One additional point: when I began to suggest to others that peer supervision might be tried by groups other than psychiatrists, one judge of a high-level court said that in at least one area of the country judges of the same type of court had group conferences which resembled peer supervision. The conferences focused on the sentences to be handed down in the courts of each of the judges, after the trials were over and decisions had been made about guilt or innocence or civil responsibility.

He reported that in such a "sentencing conference," one of the outstanding facts was the degree of difference between the judges about the lightness and severity of the sentences they recommended in cases in which the law permitted a judge a wide latitude in the sentence to be imposed. He said that in the sentencing discussion of a group of judges, it was apparent that the personality of the judge often played a major role in determining the kind of punishment he would deem logical or appropriate. Some of the comments they made to each other about the impact of their patterns of work and thinking on their decisions seem to be comparable to those suggested for peer supervision. The conferences represented in part an attempt to have an ethical partnership, an alliance, in decision-making, and to stimulate others to an ethically valuable self-scrutiny, and also to consider, even more ethically and poignantly, the value of better decisions when a judge must take a step which has a profound effect on the one judged guilty and on his family. Further, the fact of such sentencing conferences increases the confidence of society in the judiciary and in the legal system.

Such an ethical pattern has obvious limits. In the Nazi regime, a sentencing conference of judges probably only rarely would have led to sentences in line with the non-Nazi but widespread principles of contemporary jurisprudence and ethics. Peer supervision is not a substitute for the democratic process, for majority rule which provides full protection of the rights of minorities, for representative government, for strong leadership, and for loyal opposition, in social and political organizations.

The next is the *eleventh* suggestion for a technology of ethics. Whenever one talks of ethics, one seems to talk of principles, of ideas, of maxims and aphorisms, i.e. of an intellectual process. This seems inevitable, since ethics in part is based on being reasonable or rational, on thinking things through, on making a choice between types of behavior, or on making a choice to integrate types of behavior.

Also in good part, the consideration of ethics in the past has been in the intellectual tradition, has stressed the high value of words and ideas in modifying human impulses and feelings and behavior. This approach still has certain values. Therefore if one wants to work toward a technology of ethics, toward the improvement in ethical behavior that has become increasingly important for the human race, one certainly must include the technical attempts to open new doors in the intellectual approach in ethics. I have attempted to do this repeatedly in this book.

But it can no longer be doubted that in the human animal the intellect often plays second fiddle to human drives and emotions, in determining human behavior. This fact has guided much of our discussion of Id, Ego, and Superego, of Defensive Ethics and of Creative Ethics. So a consideration of new developments in the technology of ethics must emphasize emotion and drive, nonverbal communication, and patterns of good personal development, which can carry with them good patterns of ethical behavior. This emphasis is apparent also in the present work.

Hence, as this book nears its end, it seems imperative to underline further the nonintellectual factors in the further development of ethics. It is clear, for example, that the teaching of ethics should be not only by precept and maxim but also by example. Second, a generally good relation between parent and child, with its productive emphasis on selective permissiveness and selective firm limit-setting, can be of great value as a most basic technique of fostering good ethics, in the development in the child of his own standard-setting toward himself, his development of an effective conscience. And perhaps one can say, or hope, that anything which fosters the healthy development of the human being, of his drives, his emotions, his behavior, and his internal standards as well as his intellect, is likely also to foster a good development of ethical behavior.

Now as a change of pace, and as a way of ending this chapter, we shall discuss another technique of ethics which will symbolize the fact that these pages must be a beginning, not an end, to our thinking about a technology of ethics. I want to use this point, also, to indicate the fact that the technologic advances in ethics must focus on nonverbal behavior as well as on words or advice from one person to another.

By focusing on this technique, I can show my respect for the readers of this book. The technique to be suggested is not simple. It will take some feeling and thinking, which means that the readers will have to stretch a bit further their zest for living and their drive to do a good job, in order to behave in accordance with this pattern.

This final point is the *twelfth* suggestion of techniques for the further development of ethics. Its title is "The Avoidance of Double Messages."

An example is this. A parent or a teacher, who had been rather rebellious in childhood or adolescence but no longer acts rebelliously, may still have such impulses, and at times have fantasies of being rebellious and enjoying it. That parent or teacher now is in close contact with a youngster who has just become sixteen, and has a driver's license. He has become rebellious in various ways in recent months, and at times drives an automobile at high speeds, dangerous to others and to himself. The parent or teacher may do an excellent, even an outstanding, job of responding in this crisis, in words and in action, with an attitude which expresses a good selective permissiveness in certain ways, and a very good selective firm limit-setting in other ways.

But at the moment the parent or teacher responds productively, he or she also may have a facial expression of intense interest and of eagerness to hear more about the boy's quick swerving to avoid hitting a dog in the street, about what the policeman said the second time, etc. Almost inevitably the sixteen-year-old will get a second message, that the parent or teacher secretly in a way is thrilled or pleased by the boy's expression of independence and rebellion, and is getting a vicarious enjoyment. There is a fair chance that the sixteen-year-old is more likely to act in accordance with the secret message than with the message that was expressed in words and in principle and in overt behavior. He may think that the parent or teacher feels obligated to make socially approved comments but in reality would prefer to play the Russian Roulette of dangerous driving. It is clear that facial expression and the way questions are asked, and comments are made, are tremendously important in backing the message expressed verbally, or in producing a contradictory double message.

And double messages occur not only with regard to rebellion. An example is to be seen in the following interchange between a father and his fifteen-year-old son. In the past, the father had mentioned to his doctor and to his friends, not to his children, that he was afraid of girls when he was younger. Now he learns that his son is to have his first date. The father becomes very, very helpful about seeing that the son wears the right clothes and knows the right things to say or to do under all circumstances. The father reassures the son that all will go well and that he need not worry. The father several times says, with some tension, that he knows that his son is so strong that he surely will never be afraid of girls, never be ill at ease with them. The son can hardly fail to hear both messages, and to become anxious even as he listens to the words of reassurance.

In the discussion of the Golden Rule, the end-point was that an ethics based on the Golden Rule is often good enough, but that an ethics based on the Golden Rule which had been amended to include a consideration of the difference between individuals, and to include the fact of ambivalence, could do an even better job. A similar comment about the ethical issue related to the double-message pattern just mentioned is in order.

The ethical behavior of a parent or teacher, or other adviser, which consists of his behaving and speaking in the usual ethically productive ways with another person, often is good enough. But at times, when the parent or teacher or adviser is not satisfied with the way he is doing that job, he can do a bit of self-scrutiny, or have a bit of scrutiny done by others in a peer supervision group. From this, he may see that he himself enjoys the misbehavior of the others, or may see that he himself is more anxious than the next generation is, and shows it in questions or facial expression or tone of voice. When that kind of hidden message or double message can be seen, it may not be difficult to modify, and the ethics of the fathers or the mothers or the teachers or other advisers has gone to a higher level, and is more likely to be effective.

This was the *twelfth* and last of the series of suggestions for the development of a technology of ethics. These propositions obviously are not given as proven or established. They are worth further testing. But more important, they provide one way of stimulating an ongoing participation in the further development of ethical principles and ethical behavior.

11

Postscript

THIS Postscript is phrased as a series of independent items, so that each one can serve as a starting point for later discussion.

1. The widely accepted Occam's Law (of Parsimony) in philosophy and in science, good though it is, often is restrictive and blocking to further development. A Moccam's Law (of Extravagance) is suggested, with an Occam-Moccam integration as a further solution.

2. It was known for a long time that man was not the only *tool-using* animal. Now, Jane Goodall's studies of chimpanzees show, also, that man is not the only *tool-making* animal. This finding and others like it may eliminate another of the differences which seemed to show a sharp qualitative discontinuity between man and the other species.

3. Recent biologic studies, after the Post-Darwinian era, have revealed a somewhat different picture of animal life than is reflected in many of the publications about man in the first half of this century. Recent findings of an innate defense in vertebrate animals against their killing others of the same species in the process of competitive and violent fighting, and of widespread and highly developed patterns of social living in primates, force a reworking of our thinking about man's biologic drives.

4. Contemporary biology stresses genetic stability in the species and frequent genetic variations in the individuals, interacting with external forces in the process of natural selection. In this process, biologic survival, of the individual and of the species, is achieved in many species not only by competitive struggle but also by co-operation and mutual help. This, plus the well-developed systems of social organization among the higher animals, seem to provide the prototypes for social organization in man and for his Superego and Ego patterns.

5. Erik Erikson suggested that one biologic basis for Ego function in man was the pattern of the adjustment of each animal species to its ecologic niche, and its tolerance of the needs of other species in the same area. The Washburn-DeVore studies of the participation of individual primates in the organization of the group, the reports of Lorenz and many others of species-specific defenses against the killing of members of the same group, etc., offer additional convincing evidence of prototypes of Ego function in many vertebrate species.

6. The development of those functions of the brain cortex, and of those functions of the Ego, which are called inhibition, integration, central coordination, decisions, choice, etc., can be assumed to have had great biologic survival value. The flexibility and complex responsiveness, the capacity to cope and to adjust by the use of one or another alternative reaction, in biologic functioning, seems to require a concept of determinism which is not simple or rigid and which includes a flexible but limited function of decision-making. Therefore a psychodynamic formulation of the Ego functions of integration, decision-making, and choice, requires a re-definition of psychic determinism which is comparable to the re-definition of determinism in other sciences.

7. Psychiatric data stresses the power of the forces "by which we are lived," the individual's own irresistible drives and his own rigid defenses.

8. Based on the observable facts of the Ego's ability (in varying degrees) to cope with and to master some of the Id and Superego

forces, one can formulate a workable concept of Ego strength, a concept which includes an awareness of the limited nature of that Ego strength. The recognition of Ego strength is the basis for the next step, viz. the concept that the Ego in its functioning is strong and effective enough so that it need not always use the battle-axe defenses of total repression or of reversal. Instead, in its dealing with the various Id and Superego forces and with the forces of the external world, the Ego's functioning can use a more effective coping type of strength. For example, it may combine a selective permissiveness (after requiring some modification of the drives, if necessary) with a selective firm limit-setting or conscious renunciation.

9. The social pattern of *eternal vigilance* against corruption as the price of freedom can be paralleled by the concept of an Ego function of *eternal internal vigilance* against corruption as the price of internal freedom.

10. Man's killing of man, and more generally man's inhumanity toward man, no longer can be regarded as the inevitable result of his biologic heritage. One possible formulation is that man's inhumanity to man may in part have certain innate sources, but in good part is cultural in origin and is related to man's patterns of anxiety and destructive defenses, of magical thinking, of language, of fantasy, of projection, of hostility, etc., which in turn arise in good part out of man's biologic pattern of a prolonged period of dependency in early childhood.

11. A respectable case might be made for the existence of a Job complex comparable to the Oedipus complex, also for a process of overcoming the Job complex comparable to overcoming the Oedipus complex, with the end-point of a Neither-Oedipus-Nor-Job pattern of Ego adjustment.

12. The corruptibility of the Superego may be triggered by suffering (especially when that is the result of self-punishment) even more frequently than by the agents of corruption usually described, such as money and power.

13. One essential ethical problem has to do with two contra-

dictory emphases. One emphasis is that man's conscience should be the final arbiter of right and wrong, i.e. the primacy of individual conscience over law. The second emphasis is that group decisions, laws, and universal principles should be the final arbiter of what is right or wrong, i.e. the primacy of law over individual conscience. But the fact that conscience patterns (Superego functions) at times may be primitive or contradictory or corruptible, and the fact that external standards at times may be seriously unreliable, calls for three types of Ego patterns. One is the individual's stringent self-scrutiny of his conscience. The second is the individual's stringent scrutiny of external standards. The third is the development of a strong Ego pattern of cross-validation of internal standards by external standards, and the reverse. A comparable scrutiny by the group is essential as well.

14. An individual's unconscious hostile caricature of the Superego principles of his parents can produce a serious Superego distortion in himself.

15. In the resolution of conflicts, either internal or external, human beings develop many patterns of coping and of defenses. A defense can be regarded as a form of "Defensive Ethics" if the defenses are in keeping with the ongoing or mature interests of the individual himself and at the same time do no damage to others, or even at times further the interests of others. In certain extreme situations, Defensive Ethics may include an unavoidable risk of hurting others, e.g. in the process of protecting the weak against actual mistreatment by others.

16. There is an even more constructive type of Ego functioning, of interpersonal relations, and of cultural patterns, which is not merely defensive, and which can be called "Creative Ethics." Often in this, some of the essential interests of the individual himself, and of the other persons or groups, are fostered simultaneously. One interpersonal example is the mutual partnership between individuals, in productive work which has value for them and for a much larger group. An intrapsychic example is the pattern described by Freud as postambivalent object love.

17. Unfortunately, the struggle between Ego and Id often is phrased as if it were a struggle between good (the Ego) and evil (the Id) no matter how the terms, good and evil, are defined. But some of the early Ego responses (e.g. the projection of early destructive hostile impulses) can later be seen by the observing portions of the Ego, and by other persons, to be destructive to oneself and to others. Also, the Id (often phrased as essentially evil) includes forces which may indeed be destructive at times to the individual or to others, but also includes some forces which are a vital source of positive developments, e.g. the need for help and love, and the need to give help and love.

18. In Creative Ethics, the pattern of an alliance, of various types, has high value. Examples are the therapeutic alliance and the supervisory alliance. A similar pattern of alliance can have high value in other ways, e.g. in the conflict between the generations. In the honest, open attempt of older members of the tribe to help the younger members, the concept of an *ethicogenic alliance* can correspond to the concept of the therapeutic alliance in the process of psychotherapy.

19. Concurrent with the use of alliance and the other patterns in Creative Ethics, there must be patterns of Defensive Ethics to use in certain other situations. For example, there are situations in which a stand which emphasizes sharp differences or disagreement rather than alliance must be used, even though it may threaten one's career or one's safety.

20. The use of physical force, as part of Defensive Ethics, occasionally can be an absolute necessity. But many serious and dangerous mistakes are made in this type of thinking and behavior. Therefore such decisions must be subject to intensive and stringent self-scrutiny, and to other safeguards.

21. Stringent but congenial self-scrutiny, individual supervision, and peer supervision can provide essential safeguards, in many varieties of Defensive Ethics and of Creative Ethics.

22. Stringent self-scrutiny can be the first step in the resolution of a conflict between the generations. The older generation may

find that it is unrealistically controlled by myths, such as the Myth of the Wise Elder Statesman. The younger generation, on self-scrutiny, may find itself too much under the sway of the Myth of Fresh Blood and New Ideas. Such self-scrutiny can lead to a productive alliance instead of to ongoing nonproductive alienation.

23. In the conflict between the generations, one of the core issues is the fact of ambiguity with regard to the equality and inequality of the roles and functions of the generations.

24. Self-scrutiny similar to that which was reported by Darwin, which can be phrased as a pattern of observing, facing, and overcoming his pattern of forgetting those of his own observations which contradicted his own developing theory, can be very useful in the field of ethics. It is at a level which can be recommended for general use. It focuses on observable behavior and on conscious wishes or feelings which may not be acceptable to the individual or to those he respects. This type of self-scrutiny can be contrasted with the more deep-going kind of self-scrutiny which is done in individual psychotherapy and psychoanalysis, which is not to be recommended as a general technique of ethics without professional help.

25. The concept of a conflict of ethical systems within one person can be productive. It can be phrased as being a conflict between Superego patterns, or as a conflict between Ego functions, rather than as being the more usual type of conflict, between Ego (and Superego) and Id. In another frame of reference, it can be phrased as a conflict between good and good, to supplement the usual concept of a conflict between good and evil.

26. The recognition of the existence of ambivalence forces a revision of the use of the Golden Rule as a guide to Ego function.

27. There is an urgent need for a further development of ethical principles and ethical behavior. In that development, a technology of ethics can be of high value. Such a technology might use some of the patterns developed in the application of pure science to technologic innovation.

28. Techniques of psychotherapy provide many paradigms which

could be useful in the development of techniques of ethical teaching. One example is the use of the therapeutic alliance as a model for the development of a teaching-learning alliance in ethics.

29. Over the years, an unrecognized process of caricaturing one's own ethical principles may take place. Until it is seen as such, the principles are in jeopardy of being beside the point, or of being overdone, and also are in jeopardy at times of being discarded as totally mistaken, i.e. making the mistake of discarding the original value as well as the caricature.

30. The use of a number of concepts from the field of athletics can provide techniques for the teaching of ethics. One would be a striving for a high batting average rather than for perfection. A second is the concept of an ethical fairway with the rough on both sides.

31. The technique of peer supervision groups may be of value in clarifying ethical behavior and ethical principles.

32. The techniques of ethics have been predominantly intellectual, using aphorisms and maxims, with an emphasis on intellectualization and on the power of words. The further development of ethics may consist largely of the development of new concepts and new dynamic patterns of Ego activity, emphasizing emotional maturity and levels of personal and interpersonal integration, as well as intellect and reason.

33. A postscript in this book must end by referring again to the two-way working alliance between readers and author. Even an author must take the initiative and the responsibility in choosing what to include and what to exclude in a book. Often an author must defer discussion of a number of important issues in order to have space in a book of reasonable size and price for an understandable discussion of issues which to him seem most basic and crucial.

I chose those topics which seemed to merit first attention. My judgment was guided by the comments of those who have participated in my lectures, seminars, and supervision over the years, by my discussions with individuals of various generations, with members of various majority and minority groups.

In future books, the author hopes to present more extensively some of the relevant areas touched on only lightly in this book. This could include the impact of special developments in psychiatry and in psychoanalysis on the growing understanding of ethics; the variety of approaches to the study of ethics used by philosophers; the discussion by philosophers of precise points of psychoanalytic thinking about ethics; the specific contributions of anthropology, of sociology, and of social psychology to the concepts of psychoanalysis and to the concept of ethics.

April 28, 1971

•

A Memo From ML[*]

O NLY rarely do many of a group read a long memorandum, unless there is a special reason for doing so. So to make sure that you will at least begin to read this memo, I can start by saying that its topic is my recent illness and the fact that I was close to death. Knowing the topic, you probably will read a page or two, and perhaps then the rest of the memo.

This is the latest of the psychiatry department series called "Memos from M.L.," which over the past 20 years has consisted of occasional notes, comments, and freewheeling discussions of current issues. The memos have functioned in the department as a cohesive force and as a technique of communication and mutual understanding.

This memo focuses on the fact that as an older member of the tribe, a grandfather-father-uncle figure, I am more likely than you

* This memorandum was written on March 30, 1971, by Dr. Maurice Levine, Professor and Director of the Department of Psychiatry at the University of Cincinnati, to his faculty, staff, and colleagues. It was not originally meant for publication. It has been edited slightly to remove time-related comments. Maurice Levine died May 1, 1971.

are, to have or to have had, certain types of experience. At times I feel I have a responsibility to give you a chance to live through some of these experiences with me, if you care to do so. In my own development, this kind of vicarious experience had great meaning and value. (And its good practice in empathy which is one of the central patterns of our work.)

It might be an important piece of living for you to identify temporarily with me as I go through this period of serious sickness, to share some bits and pieces of this important human process. Of course, I know that often it is very difficult to listen to someone who is discussing a critical illness, of himself or of another person, and the possibility of death. But in the setting of the special atmosphere and the essentially positive set of relations in this Department, it may be possible. Again, however, I want to emphasize the fact that you have no obligation to read this memo. Some of you will simply put it aside.

To carry out my part of this deal, I must be able to talk without too much blocking about serious illness and the risk of death, in others or in myself. This is not easy to do. But I have had certain experiences which make it a bit easier.

I have seen death and dying many times, in those who were strangers, in those I had known for only a brief period, and in others I had known for a long time. Over the years I have been there at the moment of death with a number of patients, with several friends, with my father, with my mother, with a brother, and with a sister. And I have been with several members of my family and with a fair number of patients and others who were close to death but then recovered. Out of these experiences, out of my own age, and out of my discussions with others of like experience, I can think about death, feel about death, and talk about death, somewhat more easily than do many others.

The evidence is clear, from psychiatry and psychoanalysis, that it is valuable to feel and to think, and also to talk under certain conditions, about aspects of life which often are left unspoken, this is true not only about sex, but also about anger and hate, about wishes to be childlike, about guilt and shame, about anxiety and about the excessive or the insufficient inhibitions which often are linked with anxiety, and about dying, the death of others or of oneself. But there is no compulsion about this. One can live a good life and one can die a good death, without thinking or talking about death.

Most of you know by this time that my recent illnesses have been severe . . . these illnesses were indirectly the outgrowth of a recently discovered leukemia . . . an intensive treatment program has been started, aimed at the anemia and the danger of bleeding, and especially at the leukemia process itself.

To facilitate your putting yourself in fantasy momentarily in my shoes, it would help if I confessed some of my personal feelings and responses. During the sickness so far, I have had many intense emotions, of fear, of anxiety, of confusion, of disbelief, of fury, of irritability, of giving up, of feeling overwhelmed, of wanting sympathy and attention, of denial of illness, and of false hope, as well as a set of fairly good cooperative responses. In addition, I have had many other intense feelings, which also are human and perhaps inevitable, which are forgivable and forgettable since they don't really hurt others or oneself if they are not put into action. But such feelings and attitudes are of limited value.

In addition, I have been doing a great deal of thinking about some of the fantasies and myths and human patterns which may be even more productive than the kind of simple and direct reactions I just confessed. For example, we have just enjoyed the first week of spring. This time of the year seems to have had extraordinarily important meanings, realistic and symbolic, for the human being, primitive and civilized, over a long period of time. Each year in spring the apparently dead vegetation of the past year begins to grow again. What seemed dead, or close to death, seems to come alive again.

I suppose that in spring, for primitive man, the world must have seemed a warmer, safer, more secure, more promising place to be. The world must have seemed less dangerous in many ways, with the promise of food and warmth, of growing strength.

My fantasy about this, which differs slightly from the one usually given about the experience of spring in primitive man, is that in spring it may have seemed as if a new generation of plant life had begun to appear. Perhaps a new generation of animals then seemed to be possible, to be on the way. The world must have seemed vital and fertile again.

Out of this, and out of other facts and fantasies of early and of later man, there may have been stimulated the hope for, or the illusion of, personal immortality, the hope that one would not die as an individual, or that in a sense one would live on through the coming generations. And for very many, of course, the evidence indicates that spring was the period in which it was believed that the deity or the deities were revived, were alive again, benign and responsive.

In the life of a contemporary, skeptical, self-critical individual human being, there is room for a large variety of important "as-if" feelings, of symbolic responses which can be used as leads to better understanding. One can be confident enough about the strength and the validity of the realistic, scientific approach to stop being afraid of the symbolic, aesthetic, empathic moments of life. In fact, such patterns can add depth and breadth to one's realistic perceptions and responses. At times a symbolic response can lead to the resolution of blocked intellectual problems, e.g. Kekule's use of his snake circle daydream, in the carbon ring discovery, basic to organic chemistry.

I feel alive, active and revived, these first weeks of spring. Such feelings conceivably in part are an as-if component of a symbolic process, a primary process response, a set of momentary illusions of immortality or of resurrection.

But my feelings of being alive and vital are related not only to the time of the year and its symbolism, and not only to momentary illusions. I have good realistic reasons for feeling revived and active. The winter of my pneumonia and pulmonary edema is gone. The temporary heart failure and the delirium are over. I was close to death for many days, but today I am feeling alive and cantankerous, again. I feel expansive and creative.

Inevitably, but pleasurably, I've begun to concoct jokes again. I recall that about two weeks ago, several careful hospital people were checking the name-tag on my wrist against the labels on the packages of blood platelets which were about to be injected into my vein to prevent the dangerous bleeding which can be one aspect of leukemia. The first voice read the label on the package of platelets, read the date on which the blood had been drawn from the donor and the date it was delivered to my room, or some other important date. Then the second voice, I thought, read my name and the number of my Holmes Hospital room. Then one of the voices read, "Expiration Date, March 17, 1971." How dare they, I thought! I had given them the right to decide when I could move my arm, when I should open or close my mouth. Now they even had assumed the right to set my expiration date, and with damn little notice in advance!

All the time, of course, in a paralled process of perception, I knew that it was the voice of the other person, reading the expiration date of this batch of platelets, the date beyond which there would be doubt of its freshness and safety.

So I was close to death for a time, close to a permanent winter. But I am alive. Spring is here. And I know that symbolic responses are highly meaningful. But for me, the most important component of my feeling is the depth of my respect for science and medicine. The fact that I am alive as a vivid example of medical and other research proving its scientific and practical value again, e.g. the research on the transfusion of components of blood, on the life history of each type of cell in the blood, on the avoidance of hepatitis, on the process of blood clotting, on the mechanisms and treatment of heart failure. Also it is an example again of medical and related education producing a group of professionals and paraprofessionals, who in their jobs have a very high batting average, of great competence and skill. And I must emphasize the fact that in this medical center, an anonymous, perhaps penniless, man or woman of my age, of any ethnic or cultural group, who had been brought to the General Hospital across the street by the "Life Squad," would be given essentially the same service, the same application of medical research and training as I am receiving. Despite these great achievements, much more is to be done, in research, in education, and in providing better service, and for more people. . . .

Spring has come for me. But, based on the leukemia or on "complications," the winter of the threat of death may return in a week or a month or a year. The actuality of death may be with me in a month or a year or in five or ten years. At the moment, my feeling, perhaps my logic, tells me it will be a fair number of years.

At this moment, no longer winter but spring, I have a strong impulse to do things, one of which is to try to win some games of table tennis again. And when we play, anyone who won't try his best to beat me, because I am older, or because I have leukemia, or because he "may be the cause of my death," should not play with me. Until I say I don't, I want the games to be competitive.

But also if I am feeling tired, we will postpone the game or merely hit the ball around, practicing some strokes. That's an honest kind of fun, too. Whoever talks of half-a-loaf being no good, never has tasted a half-a-loaf of bread when one is hungry, never has enjoyed the fun of a table tennis to-and-fro badinage when a competitive game can't be played for one reason or another.

I hope to be active this spring in more serious ways. I want to do things for the medical center, for the psychiatry group, for the university, for my family and others, and for myself. . . .

The drive toward activity as an expression of being alive will have to be limited for several months, I am sure. Further work on the book which I have been writing this past two years may be the most suitable form of active creative living, for the immediate future. I want that book to be understandable and effective. . . .

Part of my feeling of spring and of increased well-being is related to the depth of friendship you have shown during the past few weeks. I want to thank wholeheartedly all those who sent their good wishes or expressed them in other ways. . . . If my estimate is correct, I have the blood of almost 100 of you in me. It's good to feel well enough to express my profound gratitude for that alone.

. . . I am home at the moment and feeling rather well, but I live on a rather narrow fairway, with the rough of a heavy fatigue on one side, and the rough of a variety of minor symptoms on the other side. Apparently when there is this level of anemia, talking and listening are especially fatiguing. So I'm afraid I won't feel well enough for some time to have visitors, or to respond as I'd like in other ways. And I'll probably go into the hospital, for a day or two each time, to have platelets or red blood cells from your blood streams injected into my veins. Can one ever really thank others adequately for such a gift?

If this or other antileukemia medication works, or is somewhat effective, the hope is for the first of a series of remissions which could keep me in good shape for months or years. If that happens, there's a chance that in a month or two I can resume my seminars, etc.

Finally, my special thanks to those of you who are sharing directly or indirectly in doing the work I can't do. The spirit and the carry-through, of your response to this situation, has been one of the finest experiences that a man or a woman could have.

Hope to see you soon.

Cordially,

(S)   MAURICE LEVINE

Professor and Director

PART II

SELECTED PAPERS
AND LECTURES

Biographical Note

T HE death on May 1, 1971, of Maurice Levine, Professor and Chairman of the Department of Psychiatry at the University of Cincinnati, marks the end of an extraordinary epoch in American psychiatry. It was an epoch that saw psychiatry established as a major clinical department in virtually every medical school in the country and its undergraduate and graduate educational programs become models for the entire world. True, the ground had been long in preparation, and World War II had brought in its wake a sudden wave of interest in psychiatry among physicians and the public. It was fortunate that eager to respond to the challenge were a group of talented young psychiatrists waiting only for an opportunity.

All had been nurtured in two traditions, Adolf Meyer and psychobiology and Sigmund Freud and psychoanalysis. From Meyer and psychobiology came the holistic view of man in his total environment and the clearest blueprint for the role of psychiatry in the education of the physician. From Freud and psychoanalysis came the most generative system for understanding human behavior yet devised—a system that reconciled the biological and the environmental perspectives.

Levine was the oldest of this group of young chairmen-to-be, almost too old in that era of the "boy wonder" professors. Past forty-four when appointed, he had already been settled for a dozen years in the private practice of psychoanalysis and psychiatry in Cincinnati, his native city. A graduate of the University of Cincinnati, where he received his B.A. and M.A. degrees in psychology in 1923 and 1924 respectively, he went on to Johns Hopkins University for his medical degree (1924–28), internship (1928–29), and psychiatric residency at the Henry Phipps Clinic under Adolf Meyer (1929–1932). Upon his return to Cincinnati in 1932 he was appointed an Assistant Professor of Psychiatry and supervisor of the inpatient psychiatric service at the Cincinnati General Hospital. After two years he left this full-time post to enter private practice. During the years 1932–37 he commuted to Chicago for psychoanalytic training, coming under the influence of Franz Alexander, who introduced him to the psychosomatic field as well. He graduated from the Institute in 1937 and subsequently was appointed a training analyst.

It is difficult now to picture the situation of psychiatry in the 1930s. The psychiatrist as well as the psychiatric patient were held in low regard by physicians as well as by the public. With a few notable exceptions little (or more often no) psychiatry was taught in the undergraduate medical curriculum; what teaching was done amounted to little more than a few demonstrations of institutionalized psychotic patients. Most medical schools did not even have departments of psychiatry, and there were few graduate training programs. Medical students regarded their classmates who aspired to be psychiatrists as either crazy, like their patients, or stupid and lazy, suitable only for a salaried sinecure in a state hospital. Levine no doubt was one of the crazy ones—excited and challenged by the mysteries of the mind, willing to plunge into the unknown and, worse still, to explore psychoanalysis. For the psychoanalysts were not only outside the pale of medicine, certainly academic medicine, but they were considered the craziest of all.

In that period the bright young men in psychiatry had to make it on their own. There were few ways in which they could pursue scholarship or research, no matter how talented they were, and earning a livelihood outside of private practice was out of the question. It seems clear that Levine, like many others of his generation, had largely reconciled himself to these realities when he entered private practice in 1934. But the scholar and teacher within him was not to be denied. The arduous weekly trips to Chicago for psychoanalytic education, teaching students and house officers at the medical college, presenting a highly popular course in abnormal psychology in the evening college (1933–46) and in the School of Public Administration of the University of Cincinnati (1934–36), and offering evening seminars for practicing physicians in his home—all were fitted into the interstices of a busy practice. These efforts, particularly his teaching of social workers, psychologists, and lay people, had a profound influence on the community and generated a great demand for his services as a consultant by many community agencies. Long before the present community psychiatry vogue, much of his writing and teaching were designed for the guidance of community workers. A very up-to-date title from 1935 was "Psychoanalytic Comments on Community Planning."

But his most important work of that period, truly a labor of love, was his book *Psychotherapy in Medical Practice*,[1] which is now in its 18th printing and has been translated into Swedish, Spanish, and Yugoslav. A product of ten years of thoughtful attention to the needs of the physician and other health care professionals without psychiatric background, this book in many ways epitomized his credentials to take over the chairmanship of a medical school department of psychiatry. For the main thrust of the revolution that brought psychiatry into the medical schools on a par with other clinical departments was the recognition that psychiatric knowledge and skills are indeed essential for the effective practice of medicine.

Yet who in the 1930s, least of all young Maurice Levine, would have predicted that a war would bring about such a dynamic alter-ation in attitudes toward psychiatry or that chance would provide him with the opportunity to fulfill the destiny that would have been denied him and psychiatry had he been born a scant five years earlier? Milton Rosenbaum had returned from the Massachusetts General Hospital to assume a full-time position at the medical school in 1940; and in 1942 John Romano, then a mere thirty-three, assumed the chairmanship of the department. A brilliant teacher and charismatic leader with a prophetic vision of the place of psychiatry in a medical school, Romano in four short years that were crowded with the demands, shortages, and confusion of the war created a vibrant, exciting new image and place for psychiatry in Cincinnati. Students, house officers, and physicians suddenly turned to psychiatry with excitement and enthusiasm, and a remarkable collaboration with faculty of other departments developed. I had also come, as an internist, in 1942. Eugene Ferris sponsored my appointment in medicine while Romano gave me rank in psychiatry, primarily as the internist consultant to the psychiatric inpatient service; he was more aware than I that I could be seduced into the field. During those four years collaborative teaching and research involved Romano, Rosenbaum, and Levine from psychiatry, Charles Aring from neurology, Arthur Mirsky from the May Institute (flitting in and out between military assignments), and Ferris and myself from medicine. Thus was established a pattern for the intimacy and status of psychiatry within the school that continues today. Although primarily in private practice, Levine nonetheless entered into the work of the department with devotion and enthusiasm. Very different in personality and style, Levine, Rosenbaum, and Romano were complementary to each other. Levine was the more orderly and precise one, who brought to his discussions of patients the greater rigor of observation and breadth and detail of analysis without sacrifice of sensitivity to the patient. Clear for all to see, he was the model of the teacher.

And so might things have remained had Romano not decided early in 1946 to accept an attractive offer in Rochester. After an interval of several months came the announcement that Maurice Levine was to be chairman. If the wisdom of a decision is to be measured by its ultimate results, the choice of Levine was inspired.

Levine and Cincinnati flourished in the new career. Above everything else his self-image was that of the teacher and scholar, and he responded to the opportunity like a hungry child to a dish of ice cream. No opportunity to advance the cause of scholarship in its purest sense was missed. He wanted students and residents to learn of psychiatry as an all-encompassing human endeavor. He brought to the program physiologists and philosophers, biochemists and artists, pharmacologists and religionists, neurologists and dramatists, internists and poets, pediatricians and musicians, anthropologists and mathematicians, psychologists and literary scholars, psychoanalysts and historians, economists and sociologists. Nothing that could possibly throw light on the human mind was to be overlooked, no topic to stimulate the intellect was barred. But this was no cold scholasticism, this was first and foremost in the service of the care of the sick and the relief of the troubled. He had high standards and he never permitted himself to be overawed by the visiting scholar, no matter how eminent; always he wanted to test the new and the different against his own accumulated knowledge and wisdom as a clinician. His own contribution to other disciplines was acknowledged by Hebrew Union College when it selected him for the Frank L. Weil Lectureship in Religion and Humanities for 1968–69.

And never did he fail to appreciate that the psychiatrist is a physician and must remain in the mainstream of medicine if he is to fulfill his responsibilities both to the sick and the troubled and to those who care for the sick, his fellow physicians. He clearly understood how the role and responsibility of the physician, whether psychiatrist or other, differed from the roles and responsibilities of other professionals concerned with the problems of health and disease. This was beautifully articulated in his inaugural address as professor titled "The Hippocratic Oath in Modern Dress."[2] He was not to be fooled by naïve diatribes about the irrelevancy for psychiatry of "the medical model"; he knew the physician-psychiatrist's task is to update the medical model and not permit medicine to be relegated to the status of a cold technology. In a long letter in 1952, upon the appointment of William Lotspeich, another humanist and scholar, as the new Professor of Physiology, Levine solicited my ideas as to how the course in physiology could be modified to serve as a "decent maturing experience" and provide a "better basis for the student's understanding of human behavior in a physiologic context." Thus was exemplified the attitude of a professor of psychiatry concerned with his responsibilities for the education of physicians.

In the twenty-four years of his tenure as chairman, the Department of Psychiatry at Cincinnati had a profound influence in every activity of the medical school, and the residency training program became and remains one of the most sought after in the country. Graduates of the program, who number in the hundreds, are to be found all over the world, many holding positions of importance for the future of psychiatry.

His contributions on the national scene, which were legion, were mostly in the cause of education. He served on the executive council of the National Committee for Mental Hygiene 1947–50, was consultant to the Surgeon-General of the U.S. Army 1948–52 and to the Surgeon-General of the U.S. Public Health Service 1950–58, was chairman of the Training Committee of the National Institute of Mental Health 1950–52 and of the Preparatory Commission of the Psychiatric Education Conference in 1951, was a member of the Council on Mental Health of the American Medical Association 1951–53, and was chairman of the Committee on Medical Education of the American Psychiatric Association. In 1950 he was president of the American delegation to the First International Congress of Psychiatry in Paris. From 1953 to 1957 he was a member of the National Advisory Mental Health Council of the National Institute of Mental Health. In 1960 he was co-chairman of the Committee on General Hospitals of the AMA's First Congress on Mental Health, and in 1967 he was on the Preparatory

Commission for the Conference on Psychiatry and Medical Education. He was a member of thirteen professional societies, serving as president of the Cincinnati Society for Neurology and Psychiatry and the Cincinnati Psychoanalytic Society, and was a member of the editorial boards of the *Journal of the American Psychoanalytic Association* and the *Journal of Nervous and Mental Disease*.

I last saw Maury Levine in July 1970, twenty-nine years almost to the day of our first meeting. I had come to Cincinnati at the invitation of the committee chosen to select his successor. Recalling vividly the vigorous, squalling, but quite helpless and vulnerable four-year-old we had left behind in 1946, I could enjoy and admire the healthy 29-year-old giant that had evolved under Levine's leadership. We had seen each other all too infrequently in the intervening twenty-four years—a meeting now and again and a number of visits to Cincinnati at his invitation to teach (but mostly to tell stories of those exciting old days), the last time for the celebration of the 20th anniversary of his chairmanship. We reminisced, as usual, but he also spoke with satisfaction of the health and vigor of the department he would turn over to the next chairman. He himself had set the date for his retirement and would have the satisfaction of knowing before he died that his successor would be a much-admired pupil, Robert Daniels.

His illness, acute monocytic leukemia, began in February and ran its usual rapid, malignant course. Twice he was rescued from the brink of death by the skill and devotion of his physicians and I believe by his own determination. For he had something to say before he died; he knew he was dying and he was not to be thwarted. In an extraordinary memo addressed to "the staff and a few others" dated March 30, just one month before his death, he discussed the personal psychological experience of a dying man. The teacher must teach and share. He who would learn of life, of living, and death must be willing to identify through bits of vicarious experience. "It's good practice in empathy [he wrote], which is one of the central patterns of our work. [So] it might be an important piece of living for you to identify temporarily with me as I go through this period of serious sickness, to share some bits and pieces of this important human process."

Through the memo shines his indomitable determination to turn every human experience, even his own most trying and painful ones, to use as a source of cognitive mastery for himself, but even more importantly, a source of help and strength to others. Nothing that may conceivably serve someone else should go to waste. Death is inevitable, but it is the rare human being who can turn the inevitability of his own death into a gift for others, even those who may never even have known him. For the recipients, the last "Memo from M. L." will be but the latest bits of his wisdom and insight to be incorporated into their own being. Like all the other bits it will be used in the service of the sick and imparted to the next generation who serve the sick. And so Maury Levine lives on.

GEORGE L. ENGEL, M.D.

1

Psychoanalytic Comments on Community Planning

W HEN I accepted the invitation to join in this afternoon's dicussion, I thought of the nice motives I might have for accepting —such as furthering the work of your group, which is of course admirable, and of carrying the banner of the psychoanalytic approach, which is coming to be regarded as admirable also. But one of the fundamental trends of the psychoanalytic approach is a benevolent skepticism toward all such apparently nice motives, which so often turn out to be rationalizations. When I thought over my experience, I wondered if I had not given way to some need for punishment and for punishing you. In fact it might be suggested that I was atoning for some feeling of guilt toward social work or toward some particular social worker. Anyway, self-punishment it must be, for I hereby demonstrate that I know little about family social work, and less about community planning. The purpose of self-punishment very often is to permit indulgence and satisfaction, so I shall use it to permit myself to make some comments about our fields of work that I have wanted to make.

My mention of the benevolent skepticism that is basic in the psychoanalytic approach leads to my first point. It is this skepticism about motives that so often makes people regard the psychoanalyst as a person who is always suspicious. This is not a correct judgment, however, and it is an important point for workers in your field to realize that suspicion is a hostile, antagonistic attitude, and does not have a place in the modern approach to your clients. It is true that your workers should not believe much of what is told to them—the client may be a liar or a malingerer, and, more often, when he is not, his explanations for what he thinks or does or wants will be surface rationalizations for deeper motives and reasons. But the worker's attitude, if it is to be constructive, must be benevolent in its skepticism. The worker must doubt the correctness of the things said but must doubt them not because she wants to strike back or to hurt or to show up the other, but because she wants to find the true causes in order to help, to establish a plan or a relationship that will be based on solid ground.

I regard it as urgent that in family case work the worker should never uncover the client's motives except in a spirit of neutrality and of friendliness. Certainly one great danger in social case work is that it may take techniques of human behavior from psychoanalytic formulations and use them as weapons in an attack on a client. Usually this is not a conscious attack; usually the worker is proud of her grasp of the dynamics of the situation and feels she will help the client by giving an interpretation; but if she does it with an undercurrent of hostile suspicion, or of retaliation, she will often do harm. There are no absolute rules for avoiding such a situation, but certainly an interpretation should never be given unless the worker likes the client, is at ease in his presence, is not in an irritable mood, does not feel the need to show her superiority, and does not care too much whether the client accepts the worker's interpretation or not. This point of view, which I hope that you, as executives and supervisors, emphasize to your workers, is of primary importance.

My point here is that case workers must realize the possibility that their own hostilities may lead to a misuse of good material.

This is a point that is of practical importance, but today I want to use it only as a stepping stone to a broader, more theoretical point —that social work in general, family case work in particular, and community planning in many aspects, achieve a fresh significance when viewed in the light of the major psychoanalytic discovery that a large part of human misery, unhappiness, and maladjustment is based on unconscious hostility. The field of social work, as you know, has been deeply influenced by psychoanalytic contributions, and for a group like this I need not go into detail, but to my mind there has not been a sufficient grasp or use of the discovery of the unconscious hostility. In the field of psychoanalysis itself the point has been reached where even Freud has said that analysis has forsaken sex for hostility in its formulations. Of course, by this it is not meant that sexuality is less important than was formerly thought. We still are convinced that in all cases of maladjustment, sexual conflicts play a major role, but we now realize that sexuality *per se* is a rather harmless, pleasant, enjoyable field of thought or activity and achieves its importance because it becomes entangled, especially in childhood, with hostility and aggression and hatred, and the fears and feelings of guilt which such hostility engenders. The generic term aggressions is used for the tendencies I refer to and includes such factors, largely engendered in the fantastic life of the child, as the wish to kill, to destroy, to take revenge, to eat up, to bite off, to cut off, to depreciate, to compete with destructively, to provoke, to pull down, to take away, to replace, to get rid of a rival, and so on. When sexuality is combined with such urges or their effects, it becomes a source of difficulty. When other phases of life are infiltrated with such urges, they become sources of difficulty.

I can imagine you think that I am painting an ugly picture of human beings. I can only remind you that human beings are animals —animals with a conscience. In general, we now believe that maladjustments and unhappiness are largely the result of hostile urges, originating in childhood. Symptoms, personality formation, social difficulties, and the like are most often the result of such trends or of the defenses against them. The strengths and assets of a person are largely the ways in which he has found solutions for such urges—solutions in terms of sublimations or compensations, solutions satisfactory personally and socially. I do not wish to give the impression that the concept of unconscious hostilities offers a complete formulation of human difficulties; frustration, privation, unusual stimulation, fears, guilt, shame, receptive urges, inferiority feelings, and many other factors, both socioeconomic and psychologic, play their part, but in all of these the involvement or implication of unconscious hostility plays a major, perhaps a determining, rôle.

If we are convinced of the importance of unconscious hostilities, it follows that one criterion of the success of social agencies is their ability to modify these hostilities or their effects. A successful agency in any community plan, except one preparing for a revolution, is that agency which lessens the frequency of formation of these hostilities, or provides means of channeling or sublimating them, or offers a chance for further development of those sublimations already formed. My hope today is that this formulation may lead to some practical applications on the part of you whose job, in part, is that of applying facts and theories from other fields to your field of practical social work and planning.

The problem of hostilities is big enough to justify the use of a variety of agencies for its handling. The causes of hostilities may be prevented by certain agencies; by other agencies childhood hostilities at the time of their formation may be made less intense or given a chance for sublimation. Later in life, increase in hostilities may be prevented by eliminating their sources; the hostilities may be directed in acceptable ways; the strength of the personality, that is, the well-directed aggressiveness, may be nurtured at the expense of the badly directed hostilities; and finally relationships may be established through which the unconscious hostilities may be brought to light, recognized, and dealt with in terms of adult reality instead of in terms of infantile fears, guilt feelings, and unhealthy defenses.

Let us for a moment sample the field of social work and see how some of the agencies fit in with this general scheme. The recreation agencies lessen unconscious hostility by providing physical activity through which hostile feelings are often drained—I say without being facetious that the pounding of a runner's feet in a playground race may help to drain off destructive and murderous impulses. Competitive sports in which the competition is not too destructive offer paths of sublimation for competition that would ordinarily be destructive. An opponent in a game may offer an acceptable outlet for small doses of unconscious murderous rivalry. To a slight degree, what happens here is a replica of the situation in the war: When it was not only acceptable but praiseworthy to hate the Germans, when hostility attitudes could have full sway, the suicide rate dropped sharply (of course we know that to a certain degree, suicide is a result of unconscious homicidal urges, boomeranged on the self out of fear and guilt). The evidence is not absolute, but it seems probable that the drop in the suicide rate during the war is to be explained in part by the existence of an acceptable object of hate, toward which the unconscious hostility could be drained, lessening the unconscious hostility and the self-punishment of suicide. The minor wars of sport may tap the same sources of relief.

The public agencies, whose chief function is relief, lessen unconscious hostility also. The slight increase in the feeling of security, the slight lessening of feelings of inadequacy and hopelessness, the feeling that there is a government of the good parent and not the bad parent type, lessen the sources of hostility, because insecurity, inadequacy, and hopelessness often lead to an urge to strike back. It must be recognized that in this type of work (as in others) there is only a limited lessening of hostility, and it has little influence on the hostility that lies deeply within the personality. And herein lies the shortcoming of all such palliative work—it deals with only the new and superficial hostilities. From my point of view, that of preventing maladjustment and unhappiness, the chief function of such work is the indirect effect—by making the life of parents more secure, it improves their relationship with their children, and tends to lessen the formation of hostility patterns in the child. The father who has some money—or better, some self-respect and some work— is less apt to arouse murderous impulses in his children.

And so with other agencies. Better housing, child guidance agencies, public health centers, and so on, all indirectly or directly serve to lessen hostilities. And finally, the family agency may perform an extremely vital function, for it is in the family itself that these hostilities are formed, that they are first expressed, and in which they can in some ways be best handled.

Our concept of the family must include the fact that, in our present civilization, the most important unconscious hostilities are formed in family life. The child's sense of helplessness, his need to accept the dictates of others, the discrepancy of his having an immature body and strong sexual desires, his frequent need to give up what he wants most, and the like, lead to strong hostilities which he must repress but which often persist throughout life. Some of these hostilities are more or less inevitable in any family group, but many are the result of specific external situations and specific parental attitudes. Modification at this point offers some real hope, and my impression is that it is here that a family agency, with its attempt to help the family as a whole as well as the specific individuals, can be a source of great good. It may help the parents but, even more important, it may minimize the hostilities of the child, hostilities that are the greatest source of difficulty during the rest of the life of that child. The family provides the setting for the origin, the development, and the pattern-formation of many of these aggressions. It is a consequence of this fact that in a community plan for welfare work and for lessening maladjustment we give an important place to an agency which should have the time, the money, and the training for prevention and treatment of hostilities in the family itself.

This is not the place to elaborate on the problem of techniques to be used. I can only mention the attempt by the psychiatrist or by the case worker to change the environment in the light of an understanding of the motives and emotions of the members of the family; giving some security and serenity; building on strengths and assets that are present; the use of the noncritical attitude which lessens the client's need to be hostile to a fantastically hateful and fearful world; the use of a closer transference relationship and wise interpretations in carefully selected cases.

We know that family case work along these lines is productive, but we are not sure how profound a change in the lives of maladjusted individuals may be achieved in these ways. But until our research has led to a shortening of the psychoanalytic technique, it is the best that we have to offer for those who have emotional or social difficulties and cannot afford to have an analysis.

1935

2

The Diagnosis of Normality

IN his daily work the physician must consider many problems of normality. Health as well as sickness, physiology as well as pathology, strength as well as weakness, normality as well as abnormality, are parts of his daily thinking. The problems of normality are manifold, as are the problems of abnormality, so much so that it is necessary in a short presentation to limit the discussion to one aspect of the problem. The topic chosen is that of emotional maturity, an aspect of normality which in recent years has become a central issue through the clinical study of emotionally immature patients, essentially the neurotic or psychopathic personalities.

To place the discussion of emotional maturity in its setting, the following tabular summary of a general definition of normality is presented:

Normality:

1. Never complete; only relative approximations.
2. Based on statistical averages of large or small groups, if this is not contrary to individual health.
3. Physical normality; absence of physical disease; presence of good structure and function and maturity.
4. Intellectual normality.

5. Relative freedom from neurotic or psychotic symptoms.
6. Emotional maturity (especially in contrast with neurotic character-formation).
   (a) Ability to be guided by reality rather than by wishes and fears.
   (b) Use of long-term values.
   (c) Mature conscience.
   (d) Independence.
   (e) Capability to "love" someone else, but with an enlightened self-interest.
   (f) Reasonable aggressiveness.
   (g) Reasonable dependence.
   (h) Healthy defense-mechanisms.
   (i) Good sexual-adjustment with acceptance of own gender.
   (j) Good work-adjustment.

The first five points of the definition refer to aspects of normality other than that of emotional maturity. The first indicates clearly the relative nature of the concept of normality, and the avoidance of the claim that there is a superior race of human beings to be called sane or normal or mature. The second point indicates that although statistics are helpful in determining normality, health and good function is a more important criterion than are statistical averages, e.g. that dental caries and chronic alcoholism are not normal from the point of view of good health in spite of their statistical frequency. The third point stresses the physical aspects of normality, including its relationship with intellectual and emotional development. The fourth point indicates the important topic of intellectual capacity and development. The fifth point indicates that normality includes a relative freedom from neurotic and psychotic symptoms, such as hallucinations, hysterical paralyses, compulsive handwashing, phobias, neurasthenic fatigue, and the like. The sixth point, then, refers to emotional maturity, and with its subdivisions lists some of the criteria of emotional maturity. The contrast of normality in this aspect is not a contrast with specific neuroses and psychoses but a contrast with children and with such clinical entities as psychopathic personalities, neurotic characters, immature personalities, and the like.

With regard to this set of criteria, the parenthetic remark is necessary that they are not based on experimentation or statistical treatment. They are the results of the clinical experience of psychiatrists and psychoanalysts. Of the psychiatric and psychoanalytic literature on this topic, the most pertinent are the contributions of Freud, and such specific contributions to the problems of maturity as the papers of Abraham,[1] Alexander,[2] Meyer,[3] and Glover.[4] In the present paper, a definition of emotional maturity is presented in the form of a list of criteria of emotional maturity, each of which will be discussed in turn.

The first criterion of emotional maturity is that the individual lives to a greater degree in terms of reality, of the actual facts of his life, than in terms of his fantasies and wishes and fears. If a man is in business, he is reacting maturely if he can think fairly clearly about the state of his business and can gauge fairly accurately the reality of his assets and liabilities; he is reacting immaturely if, in spite of the facts he has or could get, his wishes make him believe that his business is in excellent shape when it actually is only fair or poor, and on the other hand, he is reacting immaturely if his fears make him believe that his business is in horrible shape when actually it is fair, good or excellent. Children to a very great degree live in terms of their wishes and fears. A lonely child may deny the reality of his loneliness by pretending he has many playmates, and live in a fantasy world. In play this is good fun; in the serious aspects of adult life, it means that one is tricking oneself and seeing things crookedly. Of course, all human beings have some tendency to distort reality, to see life in terms of their own desires and needs, and probably there is no such perfectly matured individual who could react entirely and completely in terms of situations as they actually are. Again, it is a matter of degree, of being sufficiently mature in this respect. Immature people to a high degree tend to be unduly optimistic or pessimistic in spite of actual facts or probabilities. If their emotional bias is one way, they may see other people as being all sweetness and light, or if their emotional bias is the other way may see other people as devils and persecutors, in spite of the actual facts about other people or external situations. The adolescent girl or the adult woman may add to her problems by being convinced that all men are dangerous, that she is sure to be injured by any sort of contact with a man and so distort the picture that she is unable to believe in the reality of an actual situation in which there is no danger to her. If in reality a mother has a child who interrupts too frequently, she is reacting maturely if she sees that reality and tries to handle it understandingly; she is reacting immaturely if her pride makes her see the child's behavior as only cute or praiseworthy, and she is reacting immaturely if her fears make her feel convinced that the interruptions are surely the first step in a criminal career. The essence of the mature reaction in this connection is the ability to use one's intelligent appreciation of the facts fairly free of distortions that are the results of misplaced wishes and fears.

The second criterion of normality is the ability to live sufficiently in terms of long-term values instead of short-term values. The essential fact here is that as human beings grow older, as they make an adjustment to life and to other people, they have to give up certain momentary pleasures for the sake of more lasting pleasure, they have to defer immediate satisfactions when those satisfactions would block or stultify or destroy the more lasting satisfactions in life. The child gives up the pleasure of the immediate relief he feels in his wetting and soiling, for the sake of the more lasting satisfactions of avoiding punishment or the fear of punishment, or for the sake of getting love from his parents. The boy gives up the temporary pleasures of playing ball in the school yard for the more lasting pleasures of school, i.e. avoiding fear, getting praise, gaining self-respect, etc. The maturing man may give up the pleasures of casual affairs or of lack of responsibility for the more lasting pleasures of a less temporary relationship, for example, in marriage. The medical student chooses, the night before an examination, the long term values of studying and a career, to the more evanescent pleasure of a movie. But this criterion of maturity does not eliminate temporary pleasures or short-term gratifications. In correct time and place, in vacations, time-off, or when examinations are not pending, the short-term values, such as movies, playing the fool, and the like, may interfere in no way with the lasting values. Immature and neurotic individuals violate this criterion of long-term values to a degree that is destructive to themselves or others. Chronic alcoholics or drug addicts take their drugs in spite of the fact that it tends to destroy them physically, psychologically and socially, out of a largely uncontrollable compulsive need. A mother may give in to a child's pleadings for something which it actually should not have, in order to have for herself the temporary satisfaction of stopping the whining or to give herself the gratification of feeling generous, forgetting the long term values of the development in the child of greater responsibility, of a capacity to wait, to postpone, when it is necessary. In other words, one of the best criteria of maturity is the capacity to stand a necessary temporary frustration.

A third criterion of maturity is that the individual should have a grown-up conscience instead of a childhood variety of conscience. It is not easy to understand this distinction, because for most people, there still is a carryover of the idea of conscience as something fixed and unitary and given, and so not to be examined in terms of maturity and immaturity. The truth is that the "still small voice" of conscience may be too strict, too lenient, inappropriate, immature, built in childhood and not suitable for the adult.

An example may make the discussion of this point more vivid. It is this: certain individuals feel badly every Sunday or day of vacation or rest. It is called the Sunday neurosis. There are a number of causes of this "Sunday neurosis"; one cause is an immature conscience. On a Sunday or a day of rest, a mature conscience can say: "You can take the day off, for some rest or pleasure, as other people do; you work better during the week if you've had some diversion or pleasure or relaxation; and even if your work last week wasn't as good as it might have been, you can take the day off and work harder next week, and try to do a more self-respecting job. Of course if the work is urgent, you can work for a while." Thus speaks the mature conscience. Not so the immature conscience; it says: "You must never let down in your striving for perfection, as you were told in your childhood. If you take a day off, you're being bad and lazy and will come to a horrible end. You must hitch your wagon to a star. You ought never to forgive yourself for having let down last week. You should be ashamed of yourself for wanting any relaxation or pleasure and when you take it, you must suffer and feel badly, all day long."

In general one can define an infantile conscience as one which is based on threats and fear and guilt and the distorted ideas and fancies of childhood, while an adult conscience is based on real dangers and possibilities and standards. The infantile conscience has three chief sources. First, it is built out of the punishment and threats of the controlling adults. Second, the conscience of childhood is built out of the inevitable frustrations of the childhood period, because in childhood many things have to be forbidden to a child, e.g. sexual satisfaction, or independent judgment and plans and control. Third, the conscience in childhood is one that is built up to control the distorted or extreme ideas of the sort that are so frequent but unspoken in childhood, e.g. the primitive notion of being able to kill someone by a gesture or a harsh thought, or the childish fantasy of sexuality being a fight to the death. Such fearful ideas lead to the formation of a strict conscience to keep out of mind even the slightest hint of a harsh thought or of a sexual desire, because of the dangers to which it might lead. In most people, the overly strict conscience which is built up in childhood gradually loses its power as the person grows older, but occasionally it persists. An adult individual with a large residual of his infantile conscience even in his adult life will avoid those situations which for the grown-up are permitted, because in childhood or in childhood fancies they were not permitted. Such an individual may as an adult avoid sexual satisfactions even in marriage because it was forbidden or dangerous as a child, or such an individual will avoid a necessary adult independence because for the child such independence was dangerous or forbidden or seemed to be. Having an adult conscience means that the individual permits himself those satisfactions which are in keeping with adult and real possibilities, powers and dangers, with grown-up ideals and standards, and that he refuses to permit himself those satisfactions which are antagonistic to the adult reality, to his own enlightened self-interest, or which might unnecessarily hurt others who are involved. The elaboration of this distinction between a mature and an immature conscience is one of the important contributions of psychoanalysis. In this connection, the comment is necessary that popularizers of psychoanalysis give a badly distorted picture when they say that psychoanalysts advise the acting out of "repressed desires." That is simply not so. The actual recommendation is that repressed urges or unadjusted impulses should not be repressed because of infantile conscience, or acted out according to infantile impulsiveness, but should be recognized as existing, and then handled reasonably, that is, gratified or sublimated or controlled or renounced in the light of adult conscience and external realities. Not all impulses or wishes can be treated alike by a person with a grown-up conscience. Many repressed impulses such as spite or stealing are unacceptable according to adult standards and ideals and so are not to be satisfied. Other repressed impulses such as certain forms of sexuality and of independence are found to be acceptable and can be satisfied. Still other repressed impulses, such as a desire for power and prestige, can be redirected into constructive channels.

The fourth criterion of emotional maturity is the ability to be independent. This does not mean the blustering defiance of authority in the guise of independence nor an unwillingness to take advice, which may be camouflaged under the need to be self-sufficient. This does not mean the sort of independence which makes the desire to be the dominant one in a situation, which conceals the urge to run other people's lives, to play the big boss. This does mean an independence of this sort: that the individual is able to stand on his own feet when necessary, that he is not still tied to his parents' apron strings, that he is not dependent upon others for advice and guidance, that he is able to take some responsibility, and that he does not have an excessive amiability or willingness to give in. The topic of independence is one of high importance because the difficulties of being independent are far greater than is ordinarily realized. The whole setup of human development to a large degree militates against any real development of independence. Children are taken care of for a long period of time and many of them come to have deeply ingrained in them the pattern of being able to depend on someone else for the satisfaction of their wishes. Spoiling adds enormously to the problem because the spoiled child is essentially one who has been given cause to believe that it has more or less the complete right to expect to be taken care of and to have the spoiling continue. The spoiled child has had fostered to him the attitude that whenever he is helpless, somebody will come to his rescue and take over the responsibility and the management of the situation. The attitude that may be engendered is that by being helpless one can force others to help, and clinically one sees with great frequency this particular pattern in emotionally immature individuals. As one of the important sources of emotional sickness in adulthood one finds that the individual unconsciously becomes sick, makes himself helpless, may even try to destroy his success, so that somebody will take care of him. So many of the points in the development of human beings lead to an accentuation of the need and enjoyment of being dependent, that when difficulties come up in life, there is a strong tendency to swing away from independent activity and solutions of the problems, in the direction of being dependent, to trying to be "his majesty the baby," who can be taken care of. Such dependence has its pleasures; but in the mature person, there is a preference for adult pleasures over the pleasures of childhood.

The fifth characteristic of emotional maturity is that the individual has the capacity to love somebody other than himself. Here, of course, we are using the word "love" in the broad sense of being able to have a relationship of true friendliness with other human beings, of having the capacity to consider the interests of other individuals as well as oneself. It is a clinical fact that in both children and adults the lack of the capacity to give affection and love is one of the most important of the aspects of immaturity, most important in the sense of leading to unhappiness, to nervous illness, to an essential lack of success in life, and in the sense of preventing the internal peace and serenity that can be associated with the development of a true emotional maturity. This attitude of self-aggrandizement and self-love is called the narcissistic attitude, the name deriving from the story of Narcissus, who fell in love with his own image in the water. This narcissistic attitude is in the extreme degree, and in one variety, apparent in psychotic patients. For example, in schizophrenia much of the interest in the outside world is gone and the individual is interested essentially in himself and in the products of his own thinking, to such a degree that he may be stuporous, have no contact with people in the outside, and live in a world of voices which he has created and now hears. But in a smaller degree and in a different fashion, the narcissistic attitude is present in a large number of neurotic and immature human beings who miss out on much of what can be gained by the development of relationships with other people because in each relationship they are essentially able to see only what they can get out of it themselves. Other people are, in a sense, merely "stooges" for them, are parts of an audience, are persons who can pay attention and give admiration. The need to dominate and to control is central. Other people are objects who can praise them or who can be used in some way for their own self-aggrandizement. The result may be a deep sense of loneliness or emptiness. Of course, such naricissism must be contrasted with intelligent self-interest, because it is thoroughly possible to be intelligently self-interested, to be on the look-out for one's own advancement, for one's own security and best interests, and at the same time to avoid the self-aggrandizement of narcissism. Intelligent self-interest usually involves a cooperative attitude and a mutual growth and development, whereas the narcissistic attitude involves only a semblance of cooperation in which the other is used for what can be got out of him. Such a narcissistic attitude usually leads to a series of frustrations in life, in part because other people are often consciously or unconsciously aware of the attitude and so the narcissist fails to get from others some of the real things that he would like to have. In general the clinical finding is that narcissism is of high importance in the origin of personal unhappiness. There is of course no point in being moralistic about such tendencies; nothing is to be gained by using such epithets as selfish or egotistic about such individuals; instead, the narcissistic tendencies can be understood as symptoms, as reactions to events and experiences of the individual's past and present life. The finding is that it results essentially from insecurity and fear. When the individual, especially in childhood, feels that the world is essentially an unfriendly place, he is thrown back on himself and tries to find security by self-aggrandizement and self-love. When the child feels that he is rejected, when he feels that there is a lack of love for him from those who are most important in his life, or when he feels that he ought to be rejected, he may turn all of his own capacity for affection on to himself and be forced into the position of loving himself as he would like his parents to love him. Or, when a child feels extremely anxious and afraid and guilty, he may unconsciously feel that the only way he can be safe is by being all powerful, able to control any situation of danger, and hence becomes self-centered.

The sixth criterion of maturity is that the individual has only moderate reactions of anger and hatred, and that in a hateful situation, as that of working in a job with difficult or domineering associates, he can be as active and aggressive as conditions permit, and not waste energy in temper or fury which distract from a reasonable plan of action. Aggressive activity and firm self-defense are often maturely necessary; the acting out of anger is rarely mature. Acts of "righteous indignation" are often a camouflage for other motives. In some situations, effective action is possible; in others it is not, and must be deferred. Many immature individuals waste their time and energy in excessive temper, hatred, envy, anger, in trying to destroy. And others feel so full of anger that they inhibit any action they might take for fear of being too aggressive. In clinical experience, the Casper Milquestoast type of person is often one who is so afraid of his desires to be free and uninhibited and tempestuous and competitive that he is excessively timid and afraid of action. Of course, all human beings are animals, and inevitably have animal reactions of anger and fighting. Such impulses are largely outgrown and sublimated in mature persons. In immature persons such temper and anger reactions may persist, often because in their childhood their quota of anger and hate was increased by fears and cruel punishment, which made them want to fight back.

The seventh characteristic of emotional maturity is the capacity to have a reasonable dependence on others. A markedly dependent attitude, e.g. that of the clinging-vine type of women, or that of the man who expects to be babied by his wife, or of the man who can make no business decision without consulting many people, is obviously immature and a carryover of childhood attitudes. Such dependence may persist for the sake of the gratifications of the passive attitude, or for the sake of avoiding the real or fantastic danger of independence. But there is a real variety of dependent relationship that is thoroughly mature. The capacity to take advice when it is pertinent and contributory to one's own decision and responsibility, the capacity to be able to receive love and affection from others, to be able to accept when others want to give—these are mature and valid. In the give and take of human relationships, the capacity to take is as important as the capacity to give. Interpersonal relationships involve an interdependence. Cooperation involves being on the receiving as well as the giving end, in a marriage, in sexual relations, in a friendship, in social and work relationships. In some psychogenic gastric disturbances, this immaturity pattern is seen with monotonous regularity: the patient is unable to receive or be dependent, because his pride is hurt if he is not the giver; to him, giving means strength and power, and receiving or dependence means playing the second fiddle, being inferior. Such patients overwork to avoid even the faintest chance of future dependence, can not take presents, have difficulty in relaxing in a love relationship, often are overinsured, and their lives are a refrain of giving. A mature person can give a great deal but he can also enjoy receiving.

The eighth characteristic of emotional maturity is the use of healthy defense mechanisms instead of unhealthy defense mechanisms. By a mechanism of defense is meant the method by which a person tries to handle his unacceptable impulses and conflicts. Now all human beings have unacceptable impulses, some more so than others. Every person has impulses, attitudes, and ideas about which he feels guilty, or is ashamed, or has hurt pride or feeling of inferiority. When such feelings are present, the individual attempts to deal with them in some fashion. Some of the techniques used to handle unacceptable impulses are mature; some are not. One of the unhealthy mechanisms of defense is self-punishment, the method in which the person punishes himself severely for having impulses he considers to be bad, criticizes himself violently, and in an exaggerated fashion tears himself down. In this way he tries to make atonement and feel forgiven. In this group, we see people who are depressed, overly self-critical, who have persuaded themselves they are no good. Such an excessive self-punishment is immature; its value is that it makes the individual feel he has done atonement for his unacceptable impulses; but it makes no one actually any happier, does not lead to constructive work, and often makes the person feel that now he has been punished, he can be as "bad" as he wants to be. The ministers say that many a person feels that if he is cleansed of his sins on a sabbath, he can then do what he wants to do the other six days.

Another unhealthy mechanism of defense is projection. In this method of defense, the individual lessens his own inner conflicts by disowning the unacceptable impulses and claiming that they really belonged to somebody else or something else. A carpenter who is ashamed of a piece of work may blame his tools, according to the mechanism of projection. He projects on his tools his feeling of shame or the responsibility for his lack of success. Another example of projection is this: a man who has had desires to be unfaithful to his wife and who felt guilty or ashamed about those desires and tried to forget them and deny them, becomes suspicious that his wife wants to be unfaithful or has been unfaithful, when there is no justification for his suspicion. He has projected on her his own desires for infidelity, to lessen his own feeling of guilt. Another example would be that of a boy whose own procrastination has led to difficulties in his school work and who then projects the blame onto the teacher. On the other hand, the teacher, whose own preparation has been inadequate, may project the blame on the students and claim that this year's class is a singularly unresponsive one. To repeat, all human beings have unacceptable impulses. Some people react to these impulses by immature defenses, such as self-punishment and projection. Some people react to these impulses by a mature set of defense mechanisms, such as this: that the individual is able frankly to face himself and his conflicts without too much disturbance about them, is able to face his impulses for what they are without excessive self-punishment or dramatic discouragement, and then, depending on what they are, to deal with them realistically either by self-control, or renunciation in favor of something else, or by efforts to change the environment so that there will be a greater chance of satisfaction of those impulses, or by sublimating them, i.e. by using their energy in socially acceptable and constructive ways. One essential point here is that many impulses which cause defense-mechanisms and difficulties of an unhealthy sort are not fundamentally unacceptable. They arise at a time when they would be unacceptable, but at a later time they may be thoroughly in keeping with the situation. For example, sexual impulses in childhood may, because of the limitations in the life of the child at that time, have to be repressed, but later in adulthood they may be thoroughly acceptable under certain circumstances. It is necessary, therefore, to add to this consideration the fact that not only does the emotionally mature individual use healthy defense mechanisms for his really unacceptable impulses, but also that the emotionally mature individual is able to avoid using defense mechanisms when they are unnecessary, is able to arrange for the satisfaction of certain aspects of his life which are in keeping with maturity.

The ninth characteristic of emotional maturity is that the individual has a good sexual adjustment. In the mature person, sexuality involves a heterosexual partnership that is based on a good companionship, a give and take of an interpersonal relationship. The Madonna and prostitute dichotomy of many adolescents has given way to a fusion of the two; the idealized person is also the sexual object. It means that the diverse sexuality of childhood is subordinated to the primacy of genital satisfaction. The exhibitionistic, sadistic, masochistic, and other types of activities or urges or fantasies, and the mouth, anal, breast, skin and other localities of pleasure, are subordinated as incidental forepleasures to coitus with orgasm. Orgasm is followed by thorough relaxation. The desire for a quick repetition of orgasm usually is on an immature basis, indicating some underlying lack of satisfaction. The boast of having large numbers of orgasm-reactions in one night is a manifestation not of genital sexuality, but of some other emotion, e.g. pride, defense against deviate sexual desires, the urge to live up to an adolescent ideal of unending virility, or a defense against a fear of being effeminate. Similarly, promiscuity is not a sign of maturity, but of the use of genital sexuality as a drainage system for other emotions, e.g. the fear of being unlovable, which is assuaged for the moment by each affair.

Related to a good sexual adjustment is the problem of the individual's acceptance of his or her own gender. It is not only in some forms of homosexuality that one finds this denial of the gender to which the individual was born. In many other relationships in life, men want to be women and women want to be men. Men often want to reject the masculine role in sexuality and in life in general. Women's rejection of their role is more frequent, perhaps, in small part because in our culture, social and economic forces are slightly less favorable for women, in larger part because of the greater fears associated with being a woman. A woman who is emotionally mature accepts the fact that she is a woman, and does not have too much of a resentment that she is not a man. It must be emphasized that unfortunately there still are social and economic handicaps for women and an attempt to modify these handicaps realistically is a mature thing to do. But frequently the resentment over being a woman is not based on these realistic facts but on deeper and more immature resentments, which are essentially carryovers of a childhood anger at being made a girl. The mature attitude is to recognize that there is no general superiority of men over women or of women over men, that in most ways in which they are different, men have certain strengths and assets which women do not have, and women have certain strengths and assets which men do not have. The mature thing for women is to build and grow as women rather than to waste energy on the attempt to be like men.

The tenth criterion of an emotional maturity is a good work adjustment, which involves good interpersonal relationships of the sort mentioned above, and in addition involves a willingness to accept responsibilities, yet to avoid the overwork that is the result of anxiety. It means an attitude to money of regarding it as a means to an end, and not as an end in itself, and of regarding money as a means to a realistic security and self-confidence. In many persons, the gathering of money is reminiscent of the individual who, when there is a small rain cloud, wears a raincoat and rubber overshoes, and carries an umbrella, and in addition has an extra umbrella tucked away in his office to use in case he loses the umbrella he is carrying. The mature attitude to work means to be able to work for success without expecting an immediate miracle, to have a self-respect over accomplishment and creativeness, and to have as the measuring-rod of success one's growing self-respect and the respect of others, rather than one's pride and the need for admiration.

This tenth criterion of emotional maturity, a good work adjustment, is the final one of the present listing. There are other facets of maturity which might be discussed at this point, such phenomena as dependability, the capacity to meet emergencies, the acceptance of individual differences, the capacity to learn by experience, the ability to persevere and carry through, and the integration of contrary drives, but these are essentially aspects of the ten criteria listed above.

These ten criteria indicate that in the field of emotional maturity, psychodynamic understanding is developing fairly clear conceptions and formulations. In the diagnosis of normality, it is now more possible to have fairly specific concepts of emotional maturity to supplement the fairly specific concepts of physical maturity and intellectual maturity and the fairly specific concept of a relative freedom from symptoms. On this basis, a fuller understanding of normality can develop.

But it must be emphasized, as a concluding remark, that although the concepts of normality and maturity are becoming more clear, there is no attempt in the current psychiatric and psychoanalytic thinking to postulate the existence of a separate group of normal mature human beings. The concept is that of a varying and relative degree of normality and maturity. The final point to be emphasized is that through the progress of psychodynamic understanding, it is now more possible to consider the criteria of normality and maturity in positive terms as well as in negative terms, to understand normality not only in terms of the absence of difficulties and disorders but in terms of a partial achievement of growth and strength and development.

1939

3

Psychiatry for Internists

MY remarks will be limited to a single topic, a successful teaching experience from which we can abstract several points of importance. About two years ago I was approached by a small group of successful internists in Cincinnati asking that I give an informal series of discussions on the psychiatric information that might be of value in the practice of internal medicine. At that time, I was almost totally in private practice and loath to take on more obligations. I make this point because it meant that I hesitated for some time, as they urged and argued. This was quite different from the usual teaching situation, in which a psychiatrist suggests or announces a course and tries directly or indirectly to get internists to join. In a word, some of the original success of the course may have been due to the fact that the course was initiated by the internists, was urged and arranged by them, and they had a bit of a feeling of triumph when they maneuvered me into accepting. One can make the analogy with psychotherapy by saying that the usual initial resistances were not called into being.

A member of the group was asked to act as chairman, to decide with the others on eligibility, frequency of sessions, etc., again arranging the situation so that it was their course and not something superimposed on their interests.

At first a small, intimate roundtable sort of discussion of six or eight participants was planned. But the organizers talked so enthusiastically about the course in the hospital doctors' room, that eight other physicians requested to join. I was still completely in the background; it was their course. They then decided that it was only fair to others of the hospital staff to post a notice. Within twenty-four hours there was a total registration of thirty-nine, and the sponsors hurriedly removed the notice.

The course has now gone on for almost two years. During the first year we met for two hours one evening a week. The second year, because of the pressure of my work, we have met only two eveniugs per month. Of the original thirty-nine who signed for the course, about twenty-five have attended most of the sessions, and about fifteen have missed not more than one or two sessions. With the return of physicians from the armed forces, the course was thrown open to them and about fifteen joined the group, of whom seven or eight attend regularly. At present, of the thirty-five registered, twenty to twenty-five attend each session. House officers of local hospitals bring the average attendance up to thirty-five or forty. The group includes internists, dermatologists, pediatricians, orthopedists, and others.

From these figures, one can see that the group has been extraordinarily persistent. This fact can be pointed up by saying that these are busy doctors who are tired in the evening, and are not impelled to attend by the practical reasons which lead them to go to hospital staff or medical society meetings, viz., to be in touch with other doctors who might refer cases. Yet they came regularly.

Quantitatively, the course has been a success, and there are many indications to show that it has also been a success qualitatively. From their contributions to the discussion, it is obvious that about five doctors have reached a good understanding of the material, about five more have acquired a fair understanding, and there has been a safe and usable but minor increase in knowledge and skill of about ten others. It is not rare to have one of them tell about the clearing up of a patient's anxiety, of correctly estimating a suicide risk, of sensing a schizoid development and referring the patient for treatment rather than trying it himself, of correctly using a psychiatric social worker, handling the anxiety of a patient who believed he had heart disease, correctly handling a masturbation problem, etc. The enthusiasm of the group has been very great, with the expression of the same sort of emotional reaction as in the Minnesota experiment, of a tremendous change in their whole outlook. I have recognized that such expressions and reactions should not be taken at face value; in part, they are comparable to the expressions of great change, of almost miraculous salvation of which we hear in the transference cures of psychotherapeutic practice. And, of course, they are the narcissistic expression of being first on a new bandwagon. But with all this, the fact remains that in this group as in the Minnesota experiment, the verbal expressions of extraordinary change are associated with improvement in performance and skill.

We can summarize some of the points of the course, stressing in each the emotional aspects of the interplay of teacher and group. Obviously in our teaching as in our psychotherapy we must stress the emotional problems.

The first point is that I avoided, like the plague, the development of any feeling that I was talking down to them, or implying that they were inadequate as doctors. It must be remembered that these are successful practitioners, who in most of their waking lives are looked up to with respect and admiration by their patients, patients' families, and the community at large. It would not be possible to expect them to sit at the feet of another doctor, like schoolboys coming to learn. Perhaps they might do this for one lecture, when a visiting celebrity comes to town, but not as part of a continued course. The point, put simply, is that the psychiatrist must avoid dealing out unnecessary narcissistic blows.

The second point is that in the process of medical practice, these physicians are constantly giving. The receiving end of their emotional balance is inadequately satisfied. They receive money, praise, respect and idolatry, but they receive little in the way of help, protection and support, unless their wives happen to be unusually giving individuals. My impression is that they are hungry for a dependent relationship on someone, and that if such dependence can be gained without the narcissistic blow that ordinarily accompanies such dependent satisfactions in independent men and women, they respond very actively indeed. To satisfy this dependent need, I used the technique of organized lectures, especially at the beginning of the course.

I realize that lectures are at the moment somewhat in disfavor as a pedagogic technique. I agree that the preceptor system has many advantages. But the lecture system also has many advantages not lightly to be discarded, particularly if one can avoid the empty formalism into which lectures may degenerate. At this point I merely want to emphasize the fact that lectures are taken emotionally by the group as a form of receiving and in-taking which adds to their security and leads to giving responses, of understanding, acceptance, and productive discussion.

As another aspect of the satisfaction of dependence as well as good teaching technique in general, I used various visual aids, of charts, mimeographed lists, and the like.

Lectures were not the only technique used. We had group discussions of a very informal sort, in which as many as fifteen had something to say in the course of an evening. There were case presentations by myself and others of the psychiatric staff, emphasizing the type of cases likely to be seen in daily practice, as well as exemplifying general principles of psychopathology which they need as central points for their thinking. We plan next to have them present their own cases for group discussion. Now that the group has reached a friendly cohesiveness, I no longer feel the need to have them meet in my home, and we have moved to the hospital so that we can plan to present patients as well as case histories.

I gave no theoretical lectures on psychopathology as such. Material on psychopathology was given only as an outgrowth of a discussion of clinical material of the sort the group was sure to see in daily practice. For example, I used clinical material of delayed convalescence to lead to a clarification of the psychopathology of dependence; material on alcoholism to deepen their understanding of dependent trends and then of hostility; material on reaction to physical illness as an entering wedge for the discussion of the problems of anxiety, and defenses against anxiety. Material on schizophrenia was used as a starting point of the discussion of the topic of regression; material on conversion hysteria to clarify the psychopathologic concepts of internal conflict, dissociation, conversion, and some of the genetic material related to genital conflicts. In short, the approach was always from clinical material with which they were familiar, to the new concepts which could be linked with the old.

Another point to be emphasized is that internists who join such a group have mobilized in them a fair amount of anxiety. Psychiatry has certainly become more acceptable to the medical profession, but there still remains a great deal of skepticism and criticism, some of which is justified. The internist who joins such a group must meet the criticism of other internists that he is becoming unscientific, or that he now will be so interested in psychological problems that he will miss out on important physical findings. I found that it was best to deal directly with this anxiety. I stated quite explicitly the dangers of becoming interested in psychosomatic problems and psychotherapy. I agreed that the new material was so dramatic and revealing and, in a sense, so exciting, that it might lead doctors to forget the need for adequate physical studies. I was emphatic in saying that an interest in emotional problems calls for increased attention to physical factors to overcome the temptation to negligence, although decrying an unending search for improbable physical etiology. Further, I stated the danger of being so interested in psychodynamics that one misses the diagnosis of a psychosis, and used this anxiety situation as the entering wedge to include in the course an adequate description of the psychoses and the masked psychoses with which all physicians should be familiar. Still further, I agreed that physicians may become too ambitious as psychotherapists, and used this anxiety situation to bring in the concept of levels of diagnosis and treatment which I think provides a source of security for the physician. In short, I dealt with the anxiety aroused by their interest in psychiatry by recognizing its existence, by directly discussing the degree to which it might be valid, and by giving information and concepts by which the anxiety could be overcome.

We plan to continue the course so long as the group is interested in continuing. Several of the more active participants now attend my graduate seminar on psychotherapy, and we hope that some of them will take part in a psychosomatic out-patient clinic now in process of organization.

In summary, the successful outcome of this particular postgraduate course for internists was in good part the result of the fact that the emotional problems of the group were given careful consideration.

1947

4

*Dynamic Understanding of Human Behavior**

I have chosen one topic that I want to try to clarify because I think that it is unquestionably the basic concept of all modern psychiatry, one without which no attempt at any application of psychiatric understanding to other fields is possible and, I think, one which can enrich one's general thinking about human beings in an extraordinary fashion. I can talk emphatically about it because obviously I had nothing to do with its discovery or its development. This is material that antedates any work that I could do by many, many years.

This concept that I want to try to put across tonight is the concept of the three-layer approach to human beings, about which a few of you have heard. This three-layer approach is to be developed in my presentation by first trying to clarify the concept that we call "defenses against anxiety." I am going to concentrate on this psychiatric concept of defenses against anxiety because it undoubtedly

* From the transcript of a recorded address delivered February 15, 1948, at the Institute on Aspects of Religion and Psychiatry, The Hebrew Union College, Cincinnati. Unrevised except for minor deletions.

292

is the most important and because it clarifies an extraordinary variety of things. Rarely does one concept have as much of a breadth of application as this one does.

But now, in spite of my emphasis on it, I don't want to give it an unbalanced approach. This is a most fruitful concept, but definitely not the only approach; because in studies of patients and of issues, the psychiatrist must study not only psychological patterns as this, but also other things. For example, a psychiatrist will have a physical examination done on every case, since he knows that brain tumors and brain syphilis, kidney trouble, and many, many other physical disturbances, can produce psychiatric disturbances and personal problems.

The psychiatrist is mildly interested in the patient's heredity since, in the rare case, inheritance is a factor. He is interested in whether the patient has been soaking up alcohol or bromides, since these and other poisons can destroy the activity of the brain. He is interested in the patient's intelligence, since he needs to estimate the patient's fundamental ability to meet the demands that life may make on him. The psychiatrist is interested in financial strain, group pressures, and sociological factors.

But, with all of these interests, experience has taught that most of all, he must be interested in the patient's inner life—his wishes, his fears, his conflicts, his contradictions, his conscience, his ambitions, his love, his hate, his sexual feelings. These are the psychological and emotional factors in an understanding from the psychiatric point of view and, to understand these emotions, the psychiatrist has evolved the concept of defenses against anxiety.

Now, to clarify this concept, I want to start with the basic fact of animal life, namely, that all animals are confronted repeatedly—perhaps almost constantly—with great dangers: dangers of death, of starvation, of attack, of mutilation, of cold, or hunger, etc. That is one of the basic aspects of animal life.

Now, to meet such dangers and to prevent the species and the individual from dying out, animals have developed two patterns in response, or two phenomena in response. The first is the phenomenon of fear. It is, in the presence of danger, the animal reaction, the animal responses of the reaction of fear, the feeling of fear, the awareness of fear, the bodily reactions of fear such as the fast heartbeat which carries more blood to the various parts of the body—the muscles particularly—which might have to use that blood in the meeting of the fearful situation.

In general then, the first thing which animal life has as the development and responses to the dangers of life is the emotion of fear, which is a signal of the danger as well as response of it. But fear alone will not do much good if an animal must meet danger. The second thing that has to be developed is the defenses, some sorts of efficient or effective or strong defenses against the external danger; that is, defenses against his fear or responses to his fear, such things, of course, as the development of strong muscles by which one can run away from the danger, the development of strong teeth or claws by which one can fight the danger, the development of the smell of the skunk by which it meets certain dangers by repelling dangerous forces of other animals from itself, and so forth. That is, one develops, or animals develop, a variety of defenses against their fear, against the external dangers in life.

Now, human beings, as animals, of course, have many dangers to meet also. For example, there is the possibility of fire. We have individual responses to fire—of fight against the fire, or flight from the fire. Social and community resources such as the fire department and the police can be brought in. There is the fear that comes of the external danger if one happens to be held up by a robber. Or, if there is a wild animal that comes at one, one has the reaction of fear, and defenses against it of running away or of fighting or of getting help—whatever defenses may come up. Or, if one is a student and one is about to flunk an examination, there may be the healthy defense against the fear that that arouses by studying for the examination, or a variety of unhealthy defenses may be used. For example, the student may become sick in order to avoid the examination which he might be about to flunk, or, if he has a different set of defenses, he may develop the kind of thing that we call an amnesia, a forgetting of his name and address, an actual for-getting of his name and address, all of the types of identification of his own personality, so that during the period of his examina-tion, while he is sick with this kind of nervous disorder, he is un-able to take the examination because he is unable to remember who he is, where he lives, or any identifying facts about himself. . . .

External dangers lead to fear which, in turn, then leads to a variety of healthy or unhealthy defenses against the fear, against the danger, the two most primitive of the defenses being fight and flight.

Now, from that we develop the next point, which is that external dangers are not the only dangers in life for the human being. There are internal dangers as well as external dangers. Suppose, for ex-ample, that you are very tired and your heart begins to skip some beats or you have some extra beats of the heart. If you sense those extra heart beats or dropped heart beats, you develop the fear that you have heart disease. That is an internal danger to which you are reacting with fear. Or suppose that you are married and that you develop impulses to be unfaithful to your husband or to your wife. That is an internal danger. That is, the danger arises from within yourself, from your own impulse. Or suppose that you develop some impulses of hatred toward somebody whom you love. That is an internal danger. The danger arises from an impulse which is part of your own feeling, of your own inner life.

There are internal dangers as well as external dangers. And we then have, unless we have a certain particular kind of personality makeup which we call the totally uninhibited or almost criminal type of personality makeup, a certain variety of conscience. At least we have conflict about such inner impulses and problems. That is, such internal dangers lead to fear also. We have a fear when we have an impulse of hatred toward somebody whom we love. Now, for such internal fear, we use the term "anxiety." The termi-nology is this: when we are afraid of something outside of ourselves, we speak of that as "fear." When we are afraid of something within us, we speak of that as "anxiety."

Now, just as we develop defenses against fear of external things like the fight or flight when there is the external danger, so we develop defenses against our internal fear. We develop defenses against our anxiety.

This concept is so important that I don't want to talk just theoretically about it. I want to try to build up your understanding by the use of specific cases so that you can become clear, so that you can develop some feeling of the enormous importance, the enormous clarification possibilities of the approach to the understanding of human beings from the point of view of trying to say against what anxiety this particular manifestation is a defense. That is one of the central problems always to ask about human beings.

Now I want to give examples on which we can then build up this concept of defenses against anxiety. For the first example I want to go very far afield, but I want to use the example because it is so very revealing and so very clear-cut. The example is that of a severe chronic alcoholic who develops not only periods of delirium tremens, but finally develops something which has the amazing name of Korsakoff psychosis, or Korsakoff mental disease, because it was described by a Russian psychiatrist of that name a number of years ago.

What is this reaction when the alcoholic has gone to the extent of disturbing his brain by the imbibing of enough alcohol so that large areas of his brain are affected? The first thing that happens in this particular mental disorder is that the individual is unable to remember what has just happened in his life, what has happened within the last thirty seconds, minute, or five minutes. He is totally unable to remember. The phrase we use is that he has lost his power of immediate recall or of retention. He is able to remember what happened in his childhood; he is able to remember what happened ten or fifteen or five years ago. That is, his memory for remote or recent events is good; but his memory for the immediate past is blotted out almost completely because of the effects of alcohol on the brain.

Now, as an example, we may come on a ward in a hospital and

be talking to a patient who has this particular illness, talking to him for perhaps ten, fifteen minutes, thinking one has made a deep impression on him. One is called to the telephone and, two minutes later, come back to the patient's bedside and begin to talk to him again. He has totally forgotten that he has ever seen us before, has to be introduced again, has no memory whatsoever of the fact that he has been talking to us extensively the last few minutes.

Now, then, suppose that were you. I ask you to do the process which, in the practice of helping human beings, in psychiatry, or any other field, is the most important of all processes in the beginning of the attempt to be helpful. That is the process of temporarily putting oneself in the other person's shoes as a way of understanding—the process of empathy, of temporary identification. Suppose that you—and let yourself have the emotional reaction to this—suppose that you were unable to remember what had happened thirty seconds ago or a minute ago or five minutes ago? Your reaction, I think, would be obvious. It would be one of intense anxiety. The fear of disintegration, the fear of internal catastrophe, the fear of insanity, the fear of the loss of one's intelligence, one's brain, one's executive internal capacity, lead to terrific anxiety, as you know if you try temporarily to identify yourself with such a patient.

Now, what happens when one has such anxiety? What happens is exactly the same as what happens if one is confronted with a lion escaped from the zoo. One must have defenses; one must if one is not simply overwhelmed by the fear, by the external danger. One automatically develops a strong defense against such enormous anxiety.

The defense that this particular kind of patient develops is what we call "confabulation." Such a Korsakoff patient who is unable to remember what happened a minute or two ago now develops unconsciously—he doesn't do it deliberately—the technique of concocting stories, extensive stories, of what has just happened in his life. You come on to the ward at the hospital. You know that the patient has been in bed for the last two weeks. You start talking to the patient and he tells you about the fishing trip that he had this morning, about the bridge game that he had, with the tall stories that go both with bridge and with fishing. He tells you many other details of the last fifteen minutes or hour, the last two minutes also.

This is a totally unconscious automatic process, but its effect is one of completely effective defense, even though it is unhealthy in the sense of being totally untrue, even though it is a distortion of a reality and, therefore, a manifestation of a serious mental disorder, of a psychosis. But it has a completely effective function because when he now completely believes that he has been doing these things he has been talking about in the last five minutes or hour or two, he no longer has any fear about the loss of his mind, about the internal disintegration, because there is nothing to be afraid of now. He now has a totally false memory to take the place of the lost memory.

That gives you, I think, some of the feel of what we are talking about here, i.e. that individuals develop defenses against anxiety.

As a second example to try to make this issue clear, suppose that a boy has been masturbating, repeatedly masturbating, and is in great conflict about it, because he has been told the nonsense about masturbation which, I suppose, all of you know now by this time is a totally harmless procedure. The child believes that he is going to be insane, or that he has developed a physical disease, a disease of his spine or of his brain or of his genitalia, or that his genitalia will wither away, or any of the nonsense that unfortunately has been taught with so much force and domination.

Now, if the child has such conflict with regard to his masturbation, and he continues to masturbate, what happens? What happens is that he is going to have terrific anxiety, of course, of internal fear of disaster or catastrophe, and he then will automatically develop defenses of one sort or another. A typical series of defenses that would happen here is that the child would become aggressive in his attitude; he would go around with a powerful, strong attitude— pseudopowerful and pseudostrong, of course—with the attitude that "nobody can tell me anything," of being scared of nothing, of being defiant, of being sort of mean and nasty in his relationship with other people. That is, he has to build his defenses against fear of punishment and weakness and of insanity. His whole attitude is one of trying to show that he is strong, not weak; that he is not in danger of disintegration, of insanity, of physical disease, of weakness in general, but here he is the strongest one who will take nothing from anybody! It is an unhealthy defense, of course.

In human beings we are dealing unfortunately very often with unhealthy defenses, and in many individuals, as they mature, healthy defenses appear also. But the healthy defenses, of course, are not the ones which call for human helpfulness.

Now, a third example: suppose that a man has a serious heart attack. Again I ask for the process within you of temporary identification or empathy, because certainly one of the things that we hope some day if we have anything to do with the attempt at helping divinity students to understand human beings, is to point out to them that intellectual understanding is only one small facet of the understanding of human beings, that a far more productive way of understanding human beings is by this process of empathy and of temporary identification, when it is kept within control, within intellectual bounds, checked by the facts and by logic and the rest. The process is enormously more fruitful if it starts with empathy and temporary identification.

Now then, suppose you empathize with a man who has had a severe heart attack, with all of the pain that goes with it, with all of the question of what is going to happen in the future that goes with it, with the feeling of internal catastrophe and danger and disaster. Obviously the reaction is one of acute, intense anxiety, and defenses then appear to that anxiety. A typical defense that physicians—internists especially—see in the practice of medicine is that a man who has had a heart attack becomes rather babylike in his attitude, wants never to be left alone, wants attention, is difficult to get along with. He is rather irritable; he tries to dominate as a child might try to dominate a situation. He has a rather whining attitude. Now, this man is not just suddenly revealing his true nasty, ornery character. Not at all! It means that the man has so much fear about his internal danger that he has built up this particular defense, a defense for which we have the technical term of "regression," that is, of regressing, going back to a previous level of adjustment and safety. It is a man who has such a heart attack and feels terribly insecure now with all of his anxiety and his feeling of catastrophe, who now has the automatic impulse to find safety and security again somehow, somewhere in the world. Automatically within him comes up his feeling (not in his conscious mind particularly, but in his feeling—and these things are dominated particularly by feelings, not by ideas) the concept, the reaction, "Once I was safe. When I was in danger, when I was a child, my mother, my father took care of me, and I could forget my danger." And so, when he is confronted in his adult life with such terrific unexpected danger, he goes back to some of the techniques of his childhood, of trying again to revive the security of his childhood, of having somebody to lean on, by reviving his attitude and feeling and behavior of his childhood—the whining attitude, the babylike attitude, the need for attention, the begging for attention, or the dominating requests for attention, as in his particular childhood he may have attempted to get security by one or another of those methods.

That, then, is another example to indicate how the emotion of anxiety leads to automatic defenses, so that the surface appearance is one of symptoms of nervousness, of unpleasant behavior. The whining attitude of certain hospitalized patients may be a very unpleasant thing for the nurses, the doctors, the attendants, or others; certainly physicians learn that those unpleasant aspects of human beings are not so because these are unpleasant human beings—it is because they are human beings who are scared, who have terrific anxiety, and who are reacting with some type of desperate emergency ways of getting some feeling of safety and security again, some defenses against anxiety. . . .

So I can go on the basis of those three examples to a generalization. But I am not generalizing on the basis of three examples; I am generalizing on the basis of a mass of other material of which these are merely samples.

The general rule is that most of the symptoms of nervousness, most of the unpleasant surfaces of human beings, are defenses against anxiety and that, using that concept of the defenses against anxiety, we can go one step further to the statement of the three-layer approach to the problems of human beings.

The outermost layer, the first layer, is the layer of the defenses which we have been talking about, which are often manifestations which are unpleasant, which are unhealthy, which are symptoms of one sort or another.

The anxiety against which these defenses have been built is the second layer.

Now, beneath those two layers of the external unpleasant defenses and the anxiety is the third layer, the deepest layer of the human being, the fundamental personality, the fundamental decency and worthwhileness of that particular human being who has developed the anxiety and who has developed the defenses against his anxiety. In connection with my comment about this deepest layer, the fundamental decency and the worthwhileness of the human being, I can say that perhaps psychiatrists see more than any other human beings the unpleasant aspects of human beings, and yet (I think that I can speak for most psychiatrists in saying) more and more, in spite of all this experience of dealing with the unpleasant aspects of human beings, they have become more and more convinced of the fundamental decency, worthwhileness and fineness of human life and of human beings.

Now, to apply this general rule of defenses against anxiety and the three-layer material, let us try to make it more specific by applying it to the problems of children with whom not only parents and psychiatrists, but also ministers, have to deal.

We can make this general rule: misbehavior, defiance, the irritating qualities of children, are almost always defenses against anxiety; a misbehaving child is usually a scared child; and further, in the handling of the child, the ideal (and please note here that no psychiatrist ever expects people to be ideal by any means; we hold up goals without trying to say that human beings must reach those goals before they have developed their wings) is to approach the child with the intent, with the attempt to handle all three layers of the personality in the problem. That is, it is wrong for the parent to handle only the external layer, only the defenses, wrong for the parents or for the doctor to respond to the surface only. It is wrong to be too irritated or to be angry at the surface because, for the most part, it is not deliberate. It is wrong to react just to the child's misbehavior by punishment only or by aggressive, angry, hostile combative attitudes on the part of the adult or of the doctor. Further, it is wrong for the nursery school teacher, the teacher in general, the physician, or the parent to respond only to the anxiety, the second layer. Unfortunately, the unduly progressive schools made the mistake of dealing only with the anxiety; that of saying anything goes, anything can be forgiven, of responding only by knowing that this child must be loved and made secure. That was overdoing it. It had its unpleasant results. It produced new types of neuroses which are described by Anna Freud in Vienna in some of the overly progressive schools, because there was the attempt there to deal with the child only in terms of the middle layer, the anxiety.

What must happen in the ideal is that the parent or the teacher or the clergyman or the physician will respond to all three layers in this fashion: if a child is misbehaving, if a child has certain irritating, provoking qualities, one can't expect to smash down those qualities. It will do no good. One has to have an understanding attitude about them. But one must deal with those external qualities, with those external characteristics and defenses with firmness. The child must know how far it can go and how far it can not go, and if the child is unable to understand any other type of firmness, an occasional spanking may be certainly indicated. Even though most psychiatrists still are talking against spanking, I am quite convinced that an occasional spanking does no harm if it is not simply used in the service of the parents' hostility or sadism. But if it is for the sake of putting across to the child the handling of this surface layer of defenses, of putting across the fact that "so far and no further," then it certainly can be part of a legitimate firmness. Of course, other firmness is to be preferred if it can be used.

Then, simultaneously or immediately afterward, the second layer must be handled—the layer of anxiety. If one happens to know the specific anxiety, then one handles it by directly dealing with that particular kind of anxiety. If one knows that a boy, for example, is developing his ornery qualities because of terrific anxiety about his masturbation, one can deal with the masturbation and its anxiety directly.

But most of the time physicians, clergymen, or parents will not know the specific anxiety, and all that one can do is to react to the anxiety by a reassuring, kindly, decent, warm, affectionate attitude, which acts as a general reassurance against anxiety; that is, to try to give the feeling of security. Then, simultaneously, one must respond to the deepest layer. One must respond to the individual's fundamental decency and worthwhileness with warmth, with respect, with consideration. As a matter of fact, in my teaching of our psychiatrists in training at the hospital, I make the statement that no psychiatrist should ever attempt to treat anybody, any particular patient, unless he can sense that underneath the unpleasant surface defenses and the anxiety there is something about this human being he can like. Because if he does not sense that, there is something wrong within him; at least it would be unwise for him to be handling such a case because one of the vital parts—perhaps the absolutely essential part—of any attempt at human helpfulness is of somehow putting across from the one person to the other, from the one helping to the one being helped, that there is a fundamental respect and liking for that other person—not necessarily in terms of his actual behavior—but in terms of his potentialities and fundamental decency and humanity. . . .

So far then, I have put across, I hope, without too much jargon or confusion, the essential importance of the emotional interplay between the person who attempts to help and the person being helped—the patient-physician relationship. Secondly, I have tried to put across this central and absolutely essential point that is basic to all human helpfulness and understanding, of the other human being, of the person to be helped, in terms of the concepts of defenses against anxiety and three-layer approach which, if really used and really understood, will prevent many, many mistakes in human helpfulness.

Now, I have some material about the study and understanding of any particular human being. . . . You can call this the six-point approach to the study of any particular patient or to the understanding of any particular human being, and we hope some day to make the application to the work of the pastor.

First of all, before I list my six points I should like to put across this point: that in the work of the minister who is trying to deal specifically with a particular human being, he is not to make the old mistake of having blanket principles of treatment which he applies to people in general. That probably is the most frequent and most devastating mistake—that one has certain fixed ideas of how to handle human beings, that one uses them without any attempt at a specific understanding of the human being.

Now, you wouldn't want a doctor to do that with you. You wouldn't have much respect for a doctor who treats all kinds, let's say, of abdominal pain, in the same fashion, or all kinds of headache, every case of headache with the same method of treatment. The thing that must precede any method or any attempt at human helpfulness is an attempt at undertaking the specific problem before one. Any attempt on the part of a minister to help a human being must be preceded by, what we can call, a diagnostic understanding of that person. It sounds obvious, but it is amazing how infrequently it actually is done. . . . Suppose that a mother might ask a minister for help or advice in the handling of a disobedient child. It's awfully easy to give advice that is based on general principles. That would be, in many cases, devastatingly wrong, no matter what the depth of the understanding may be. Understanding must come before one gives advice to a mother about the handling of a child or before one attempts to help in the handling. One must try to have some understanding first to come to some sort of a diagnosis.

On that basis, these are the six points. We have them in a psychiatric case workup, and you can see the possibilities of application
in the work of the minister: first, clinical diagnosis; second, dynamic
diagnosis; third, genetic diagnosis; fourth, transference; fifth,
counter-transference; and sixth, the treatment possibilities. . . .

Any minister, anybody who works from a point of view of a
religious agency, must have a certain amount of understanding of
clinical diagnosis, by which we mean the entities which can occur
in unhealthy, unhappy human beings. There must be a limited
amount of understanding of just that one point. The minister must
have a small amount of understanding, for example, of the entity
that we call schizophrenia. There can be no getting away from it.
It's not possible to fool around in dealing with human beings. One
must know something of what actually has been worked out and
discovered. For example, if a minister is asked to help out with a
disobedient or a masturbating child who is providing any sort of
difficulty, he must know of the possibility that in adolescence certain of these difficulties indicate a very serious disorder, whereas in
other cases the disorder might be quite superficial and should be
handled in a totally different fashion.

The clergyman must know of the possibility that some individuals
may have their personal difficulties because they have syphilis of the
brain. And in any adequate curriculum in a divinity school which
is going to emphasize the possibility of human helpfulness on an
individual basis a certain amount of this material must be put
across so that there will not be the possibility of missing up on the
early helpfulness in such cases. Every minister, I think, should be
taught the early manifestations of schizophrenia, for example, not
because he is going to treat it, not because he has to be a psychiatrist, not because he must know a great amount about schizophrenia,
but to be able, as a matter of mental hygiene and human helpfulness, to ask for cooperative help when the time comes.

The second is the dynamic diagnosis. By the dynamic diagnosis
we mean—what is eating the individual at this time. What are the

forces that are at work to produce his problems? "Dynamics" here, psychodynamics, dynamic diagnosis, has the same sort of root as thermodynamics, that is, the forces of heat; hydrodynamics, the forces of water. We mean in psychodynamics or in dynamic diagnosis, what are the forces at work within the human being that are causing him to have his problems at this particular moment? What are his anxieties? What are his defenses? What are his conflicts? What are the forces at work? For example, in back of a prolonged convalescence might be the forces of anxiety about whether one is acceptable or the desire for attention. In back of some cases of high blood pressure may be the force of inhibited hatred. In back of the accusation, which the clergyman might hear with some frequency, that a man might make that his wife has been unfaithful or that she might be unfaithful, may be the force of the man's own impulse to be unfaithful. That is, if he has an impulse to be unfaithful which has aroused anxiety in him, one of his defenses may be of projecting that impulse, that activity on to the other person, as if he were saying, "It is not I who am guilty, but the other person who is guilty." The force there is the force of the impulse to be unfaithful himself, the force of the defense of projection on to somebody in the outside world to lessen the anxiety.

The dynamic diagnosis has to do with the internal forces which are operating in the individual at this time, and the keynote in the understanding is what I have given on the anxiety and its defenses.

Genetic diagnosis has to do with how the forces within the individual got to be this way. How does it happen that this particular man has the impulse to be unfaithful, his particular type of conflict with it, and his particular defense against it? What things of his past life or of his childhood or adolescence led him to have this particular set of forces which are operative at the present time? What in one man makes him so much more prey to anxiety and necessary defenses than another man who has much less frequent anxiety or much less intense anxiety? The genetic diagnosis has to do with the genesis of the forces at work in the individual at this time. It has to do chiefly with the childhood experiences, the childhood influences of that individual. It has to do with such things as childhood insecurity, broken homes, the fears in childhood, sexuality in childhood, the problems of the only child or of the preferred child or of the rejected child; the problems that have to do with the feelings of the child that are engendered by an over-solicitous or over-indulgent parent, that is, the things that happen in the child in response to the problems of its parents; the things that happen in children because of upsurges of impulses which they are unable to handle in terms of their intelligence and strength at that time.

Now, many, many books have been written about the forces in childhood which lead to the later problems. One that I can recommend to you perhaps as giving you more than any other is the book by English and Pearson called *Emotional Problems of Living*,[1] a book has more to do with the topic of the genetic diagnosis than with any of the other topics.

What we are saying here is this: if the minister is to attempt to have some human helpfulness, he must learn to have some idea or understanding, not merely of what the diagnosis might be in semimedical terms, not only of what the dynamics, the forces are at the present time, but also what bad and good mental hygiene is in childhood and what effect such experiences may have on the later development of the individual. It may help him in the handling of the individual case, but more than that, it may help him in his attempts at prevention, in his attempts at joining with all of the other groups and agencies which are involved in the mental hygiene program of today.

Enough for those three hints as to what might develop out of an interrelationship of psychiatric understanding and religious groups along the line of increased clinical understanding, of dynamic understanding, and of genetic understanding. The fourth of the points was the transference, which I elaborated on sufficiently before.

The fifth is the countertransference. Here I want to give one more example to try to make sure that all you have some impression as to why, in any human helpfulness, a stringent honesty about oneself is an essential and important point. In connection with the work of the clergyman, let's say, problems of the interrelationship of parents and children are, of course, frequent. Problems, let us say, of a mother and her son or daughter come up repeatedly in the life of any minister who is able to evoke that sort of confidential attitude on the part of his parishioners.

Now, always there is the question in the interrelationship of a mother and the child of what, in old-fashioned terms, can be called "Who is to be blamed?" That we consider to be a very inadequate concept. We now much prefer the concept of allocation of responsibility—not because of any desire to punish or criticize, but for the sake of merely trying to understand where it may be more helpful to try to put one's emphasis in changing the situation. One has to try to see where the responsibility is if one wants to see at what point the situation is most modifiable. It is necessary not to blame one or both—the mother or the child—but to try to get some idea of the various types of responsibility that are involved in the difficult relationship that may have developed between a mother and a child.

Now then, a clergyman, like a psychiatrist or a physician in general, who has, out of his own childhood, his own genetics, and out of his own dynamics, a tendency to be excessively sympathetic with children, will rarely be able to come to a correct estimate of the responsibilities in this difficult relationship between the mother and the child whom he is trying to help. On the other hand, another clergyman, like another psychiatrist, whose own genetic problems and own dynamic problems has led him to an undue identification with and sympathy for parents rather than with children, may also be unable to come to any sort of an objective understanding of the situation because of automatic tendencies to side with one rather than the other.

That is the type of stringent self-scrutiny and honesty which is an absolute urgent necessity in the development of any type of human helpfulness.

Now, on the basis of those five points which we have barely touched upon here—clinical diagnosis, the dynamic diagnosis, the genetic diagnosis, transference, and countertransference—we then come to the sixth point. What are the treatment possibilities with this particular individual? Is the clergyman able to help, or is the physician or psychiatrist able to help? And we would make the decision in terms of what the previous points had revealed: what the dynamics are, what the diagnosis is, what the transference is, etc. We would make the choice and decision as to what sort of work to do on the basis of those preceding five points, plus what are the practical responsibilities in the case. Is this one in which there is the possibility of helping merely by manipulating the situation, or does one have to do some other more deep-going treatment? Further, one would make the decision as to the treatment possibilities on the basis of the skill, the ability, and the training of the person doing the treating. We would have to decide what level of treatment was called for and decide who should be doing the treatment in such a case.

Now, let us conclude by saying that in his work with people, the clergyman may be able to take advantage of some of the discoveries in the field of psychiatry about human helpfulness in general, and to apply them within the strict field of his own competence, of his own training, and within the strictness of what applies to the work of the clergyman, rather than to the work of the psychiatrist.

Mr. Lillienthal's[2] recent report on atomic energy indicated his own conviction that it was not the atomic bomb that was the central problem of today; that the future of our civilization was rather dependent on economic improvements and political and social progress, but also on the emotional attitude of human beings, which can lead to a greater cooperation and to more mutually constructive relations between individuals and between groups. As I see it, an enormous mental hygiene program is needed. Psychiatrists can't do the job alone, whether it is of individual handling of human beings or of the mental hygiene program. And consequently, we hope for the sincere and lasting and informed cooperation of religious agencies and leaders.

5

Oedipus, Cain and Abel, and the Geographic Full-Time System

MANY psychiatrists today are convinced that the modern study of psychiatric patients has led not only to a workable understanding of neurotic and psychotic problems but also to a more general understanding of human behavior. Two points in support of this thesis can be mentioned. One is that patients are not members of a separate species but rather are slightly variant examples of human beings. And, second, patients are those men and women and children who, because of their hope of a cure or a lessening of their distress, are more willing than others to reveal the truths of their secret lives and the essence of their humanity. Hence, the intensive and extensive studies of patients have led to a greater understanding of men and women in general.

From this it could follow that our understanding of patients as persons provides a greater understanding of those men and women who are medical students, interns, residents, and faculty members. The findings of psychiatry, then, may suggest some additional points of understanding of medical students and faculty members, and of the agencies and patterns which they create and use; or, put in the form of a question, we shall ask, in this essay, whether present-day psychiatry has something to contribute to our thinking about medical education and about the policies of departments in a medical school.

The title of the essay has three parts, apparently unrelated. The first item of the title indicates that the essay will refer to the set of feelings and impulses named in psychiatry after Oedipus Rex, and will refer to the impulses, usually unconscious, of associate professors, assistant professors, and instructors, to murder the professor, the director of the department, as Oedipus murdered his father. The Oedipus complex, as the readers of this *Journal* know, has two components—the son's wish to be rid of his father and the son's wish to marry his mother. In medical school circles, the evidence is overwhelming that all, from instructors to associate professors, consciously or unconsciously want to murder the father-director. If also they want to marry his wife, or his widow, we can not be sure. Our evidence is incomplete. (And, of course, we must not mention that old devil sex in a medical essay.)

The second part of the title refers to the Cain and Abel problem in our medical faculties, in which associate professors, assistant professors, and instructors want to murder their brother faculty members as Cain murdered his brother Abel.

The third part of the title indicates that the essay will focus on the geographic full-time system, which many of us believe is one of the most important and productive patterns of medical school organization and structure. It can be defined as the system under which medical faculty members give their primary interest, time, and energy to their academic appointments, are paid by the school, are permitted also to participate to a limited extent in private practice, but are not permitted to have offices for private practice outside the medical school or university hospital geographic center.

The title, then, is an amalgam of medical college organizations; the Bible story of Cain and Abel; the great Greek drama of Oedipus;

and the psychiatric finding that, hidden in the most mature and intelligent men and women, the members of a medical school faculty, are impulses similiar to the violent and primitive behavior portrayed in great dramas and historical documents.

The Bible and Sophocles are included in the presentation. Inevitably, we now must include some poetry, or, rather, we now can refer to a comment attributed to the great American poet, Robert Frost. When he had reached a fairly mature age, Mr. Frost was asked whether he had come to some brief definition of "wisdom." His response was that he had tried many times to devise some simple phrase that for him would come close to defining the essence of wisdom. His final version, he said, was a paraphrase of a comment of many others throughout the ages, that true wisdom was the ability to act, when it was necessary, on the basis of incomplete information.

His principle of true wisdom is of the highest value in the everyday practice of medicine. It means that, even though we try earnestly to have a good solid foundation of scientific and experimentally verifiable data for all of our medical procedures and methods of treatment, we still not infrequently are faced with a situation in which our scientific information is incomplete, but in which we must act without hesitation and with a high degree of responsibility. In Mr. Frost's terms, our actions as such times must be based on incomplete information. In our teaching of the resident group we often emphasize the point that the practice of medicine involves a delicate balance between high scientific standards, with an emphasis on experimental and verifiable data, on predictability and accuracy, and the second fundamental requirement, the need for responsible medical action even when all the scientific facts are not yet available.

Similarly, in the field of ideas and principles, there must be two kinds of conclusions—one which is the result of research, of experimentation, and of statistical validation, and another kind which is incomplete but is probable and is worth using and trying. One must, in Mr. Frost's terms, have the courage to go forward on the basis of ideas which are incomplete but are the best we have.

Hence, this paper is presented as an essay, in first-person terms. It is not a report of a well designed and statistically validated research, but rather a discussion of ideas which are the precipitate of some thirty years of work as a psychiatrist plus a large variety of more casual observations, from the psychiatrist's point of view, of the patterns and persons in the field of medical education and administration.

The thesis of the essay can be phrased in this fashion: that, for certain specific psychologic reasons which we will discuss in a moment, the geographic full-time system has tremendous advantages over the pure full-time system in the organization of medical schools; and, further, that some specific ways of handling the geographic full-time system may add even more to its value.

The fundamental psychologic factors to which I refer are the following. A department of a medical school usually has one man as the director of the department. He is in a position of fairly great authority and responsibility. Usually, in addition, there are a number of associate professors, assistant professors, and instructors. As their careers develop, the instructors and the assistant and associate professors inevitably compete with each other, or at least want very strongly to compete with each other. In addition, these members of the faculty often have competitive impulses toward the director as well; and some of these competitive impulses can be extreme.

Surely we need no longer pretend that human relations are altogether sweetness and light and that all members of medical faculties are well-bred gentlemen. We know that for the most part their actual behavior is very acceptable indeed; but we know also that individuals of the greatest maturity and decency have a variety of unacceptable impulses, some conscious but most unconscious. In the year 1960 it no longer is possible to think of human beings as being either all nice or all bad. Such a concept is possible only if one adheres to the old-fashioned and primitive notion of "good guys and bad guys," such as children must have in watching a Western program on television. One of the points of psychodynamic understanding is that all good guys, e.g. all members of the medical school faculty, have some bad-guy impulses.

It is a commonplace observation that the director of a department by virtue of his authority arouses a series or a variety of emotional responses on the part of many other members of the department faculty. Some of the staff come to be deeply dependent on the director's leadership and come to feel that their security is in good part based on their relationship with him as a fatherly person who will take care of them, foster their careers, and shield them from criticism.

In college departments one can observe a variety of relationships within the departments, some healthy and some unhealthy; and in some departments one can see the effects of the authoritative role of the director on the rest of the group. In some faculty members, one can see an undue passivity and submissiveness, in some one can see an undue competition with the authority figure, and in some one can see an undue competition with others for the favor of the one in authority. Moreover, all three of these reactions may occur in one man.

To make the point, we can use an analogy which may be more than an analogy. A small group in which one individual has a sharply structured and demarcated position of strength and leadership has a great similarity to a family group, a father and his children. Much of the emotional interplay characteristic of family life holds true also for other small groups. Many people respond in a group as they first learned to respond in childhood, in the family group. There is no doubt that the director of a department often is regarded as a kind of father-figure by the other members of the faculty, and that toward him they have responses of obedience, submission, loyalty, passivity, rebellion, defiance, competition, and hostility, as they might, or did, have to a father-figure in a family.

A medical school department head may have an authoritarian personality. If this be true, he will have some of the reactions directed toward him which go toward an authoritarian father in a family. Excessive dependence and excessive rebellion against authority often will occur in such a department. This is true, but, more important for the thesis of this paper, is the fact that in some departments the director is forced into the role of being an authoritarian person even though his personality may not be authoritarian in its fundamental structure. For example, if he is the head of a department in which the total income of the assistant professors is dependent on his leadership, if their promotion is largely dependent on his good will, if their careers are in good part dependent on the kind of letters of recommendation that he may write, he is in a position of very great authority indeed. Almost inevitably he will have directed toward him very strong feelings of dependence and passivity.

If, then, a member of the faculty is not able to rest easily with being in such a dependent and passive position, he will tend to react against the situation and perhaps against his own impulses to be dependent. If he regards a dependent role with another man as being a blow to his masculinity he may develop pseudomasculine reactions, e.g. may have serious and aggressive quarrels with the head of the department or in some other way emphasize his independence of the professor. In other instances he may not react directly to the head of the department but rather to the other members of the faculty. He may need to show the other assistant professors that he is not a passive person, when they make suggestions, but is very independent indeed. This can lead to aggressive differences of opinion with other members of the faculty group as a demonstration of his superiority and strength in argument or in intellect, as a denial of the dependent position, and of the wish to be dependent.

This is the sort of pattern which occurs with some frequency in childhood, when a boy who is ashamed of his good-little-boy impulses to be dependent on his mother or father, tries then to be the bad-little-boy, arguing endlessly and defiantly with his parents, or getting into fights with neighbor boys in order to show how strong, how independent, and how manly he can be.

The question of tenure of office is relevant at this point. The authority and power of the director of the department are lessened to some degree when the department members have university tenure. Under such circumstances, the passivity and dependence on the director are somewhat less, and the subsequent aggressive and hostile impulses may be lessened as well. Tenure of office gives the members of the department some feeling of security beyond their relationships with the director. Unfortunately, however, the growth of temproray grants, of soft money in the budget, and the like, has lessened the percentage of endowment money on which tenure of office must be based; and one must add, with emphasis, that even when there is tenure of office it often is not enough. The career of an instructor or assistant professor still is dependent to some degree upon the favor of the director, his recommendation for promotion, his letters of reference to others, and his division of available department funds.

It seems clear to some of us that the geographic full-time system prevents many of the disastrous developments of passivity and aggressiveness in a medical school department. When the department is structured as it is in Cincinnati, in which "full-time" is defined as meaning that the members of the faculty of the Department of Psychiatry must give twenty-five to thirty hours per week to departmental activities and then may do private referral work in additional hours, one has avoided many of the problems outlined in the preceding paragraphs.

Under such an arrangement, the geographic full-time man has a very deep-going independence of the director of the department, in a real and adult sense. He starts with a moderate salary that is to a certain degree at the discretion of the director. If, however, he has tenure of office he is more independent of the director for this portion of his income. However, more to the point, he knows that the rest of his total income comes from his part-time private work. He knows that, if necessary, he could thumb his nose politely at the director of the department. He and his wife and children would not be victims of financial stringency if he had a disagreement with the director which would lead to his leaving the department. He would simply continue with his limited private practice, have enough income to be able to open an office, and then permit his practice to increase up to the size that he would want it, or have time enough and money enough to look around for another academic position. This is a self-respecting type of partial but secure independence in which he not only has an academic career but also has a large and valid degree of security based on his own independent earnings.

In this variety of geographic full-time arrangement, when the man has a realistic degree of independence of the director, he is no longer, or not so deeply, tempted in the direction of having to behave like a child in a family with a father who is in a powerful position of authority. Consequently, the younger members of the faculty are much less tempted to develop attitudes of little-boy dependency on the head of the department as a child might develop a dependence on a father. Further, they would not be in a position of having as men to be dependent on another man, a situation which by many men is regarded as a blow to their masculinity.

In some men such a dependent role unconsciously has certain feminine implications. I now have accumulated a series, relevant to this issue, of twenty-seven experiences with faculty men, some of them as patients and some not. I have heard the faculty men speak of directors of departments in terms that indicated clearly that his authority is felt as a castrating and feminizing experience. "He's got me by the ———" (five letter word), "He's got me cornered," "He can't do this to me," or "He can't ——— me" (four letter word), or "He can't cut me down" are typical phrases, when the veneer of civilized conversation is put aside for the moment.

If the associate professor, assistant professor, or instructor in a geographic full-time system is not forced, as he might be otherwise, into feelings of passivity, or dependency, or pseudofemininity, he may be relatively free of such passive attitudes and of the anxiety and shame that goes with them. Consequently, he is free of some of the need to behave in a pseudomasculine and aggressive and hostile fashion toward the director of the department and toward his colleagues and contemporaries, free of some of the need to be Oedipus or Cain.

Most of my comments so far have had to do with the favorable impact of the geographic full-time system on the dynamics of the assistant professor and others. However, I must make a parallel remark about the director as well. Under the pure full-time system, the director may be tempted into having a dominating, excessively controlling attitude. Or, under such circumstances, the director may feel so guilty over having such power that he veers then in the opposite direction, of being too gentle in the use of his authority. In the geographic full-time system, the director is not so tempted to a neurotic use of power or to a guilty avoidance of power. His power is limited. His authority is more easily questioned. He must develop techniques of leadership that evoke respect and collaboration rather than submission or rebellion. He must stimulate a deep-going cooperation based on the motivation of the members of his faculty rather than expect them to obey.

It is my impression that under the geographic system one often sees a very great development of congeniality, mutual loyalty, mutual interdependence, mutual responsibility, mutual respect, freedom from back-biting, and freedom from the development of cliques and pressure-groups. Perhaps this means that the success of a department within a medical school is only in part dependent on the assets and liabilities of the personality of the director and of the members of the department. Of great importance, also, is the structure of the department, particularly the specific variation of the geographic full-time system which is in use.

Let me not be misunderstood. I know that there are great values in having some pure full-time positions with no need to devote time to private work, if the salaries are adequate. Also, I know that permission for limited private work can be abused. Further, I know that neurotic sequences are not inevitable in departments organized on a pure full-time basis. The maturity of the director of a strictly full-time department and of the members of his department may prevent the development of disruptive interactions. Rather, my point in a way is that the director of a geographic full-time department need not be so mature as directors in other departments. The structure of such a department does most of the job; or, phrased in another way, the structure of a preclinical department which cannot use the geographic full-time system, or a clinical department which does not, puts an additional stress on the director of the department and on the rest of the faculty. I have the highest respect for the members of a strictly full-time department in which there is only a minimum of destructive passivity and of destructive hostility; they have overcome a structural obstacle which is very great indeed. Perhaps I can summarize my observations this way, that the danger of disruptive personal reactions in a pure full-time situation often is greater than the danger of being distracted by private work in the geographic full-time system.

At this point, a comment is in order about the varieties of the geographic full-time system. I have mentioned that in the Cincinnati Department of Psychiatry we have a strict requirement of a twenty-five to thirty-hour allocation of time to academic responsibilities and then freedom for referral practice in additional time. Such an arrangement holds true for other departments. However, some other schools and departments have private practice arrangements in which the private practice is done as a group, with fees collected centrally and the distribution of fees allocated by a central authority. This arrangement has many assets, but it violates the central principle advocated in this paper, viz. the high value to the faculty man of having as an individual a partial independence of the central authority within the school or hospital.

Still other schools which use the geographic full-time system place a limit on private practice earnings. Some, for example, have a rule that a man may earn in his private work as much as he receives in salary, with a surplus over such an amount reverting to the school or department. This, too, in terms of the thesis of this paper, is an excessive centralization of authority in a way that limits adult independence. A similar result can be achieved by the simpler procedure used in Cincinnati and elsewhere, of a group scrutiny of whether or not the man's academic performance is such that he obviously is fulfilling his responsibility to devote twenty-five to thirty hours to department activities. This he must do; and in addition he has the feeling of independence that goes with the realization that, if he needs some additional money, he can work a few hours more and earn it for himself.

The town-gown problem is relevant at this point. It would seem that the university position is on very safe ground if it is clear that a man is working twenty-five to thirty hours, for a modest salary, and so could not possibly have time enough to compete in private work with a man in full private practice, either for a sizeable number of patients or for a high level of income. Under this variant of the geographic full-time system, the faculty man has made a clear choice: He reserves most of his time and energy for his academic career; he has enough private work to give him a fair degree of mature independence; his income is larger than that of most men in pure full-time positions; but his income will never approximate that of a man in full-time private practice.

In this paper the actual figures of twenty-five to thirty hours to be devoted to academic work are emphasized not only as a way of indicating a solution to town-gown and other problems. Such an emphasis on twenty-five to thirty hours is important also in terms of a psychodynamic problem. A geographic full-time system which requires less than this, which requires too little academic time, not only runs the risk of stirring town-gown problems; it also, with high frequency, stirs serious guilt feelings in the man himself. A man who regards himself as having some variety of full-time post, and yet spends the major part of his time with his private patients, develops, according to my professional and casual observations, a load of guilt that must be prevented. The requirement of a twenty-five to thirty-hour work week of department responsibilities prevents the misuse of the permission for a limited private practice.

A passing thought: If the faculty person is a woman rather than a man, some of the dynamic formulations I have presented would need to be changed in certain ways. However, my experience with faculty women who, in therapy or otherwise, revealed their more deeply rooted feelings, would indicate that for them, too, a good variant of the geographic full-time system is, or would be, productive.

I recognize that the idea presented in this paper, viz. that the geographic full-time system provides an extremely favorable pattern for medical school departments because the system facilitates an avoidance of destructive neurotic developments, is an impressionistic idea. We then would say that, if such an idea seems important, it could be the subject of a well designed research project. It then would be checked for its accuracy and be evaluated quantitatively.

It would not be too difficult to devise a research design which would test some of the details of my thesis. For example, it might be possible to get records of faculty turnover in a number of departments and records of the hour and salary arrangements for the members of the faculty of the same group of departments. These then might be correlated in an adequately controlled statistical fashion, by using, for example, the well-known Lehrer Lobachevsky Pi-Square technique. Or, it might be possible to get facts as to faculty satisfaction by some sort of anonymous questionnaire or by interviewing techniques and again to correlate the findings of such a study with the variety and sources of faculty income. Further, research productiveness, job satisfaction, the happiness of faculty wives, hidden feelings of rage, are all measurable quantities and can be correlated with the type of departmental structure. For fuller accuracy, it would be necessary to consider also the question of whether one or more types of persons are drawn to the geographic full-time system and so accept a job offer in such a department, and whether one or more types of persons are drawn to the strictly full-time system.

However, statistical or experimental verification of an impressionistic idea is not the only fate which may be in store for it. It probably will be forgotten if it does not click with the impressionistic ideas of others in the field. Further, if the idea is not sufficiently central or vital to require that it be checked in an accurate and controlled study, it may have value chiefly as a stimulant to productive thinking on the part of others, and gradually lead to an improvement in concepts or in performance or in technique. Even without exact research design or experimental proof of the value of a change, a good craftsman accepts and uses new principles in his productive workmanship. A valuable type of know-how develops from flexible experience with changes based on convictions which have not been validated with a high degree of accuracy. Similarly, in medical affairs, administrative know-how and well digested experience provide a sound basis for planning by those in positions of leadership and authority.

Perhaps a final comment is in order. In many instances in recent years great stress has been placed on the importance of morale and of good leadership, in the armed forces, in industry, and elsewhere. The discussion in this paper is pertinent to this crucial problem. The generalization can be phrased this way, that plans and patterns based on some awareness of psychodynamics will improve the morale of the group and the effectiveness of its leadership. Psychodynamic observations indicate that strong leadership is crucial, a leadership which avoids the Scylla of dictatorial power and the Charybdis of the abdication of responsibility and initiative. However, perhaps even more important than the character of the leader is the structuring of an institution so that the leader does not have too great a final authority and so that others working with him have adequate feelings of independence. In medical education, the geographic full-time system fosters such a pattern of human relations. Such a structure may lessen the stimulation of childhood residuals in the group, may lessen the drive toward being dependent and cared for and protected, and so may lessen the destructive hostilities which arise as a defense. The diminution of excessive patterns of passivity and aggressiveness may lead to a more creative interplay within the group and with its director, and so to a greater stability and productiveness.

1960

6

A Hippocratic Oath
for Psychiatrists*

T HE Oath of Hippocrates is one of the famous documents in the history of mankind which seem to stimulate and to justify the use of dramatic terms and phrases. One can say, for example, that it contains a distillate of much of the medical wisdom of previous centuries. It is symbolic of a tremendous surge upward in the growth of our civilization. It seems to have crystallized a new pattern of man's conscience. For over two thousand years it has been quoted, has been the focus of medical ethics and standards, and has acted as a cohesive force in the medical world. In a true sense, it is profoundly religious. It calls for an attitude of dedication that is more than lip service. It has been a vital force in the development of the science and the art of medicine.

All of you remember enough of the original Hippocratic Oath so that it need not be read again at this meeting. We can summarize it briefly. The first third of the Oath and the last paragraph are

* Paper delivered at a meeting of the Ohio Psychiatric Association in Cincinnati, April 12, 1961.

part of the ritual of taking the oath and of preserving the fraternal aspect of the profession of the Greek era. The body of the Oath consists essentially of the following points: Physicians commit themselves to use methods of treatment that are beneficial and not injurious; to give no deadly medicine; to avoid abortions; to avoid cutting a person who has a stone, leaving this to be done by the practitioners of cutting; to avoid mischievous activity in the houses of patients and to go there for the benefit of the sick; to avoid seducing patients of the opposite sex or of the same sex; and to avoid revealing the secrets of one's patients.

I must add, however, that there are some unsettled issues with regard to the meaning of some phrases of the Hippocratic Oath. For example, the famous injunction that physicians should not cut the stone usually is interpreted as meaning that the physician should not do a surgical procedure, such as the removal of a kidney stone, for which he might not be trained. There are, however, some indications that in actuality the injunction against the cutting of the stone represented an injunction against the castration of patients, against cutting the testicles, phrased as stones.

Further, Wilder Penfield, the Montreal neurosurgeon, has just written a novel called *The Torch*, with Hippocrates as the central figure. One of the theses of the novel is that the prohibition against helping a woman to induce an abortion was put into the Oath by Hippocrates not because of the ethical problems connected with abortion, as the murder of the child, but because of the recognition by physicians, even at that time, of the danger of serious infection associated with induced abortion.

But the most fascinating recent comment on the Hippocratic Oath is one which originated with Margaret Mead, the great anthropologist. Her major insight was that the Hippocratic Oath marked one of the turning points in the history of man. She says, "For the first time in our tradition there was a complete separation between killing and curing. Throughout the primitive world the doctor and the sorcerer tended to be the same person. He with power to kill had power to cure, including specially the undoing of his own killing activities. He who had power to cure would necessarily also be able to kill.

"With the Greeks," says Margaret Mead, "the distinction was made clear. One profession, the followers of Asclepius, were to be dedicated completely to life under all circumstances, regardless of rank, age, or intellect—the life of a slave, the life of the Emperor, the life of a foreign man, the life of a defective child." Dr. Mead emphasizes the fact that "this is a priceless possession which we cannot afford to tarnish, but society always is attempting to make the physician into a killer—to kill the defective child at birth, to leave the sleeping pills beside the bed of the cancer patient," and she is convinced that "it is the duty of society to protect the physician from such requests."

My purpose today is to carry further the discussion of the Hippocratic Oath and to look at it from a new angle. My first point will be that we can regard the Hippocratic Oath as the earliest important historical document about a phenomenon which is central in the practice of contemporary psychiatry, the phenomenon of countertransference. My second thesis will be that the Hippocratic Oath, grand and impressive though it is, belongs to the simple beginnings of our understanding of the problems that occur in the relationship of doctors and patients. It is time now for a much more far-reaching statement of these problems. In today's presentation, I shall give some vignettes of our understanding of the relationship between patients and psychiatrists, as one group of physicians. Then I shall go to my third topic, a preliminary phrasing of the ways in which a new set of affirmations and renunciations can be made, which can be called a Hippocratic Oath for Psychiatrists.

Our consideration of these problems must start with the central fact that the human species has made tremendous strides in its development, but along with the increased strength there are many residuals of imperfection. Human beings strive to be rational and well-adjusted, to be logical, and to be governed by facts alone. To an amazing degree they can do so, but to an amazing degree also they still are governed by nonrational forces, by their wishes and their fears, by the residuals of their childhood, by the fact that other human beings in their current lives somehow are seen largely as duplicates of persons in their past.

Even the simplest usual one-to-one relationships in human life demonstrate this extraordinary mixture of logic, and of lack of logic. For example, in a conversation between an average pair of good friends, a statement made by one of the two will be considered by the other in the light of facts and reality, but also very often it will be accepted more or less uncritically. If there is some lack of logic in the statement made by the first of the friends, the second may be aware of its lack of logic but often will have a strong need to see it as being true, out of loyalty, out of affection, out of identification, out of the simple fact of being a friend.

Similarly, if two individuals are somewhat antagonistic, a statement made by one of the two will be evaluated by the second in terms of whether it is correct and factual and logical, but in addition, it often will have two strikes against it. The antagonistic listener is all set to find points to criticize in any statement of the speaker, and often would prefer that the speaker be mistaken rather than correct.

In these two pairs, we have just focused on the responses of the second of the pair. Now we can change our focus and concentrate on the first of each pair. In the case of the two friends, the first of the pair is likely to say something with which the second will agree, since the two are friends and the first enjoys saying things which would indicate that they have ideas in common or think in a similar fashion. Similarly, in the pair of somewhat antagonistic acquaintances, the first is rather likely to say things with which the second would be in disagreement, because the first one, out of his antagonism, would like to differ with the second, would like to show that they are not in agreement, and often might want to provoke an argument.

Usually in two such pairs, all four individuals are in good part reasonable and factual and logical. But in the two pairs, there usually are four other items. The first friend wants to say things which would please his friend. The second friend wants to hear things with which he could agree. The first of the antagonistic pair wants to provoke the second. The second of the antagonistic pair wants to hear things with which he could disagree. In all four instances we have situations in which the reasonable, logical, well-adjusted way of interacting with another person may be vitiated and distorted by specific emotional patterns.

To a group of psychiatrists, and now their wives, it must be obvious that I am saying that the phenomena of transference and countertransference, which are so crucial in the overall field of psychiatry, are essentially manifestations of a far broader tendency in human beings, the tendency to react in various nonlogical modalities to situations which ideally would call for reactions that would be logical and mature.

I phrase it this way because I want it to be clear that the medical problems on which we will focus today are problems of all human beings, are examples of the fact that in any relationship of two human beings there will be a combination of logical and mature responses along with some nonlogical or immature responses. A patient is simply being human when he has some nonlogical responses to any physician, including his psychiatrist. Further, the physician, the psychiatrist, who has certain nonlogical responses to a patient also is responding in a way that holds true generally with human beings.

The Oath as formulated by Hippocrates and his predecessors is a clear statement of the difficulties in having a persistently good medical attitude toward patients. When the early Greek physicians tried to be physicians in a real sense, or using Margaret Mead's concept, when the tradition developed of separating the curing power of the sorcerer from his killing power, a number of renunciations of strong drives had to take place. Using psychiatric terminology, we would say that a number of conscious renunciations, a number of reaction-formations, a number of sublimations, a number of total denials, a number of attempts at having a performance that would be reliable and trustworthy, had to be developed. The

Oath provides a written expression of the strong resolve of the physician to avoid doing various actions which would be damaging or destructive, which would be seriously illogical and incorrect in his role as good leader or good physician.

But now it is more than two thousand years since Hippocrates. In these years there have been tremendous advances in the understanding of anatomy, of physiology and of the other somatic aspects of the practice of medicine. But also there have been tremendous advances in the understanding of the psychologic aspects of medical work. Especially in the past hundred years there has developed a deep-going understanding of psychodynamics and psychopathology as they affect the development of personality disorders and as they affect the course and the severity of the physical disorders themselves.

In the course of such studies of psychodynamics, tremendous strides have been made in the understanding of the relationship of patients and physicians. In fact, no other relationship has been studied so carefully as the relationship between patients and one group of physicians, the psychiatrists. The two-way relationship between parents and children, with the logical and well-adjusted aspects of the responses of each to the other, and the illogical and maladjusted aspects of the relationship of the two, have been studied very thoroughly indeed. The logical and the illogical aspects of the interactions within a marriage, of husband and wife, have been studied thoroughly from the point of view both of the husband and of the wife. But the interaction between patients and psychiatrists has been studied even more extensively and intensively than the other two-way relationships, essentially because along this route has been found the great high-road to improvement and cure. And difficulties in the relationship have been found to be one of the chief stumbling blocks in the process of improvement and cure.

It was found routinely that even relatively normal and moderately neurotic patients respond to psychiatrists with varying mixtures of logic and lack of logic, various degrees of ability to see facts clearly and various tendencies to distort facts. This, as you know, has been called the transference, since in good part, the non-logical responses have been the result of transferring to the psychiatrist some of the feeling tones and responses which the patient originally had developed toward important figures early in his life. If a patient, when he was a child, had a hidden distrust of his father, he is likely to develop a hidden distrust of his psychiatrist who is in part a contemporary substitute for his father. Parenthetically, it is important to mention that patterns other than that of transferring from important figures of early life also may play an important role. For example, a patient who had little or no distrust of his father in childhood but out of other conflicts and problems gradually developed a generalized attitude of distrust and suspicion, may be suspicious and hostile to the psychiatrist as to others, even when the fact points otherwise. This type of reaction also is included in the general rubric of transference. And with regard to this topic, the transference, we must emphasize that the study of the reactions of human beings as patients has been one of the most productive of all research areas in the history of science and of medicine.

So much for the transference. Further discoveries then were made, when courage and honesty were added to open-minded observation. Gradually it was discovered that in part the relationship of psychiatrists to some patients also was a combination of logical and well-adjusted attitudes with some attitudes which were not so logical. But a word of warning at this point: Honesty in self-scrutiny should not become a self-depreciation or a new kind of hairshirt. Fundamentally most psychiatrists can use maturity and logic to a sufficient degree in their attitudes toward patients.

Further, since this talk will focus on the difficulties of being a psychiatrist, it is imperative to say that one of the greatest assets of psychiatrists has been their attempt to be honest with themselves. I know of no other group in man's history in which the members of the group have shown as extensive an attempt to be honest in looking at themselves, honest not only about major issues, but honest also about minor and subtle issues. This was so from the early days in which Freud found that certain of his own attitudes were interfering with his work with patients and realized that he must do something about it and do it quickly, to the later days in which he found that some of his pupils were having some feelings and attitudes toward patients which were hindering their treatment, and to this decade in which a resident-in-training in psychiatry is expected to be honest with the faculty about his own feelings throughout his long period of training.

The items about which he must be honest, his nonlogical feelings and attitudes toward patients, are, as you know, given the label of countertransference, a term chosen to designate the fact that there is a stream of possibly disturbing or blocking attitudes going from psychiatrist to patient, counter to the direction of the transference, which is from patient to psychiatrist.

In this setting, of trying with honesty to see and to deal with countertransference feelings, there developed the extraordinary process of supervision, in which the psychiatrist-in-training exposes his strengths and his weaknesses, his personal feelings and responses, to his supervisor, so that through honesty he can learn to be stronger and more effective.

Then came a period that seemed devastating. Psychiatrists learned more and tried to help more kinds of patients, and succeeded with many, fully or in part. But an increase in the positives was found to be associated with an increase in the negatives. The profound and far-reaching increase in the ability of the psychiatrist to help his patients through a new version of psychotherapy (as well as with other techniques, such as the use of drugs) was associated with the recognition that in many small and subtle and complex ways certain of the attitudes of the psychiatrist might interfere with the process as he wanted to have it go for the sake of the patient. No longer was it enough for the psychiatrist as physician merely to be guided by the good but simple admonitions of the Hippocratic Oath. There was only an infinitesimal danger now that he would seduce a patient of the same or of the opposite sex during the process of psychotherapy. There was no real danger that he deliberately would give a medicine which would hurt or kill the patient. Rarely were these gross problems, which were so emphasized in the Hippocratic Oath, actually of concern to the psychiatrist. Rather as his power to help patients increased, the number of hidden and subtle booby-traps in the process of psychotherapy increased.

Let me give a few examples of countertransference, to make sure we are traveling the same road and are preparing the groundwork for our own Oath for Psychiatrists. And, approaching our material from a slightly different angle, let me start with some examples which appear in general medical practice, and in psychiatry as well.

The essence of professional work is human helpfulness, and the essence of the work of the physician, including the psychiatrist, is that he has sympathy and that he wants to help those in pain, in sickness, in trouble. Yet the first booby-trap to mention is the danger of excessive sympathy. Time after time it is clear that a physician who is too sympathetic with sick people may pamper his patients, may make them realize too vividly that sickness has its pleasures and values, and so may delay their recovery.

Conversely, a physician who is overdemanding that his patients be strong and mature and self-reliant may do damage by holding up to his patients an impossible ideal. Patients of such a physician may become excessively critical of their own human limitations, may ignore their actual need for rest, for leisure, and for recuperation, and may struggle too strenuously to be as strong as the physician seems to expect them to be.

Another type of mistake can be called excessive therapeutic ambition. All professional people should have ambition, should try to help others improve, and legitimately should try to build their own security and prestige in part by being successful, by developing a reputation for helping their patients or their clients quickly and thoroughly. Such an ambition is of real value to a doctor and to his patient, and of value to a lawyer and his client. But in medical work, including psychiatry, therapeutic ambition may be excessive and so defeat its own ends. If the physician is insecure and has too great a need for fame and fortune, he then may have too great a need for cured cases, for the kind of case which gives a big boost to his prestige. He then may become impatient with patients who do not respond, or in an open or concealed fashion may be angry and resentful toward them. The emotions of anger and resentment that arise when excessive therapeutic ambition is thwarted are not conducive to clear thinking nor to the gradual working through of a difficult problem. And further, a patient may sense the physician's impatience and resentment, and become anxious or resentful or self-critical, so that a secondary conflict is superimposed on the primary problem which still is unsolved.

Another countertransference problem has to do with the temptation to reveal a patient's personal confidences. The problem of confidentiality is more urgent in psychiatry than in the general practice of medicine either in the age of Hippocrates or in the twentieth century. This is so because the essence of psychiatry is the discussion of private and confidential material. In fact, it may amuse you to know that in the famous case several years ago in which the psychiatrist Roy Grinker almost went to jail for contempt of court when he refused to give a hospital psychiatric record to a presiding judge he was saved from the jail sentence by the fact that Judge Fisher decided that the process of psychiatric work was based on the patient having enough trust in the psychiatrist so that he, or she, could tell things to the psychiatrist which he might tell no one else. Judge Fisher's decision was that confidentiality must be completely preserved when it was confidential material given either to a psychiatrist or to a lawyer, and that the degree of confidentiality to be expected was far greater in those two instances than it was in connection with the confidences given to a clergyman or to a nonpsychiatrist physician. Of course, this contrast may be questioned, but I give it as a pertinent example of the fact that in the practice of psychiatry the patient is forming a relationship with another human being which in a way is unique, is similar in Judge Fisher's decision only to that of a client with a lawyer. And between these two there are obvious differences.

The uniqueness of the relationship then calls for a high degree of maturity of response on the part of the psychiatrist. And he must recognize that in the practice of psychiatry he may be tempted at times by his extensive knowledge of personal confidential material to break confidence.

But the problems posed by the trusting attitude of the patient go far beyond the problem of confidentiality. The process of psychotherapy, which requires the patient to entrust the psychiatrist with shame-connected or guilt-connected confidential facts and fantasies, sometimes means that the patient has decided deeply to trust another human being. Such a process of trust is for many patients identical with the process of being deeply dependent on the other person. And some patients feel that their trusting attitude should bring the reward of their being completely cared for by an all-powerful helper and leader, on whom they can be dependent. The psychiatrist wants the patient to trust him and wants him to have a limited dependence during a limited period, but not to have a far-reaching dependence on him. This is the logic of the situation. But when the patient repeatedly wants to be excessively dependent on the psychiatrist and wants to think of the psychiatrist as a god-like person, as marvelously wise and strong and powerful, there may develop in the psychiatrist the nonlogical temptation to feel as if he were in truth all-powerful, as if he were an Atlas who could hold up the whole world of patients, or an all-giving mother with an ever-flowing breast. Surely in an important part of his Hippocratic Oath the psychiatrist must resolve deeply to withstand the temptation to play the role of being one on whom other human beings become so dependent that they will use him unendingly as a crutch, to their own detriment and to his eventual defeat in his prime purpose of improvement and cure.

It becomes clear that the problems faced by the psychiatrist are several thousand years beyond the problems mentioned in the Oath of Hippocrates. In the twentieth century, the psychiatrist must have a much more sophisticated kind of Oath, must say that he will do his best not to let any of his human imperfections interfere with his psychotherapy and with the decency and maturity of his attitude toward his patients. And he must do so even under those circumstances in which patients are searching for his weak spots. And such is a typical day-by-day experience in the life of a psychiatrist. The man psychiatrist who is bald must expect to hear many times about his baldness and about the fact that this to the patient represents a lack of masculinity. The psychiatrist must be able to deal with such remarks without a personalized comment, with a full recognition of the fact that it has to do with the patient's conflicts and needs at the moment. The psychiatrist knows that if he is able to respond in such a fashion, he then may set in motion a process that can be far-reaching. Patients thereby may learn that verbal attacks and impulses of hostility to others are not as death-dealing or devastating or humiliating as they always had thought. Patients may come to see that sincere and well-motivated responses actually exist in life, and this may be the starting point for an identification on their part with the simple decency of the response of the psychiatrist.

A psychiatrist who is a member of a minority group must expect to have that fact be mentioned to him in hostile fashion many times indeed and be able to deal with such comments on the basis of responses which are best for the patient rather than those which would give him relief by some sort of counterattack. Surely a part of the Hippocratic Oath for psychiatrists must be that he develop a capacity for being nonpunitive and nonjudgmental and have the capacity to absorb without much turmoil, and clearly without counterattack, the hostility directed toward him from patients who have been stirred by the process of psychotherapy, and by the processes of life. And he must never confuse the issue by failing to recognize the fundamental decency of the patient which underlies his anxiety and his unpleasant defenses.

Further, in the good leadership of the psychiatrist, a realistic limit-setting is necessary. Patients are not to be permitted to insult the secretary when the patient is angry at the psychiatrist for repeating an interpretation which the patient does not want to hear. In fact, one goal should be to set limits on the verbal sallies at the psychiatrist under such circumstances and to have the patient reach the point of being able to say, "It's at this point I know I'd like to try to insult you again." In differing ways in different patients, limit-setting and strong leadership may be essential, but a punitive attitude would be countertransference nonsense.

And as another example, the problem of permissiveness can be mentioned. A permissiveness to patients to express in words the hidden fantasies and impulses that are not put into action is of high value as part of the curative process. But a permissiveness to patients to act out destructively toward others or toward themselves is a countertransference mistake.

Another frequent countertransference mistake is that of "taking sides" in a disagreement between a patient and his relatives. Often an inexperienced psychiatrist-in-training "sides with" an adult patient who gives a vivid story of the mistakes made by his or her children. And often a resident in his first experience in child psychiatry "sides with" the child who seems to have been badly rejected and frustrated by one of its parents. In either case, the evaluation made by the psychiatrist-in-training may be right or may be wrong, but the "taking sides" attitude rarely is productive.

I vividly remember one day when I made ward-rounds with one and then the other of two residents in their first month of training. Each was to give a ten-minute summary of each of five of his ward-patients. The first resident, in his separate summaries of his five patients, told me, without noticing the pattern, that in four of the five cases, the patients had become disturbed because of the unfair attitudes and pressures of their families and their supervisors at work. The second resident, in his separate summaries of his five patients, told me, without noticing the pattern, that in four of his five cases, the patients had been very difficult indeed in their unfair attitudes toward their families and toward their associates at work. I was amused by the happenstance of the sharp contrast. I knew that it might have been a chance affair, so I arranged a month later for a presentation by the same two residents, each to give summaries of five patients. This time the first resident mentioned that three of the five had been disturbed by their families and others. And this time the second resident mentioned that two or three had been very difficult to their families and others. So in all probability, the pattern of each was one for the faculty and for the residents to work on carefully. And in addition, the lower percentage, hopefully, could have been a measure of the growth of the residents during a month's period in the training program.

In this problem in psychotherapy, the issue is clear. If there is a "taking of sides" by the psychiatrist, he limits his effectiveness. For example, if we consider only the countertransference pattern in which the psychiatrist is too identified with his patient, it becomes clear that the patient gets some temporary relief in having a person in authority agree with him, take sides with him. But in so doing, an important opportunity may be missed. The real improvement and the cure of the patient may be dependent on his having someone who can say to him, "Of course your relative or your business associate made some mistakes. But hold on, now, take a look at yourself in this. Usually mistakes are made on both sides. Your halo might be too tight. You too might have contributed to some of the turmoil. Let's take a look inside as well as outside."

So much for my first thesis, of the Hippocratic Oath as a document about countertransference, and for my second thesis, of the far greater subtlety and complexity in the responses of the psychiatrist than is outlined for the physician in the Hippocratic Oath. We come now to my third thesis, the need for an attempt to put into words a contemporary Hippocratic Oath for psychiatrists, and a statement of our group's attempt to deal with such problems.

One of the ways in which a serious effort has been made to prevent countertransference mistakes is by having the psychiatrist undergo psychotherapy himself. In that area of psychiatry which is called psychoanalysis, and the training for which is done in one of the recognized institutes for psychoanalysis, the psychoanalysis of the psychiatrist who is to do psychoanalysis is a routine and absolute requirement. In the institutes this is followed by extensive formal and informal education and by intensive and close supervision, in which again there is a process of observing the various indications of countertransference and of helping the psychoanalyst-in-training in his attempt to minimize or eliminate them, or to use them constructively. This is the process of training in psychoanalysis which may be undertaken after residency training in general psychiatry.

But these days, such full training in psychoanalysis is only one of the accepted and respected patterns. In the past twenty-five years there has been a widespread and successful attempt to introduce a large amount of psychoanalytic understanding and principles into the general practice of psychiatry. There has emerged a kind of training in dynamic psychotherapy which can be done by a psychiatrist who has not had full training in a psychoanalytic institute, a psychotherapy which in a large number of instances can be very effective indeed, a psychotherapy which makes broad and general use of the principles of psychoanalytic understanding and of psychoanalytic therapy, but which differs from psychoanalysis *per se* in a number of significant ways. It deals with the problems of patients on a less deep-going level, and with much less development of transference-neurotic responses. And in the training for such a psychoanalytically oriented variety of psychotherapy in the hands of the general psychiatrist, it has been found possible to avoid a large number of the countertransference mistakes without requiring the psychiatrist to have psychotherapy for himself. In some instances psychotherapy of the psychiatrist is called for and may be tremendously valuable. But in the majority of cases it now seems probable that the tendency to make countertransference mistakes in dynamic psychotherapy can be minimized sufficiently by intensive supervision by experienced psychiatrists, in the form both of individual supervision and group supervision, plus extensive education in clinical and dynamic psychiatry. And the training in dynamic psychotherapy is only part of his total training, since he must have adequate expertness in diagnosis, in work with in-patients as well as out-patients, in the use of drugs and other physical techniques, and in all of the other aspects of contemporary psychiatry.

And in the total process, the training center deals with the problem of countertransference in a number of ways. It exercises great care in the selection of applicants for training in psychiatry. It emphasizes teaching by individual supervision. It provides organized teaching sessions for the psychiatrists-in-training about the problems of countertransference as well as the other aspects of the practice of psychiatry. And especially it provides large numbers of conferences in which the psychiatrists-in-training observe their colleagues, the other psychiatrists-in-training, present their work, with the leader of the seminar and the others of the group discussing the various aspects of the treatment process, including any indications of countertransference, followed then by intensive discussion of the methods of improving the process of therapy.

Then, his training over, he begins work as psychiatrist in one of the armed forces, or he takes a position in a medical school, in a hospital, in a clinic, in research, in teaching, or in private practice, or in some combination of these. What must he say; what must he do? What kind of an oath might he take?

My suggestion is that in an implicit, unspoken way each psychiatrist does take a sort of oath, does say something to his own conscience, to his own need for self-respect and the respect of others. Unfortunately, for this paper, such a Hippocratic Oath for Psychiatrists cannot be as succinct and pointed as was the original oath, since the issues are immeasurably more subtle and sophisticated. This might be the Psychiatrist's Oath:

> I am deeply moved by the fact that my profession is one which has high human ideals and aspirations. I know that psychiatrists are not perfect and need not be, but I profoundly honor their attempt to do a good job and to practice their profession with honesty and self-respect. I know that I too am far from perfect, but I will make a sincere attempt to do a really decent job. I shall

certainly follow the good advice of the Hippocratic Oath. I shall avoid the felonies, the misdemeanors, and the misbehavior referred to in the original oath. And if ever I find myself doing a medical treatment for which I am not prepared, or trying to be seductive to a patient, I will recognize that I have a serious neurotic disorder, and try to get treatment. If I am unable to bring myself to treatment, I will give up my work with patients or confine my activities to fields in which there will be no temptation.

And even though I have no such obvious neurotic reactions to my patients, I often will turn my eyes and ears inward, to see if in any way my own emotional attitudes are keeping me from functioning at my best level. I know that patients will respond inappropriately far more often than I will, but I will not hide behind that fact. Indeed, each physician of any specialty or in general practice must be aware of his own attitudes and thoughts and feelings, to see if at any time they are interfering with the quality of his work with patients. As a psychiatrist, I have that obligation even more than do other physicians. And no matter what treatment I use, I will examine my choice with care. I will not give drugs because I am impatient, nor use psychotherapy because I have free time.

I will observe myself as well as my patients. And if, in this recurrent process of stringent self-scrutiny, at any time I detect in myself too much anxiety, too much sympathy, too much coolness, or too much conceit, or diffidence, or leniency, or strictness, or any other excessive attitudes, I will make an honest attempt to modify them by my own efforts.

But I shall not permit such a stringent honesty to become a new kind of scrupulosity, a new kind of hairshirt, or a striving for superhuman perfection. I know that training in medicine, and training in psychiatry, these days is good enough so that the relationship of most psychiatrists with most patients, even in the more subtle issues, is very workable indeed. But if an inappropriate attitude or response to a patient persists in spite of my efforts, I will arrange at my own expense for a period of the kind of consultation which is called supervision, in which another experienced psychiatrist will consider thoroughly my work with the patient. And fortunately such an expense is tax-deductible!

Further, in such supervision I will avoid breaking confidentiality. I will change the identifying facts about the patient so as to conceal his identity and the identity of anyone mentioned by him.

If, however, even after a stringent self-scrutiny, I do not see any issues in my own personality that interfere with my work, I shall breathe a sigh of relief.

But, if my self-scrutiny does not convince me definitely one way or the other, but, as a third possibility, leaves me uncertain and uncomfortable, I shall consider the various ways of having a check by others on my work. Under these circumstances, I could arrange for some hours of supervision, of the sort mentioned above. Or, I could discuss my work, preserving confidentiality, with a contemporary who, I know, will not withhold criticism and suggestions out of his friendship with me.

Or, if I work in a group or in a hospital or in a clinic in which there are active staff discussions of patients in treatment, I shall arrange to present my case-material for critical discussion and suggestions—again preserving confidentiality.

And I shall give serious consideration to a plan which may be the best of the alternatives. This would be to join, or to organize, a small seminar group of peers, to present and to discuss the work of each in rotation. Such a seminar might consist of three to five psychiatrists, meeting at regular intervals, in an arrangement which could continue for many years after my training is over. The psychiatrists of such a group would be chosen on the basis of competence and congeniality and friendship, so that each can feel that the comments of the others are essentially helpful even when they are critical.

In such a seminar, I will present samples of my work for evaluation, hoping that the others will comment on the strong points of my work which I then can develop further, and hoping further that they will notice any mistakes which I had not noticed, and make productive suggestions for a change. Such a group could play a vital role in my continuing development.

Before joining such a seminar, I will take an oath far more difficult than any portion of the Oath as written by Hippocrates. I promise to present to the group not only examples of work which I think were good, but also examples of work about which I was doubtful, and especially examples of my work taken at random. And in such a seminar, as in the other plans, I will preserve confidentiality.

And I hope very deeply that I will retain perspective about myself, that I never will think that being a psychiatrist means living on Mount Olympus. Rather I will use images about myself that are far from godlike. I will merely hope that in my work I can improve my batting average, that I can stay on the fairway, and that the patient and I can form a cooperative team to work toward his improvement and cure.

For I know that it is not necessary to feel that I am Olympian, nor to feel small and helpless. I know that it is enough to belong to the human species, to be at the level of men and women, strengthened by thorough training. Then the practice of psychiatry can be infinitely rewarding in the satisfactions of human helpfulness.

We, as psychiatrists, will not give up when we stumble. Our job has rough moments, but it is enormously worth doing, it is idealistic but practical, and it is thoroughly alive. We hope deeply that we can grow in stature as we practice, not only in our scientific and technical knowledge and ability, but also in our strength, our maturity, and our integrity. This is our hope, our Oath.

NOTES AND BIBLIOGRAPHIES

Notes to Introduction by Margaret Mead

1. See p. 251.
2. See p. 259.
3. The contents of this memorandum are largely incorporated in the Postscript.

Notes to Part I

1. Darwin, Charles, *Autobiography and Selected Letters*, p. 45.
2. See Edel, Abraham, *Science and the Structure of Ethics*, and Feuer, Lewis, *Psychoanalysis and Ethics*.
3. Abraham, Karl, *Selected Papers*, p. 480.
4. A similar conclusion was reached by C. H. Waddington, in *The Ethical Animal*, p. 26, footnote 1.
5. Related in conversation with Maurice Friedman, his translator.
6. *International Journal of Psycho-Analysis*, Vol. 49, pp. 109–112.
7. Huxley, T. H., and Huxley, J. S., *Touchstone for Ethics;* Hofstadter, Richard, *Social Darwinism in American Thought.*
8. For extensive reports of the group behavior of the primates, the animals most closely related to man, see the books listed in the Selected Bibliography by Roe and Simpson, Washburn, DeVore, Hinde, Altman, Jay, Goodall, and others.
9. See the books in the Selected Bibliography by Lorenz, Chauvin, and Tinbergen.
10. Clough, Garret C., *American Scientist*, 53:199–212, 1965.
11. *American Scientist*, 54:244–272, 1966.
12. *My Friends the Wild Chimpanzees.*
13. For a discussion of various patterns of interrelating the studies of nonhuman primates to the study of man, see Mason, W. A., "Scope and Potential of Primate Research," in *Animal and Human*, p. 101.
14. Cannon credits the phrase to E. R. Starling in his Harvey Lecture of 1923.
15. Mason, W. A., *Science and Psychoanalysis*, Vol. 12.
16. *Childhood and Society*, p. 253; *Identity, Youth, and Crisis*, p. 136.
17. Waelder, Robert, "The Principle of Multiple Function: Observations on Over Determinism."
18. For important basic studies of the conflict between the generations, see Mead, Margaret, *Culture and Commitment*; Feuer, Lewis, *The Conflict of Generations*; Keniston, Keith, "Student Activism, Moral Development, and Morality."
19. In Margaret Mead's *Male and Female*, p. 65, she deals with a comparable ambiguity by a productive discussion of symmetry in the relations between men and women.
20. Fortes, Meyer, *Oedipus and Job* . . . , p. 11.
21. *Ibid.*, pp. 31, 27, 31.
22. *Ibid.*, pp. 31, 68.
23. A comparable reformulation of the problem of determinism and freedom is underway in other sciences. See, for example, the publications of two biologists: Wald, George, chapter on "Determinacy, Individuality and the Problem of Free

Will," in Platt's *New Views of the Nature of Man*, p. 17; Dobzhansky, Theodosius, *The Biology of Ultimate Concern*.

24. For a further discussion of this aspect of work with patients, see the author's chapter on "Psychiatric Treatment," in Alexander, F. and Ross, H., *Dynamic Psychiatry*, and in *The Impact of Freudian Psychiatry*. See also Mark, V. H., and Ervin, F. R., *Violence and the Brain*.

25. See Fletcher, Joseph, *The Situation Ethics Debate*.

26. Kekule, Friedrich A., *Zeitschrift Für Chemie*, 3:217. Also *Dreams and Visions in a Century of Chemistry*, Edward Farber.

27. This is similar to what has been called lateral thinking, by DeBono, in several recent books.

28. See Waddington's concept of man as an ethicizing animal.

Bibliography to Part I

THE following list is presented essentially as a guide for the general reader, rather than for the specialist. It consists largely of a selection of books which are closely related either to the overall thesis of this book or to the specific topics discussed in the individual chapters.

In addition, the list includes the articles and books which are cited as references in the text:

Abraham, Karl: "Origins and Growth of Object Love," in *Selected Papers of Karl Abraham, M.D.*, trans. by Douglas Bryan and Alix Strachey, London: Hogarth Press and the Institute of Psychoanalysis, 1927.

Academy of Religion and Mental Health—Proceedings of the 6th Academy: *Moral Values in Psychoanalysis*, New York, 1965.

Adler, Mortimer J.: *The Difference of Man and the Difference It Makes*, New York: Holt, Rinehart and Winston, 1967.

Adler, Mortimer J.: *The Time of Our Lives*, New York: Holt, Rinehart & Winston, 1970.

Albert, Ethel M., and Kluckhohn, C. K. M.: *A Selected Bibliography on Values, Ethics, and Esthetics in The Behavioral Sciences and Philosophy, 1920–1958*, New York: Free Press, 1959.

Alexander, Franz: "The Logic of Emotions and Its Dynamic Background," *International Journal of Psychoanalysis*, 16:399–413, 1935.

Alexander, Franz: "The Voice of the Intellect Is Soft," *Psychoanalytic Review*, 28(1): 12–29, Jan. 1941.

Alexander, Franz: *Fundamentals of Psychoanalysis*, New York: W. W. Norton, 1948.

Alexander, Franz: *Psychosomatic Medicine*, New York: W. W. Norton, 1950.

Alexander, Franz: *Twenty Years of Psychoanalysis*, New York: W. W. Norton, 1953.

Alexander, Franz: *Psychoanalysis and Psychotherapy: Developments in Theory, Technique and Training* (1st edition), New York: W. W. Norton, 1956.

Alexander, Franz: *Western Mind in Transition*, New York: Random House, 1960.

Alexander, Franz, (ed.): *The Scope of Psychoanalysis*, New York: Basic Books, 1961.

Alexander, Franz, and Healy, William: *Roots of Crime: Psychoanalytic Studies*, New York: Alfred A. Knopf, 1935.

Alexander, Franz; Eisenstein, Samuel; and Grotjahn, Martin (eds.): *Psychoanalytic Pioneers*, New York: Basic Books, 1966.

Alexander, Peter: "Rational Behaviour and Psychoanalytic Explanation," *Mind*, LXXI:326–341, July 1962.

Al-Issa, Ihsan, and Dennis, Wayne (eds.): *Cross-Cultural Studies of Behavior*, New York: Holt, Rinehart and Winston, 1970.

Alland, Alexander, Jr.: *Evolution and Human Behavior*, Garden City: Natural History Press, 1967.

Alland, Alexander, Jr.: *Adaptation in Cultural Evolution: An Approach to Medical Anthropology*, New York: Columbia University Press, 1970.

Allee, Warder C.: *The Social Life of Animals*, Boston: Beacon, 1958.

Alsberg, Paul: *In Quest of Man: A Biological Approach to the Problem of Man's Place in Nature*, Elmsford, New York: Pergamon, 1970.

Altmann, Stuart A. (ed.): *Social Communication Among Primates*, Chicago: University of Chicago Press, 1967.

Anthony, E. James, and Benedek, Therese (eds.): *Parenthood: Its Psychology and Psychopathology*, Boston: Little, Brown, 1970.

Ardrey, Robert: *The Social Contract*, New York: Atheneum, 1970.

Arendt, Hannah: *The Human Condition*, Chicago: University of Chicago Press, 1958.

Arendt, Hannah: *On Violence*, New York: Harcourt, Brace and World, 1970.

Arieti, Silvano (ed.): *American Handbook of Psychiatry*, 3 vols., New York: Basic Books, 1959.

Aring, Charles (ed.): *Man and Life*—Sesquicentennial Year, University of Cincinnati, Occasional Paper No. 7, 1969.

Arlow, Jacob: "Ego Psychology," in *The Annual Survey of Psychoanalysis*, Vol. I, Frosch, J. (ed.), New York: International Universities Press, 1952.

Arlow, Jacob, and Brenner, Charles: *Psychoanalytic Concepts and the Structural Theory*, New York: International Universities Press, 1964.

Arlow, Jacob: *The Legacy of Sigmund Freud*, New York: International Universities Press, 1956.

Aronfreed, Justin: *Conduct and Conscience*, New York: Academic Press, 1968.

Aronson, L. R., Tobach, E., Lehrman, D. S., and Rosenblatt, J. S. (eds.): *Development and Evolution of Behavior: Essays in Memory of T. C. Schneirla*, San Francisco: W. H. Freeman, 1970.

Balint, Michael: "The three areas of the mind," *International Journal of Psychoanalysis*, 39, Part 5:328–340, 1958.

Balint, Michael: "Ego Strength and Education of the Ego," *Psychoanalytic Quarterly*, (11):87–95, 1942.

Balint, Michael: *Primary Love and Psychoanalytic Technique*, London: Hogarth, 1952.

Balint, Michael: *The Doctor, His Patient and the Illness*, New York: International Universities Press, 1957.

Balint, Michael: *Thrills and Regressions*, New York: International Universities Press, 1959.

Balint, Michael: *The Basic Fault*, London: Tavistock Publications, 1968.

Banfield, Edward C.: *The Moral Basis of a Backward Society*, Glencoe: Free Press, 1958.

Bang, Frederik B.: "Introduction to Behavior Studies," in *Biology of Populations*, Sladen, B. K., and Bang, F. B., New York: American Elsevier, 1969.

Barbour, Ian: *Issues in Science and Religion*, Englewood Cliffs: Prentice-Hall, 1966.

Barbour, Ian: *Science and Secularity: The Ethics of Technology*, New York: Harper and Row, 1970.

Barnett, Homer G.: *Innovation: The Basis of Cultural Change,* New York: McGraw-Hill, 1953.

Barnett, S. A.: *A Century of Darwin,* Cambridge, Mass.: Harvard University Press, 1958.

Barnett, S. A.: *Instinct and Intelligence,* Englewood Cliffs: Prentice-Hall, 1967.

Barrett, William, and Aiken, Henry D. (eds.); *Philosophy in the 20th Century,* New York: Random House, 1962.

Bates, Marston, and Humphrey, Philip S. (eds.): *The Darwin Reader,* New York, Charles Scribner's Sons, 1956.

Bateson, William, F. R. S.: "Biological Fact and the Structure of Society," pp. 334-355 in *Wm. Bateson, F. R. S., Naturalist, His Essays and Addresses,* Cambridge University Press, 1928.

Bayles, Michael D. (ed.): *Contemporary Utilitarianism,* Garden City: Anchor Books, 1968.

Beadle, George, and Beadle, Muriel: *The Language of Life,* New York: Doubleday, 1966.

Becker, C. L.: *Progress and Power,* Stanford: Stanford University Press, 1935.

Becker, Ernest: *The Structure of Evil,* New York: George Braziller, 1968.

Beckner, Morton: *The Biological Way of Thought,* Berkeley: University of California Press, 1968.

Bell, Daniel: *The End of Ideology,* Glencoe: Free Press, 1960.

Bell, Daniel (ed.): *Toward the Year 2000: Work in Progress,* Boston: Houghton Mifflin, 1968.

Bell, Peter R. (ed.): *Darwin's Biological Work: Some Aspects Reconsidered,* London: Cambridge University Press, 1959.

Bendix, Reinhard: *Embattled Reason. Essays on Social Knowledge,* New York: Oxford University Press, 1970.

Benedict, Ruth: *Patterns of Culture,* Boston: Houghton Mifflin, 1934.

Benedict, Ruth: "The Natural History of War," pp. 369–382, in *An Anthropologist at Work,* Mead, Margaret, Boston: Houghton Mifflin, 1959.

Benjamin, Abram Cornelius: *Science, Technology, and Human Values,* Columbia: University of Missouri Press, 1965.

Berdyaev, Nicolas: *The Destiny of Man,* New York: Harper & Row, 1960.

Beres, David: "Psychoanalytic Notes on the History of Morality," *Journal of the American Psychoanalytic Association,* 13(1):3–37, 1965.

Bergler, Edmund: *The Superego: Unconscious Conscience,* New York: Grune and Stratton, 1952.

Berkowitz, Leonard: *Aggression: A Social Psychological Analysis,* New York: McGraw-Hill, 1962.

Berkowitz, Leonard: "Aggressive Stimuli, Aggressive Responses and Hostility Catharsis," in *Science and Psychoanalysis,* Vol. VI, *Violence and War,* Masserman, Jules H. (ed.), New York: Grune and Stratton, 1963.

Berkowitz, Leonard (ed.): *Advances in Experimental Social Psychology,* New York: Academic Press, 1964.

Berkowitz, Leonard: *The Development of Motives and Values in the Child,* New York: Basic Books, 1964.

Berle, Adolf A.: *Power Without Property,* New York: Harcourt, Brace, 1959.

Bernal, John D.: *The World, the Flesh and the Devil*, Bloomington: Indiana University Press, 1969.

Berrill, N. J.: *Man's Emerging Mind: Man's Progress Through Time*, New York: Dodd, Mead, 1955.

Bettelheim, Bruno: *The Informed Heart: Autonomy in a Mass Age*, Glencoe: Free Press, 1960.

Bidney, David: *The Concept of Freedom in Anthropology*, The Hague: Mouton, 1963.

Binkley, Luther J.: *Contemporary Ethical Theories*, New York: Philosophical Library, 1961.

Bishop, W. W., and Clark, J. D. (eds.): *Background to Evolution in Africa*, Chicago: University of Chicago Press, 1967.

Blackett, Patrick M. S.: *The Gap Widens*, London: Cambridge University Press, 1970.

Blest, A. D.: "The concept of 'ritualization,'" in *Current Problems in Animal Behavior*, Thorpe and Zangwill (eds.), Cambridge: Cambridge University Press, 1961, pp. 102–24.

Bliss, Eugene L. (ed.): *Roots of Behavior*, New York: Harper and Row, 1962.

Bloch, H. A., and Geis, G.: *Man, Crime and Society*, New York: Random House, 1962.

Blos, P.: *On Adolescence*, New York: Free Press, 1962.

Boelkins, R. C., and Heiser, J.: "Biological Bases of Aggression," in *Violence and the Struggle for Existence*, Daniels, D. N., Gilula, M. F., and Ochberg, F. M. (eds.), Boston: Little, Brown, 1970.

Bohannan, Paul (ed.): *Law and Warfare*, New York: Natural History Press, 1967.

Bohannan, Paul: *Love, Sex and Being Human*, New York: Doubleday, 1969.

Bohr, Aage: "Concepts of Nuclear Structure," in *Science*, 172 (3978):17–21, April 2, 1971.

Booth, Verne H.: *Elements of Physical Science: The Nature of Matter and Energy*, New York: Macmillan, 1970.

Boulding, Kenneth E.: *A Primer on Social Dynamics: History as Dialectics and Development*, New York: Free Press, 1970.

Boulding, Kenneth E.: *Conflict and Defense: A General Theory*, New York: Harper and Row, 1962.

Boulding, Kenneth E.: *Beyond Economics: Essays on Society, Religion and Ethics*, Ann Arbor: University of Michigan Press, 1968.

Bourke, Vernon J.: *History of Ethics*, Garden City: Doubleday, 1968.

Bowker, John: *Problems of Suffering in Religions of the World*, Cambridge: Cambridge University Press, 1970.

Bowlby, J.: "An Ethological Approach to Research in Child Development," *British Journal of Medical Psychology*, London, 30(4) December 9, 1957, pp. 230–240.

Boyko, Hugo (ed.): *Science and the Future of Mankind*, The Hague: W. Junk, 1964.

Braidwood, Robert J.; "Archeology and Evolutionary Theory," in *Evolution and Anthropology: A Centennial Appraisal*, Meggers, Betty J. (ed.): Anthropological Society of Washington, 1959.

Braidwood, Robert J., and Wiley, Gordon R. (eds.): *Courses Toward Urban Life*, Chicago: Aldine, 1962.

Brain, Walter Russell: *Science and Man*, New York: American Elsevier, 1966.

Breggin, Peter: "Psychotherapy as Applied Ethics," in *Psychiatry*, 34(1):59–74, Feb. 1971.

Bridgman, P. W.: *The Way Things Are*, Cambridge: Harvard University Press, 1959.

Bridger, W. H.: "Ethological Concepts and Human Develpoment," pp. 95–107, in *Recent Advances in Biological Psychiatry*, Vol. IV, Wortis, J. (ed.), New York: Plenum, 1962.

Brierley, Marjorie: *Trends in Psycho-Analysis*, London: Hogarth, 1951.

Broad, C. D.: *Five Types of Ethical Theory*, New York: Harcourt Brace, 1930.

Broad, C. D.: "Symposium on the Relations Between Science and Ethics," by C. H. Waddington, A. C. Ewing, and C. D. Broad, *Proceedings of the Aristotelian Society*, 65–100H, London: Harrison & Sons, 1942; C. D. Broad's contribution pp. 100A–100H.

Bronowski, Jacob: *Science and Human Values*, New York: Harper and Row, 1965.

Bronowski, Jacob: *The Identity of Man*, Garden City: Natural History Press, 1965.

Bronowski, Jacob: *The Face of Violence*, Cleveland: World, 1967.

Bronwell, Arthur B. (ed.): *Science and Technology in The World of the Future*, New York: Wiley-Interscience, 1970.

Brown, Norman O.: *Life Against Death: The Psychoanalytic Meaning of History*, Middletown, Conn.: Wesleyan University Press, 1959.

Brown, Roger: *Social Psychology*, New York: Free Press, 1965.

Brunswik, Egon: "The Conceptual Framework of Psychology," in *International Encyclopedia of Unified Science*, Vol. 1, No. 10, Chicago: University of Chicago Press, 1952.

Buber, Martin: "Distance and Relation," *Psychiatry* 20:97–104, 1941.

Buber, Martin: "Guilt and Guilt Feelings," *Psychiatry* 20:114–129, 1957.

Buber, Martin: *I and Thou*, New York: Charles Scribner's Sons, 1958.

Buber, Martin: *Between Man and Man*, New York: Macmillan, 1965.

Burke, John G. (ed.): *The New Technology and Human Values*, Belmont, California: Wadsworth Publishing Co., 1966.

Burnham, John: "Psychoanalysis and American Medicine: 1894–1918: Medicine, Science and Culture," *Psychological Issues*, Vol. V, No. 4, Monogr. 20, 1967.

Burnshaw, Stanley: *The Seamless Web*. Language-Thinking. Creative Knowledge. Art-Experience. New York: George Braziller, 1970.

Bush, V.: *Endless Horizons*, Washington, D. C.: Public Affairs Press, 1946.

Bychowski, Gustav: *Evil in Man: The Anatomy of Hate and Violence*, New York: Grune & Stratton, 1968.

Calder, N. (ed.): *Unless Peace Comes: A Scientific Forecast of New Weapons*, New York: Viking, 1968.

Calhoun, J. B.: "The Lemmings' Periodic Journeys Are Not Unique," *Smithsonian*, 1(10):6–12, Jan. 1971.

Callan, Hilary: *Ethology and Society*, Oxford: Oxford University Press, 1970.

Campbell, Bernard: *Human Evolution, an Introduction to Man's Adaptations*, Chicago: Aldine, 1966.

Cannon, W. B.: *Bodily Changes in Pain, Anger, Fear, and Rage*, 2nd edition, New York: D. Appleton, 1929.

Cannon, W. B.: *The Wisdom of the Body*, New York: W. W. Norton, 1939.

Cardozo, Benjamin N.: *The Nature of the Judicial Process*, New Haven: Yale University Press, 1921.

Carleton, William G.: *Technology and Humanism*, Nashville: Vanderbilt University Press, 1970.

Carthy, John D., and Ebling, F. J. (eds.): *The Natural History of Aggression*, New York: Academic Press, 1964.

Caspari, E. W.: "Some Genetic Implications of Human Evolution" in *Social Life of Early Man*, Washburn, Sherwood (ed.), Chicago: Aldine, 1961.

Cassidy, Harold G.: *Knowledge, Experience and Action: An Essay on Education*, New York: Teachers College Press, Columbia University, 1969.

Cassirer, Ernst: *An Essay on Man*, New Haven: Yale University Press, 1944.

Cassirer, Ernst: *Language and Myth*, New York and London: Harper and Bros., 1946.

Caudill, W.: "Anthropology and Psychoanalysis: Some Theoretical Issues," in *Anthropology and Human Behavior*, Gladwin, T. and Sturtevant, W. (eds.), Washington: Anthropological Society of Washington, 1962.

Chapple, Eliot D.: *Culture and Biological Man*, New York: Holt, Rinehart and Winston, 1970.

Chauvin, Remy: *Animal Societies*, New York: Hill and Wang, 1968.

Chein, I.: "The Awareness of self and the structure of the ego," *Psychological Review*, 51(4):304–314, July 1944.

Chein, I.: "The image of man," *Journal of Social Issues*, 18(4), 1–35, 1962.

Childe, V. Gordon: *Social Evolution*, London–New York: World, 1963.

Chisholm, George B.: *The Psychiatry of Enduring Peace and Social Progress*, William Alanson White Memorial Lectures, 2nd ser., Washington, D. C.: William Alanson White Psychiatric Foundation, 1946.

Clausen, John A. (ed.): *Socialization and Society*, Boston: Little, Brown, 1968.

Clemente, C., and Lindsley, D. (eds.): *Aggression and Defense*, Berkeley: University of California Press, 1967.

Clough, Garret C.: "Lemmings and Population Problems," in *American Scientist*, 53, 199–212, 1965.

Cogan, L. Peter: *The Rhythmic Cycles of Optimism and Pessimism*, New York: William-Frederick, 1969.

Cohen, Felix S.: *Ethical Systems and Legal Ideas: An Essay on the Foundation of Legal Criticism*, New York: Falcon, 1933.

Cohen, Felix S.: *The Legal Conscience*, New Haven: Yale University Press, 1960.

Cohen, Morris Raphael: *Reason and Nature*, New York: Harcourt, Brace, 1931.

Cohen, Yehudi A.: *Man in Adaptation: The Biosocial Background*, Chicago: Aldine, 1968.

Colbert, Edwin H.: *Evolution of the Vertebrates*, 2nd ed., New York: Wiley, 1969.

Colby, Kenneth M.: *Energy and Stucture in Psychoanalysis*, New York: Ronald, 1955.

Coles, Robert: *Erik H. Erikson: The Growth of His Work*, Boston: Little, Brown, 1970.

Collias, N. E.: "Problems and Principles of Animal Sociology," in *Comparative Psychology*, Stone, C. P. (ed.), New York: Prentice-Hall, 1951.

Comfort, Alexander: *The Nature of Human Nature*, New York: Harper and Row, 1966.

Commoner, Barry: *Science and Survival*, New York: Viking, 1966.

Cooper, Joseph B., and McGaugh, James L.: *Integrating Principles of Social Psychology*, Cambridge: Schenkman, 1963.

Coser, Lewis A.: *The Functions of Social Conflict*, Glencoe: Free Press, 1956.

Cox, Harvey (ed.): *The Situation Ethics Debate*, Philadelphia: Westminster, 1968.

Cox, Harvey: *The Feast of Fools*, Noble Lectures, Cambridge: Harvard University Press, 1969.

Cranberg, L.: "Science, Ethics, and Law," *Zygon* 2(3), 262–271, Sept. 1967.

Crick, F.: *Of Molecules and Men*, Seattle: University of Washington Press, 1966.

Critchley, M.: "The Evolution of Man's Capacity for Language," in *Evolution After Darwin*, Tax, Sol (ed.), Chicago: University of Chicago Press, 1960.

Crockett, Campbell: "Ethics, Metaphysics, and Psychoanalysis," *Inquiry* 4(1):37–52, Spring 1961.

Crook, John Hurrell (ed.): *Social Behaviour in Birds and Mammals*, New York: Academic Press, 1970.

Crook, John Hurrell: "The Basis of Flock Organization in Birds," *Current Problems in Animal Behaviour*, Thorpe, W. H., and Zangwill, O. L. (eds.), Cambridge: Cambridge University Press, 1961.

Crovitz, Herbert F.: *Galton's Walk: Methods for the Analysis of Thinking, Intelligence, and Creativity*, New York: Harper and Row, 1970.

Crowe, Beryl L.: "The Tragedy of the Commons Revisited," *Science*, 166: 1103–1107, November 28, 1969.

Daedalus: *Science and Technology in Contemporary Society*, 91, (2), Spring 1962.

Dalberg-Acton, John Emerich Edward: *Essays on Freedom and Power*, Boston: Beacon, 1948.

D'Amato, M. R.: "Instrumental Conditioning," in *Learning Processes*, Marx, M. H. (ed.), London: Macmillan, 1969.

Daniels, D. N., Gilula, M. F., and Ochberg, F. M. (eds.): *Violence and the Struggle for Existence*, Boston: Little, Brown, 1970.

Darlington, Cyril D.: *Darwin's Place in History*, New York: Macmillan, 1961.

Darlington, Cyril D.: *The Evolution of Man and Society*, New York: Simon and Schuster, 1969.

Darwin, Charles: *On the Origin of Species*, London: J. M. Dant, 1956. Several other editions.

Darwin, Charles: *The Descent of Man*, 1871, 2nd edition, 1896. Several other editions. New York: D. Appleton.

Darwin, Frances (ed.): *The Autobiography of Charles Darwin and Selected Letters*, New York: Dover, 1958.

DeBono, Edward: *New Think*, New York: Basic Books, 1968.

Delgado, J. M. R.: *Physical Control of the Mind: Toward a Psychocivilized Society*, World Perspectives, Vol. 41, New York: Harper and Row, 1969.

DeReuck, Anthony V. and Knight, Julie (eds.): *Conflict in Society*, A CIBA Foundation Symposium, Boston: Little, Brown, 1966.

DeReuck, Anthony V., and Porter, Ruth (eds.): *Transcultural Psychiatry*, A CIBA Foundation Symposium, Boston: Little, Brown, 1965.

Dethier, V. G., and Stellar, Eliot: *Animal Behavior*, Englewood Cliffs: Prentice-Hall, 1970. 3rd edition.

Devereux, G.: "Normal and abnormal: The key problem of psychiatric anthropology," in *Some Uses of Anthropology: Theoretical and Applied*, Casagrande, J. B., and Gladwin, T. (eds.), Washington: Anthropological Society of Washington, 1956.

DeVore, Irven: "A Comparison of the Ecology and Behavior of Monkeys and Apes," in *Classification and Human Evolution*. Washburn, Sherwood L., (ed.), Chicago: Aldine, 1963.

DeVore, Irven, and Washburn, S. L.: "Baboon Ecology and Human Evolution," in *African Ecology and Human Evolution*, Howell, F. Clark, and Bourliere, F. (eds.), Chicago: Aldine, 1963.

DeVore, Irven (ed.): *Primate Behavior: Field Studies of Monkeys and Apes*, New York: Holt, Rinehart and Winston, 1965.

349

Dewey, John: *Human Nature and Conduct*, New York: H. Holt & Co., 1922.

Dewey, John: "Theory of Valuation," Vol. II, No. 4, *International Encyclopedia of Unified Science*, Chicago: University of Chicago Press, 1939.

Dobzhansky, Theodosius: *The Biological Basis of Human Freedom*, New York: Columbia University Press, 1956.

Dobzhansky, Theodosius: *Mankind Evolving*, New Haven: Yale University Press, 1962.

Dobzhansky, Theodosius: *The Biology of Ultimate Concern*, New York: New American Library, 1967.

Dobzhansky, Theodosius; Hecht, G.; Max, K.; and Steere, William C. (eds.): *Evolutionary Biology*, Vol. II, New York: Appleton-Century-Crofts, 1968.

Dobzhansky, Theodosius: *Genetics of the Evolutionary Process*, New York: Columbia University Press, 1970.

Dodds, E. R.: *The Greeks and the Irrational*, Boston: Beacon, 1957.

Douglas, Mary: *Purity and Danger*, New York: Praeger, 1966.

Dröscher, Vitus B.: *The Friendly Beast*, New York: Dutton, 1971.

Drucker, Peter F.: *The Age of Discontinuity: Guidelines to Our Changing Society*, New York: Harper and Row, 1969.

Drucker, Peter F.: *Technology, Management and Society*, New York: Harper and Row, 1970.

Dubos, René J.: *The Dreams of Reason*, New York: Columbia University Press, 1961.

Dubos, René J.: *Man Adapting*, New Haven: Yale University Press, 1965.

Dubos, René J.: *So Human an Animal*, New York: Charles Scribner's Sons, 1968.

Dubos, René J.: *Man, Medicine and Environment*, New York: New American Library, 1968.

Dubos, René J.: *Reason Awake—Science for Man*, New York: Columbia University Press, 1970.

Eaton, Theodore H., Jr.: *Evolution*, New York: W. W. Norton, 1970.

Eccles, John C.: *Facing Reality; Philosophical Adventures by a Brain Scientist*, New York: Springer-Verlag, 1970.

Eckstein, Gustav: *The Body Has a Head*, New York: Harper and Row, 1970.

Edel, Abraham: *Ethical Judgment*, Glencoe: Free Press, 1955.

Edel, Abraham: "Science and the structure of ethics," *International Encyclopedia of Unified Science*, Vol. 2, No. 3, Chicago: University of Chicago Press, 1961.

Edel, Abraham: *Method in Ethical Theory*, Indianapolis: Bobbs-Merrill, 1963.

Edel, May and Edel, Abraham: *Anthropology and Ethics*, Springfield: Charles C. Thomas, 1959.

Edelman, J. M.: *The Symbolic Uses of Politics*, Urbana: University of Illinois Press, 1964.

Ehrlich, Paul R., and Ehrlich, Anne H.: *Population, Resources, Environment*, San Francisco: Freeman, 1970.

Ehrlich, Paul R., and Ehrlich, Anne H., in *Global Ecology: Readings Toward a Rational Strategy for Man*, Holden, J. P. and Ehrlich, P. R. (eds.): New York: Harcourt, Brace, Jovanovich, 1971.

Eibl-Eibesfeldt, Irenäus: "Aggressive Behavior and Ritualized Fighting in Animals," in *Science and Psychoanalysis*, Vol. VI, *Violence and War*, Masserman, Jules H. (ed.), New York: Grune and Stratton, 1963.

Eibl-Elbesfeldt, Irenäus: (Trans. from German by Klinghammer, E.): *Ethology: The Biology of Behavior*, New York: Holt, Rinehart, and Winston, 1970.

Eimerl, Sarel, and DeVore, Irven (eds.) and the editors of LIFE: *The Primates,* New York: Time, Inc.. 1965.

Eiseley, Loren: *The Immense Journey,* New York: Random House, 1957.

Eiseley, Loren: *Darwin's Century: Evolution and the Men Who Discovered It,* Garden City: Doubleday, 1958.

Eiseley, Loren: *The Firmament of Time,* New York: Atheneum, 1960.

Eiseley, Loren: *The Unexpected Universe,* New York: Harcourt, Brace and World, 1969.

Eiseley, Loren: *The Invisible Pyramid,* New York: Charles Scribner's Sons, 1970.

Eleftheriou, Basil E., and Scott, J. P. (eds.): *The Physiology of Aggression and Defeat,* New York: Plenum Press, 1971.

Ellenberger, H.: *The Discovery of the Unconscious,* New York: Basic Books, 1970.

Elsasser, W. M.: "The Role of Individuality in Biological Theory" in *Towards a Theoretical Biology,* Vol. III, Waddington, C. H. (ed.), Edinburgh: Edinburgh University Press, 1970.

Elton, Charles S.: *The Pattern of Animal Communities,* New York: Wiley, 1966.

Empson, William: *Seven Types of Ambiguity,* New York: Harcourt, 1931.

Engel, George L.: *Psychological Development in Health and Disease,* Philadelphia: Saunders, 1962.

Erikson, Erik H.: *Childhood and Society,* New York: W. W. Norton, 1950.

Erikson, Erik H.: "The Problem of Ego Identity," *Journal of the American Psychoanalytic Association,* 4:56–121, 1956.

Erikson, Erik H.: *Insight and Responsibility,* Lectures on the Ethical Implications of Psychoanalytic Insight, New York: W. W. Norton, 1964.

Erikson, Erik H.: *Young Man Luther: A Study in Psychoanalysis and History,* New York: W. W. Norton, 1958.

Erikson, Erik H.: "Identity and the Life Cycle," *Psychological Issues,* Vol. 1, No. 1, Monograph 1, 1959.

Erikson, Erik H.: "The Golden Rule and the Cycle of Life," *Harvard Medical Alumni Bulletin,* 37(2), Winter 1963; 1962 George W. Gay Lecture.

Erikson, Erik H.: *Identity, Youth and Crisis,* New York: W. W. Norton, 1968.

Erikson, Erik H.: *Gandhi's Truth,* New York: W. W. Norton, 1969.

Esser, Aristide H. (ed.): *Behavior and Environment: The Use of Space by Animals and Men,* New York: Plenum, 1971.

Etkin, William: "Social Behavioral Factors in the Emergence of Man," in *Culture and the Direction of Human Evolution,* Garn, S. M. (ed.), Detroit: Wayne State University Press, 1964.

Etkin, William (ed.): *Social Behavior and Organization Among Vertebrates,* Chicago: University of Chicago Press, 1964.

Etkin, William: *Social Behavior—From Fish to Man,* Chicago: University of Chicago Press, 1967.

Etkin, William: "Cooperation and Competition in Social Behavior," in *Social Behavior and Organization Among Vertebrates,* Etkin, William (ed.), Chicago: University of Chicago Press, 1964.

Etkin, William: "Types of Social Organization in Birds and Mammals," in *Social Behavior and Organization Among Vertebrates,* Etkin, William (ed.), Chicago: University of Chicago Press, 1964, pp. 256–296.

Eucken, Rudolf Christof: *Ethics and Modern Thought.* Deem Lectures, New York

University, 1913 (also in The Nobel Prize Library, 20 Commemorative Volumes). New York: Putnam, 1913.

Ewer, R. F.: *Ethology of Mammals*, New York: Plenum, 1968.

Farb, Peter: *Man's Rise to Civilization*, New York: Dutton, 1968.

Farber, Eduard: "Dreams and Visions in a Century of Chemistry," in *The Kekule Centennial, Advances in Chemistry Series*, American Chemical Society, Washington, D. C., 61:129–139, 1966.

Farrington, Benjamin: *What Darwin Really Said*, New York: Schocken, 1966.

Feibleman, J. K.: *Mankind Behaving*, Springfield, Ill.: Charles C Thomas, 1963.

Feigl, H., and Scriven, M. (eds.): *The Foundations of Science and the Concepts of Psychology and Psychoanalysis*, Minneapolis: University of Minnesota Press, 1956.

Feinberg, Joel: *Doing and Deserving: Essays in the Theory of Responsibility*, Princeton: Princeton University Press, 1970.

Fenichel, Otto: *The Psychoanalytic Theory of Neurosis*, New York: W. W. Norton, 1945.

Fenichel, Otto: "Ego strength and ego weakness," in *The Collected Papers*, 2nd edition, Fenichel, Hanna and Rapaport, David (eds.), London edition, Routledge & Paul, 1955.

Ferkiss, Victor: *Technological Man*, New York: George Braziller, 1969.

Feuer, Lewis S.: *Psychoanalysis and Ethics*, Springfield: Charles C Thomas, 1955.

Feuer, Lewis S.: *The Conflict of Generations*, New York: Basic Books, 1969.

"Fields Within Fields . . . Within Fields: The Methodology of the Creative Process," *Man's Emergent Evolution*, World Institute Council, 3(1), 1970.

Fingarette, Herbert: "Psychoanalytic Perspectives on Moral Guilt and Responsibility: A Reevaluation," *Philosophy and Phenomenological Research*, 16(1):18–36, September 1955.

Fingarette, Herbert: *On Responsibility*, New York: Basic Books, 1967.

Fischer, Robert B.: *Science, Man and Society*, Philadelphia: W. B. Saunders, 1971.

Fletcher, Joseph F.: "Reflection and Reply" in *The Situation Ethics Debate*, Harvey Cox (ed.), Philadelphia: Westminster, 1968.

Flugel, J. C.: *Man, Morals, and Society*, New York: International Universities Press, 1945.

Flugel, J. C.: *A Hundred Years of Psychology: 1833–1933*, with an additional part: *1933–1963* by West, Donald J., New York: Basic Books, 1964.

Forbes, R. J.: *The Conquest of Nature*, New York: Praeger, 1968.

Fortes, Meyer: *Oedipus and Job in West African Religion*, Cambridge, England: Cambridge University Press, 1959.

Foss, B. M. (ed.): *Determinants of Infant Behavior*, Vol. II, New York: Wiley, 1963.

Francoeur, Robert: *Evolving World: Converging Man*, New York: Holt, Rinehart, and Winston, 1970.

Frank, Jerome D.: *Sanity and Survival*, New York: Random House, 1967.

Frank, Jerome D.: "Human Group Aggression," in *Biology of Populations*, Sladen, B. K., and Bang, F., New York: American Elsevier, 1969.

Frank, Lawrence K.: *Cultural Determinism and Free Will*, Cincinnati: Hebrew Union College, Jewish Institute of Religion, 1951.

Frankel, Charles: *The Case for Modern Man*, New York: Harper, 1956.

Freedman, Alfred M., and Kaplan, Harold I. (eds.): *Comprehensive Textbook of Psychiatry*, Baltimore: Williams and Wilkins, 1967.

Freedman, D. G.: "The ethological study of man," in *Genetic and Environmental*

Influences on Behavior, Thoday, John M., and Parkes, A. S. (eds.), New York: Plenum, 1968.

Freud, Anna: *The Ego and the Mechanisms of Defense,* New York: International Universities Press, 1946.

Freud, Anna: *Normality and Pathology in Childhood: Assessments of Development,* New York: International Universities Press, 1965.

Freud, Sigmund: *The Problem of Anxiety,* New York: W. W. Norton, 1936.

Freud, Sigmund: *Civilization, War and Death: Selections from Three Works by Sigmund Freud,* Rickman, J. (ed.), London: Hogarth, 1939.

Freud, Sigmund: *An Outline of Psychoanalysis,* New York: W. W. Norton, 1949.

Freud, Sigmund: *New Introductory Lectures on Psychoanalysis,* New York: W. W. Norton, 1933.

Freud, Sigmund: *Civilization and Its Discontents,* London: Hogarth, 1930.

Freud, Sigmund; *Three Contributions to the Theory of Sex,* 4th edition, New York: Nervous and Mental Disease Publishing Co., 1930.

Freud, Sigmund: *The Complete Psychological Works of Sigmund Freud,* Standard Edition (J. Strachey, trans.), London: Hogarth, 1953–1964.

Fried, Charles: *An Anatomy of Values: Problems of Personal and Social Choice,* Cambridge: Harvard University Press, 1970.

Fried, Morton; Harris, Marvin; and Murphy, Robert (eds.): *War: The Anthropology of Armed Conflict and Aggression,* Garden City: Natural History Press, 1968.

Friedman, L.: "The Therapeutic Alliance," *International Journal of Psychoanalysis,* 50(2):139–153, 1969.

Fromm, Erich: *Escape from Freedom,* New York: Farrar and Rinehart, 1941.

Fromm, Erich: *Man for Himself,* New York: Farrar and Rinehart, 1947.

Fromm, Erich: *Psychoanalysis and Religion,* New Haven: Yale University Press, 1950.

Fromm, Erich: *The Revolution of Hope,* New York: Harper and Row, 1968.

Fromm–Reichmann, Frieda: *Principles of Intensive Psychotherapy,* Chicago: University of Chicago Press, 1950.

Fuller, Lon L.: *The Morality of Law,* New Haven: Yale University Press, 1964.

Fuller, R. Buckminster; Walker, Eric A.; and Killian, James R., Jr.: *Approaching the Benign Environment,* The Franklin Lectures in the Sciences and Humanities. First Series. Published for Auburn University by University of Alabama Press, 1970.

Galdston, Iago (ed.): *Freud and Contemporary Culture,* Freeport, New York: Books for Libraries Press, 1957.

Garattini, S., and Sigg, E. (eds.): *Aggressive Behavior,* New York: Wiley, 1969.

Garcia, John David: *The Moral Society: A Rational Alternative to Death,* New York: Julian, 1971.

George, Jean Craighead: *Beastly Inventions: A Surprising Investigation into How Smart Animals Really Are,* New York: McKay, 1970.

Gerard, R. W.: "A Biological Basis for Ethics," *Philosophy of Science,* 9(1): 92–120, Jan. 1942.

Gerard, R. W.: "Becoming: The Residue of Change," in *Evolution After Darwin, 2, The Evolution of Man,* Tax, Sol (ed.), Chicago: University of Chicago Press, 1960.

Gerard, R. W.: "The Biology of Ethics," in *Society and Medicine,* Galdston, I., New York: International Universities Press, 1955.

Gert, Bernard: *The Moral Rules,* New York: Harper and Row, 1966.

Ghiselin, Michael T.: *The Triumph of The Darwinian Method,* Berkeley: University of California Press, 1969.

Ginsburg, B.: "Social Behavior and Social Hierarchy in the Formation of Personality Profiles in Animals," in *Comparative Psychopathology, Animal and Human,* Zubin, Joseph, and Hunt, Howard (eds.), New York: Grune and Stratton, 1967.

Gitelson, M.: "On ego distortion," *International Journal of Psychoanalysis,* 39 (Parts II–IV):245–257, Mar.–Aug. 1958.

Glass, Bentley: *Science and Ethical Values,* Chapel Hill: University of North Carolina Press, 1965.

Glass, Bentley: *Science and Liberal Education,* Davis Washington Mitchell Lectures, Tulane University, 1959; Baton Rouge: Louisiana State University Press, 1959.

Glass, Bentley: *The Timely and the Timeless: The Interrelationships of Science, Education, and Society,* New York: Basic Books, 1970.

Glass, Bentley: "Biological Aspects of Technology Assessment," *Science,* 165:755, Aug. 22, 1969; also in *Quarterly Review of Biology,* 45(2):168–172, June 1970.

Glass, Bentley: "Science: Endless Horizons or Golden Age?", *Science,* 171:23–29, January 8, 1971.

Glazer, Nathan: *Remembering the Answers,* New York: Basic Books, 1970.

Goffman, Erving: *The Presentation of Self in Everyday Life,* Garden City: Doubleday, 1959.

Goffman, Erving: *Asylums: Essays on the Social Situation of Mental Patients and Other Inmates,* Chicago: Aldine, 1961.

Goffman, Erving: *Interaction Ritual: Essays on Face-to-Face Behavior,* Garden City: Anchor, 1967.

Goldschmidt, Walter (ed.): *Ways of Mankind,* Boston: Beacon, 1954.

Goldstein, Kurt: *Human Nature in the Light of Psychopathology,* William James Lectures at Harvard University, 1938–39; New York: Schocken Books, 1963.

Goodall, Jane: "Chimpanzees of the Gombe Stream Reserve," in *Primate Behavior,* DeVore, Irven (ed.), New York: Holt, Rinehart and Winston, 1965.

Goodall, Jane: *My Friends the Wild Chimpanzees,* Washington; National Geographic Society, 1967.

Goodman, Paul: *Growing Up Absurd,* New York: Random House, 1960.

Gorer, G.: *The American People,* Revised edition, New York: W. W. Norton, 1964.

Gorer, G.: *The Danger of Equality,* New York: Weybright and Talley, 1966.

Graubard, Stephen R. (ed.): *Theory in Humanistic Studies,* Bloomfield, Morton. *et al.,* Cambridge: American Academy of Arts and Sciences, 1970.

Greene, John C.: *Darwin and the Modern World View,* Baton Rouge: Louisiana State University Press, 1961.

Greenfield, Norman S., and Lewis, William C. (eds.): *Psychoanalysis and Current Biological Thought,* Madison: University of Wisconsin Press, 1965.

Greenson, Ralph R.: "The Working Alliance and the Transference Neurosis," *Psychoanalytic Quarterly,* 34:155–181, 1965.

Greenson, Ralph R.: *The Technique and Practice of Psychoanalysis,* Vol. I, New York: International Universities Press, 1967.

Grene, Marjorie: *Approaches to a Philosophical Biology,* New York: Basic Books, 1968.

Grinker, R. R., Sr. (ed.): *Toward a Unified Theory of Human Behavior,* 2nd ed., New York: Basic Books, 1967.

Grinstein, Alexander: *The Index of Psychoanalytic Writings,* 5 vols., 1956–60, New York: International Universities Press.

Grotjahn, M.: *Beyond Laughter,* New York: McGraw-Hill, 1957.

Group for the Advancement of Psychiatry: "Some Consideration of Early Attempts in Cooperation Between Religion and Psychiatry," Symp. No. 5, March, 1958.

Group for the Advancement of Psychiatry: "Psychiatry and Religion," Report No. 48, Dec. 1960.

Group for the Advancement of Psychiatry: "The Psychic Function of Religion in Mental Illness and Health," VI, Report No. 67, Jan. 1968.

Gustafson, James M.; Peters, Richard S.; Kohlberg, Lawrence; Bettelheim, Bruno; and Keniston, Kenneth: *Moral Education,* Five Lectures, Cambridge: Harvard University Press, 1970.

Hall, K., and DeVore, Irven: "Baboon Social Behavior," in *Primate Behavior,* Devore, Irven (ed.): New York: Holt, Rinehart and Winston, 1965.

Halleck, Seymour L.: *Psychiatry and the Dilemmas of Crime: A Study of Causes, Punishment and Treatment,* New York: Harper and Row, 1967.

Hallowell, A. I.: "Self, Society, and Culture in Phylogenetic Perspective," in *Evolution After Darwin,* Vol. II, Tax, Sol (ed.), Chicago: University of Chicago Press, 1960.

Hallowell, A. I.: "Hominid Evolution, Cultural Adaptation and Mental Dysfunctioning," in *Transcultural Psychiatry,* DeReuck, A. V. S., and Porter, R. (eds.), A CIBA Foundation Symposium, Boston: Little, Brown, 1965.

Hamburg, David A.: "The Relevance of Recent Evolutionary Changes to Human Stress Biology," in *Social Life of Early Man,* Washburn, Sherwool (ed.), Chicago: Aldine, 1961.

Hamburg, David A.: "Emotions in the perspective of human evolution," in *Expression of the Emotions in Man,* Knapp, P. D. (ed.), New York: International Universities Press, 1963.

Hamburg, David A.: "Evolution of Emotional Responses: Evidence from Recent Research on Nonhuman Primates," in *Science and Psychoanalysis,* Vol. XII, *Animal and Human,* Masserman, Jules H. (ed.), New York: Grune and Stratton, 1968.

Hamburg, David A. (ed.): *Psychiatry As a Behavioral Science,* Englewood Cliffs: Prentice-Hall, 1970.

Handler, Philip (ed.): *Biology and the Future of Man,* New York: Oxford University Press, 1970.

Hardin, Garrett (ed.): *Populations, Evolution and Birth Control,* San Francisco: Freeman, 1964.

Hardin, Garrett: "The Tragedy of the Commons," *Science,* 162: 1243–1248, December 13, 1968.

Hare, R. M.: *The Language of Morals,* Oxford: Clarendon, 1952.

Harlow, Harry F.: "The Evolution of Learning," in *Behavior and Evolution,* Roe, A., and Simpson, G. G. (eds.), New Haven: Yale University Press, 1958.

Harlow, Harry F., and Zimmerman, R. R.: "Affectional Responses in the Infant Monkey," *Science* 130:421–432, Aug. 21, 1959.

Harlow, Harry F.: "The Maternal Affectional System," in *Determinants of Infant Behavior* II, Foss, B. M. (ed.), London: Methuen, 1963.

Harlow, Harry F., and Harlow, M. K.: "The Effect of Rearing Conditions on Behavior," *Bulletin of the Menninger Clinic* 26(5):213–224, Sept. 1962.

Harlow, Harry F.: "Social Deprivation in Monkeys," *Scientific American,* 207(5): 136–146, November 1962.

Harlow, Harry F.: "Development of the Second and Third Affectional Systems in

Macaque Monkeys," in *Research Approaches to Psychiatric Problems: A Symposium*, Tourlentes, T. T.; Pollock, S. L.; and Himwich, H. E. (eds.), New York: Grune and Stratton, 1962.

Harlow, Harry F., and Harlow, M.: "The affectional systems," in *Behavior of Nonhuman Primates*, Vol. II, Schrier, A.; Harlow, H.; and Stollnitz, F. (eds.), New York: Academic Press, 1965.

Harlow, Harry F., and Harlow, M. K.: "Learning to Love," *American Scientist*, 54: 244–272, Sept. 1966.

Harlow, Harry F.: "The Primate Socialization Motives," in *Transactions and Studies of the College of Physicians of Philadelphia*, Fourth series, 33(4):224–237, April 1966.

Harlow, Harry F., and Woolsey, C. N. (eds.): *Biological and Biochemical Bases of Behavior*, Madison: University of Wisconsin Press, 1958.

Harré, Romano: *The Principles of Scientific Thinking*, Chicago: University of Chicago Press, 1970.

Hartmann, Heinz: "Comments on the Psychoanalytic Theory of the Ego," *Psychonalytic Study of the Child*, 5:74–96, 1950.

Hartmann, Heinz: "The Mutual Influences in the Development of Ego and Id," *Psychonalytic Study of the Child*, 7:9–30, 1952.

Hartmann, Heinz: *Ego Psychology and the Problem of Adaptation*, New York: International Universities Press, 1958.

Hartmann, Heinz: *Psychoanalysis and Moral Values*, New York: International Universities Press, 1960.

Hartmann, Heinz: *Essays on Ego Psychology*, New York: International Universities Press, 1964.

Hartmann, Heinz; Kris, Ernst; and Loewenstein, Rudolph: "Papers on Psychoanalytic Psychology," in *Psychological Issues*, Vol. IV, No. 2, Monograph 14, New York: International Universities Press, 1964.

Hartogs, Renatus, and Artzt, Eric: *Violence: Causes and Solutions*, New York: Dell, 1970.

Haselden, Kyle, and Hefner, Philip (eds.): *Changing Man: The Threat and the Promise*, Garden City: Doubleday, 1968.

Hastings, William Thomson (ed.): *Man Thinking*, Ithaca, New York: Cornell University Press, 1962.

Hazlitt, Henry: *The Foundations of Morality*, Princeton, New Jersey: Von Nostrand, 1964.

Helfer, R. E. and Kempe, C. H. (eds.): *The Battered Child*, Chicago: University of Chicago Press, 1968.

Helfrich, Harold W. (ed.): *The Environmental Crisis: Man's Struggle to Live with Himself*, New Haven: Yale University Press, 1970.

Hempel, Carl: *Aspects of Scientific Explanation: and Other Essays in the Philosophy of Science*, New York: Free Press, 1965.

Hendrick, Ives: *Facts and Theories of Psychoanalysis*, 3rd edition, New York: Knopf, 1958.

Henry, Jules: *Culture Against Man*, New York: Random House, 1963.

Herrick, C. J.: *The Evolution of Human Nature*, Austin: University of Texas Press, 1956.

Hess, E.: "Imprinting and the 'Critical Period' Concept," in *Roots of Behavior*, Bliss, E. L. (ed.), New York: Harper, 1962.

Hess, E.: "Ethology," in *Comprehensive Textbook of Psychiatry*, Freedman, A. M. and Kaplan, H. I. (eds.), Baltimore: Williams and Wilkins, 1967.

Hilgard. Ernest R.; Kubie, L.; and Pumpian-Mindlin, E.: *Psychoanalysis as Science*, Pumpian-Mindlin, Eugene (ed.), Palo Alto: Stanford University Press, 1952. Hixon Lectures on the Scientific Status of Psychoanalysis.

Hinde, R. A., and Tinbergen, N.: "The Comparative Study of Species-Specific Behavior," in *Behavior and Evolution*, Roe, A., and Simpson, G. G. (eds.), New Haven: Yale University Press, 1958.

Hinde, R. A.: "The Relevance of Animal Studies to Human Neurotic Disorders," in *Aspects of Psychiatric Research*, Richter, D.; Tanner, J. M.; Taylor, L.; and Zangwill (eds.), New York: Oxford University Press, 1962.

Hinde, R. A.: *Animal Behavior*, New York: McGraw-Hill, 1966.

Hoagland, H., and Burhoe, R. W.: *Evolution and Man's Progress*, New York: Columbia University Press, 1962.

Hockett, C. F.: "Animal 'languages' and human language," in *The Evolution of Man's Capacity for Culture*, Spuhler, J. N. (ed.), Detroit: Wayne State University Press, 1959.

Hockett, C. F. and Ascher, Robert: "The Human Revolution," *American Scientist*, 52:70–92, March 1964.

Hodges, Henry: *Technology in the Ancient World*, New York: Knopf, 1970.

Hoffman, Frederick J.: *Freudianism and the Literary Mind*, Baton Rouge: Louisiana State University Press, 1945.

Hoffmann, Stanley: "The Sound and the Fury: The Social Scientist Versus War in History," in *The State of War, Essays in the Theory and Practice of International Politics*, Hoffmann, Stanley, New York: Praeger, 1965.

Hofstadter, R.: *Social Darwinism in American Thought*, Boston: Beacon, 1955.

Hohfeld, Wesley Newcomb: *Fundamental Legal Conceptions, As Applied in Judicial Reasoning*, Edited by Cook, W. W., New Haven: Yale University Press, 1919.

Hollingsworth, Harry L.: *Psychology and Ethics*, New York: Ronald, 1949.

Holt, Edwin B.: *The Freudian Wish and Its Place in Ethics*, New York: Henry Holt, 1915.

Holt, Robert: "Ego Autonomy Re-evaluated," *International Journal of Psychoanalysis*, 46(Part 2):151–167, April 1965.

Holton, Gerald (ed.): *Science and Culture*, Boston: Houghton Mifflin, 1965.

Holzman, Philip S., *Psychoanalysis and Psychopathology*, New York: McGraw-Hill, 1970.

Hook, Sidney (ed.): *Determinism and Freedom*, New York: New York University Press, 1958.

Hook, Sidney (ed.); *Psychoanalysis, Scientific Method and Philosophy, A Symposium*, New York: New York University Press, 1959.

Hook, Sidney: *Religion in a Free Society*, Lincoln: University of Nebraska Press, 1967.

Hook, Sidney (ed.): *Human Values and Economic Policy*, New York: New York University Press, 1967.

Horsburgh, H. J. N.: *Non-Violence and Aggression: A Study of Gandhi's Moral Equivalent of War*, London: Oxford University Press, 1968.

Hospers, John: "Free-will and Psychoanalysis," in *Readings in Ethical Theory*, Sellers, Wilfred and Hospers, John (eds.), New York: Appleton-Century-Crofts, 1952.

357

Hospers, John: *Human Conduct,* New York: Harcourt, Brace and World, 1961.

Howell, F. Clark, and Bourlière, Francois (eds.): *African Ecology and Human Behavior,* Chicago: Aldine, 1963.

Howell, F. Clark and the editors of Time-Life Books: *Early Man,* New York: Time-Life Books, 1968.

Howells, W. W.: *Mankind in the Making,* New York: Doubleday, 1959.

Hutchings, Edward and Elizabeth (eds.): *Scientific Progress and Human Values,* New York: American Elsevier, 1967.

Huxley, J. S.: *Evolution, The Modern Synthesis,* New York: Harper, 1942.

Huxley, J. S. (ed.): "A Discussion on Ritualization of Behavior in Animals and Man," *Philosophical Transactions of the Royal Society,* London, (1) Series B:247–526, Dec. 1966.

Huxley, J. S.: *The Human Crisis,* Seattle: University of Washington Press, 1963.

Huxley, J. S. (ed.): *The Humanist Frame,* New York: Harper, 1961.

Huxley, T. H. and Huxley, J. S.: *Touchstone for Ethics,* New York: Harper, 1947.

Ichheiser, Gustav: *Appearances and Realities,* San Francisco: Jossey-Bass, 1970.

Jaques, Elliott: *Work, Creativity, and Social Justice,* New York: International Universities Press, 1970.

Jaspers, Karl, (Trans. by Ashton, E. B.): *The Future of Mankind,* Chicago: University of Chicago Press, 1961.

Jay, Phyllis C.: "Field Studies" in *Behavior of Nonhuman Primates,* Vol. II, Schrier, A. M.; Harlow, H. F.; and Stollnitz, F. (eds.), New York: Academic Press, 1965.

Jay, Phyllis C. (ed.): *Primates: Studies in Adaptation and Variability,* New York: Holt, Rinehart and Winston, 1968.

Jennings, H. S.: *The Biological Basis of Human Nature,* New York: W. W. Norton, 1930.

Jennings, B. H., and Murphy, J. E. (eds.): *Interactions of Man and His Environment,* New York: Plenum, 1966.

Jensen, Gordon D., and Bobbitt, Ruth A.: "Implications of Primate Research for Understanding Infant Development," in *Science and Psychoanalysis,* Volume XII, *Animal and Human,* Masserman, Jules H. (ed.), New York: Grune and Stratton, 1968.

Johnson, Adelaide: "Sanctions for Superego Lacunae of Adolescents," in *Searchlights on Delinquency,* Eissler, Kurt R. (ed.), New York: International Universities Press, 1949.

Johnson, Adelaide, and Szurek, S. A.: "The Genesis of Antisocial Acting Out in Children and Adults," in *Psychoanalytic Quarterly,* 21(3):323–343, 1952.

Johnson, Oliver, A. (ed.): *Ethics: A Source Book,* New York: Dryden, 1958.

Jones, Ernest: *Life and Work of Sigmund Freud* (3 Volumes), New York: Basic Books, 1953–57.

Jones, H. M.: *Violence and Reason: A Book of Essays,* New York: Atheneum, 1969.

Jones, W. T.; Sontag, Frederic; Beckner, Morton; and Fogelin, Robert (eds.): *Approaches to Ethics,* New York: McGraw-Hill, 1962.

Jung, Carl Gustav (ed.): *Man and His Symbols,* Garden City: Doubleday, 1964.

Jung, Carl Gustav: *Satan in the Old Testament,* Tr. by Hildegard Nagel, Evanston: Northwestern University Press, 1967.

Kagan, Jerome (ed.): *Creativity and Learning,* Boston: Houghton, Mifflin, 1967.

Kaplan, A., and Kris, E.: "Aesthetic Ambiguity," *Philosophy and Phenomenological Research* 8(3): 415–435, March 1948.

Kaplan, Abraham: "Freud and Modern Philosophy," in *Freud and the 20th Century*, Nelson, B. (ed.), New York: Meridian, 1957.

Kaplan, Abraham: *The Conduct of Inquiry, Methodology for Behavioral Science*, San Francisco: Chandler, 1964.

Kaplan, Abraham: *The New World of Philosophy*, New York: Random House, 1961.

Kaplan, Abraham: *American Ethics and Public Policy*, New York: Oxford University Press, 1963.

Kaplan, Abraham (ed.): *Individuality and the New Society*, Seattle: University of Washington Press, 1970.

Kardiner, A.: *The Individual and His Society*, New York: Columbia University Press, 1939.

Kardiner, A.: *Psychological Frontiers of Society*, New York: Columbia University Press, 1945.

Karush, A.; Easser, B. R.; Cooper, A.; and Swerdlof, B.: "The evaluation of ego strength. A profile of adaptive balance," *Journal of Nervous and Mental Disease*, 39: 332–349, 1964.

Karush, Aaron: "Ego strength: An unsolved problem in ego psychology," in *Science and Psychoanalysis*, Vol. XI, *The Ego*, Masserman, Jules (ed.), New York: Grune and Stratton, 1967.

Katz, D.; Sarnoff, I.; and McClintock, C.: "Ego-defense and attitude change," *Human Relations*, 9:27–45, 1956.

Katz, Jay; Goldstein, Joseph; and Dershowitz, Alan: *Psychoanalysis, Psychiatry*, and *Law*, New York: Free Press, 1967.

Katz, Milton: *The Relevance of International Adjudication*, Cambridge: Harvard University Press, 1968.

Katz, R. L.: *Empathy*, New York: Free Press, 1963.

Kaufman, I. C.: "Some ethological studies of social relationships and conflict situations," *Journal American Psychoanalytic Association*, 8:671–685, 1960.

Kaufman, I. C.: "Symposium on 'Psychoanalysis and Ethology': III Some theoretical implications from animal behavior studies for the psychoanalytic concepts of instinct, energy, and drive," *International Journal Psychoanalysis*, 41 (Parts 4 & 5): 318–326, July–Oct. 1960.

Kaufmann, Walter: *The Faith of a Heretic*, Garden City: Doubleday, 1961.

Kaufmann, Walter: *Tragedy and Philosophy*, Garden City: Doubleday, 1968.

Kaul, R. N.: "Freud's Contribution to Ethical Theory," *Psychoanalytic Review*, 51(4): 72–78, Winter, 1964–65.

Keith, Arthur: *Evolution and Ethics*, New York: Putnam, 1947.

Kekule, Friedrich A.: *Zeitschrift für Chemie*, 3, p. 217, 1867.

Kelman, Herbert C.: "Social-Psychological Approaches to the Study of International Relations," in *International Behavior*, Kelman, Herbert C. (ed.), New York: Holt, Rinehart and Winston, 1965.

Keniston, K.: *The Uncommitted: Alienated Youth in American Society*, New York: Harcourt, Brace, and World, Inc., 1965.

Keniston, K.: "Morals and ethics," *American Scholar*, 34(4):628–632, Autumn, 1965.

Keniston, K.: "Student Activism, Moral Development and Morality," *American Journal Orthopsychiatry*, 40(4):577–592, July 1970.

Kiefer, Howard E., and Munitz, Milton K. (eds.): *Mind, Science, and History*, Albany: State University of New York Press, 1970.

Klein, M.: "A Comment by Mrs. Melanie Klein," in *Science and Ethics*, Waddington, C. H., London: Allen and Unwin, 1942.

Klein, M., and Riviere, Joan: *Love, Hate and Reparation*, London: Hogarth, and Institute of Psychoanalysis, 1937.

Klopfer, Peter H., and Hailman, J. P.: *An Introduction to Animal Behavior: Ethology's First Century*, Englewood Cliffs: Prentice-Hall, 1967.

Klopfer, Peter H.: *Habitats and Territories*, New York: Basic Books, 1969.

Klopfer, Peter H.: *Behavioral Ecology*, Belmont, California: Dickenson, 1970.

Kluckhohn, C.: "The Influence of Psychiatry on Anthropology in America During the Past One Hundred Years," in *One Hundred Years of American Psychiatry*, New York: Columbia University Press, 1944.

Kluckhohn, C.: "The Limitations of Adaptation and Adjustment as Concepts for Understanding Cultural Behavior," in *Adaptation*, Romano, J. (ed.), Ithaca: Cornell University Press, 1949.

Kluckhohn, C.: "Value and value orientations in the theory of action," in *Toward a General Theory of Action*, Parsons, T., and Shils, E. A. (eds.), pp. 388–433, Cambridge, Mass.: Harvard University Press, 1954.

Kluckhohn, C.: "Ethical Relativity; Sic et Non," *Journal of Philosophy*, LII: esp. 633ff, 676, 1955.

Kluckhohn, C.: "The Scientific Study of Values," in Proceedings of American Philosophical Society, 102:469–476, 1958.

Knapp, P. H. (ed.): *Expression of the Emotions in Man*, New York: International Universities Press, 1963.

Knight, James Allen: *Conscience and Guilt*, New York: Appleton-Century-Crofts, 1969.

Knight, R. P.: "Determinism, 'Freedom,' and Psychotherapy," *Psychiatry*, 9(3): 251–262, Aug. 1946.

Koestler, Arthur: *Insight and Outlook: An Inquiry into the Common Foundations of Science, Art and Social Ethics*, New York: Macmillan, 1949.

Koestler, Arthur: *The Act of Creation*, New York: Macmillan, 1964.

Koestler, Arthur: *The Ghost in the Machine*, New York: Macmillan, 1967.

Kohlberg, L.: "Development of moral character and moral ideology," in *Review of Child Development Research*, Hoffman, Martin L. and Lois W. (eds.), Vol. I, Russell Sage Foundation, 1964.

Kohlberg, L.: *Moral Development*, New York: Holt, Rinehart and Winston, 1972.

Kohler, Wolfgang: *The Place of Value in a World of Facts*, New York: Meridian, 1959.

Konorski, Jerzy: *The Integrative Activity of the Brain*, Chicago: The University of Chicago Press, 1967.

Kris, E.: *Psychoanalytic Explorations in Art*, New York: International Universities Press, 1952.

Kris, E.: "Neutralization and Sublimation: Observations on Young Children," *Psycho-Analytic Study of the Child*, 10:30–46, 1955.

Kruskal, William (ed.): *Mathematical Sciences and Social Sciences*, Englewood Cliffs: Prentice-Hall, 1970.

Kubie, Lawrence: *Neurotic Distortion of the Creative Process*, Lawrence, Kansas: University of Kansas Press, 1958.

Kubie, Lawrence: "Freud's Legacy to Human Freedom," in *Perspectives in Biology and Medicine*, 1:105–118, 1957.

Kuhn, Alfred: *The Study of Society: A Unified Approach,* Homewood, Illinois: R. D. Irwin, 1963.

Kuhn, Thomas S.: *The Structure of Scientific Revolutions,* Chicago: The University of Chicago Press, 1962.

Kuo, Z. Y.: "Studies on the basic factors in animal fighting," *Journal Genetic Psychology,* 96:201–239, June 1960; 97:181–225, Dec. 1960.

Kurtz, Paul (ed.): *Moral Problems in Contemporary Society: Essays in Humanistic Ethics,* Englewood Cliffs: Prentice-Hall, 1969.

LaBarre, Weston: *The Human Animal,* Chicago: University of Chicago Press, 1954.

Lambert, Karel, and Brittan, Gordon G., Jr.: *An Introduction to the Philosophy of Science,* Englewood Cliffs: Prentice-Hall, 1970.

Landes, David S. and Tilly, Charles (eds.): *History As Social Science,* Englewood Cliffs, New Jersey: Prentice-Hall, 1971.

Langer, Susanne: *Philosophy in a New Key: A Study in the Symbolism of Reason, Rite and Art,* 3rd edition, Cambridge: Harvard University Press, 1957.

Langer, Susanne: *Mind: An Essay on Human Feelings,* Baltimore: Johns Hopkins Press, 1967.

LaPiere, R.: *The Freudian Ethic,* New York: Duell, Sloan and Pearce, 1959.

Lasswell, Harold D., and Kaplan, Abraham: *Power and Society,* New Haven: Yale University Press, 1950.

Laughlin, Henry P.: *The Ego and Its Defenses,* New York: Appleton-Century-Crofts, 1970.

Lazarsfeld, Paul; Sewell, William H.; and Wilensky, Harold L. (eds.): *The Uses of Sociology,* New York: Basic Books, 1967.

Leach, Edmund R.: "Ritualization in man in relation to conceptual and social development," in *Ritualization of Behaviour in Animals and Man,* Huxley J. S. (ed.), *Philosophical Transactions of the Royal Society of London,* 251 (772) Series B.: 403–408, Dec. 1966.

Leach, Edmund R.: *A Runaway World?* New York: Oxford University Press, 1968. BBL Reith Lectures, 1967.

Leake, C. D.: "Ethicogenesis," *Scientific Monthly,* 60:245–253, April 1945.

Leakey, L. S. B.: "Development of Aggression as a Factor in Early Human and Pre-Human Evolution," in *Aggression and Defense,* Clemente, C., and Lindsley, D. (eds.), Los Angeles: University of California Press, 1967.

Leakey, L. S. B.: *Adam's Ancestors: The Evolution of Man and His Culture,* 4th edition, New York: Harper and Row, 1960.

Lederberg, Joshua: "Biological Future of Man" in *Man and His Future,* Wolstenholme, Gordon (ed.), a CIBA Foundation Volume, Boston: Little, Brown, 1963.

Lederer, Wolfgang: "Dragons, Delinquents, and Destiny—an Essay on Positive Superego Functions," in *Psychological Issues,* Vol. IV, No. 3, Monograph 15, New York: International Universities Press, 1964.

Lederer, Wolfgang: "Some Moral Dilemmas Encountered in Psychotherapy," in *Psychiatry,* 34(1):75–85, February 1971.

Lee, Richard, and DeVore, Irven (eds.): *Man the Hunter,* Chicago: Aldine, 1968.

Lenneberg, E. H.: "Language, Evolution, and Purposive Behavior," in *Culture in History,* Diamond, S. (ed.), New York: Columbia University Press, 1960.

Lenneberg, E. H.: "A Biological Perspective of Language," in *New Directions in the Study of Language,* Lenneberg, E. H. (ed.), Cambridge, Massachusetts: M.I.T., 1964.

Lenneberg, E. H.: *Biological Foundations of Language*, New York: Wiley, 1967.

L'Etang, Hugh: *The Pathology of Leadership*, New York: Hawthorn, 1970.

Levine, George and Thomas, Owen (eds.): *The Scientist Vs. the Humanist*, New York: W. W. Norton, 1963.

Levine, Maurice: "Principles of Psychiatric Treatment," in *Dynamic Psychiatry*, Alexander, F. and Ross, H. (eds.), Chicago: University of Chicago Press, 1952.

Levine, Maurice: Introductory Chapter, in *Surgery As a Human Experience*, Titchener, James, New York: Oxford University Press, 1960.

Levine, Sol, and Scotch, Norman A. (eds.): *Social Stress*, Chicago: Aldine, 1970.

Lévi-Strauss, Claude: "The Family," in *Man, Culture and Society*, Shapiro, H. L. (ed.), New York: Oxford University Press, 1956.

Lévi-Strauss, Claude: *The Savage Mind*, Chicago: University of Chicago Press, 1966.

Levy, David M.: "Animal psychology in its relation to psychiatry," in *Dynamic Psychiatry*, Alexander, F. and Ross, H. (eds.), Chicago: University of Chicago Press, 1952.

Lewy, E.: "Responsibility, Free Will, and Ego Psychology," *International Journal Psychoanalysis*, 42(3):260–270, May & June 1961.

Lichtheim, George: *The Concept of Ideology and Other Essays*, New York: Random House, 1967.

Lidz, Theodore: *The Family and Human Adaptation*, New York: International Universities Press, 1963.

Lifton, Robert Jay: *Thought Reform and the Psychology of Totalism: A Study of "Brain-washing" in China*, New York: W. W. Norton, 1961.

Lifton, Robert Jay: *Death in Life: Survivors of Hiroshima*, New York: Random House, 1967.

Lifton, Robert Jay: *Boundaries: Psychological Man in Revolution*, New York: Random House, 1969.

Lifton, Robert Jay: *History and Human Survival*, New York: Random House, 1970.

Lifton, Robert Jay: "Protean Man," in *The Psychoanalytic Interpretation of History*, Wolman, Benjamin B. (ed.), New York: Basic Books, 1971.

Lindsay, R. B.: *The Role of Science in Civilization*, New York: Harper and Row, 1963.

Lindzey, Gardner, and Aronson, Elliot (eds.): *The Handbook of Social Psychology*, 2d edition, Reading, Mass: Addison-Wesley, 1968–69.

Lion, J. R.; Bach-y-Rita, G.; and Ervin, F. R.: "Enigmas of Violence," *Science*, 164:1465, June 27, 1969.

Loewenberg, Peter: "Theodore Herzl: A Psychoanalytic Study in Charismatic Political Leadership," in *The Psychoanalytic Interpretation of History*, Wolman, Benjamin B. (ed.), New York: Basic Books, 1971.

Loewenstein, R. M.: *On the Theory of the Superego*, New York: International Universities Press, 1966.

Loewenstein, R. M.; Newman, L. M.; Schur, M.; and Solnit, A. J. (eds.): *Psychoanalysis—a General Psychology*, New York: International Universities Press, 1966.

Logan, F. A.: *Fundamentals of Learning and Motivation*, Dubuque, Iowa: Brown, 1970.

Lorenz, Konrad: *Evolution and Modification of Behavior*, Chicago: University of Chicago Press, 1965.

Lorenz, Konrad: *On Aggression*, New York: Harcourt, Brace, and World, 1966.

Lovejoy, Arthur O.: *Reflections on Human Nature,* Baltimore: Johns Hopkins Press, 1961.

Lowe, C. M.: "Value Orientations—An Ethical Dilemma," *American Psychologist,* 14(11):687–693, 1959.

Lustman, Seymour L.: "Rudiments of the Ego," *The Psychoanalytic Study of the Child,* Vol. XI, New York: International Universities Press, 1956.

Lynd, Helen Merrell: *On Shame and the Search for Identity,* 1st edition, New York: Harcourt, Brace, 1958.

Macaulay, J., and Berkowitz, L. (eds.): *Altruism and Helping Behavior: Social Psychological Studies of Some Antecedents and Consequences,* New York: Academic Press, 1970.

Maccoby, Eleanor: "The Development of Moral Values and Behavior in Childhood," in *Socialization and Society,* Clausen, John A. (ed.), Boston: Little, Brown, 1968.

Maddox, John: *Revolution in Biology,* New York: Macmillan, 1964.

Mandelbaum, Maurice: *The Phenomenology of Moral Experience,* Glencoe, Illinois: Free Press, 1955.

Mann, Kenneth W.: *Deadline for Survival: A Survey of Moral Issues in Science and Medicine,* Academy of Religion and Mental Health, New York: Seabury Press, 1970.

Mannoni, O.: *Freud,* New York: Pantheon, 1971.

Marais, Eugene: *The Soul of the Ape,* New York: Atheneum, 1969.

Marcuse, Herbert: *Eros and Civilization: A Philosophical Inquiry into Freud,* Boston: Beacon, 1966.

Marcuse, Herbert: *One-Dimensional Man,* Boston: Beacon, 1964.

Marcuse, Herbert: *Five Lectures: Psychoanalysis, Politics and Utopia,* Boston: Beacon, 1970.

Margenau, Henry: *The Nature of Physical Reality: A Philosophy of Modern Physics,* New York: McGraw-Hill, 1950.

Margolis, Joseph (ed.): *Contemporary Ethical Theory,* New York: Random House, 1966.

Margolis, Joseph: *Psychotherapy and Morality: A Study of Two Concepts,* New York: Random House, 1966.

Mark, Vernon H. and Ervin, Frank R.: *Violence and the Brain,* New York: Harper and Row, 1970.

Marmor, J.: "Psychoanalysis," in *Philosophy for the Future: the Quest of Modern Materialism,* Sellars, R. W.; McGill, V. J.; et al. (eds.), New York: Macmillan, 1949.

Maslow, A. H. (ed.): *New Knowledge in Human Values,* New York: Harper, 1959.

Mason, W. A.: "Determinants of Social Behavior in Young Chimpanzees," in *Behavior of Nonhuman Primates,* Vol. II, Schrier, A. M.; Harlow, H. F.; and Stollnitz, F. (eds.), New York: Academic Press, 1965.

Mason, W. A.: "The social development of monkeys and apes," in *Primate Behavior,* DeVore, I. (ed.), New York: Holt, Rinehart and Winston, 1965.

Mason, W. A.: "Motivational aspects of social responsiveness in young chimpanzees," in *Early Behavior: Comparative and Developmental Approaches,* Stevenson, Harold W.; Hess, Eckhard H.; and Rheingold, Harriet L. (eds.), New York: Wiley, 1967.

Mason, W. A.: "Scope and Potential of Primate Research," in *Science and Psychoanalysis,* Vol. XII, *Animal and Human,* Masserman, Jules H. (ed.), New York: Grune and Stratton, 1968.

Masserman, Jules H. (ed.): *Science and Psychoanalysis*, Vol. VI, *Violence and War*, New York: Grune and Stratton, 1963.

Masserman, Jules H. (ed.): *Science and Psychoanalysis*, Vol. XI, *The Ego*, New York: Grune and Stratton, 1967.

Masserman, Jules H. (ed.): *Science and Psychoanalysis*, Vol. XII, *Animal and Human*, New York: Grune and Stratton, 1968.

Matson, Floyd W.: *The Broken Image: Man, Science and Society*, New York: George Braziller, 1964.

Matson, Floyd W. and Montagu, Ashley (eds.): *The Human Dialogue*, New York: Free Press, 1967.

Matthews, L. Harrison: "Overt Fighting in Mammals." *The Natural History of Aggression*, Carthy, J. D. and Ebling, F. J. (eds.), London: Academic Press, 1964.

May, Rollo: *Love and Will*, New York: W. W. Norton, 1969.

Mayer, Milton: *On Liberty: Man vs. the State*, Santa Barbara: Center for the Study of Democratic Institutions, 1969.

Mayer, Philip (ed.): *Socialization: The Approach from Social Anthropology*, New York: Tavistock Publications, 1970.

Mayr, E.: "Cause and Effect in Biology," *Science*, 134:1501–1506, Nov. 10, 1961.

Mayr, E.: *Populations, Species, and Evolution*, Cambridge: Harvard University Press, 1970.

Mazlish, Bruce: *The Riddle of History*, New York: Harper and Row, 1966.

McLean, A. A. (ed.): *Mental Health and Work Organizations*, Chicago: Rand-McNally, 1970.

McNeil, Elton (ed.): *The Nature of Human Conflict*, Englewood Cliffs: Prentice-Hall, 1965.

Mead, Margaret: "Warfare is Only an Invention—Not a Biological Necessity," in *Asia*, 40:402–405, Aug. 1940.

Mead, Margaret: "World Culture," in *The World Community*, Wright, Q. (ed.), Chicago: University of Chicago Press, 1948.

Mead, Margaret: *Male and Female*, New York: William Morrow, 1949.

Mead, Margaret: "Violence in the Perspective of Culture History," in *Science and Psychoanalysis*, Vol. VI, *Violence and War*, Masserman, Jules H. (ed.), New York: Grune and Stratton, 1963.

Mead, Margaret: *Continuities in Cultural Evolution*, New Haven: Yale University Press, 1964.

Mead, Margaret, and Metraux, R.: "The Anthropology of Human Conflict," in *The Nature of Human Conflict*, McNeil, E. B. (ed.), Englewod Cliffs: Prentice-Hall, 1965.

Mead, Margaret: "Alternatives to War," in *War*, Fried, Morton; Harris, Marvin; and Murphy, Robert (eds.), Garden City: Natural History Press, 1968.

Mead, Margaret: *New Lives for Old: Cultural Transformation, Manus, 1928–53*, New York: Morrow, 1956; New York: Dell, 1968.

Mead, Margaret: *Culture and Commitment*, Garden City: Natural History Press, 1970.

Medawar, Peter B.: *The Uniqueness of the Individual*, New York: Basic Books, 1957.

Medawar, Peter B.: *The Future of Man*, New York: Basic Books, 1960.

Medawar, Peter B.: *The Art of the Soluble*, London: Methuen, 1967.

Medawar, Peter B.: *Induction and Intuition in Scientific Thought* (Jayne Lectures for 1968), Philadelphia: American Philosophical Society, 1969.

Meehl, P. E. and Sellars, Wilfrid: "The Concept of Emergence," in *The Foundations of Science and the Concepts of Psychology and Psychoanalysis*, Feigl, H., and Scriven, M. (eds.), Minneapolis: University of Minnesota Press, 1956.

Megargee, Edwin I., and Hokanson, Jack E. (eds.); *The Dynamics of Aggression: Individual, Group and International Analyses*, New York: Harper and Row, 1970.

Menaker, E., and Menaker, W.: *Ego in Evolution*, New York: Grove, 1965.

Menninger, Karl: *Man Against Himself*, New York: Harcourt, Brace, 1938.

Menninger, Karl: *Love Against Hate*, New York: Harcourt, Brace, 1942.

Menninger, Karl: *Theory of Psychoanalytic Technique*, New York: Basic Books, 1958.

Menninger, Karl: *The Vital Balance*, New York: Viking, 1963.

Menninger, Karl: *The Crime of Punishment*, New York: Viking, 1966.

Merton, Robert K.: *Social Theory and Social Structure*, Glencoe, Free Press, 1957.

Merton, Robert K.; Broom, Leonard; and Cottrell, Leonard, Jr., (eds.), *Sociology Today*, New York: Basic Books, 1959.

Mestheme, Emmanuel G.: *Technological Change—Its Impact on Man and Society*, Cambridge: Harvard University Press, 1970.

Meyer, L. B.: *Music, the Arts and Ideas*, Chicago: University of Chicago Press, 1967.

Middleton, W. E. K.: *The Scientific Revolution*, Cambridge, Mass.: Schenkman, 1965.

Miller, Stephen J.: *Prescription for Leadership: Training for the Medical Elite*, Chicago: Aldine, 1970.

Milne, Lorus, and Milne, Margery: *The Nature of Life*, New York: Crown Publishers, 1970.

Milne, Lorus, and Milne, Margery: *Patterns of Survival*, Englewood Cliffs: Prentice-Hall, 1967.

Mirsky, I. Arthur: "Psychoanalysis and the Biological Sciences," *Twenty Years of Psychoanalysis*, Alexander, F. and Ross, H. (eds.), New York: W. W. Norton, 1953.

Mischel, T.: "Concerning Rational Behaviour and Psychoanalytic Explanation," *Mind*, 74 (293), January 1965.

Mitscherlich, Alexander: *Society Without the Father*, New York: Harcourt, Brace and World, 1969.

Modell, Arnold H.: *Object Love and Reality*, New York: International Universities Press, 1968.

Money-Kyrle, R.: "Psycho-Analysis and Ethics," in *New Directions in Psychoanalysis*, Klein, Melanie (ed.), London: Tavistock, 1955.

Money-Kyrle, R.: *Man's Picture of His World*, New York: International Universities Press, 1961.

Monroe, Russell: "Man and Morals In Crisis," presented at a meeting on Psychiatry and Religion, 5th Province Episcopal Community Service, Indianapolis, Indiana, November 30, 1964. Unpublished paper.

Montagu, Ashley: *The Humanization of Man*, New York: World, 1962.

Montagu, Ashley: *On Being Human*, New York: Hawthorn, 1967, 2nd edition.

Montagu, Ashley: *Man Observed*, New York: Putnam, 1968.

Montagu, Ashley: *Culture: Man's Adaptive Dimension*, New York: Oxford University Press, 1968.

Montagu, Ashley: *Man and Aggression*, New York: Oxford University Press, 1968.

Moore, John A. (ed.): *Ideas in Evolution and Behavior*, Garden City: Natural History Press, 1970.

Morgan, William P. (ed.): *Contemporary Readings in Sport Psychology*, Springfield, Illinois: Charles C Thomas, 1970.

Morris, C. W.: *Varieties of Human Value*, Chicago: University of Chicago Press, 1956.

Morris, Desmond: *The Naked Ape*, New York: McGraw-Hill, 1967.

Morris, Desmond: *Primate Ethology*, Garden City: New York: Doubleday, 1969.

Moses, Leon: "An Evolutionary-Adaptational-Ecologic View of Human Behavior," in *Science and Psychoanalysis*, Vol. XII, *Animal and Human*, Masserman, Jules H. (ed.), New York: Grune and Stratton, 1968.

Moses, Leon: "The Evolution of Human Behavior," in *Science and Psychoanalysis*, Volume XII, *Animal and Human*, Masserman, Jules H. (ed.), New York: Grune and Stratton, 1968.

Muensterberger, Warner (ed.): *Man and His Culture: Psychoanalytic Anthropology after 'Totem and Taboo,'* New York: Taplinger, 1970.

Muller, Herbert Joseph: "Human Values in Relation to Evolution," *Science*, 127: 625–629, March 1958.

Muller, Herbert Joseph: *Religion and Freedom in the Modern World*, Chicago: University of Chicago Press, 1963.

Muller, Herbert Joseph: *Freedom in the Modern World*, New York: Harper and Row, 1966.

Muller, Herbert Joseph: *The Children of Frankenstein: A Primer on Modern Technology and Human Values*, Bloomington: Indiana University Press, 1970.

Mumford, Lewis: *The Myth of the Machine: The Pentagon of Power*, New York: Harcourt, Brace, 1970.

Murray, Henry: "Beyond Yesterday's Idealisms," in *Man Thinking*, Hastings, William Thomson (ed.), Ithaca, New York: Cornell University Press, 1962.

Nagel, E.: *The Structure of Science*, New York: Harcourt, Brace, and World, 1961.

Napier, John: "The evolution of the hand," *Scientific American*, 207(6):56–62, Dec. 1962.

Napier, John: *The Roots of Mankind*, Washington, D. C.: Smithsonian Institution Press, 1970 (distributed by Braziller, New York, 1970).

Nass, M. L.: "The Superego and Moral Development in the Theories of Freud and Piaget," *Psychoanalytic Study of the Child*, 21:51–68, 1966.

National Academy of Science (ed.): *The Behavioral and Social Sciences: Outlook and Needs*, Englewood Cliffs: Prentice-Hall, 1969.

National Institute of Child Health and Human Development: *The Acquisition and Development of Values: Perspectives on Research: Conference Reports*, May 15–17, 1968, Washington, D.C.: U.S. Government Printing Office, 1969.

National Psychological Association for Psychoanalysis: *Psychoanalysis and the Future —A Centenary Commemoration of the Birth of Sigmund Freud*, Foreword by Benjamin Nelson, New York, 1957.

Nelson, Benjamin (ed.): "The Future of Illusions," in *Man in Contemporary Society*, A Source Book by the Contemporary Civilization Staff of Columbia College, Vol. II, New York: Columbia University Press, 1955.

Nelson, Benjamin: *Freud and the Twentieth Century*, New York: Meridian, 1957.

Newman, J. R.: "A Review of E. Cassirer's Determinism and Indeterminism in Modern Physics," *Scientific American*, 196(3):147–152, March 1957.

Ng, Larry (ed.): *Alternatives to Violence*, New York: Time-Life Books, 1968.

Nielsen, N.: "Value Judgments in Psychoanalysis," *International Journal of Psychoanalysis,* 41 (Parts 4 and 5):425–429, July–Oct. 1960.

Nogar, Raymond: *The Lord of the Absurd,* New York: Herder and Herder, 1966.

Northrop, F. S. C.: *The Complexity of Legal and Ethical Experience,* Boston: Little, Brown, 1959.

Northrop, F. S. C., and Livingston, H. H. (eds.): *Cross-Cultural Understanding,* New York: Harper and Row, 1964.

Novey, S.: "Some Philosophical Speculations About the Concept of the Genital Character," *International Journal of Psychoanalysis,* 36 (Part 2):88–94, Mar.–April 1955.

Nowell-Smith, P. H.: *Ethics,* New York: Philosophical Library, 1957.

Nunberg, H.: "Ego strength and ego weaknesses," *American Imago,* 3(3):25–40, 1942.

Nunberg, H.: *Principles of Psychoanalysis,* New York: International Universities Press, 1955.

Oakley, Kenneth P.: *Man the Tool-Maker,* London: British Museum, 1949.

Offer, D., and Sabshin, M.: *Normality, Theoretical and Clinical Concepts of Mental Health,* New York: Basic Books, 1966.

Olson, M., Jr.: *The Logic of Collective Action,* Cambridge: Harvard University Press, 1965.

Ong, Walter J.: *The Presence of the Word: Some Prolegomena for Cultural and Religious History,* New Haven: Yale University Press, 1967.

Ong, Walter J. (ed.): *Knowledge and the Future of Man: An International Symposium,* New York: Holt, Rinehart and Winston, 1968.

Opler, Morris: "Fact and Fallacy Concerning the Evolution of Man," *Philosophy and Phenomenological Research,* 7(4):635–642, June 1947.

Opler, Marvin K.: *Culture, Psychiatry and Human Values,* Springfield, Illinois: Charles C Thomas, 1956.

Oppenheim, Felix E.: *Dimensions of Freedom: An Analysis,* New York: St. Martin's, 1961.

Ostow, M.: "Biological basis of human behavior," in *American Handbook of Psychiatry,* Vol. I., Arieti, S. (ed.), New York: Basic Books, 1959.

Parsegian, V. Lawrence, et al.: *Introduction to Natural Science, Part 2: The Life Sciences,* New York: Academic Press, 1970.

Parsons, Anne: *Belief, Magic and Anomie, Essays in Psychosocial Anthropology,* New York: Free Press, 1969.

Parsons, Talcott, and Bales, Robert F.: *Family, Socialization, and Interaction Process,* Glencoe: Free Press, 1955.

Parsons, Talcott: "The Incest Taboo in Relation to Social Structure and the Socialization of the Child," in *Social Structure and Personality,* New York: Free Press, 1964.

Passmore, John: *Philosophical Reasoning,* New York: Basic Books, 1969.

Pattison, E. Mansell (ed.): *Clinical Psychiatry and Religion,* Boston: Little, Brown, 1969.

Pearson, G. H. J.: *Adolescence and the Conflict of Generations,* New York: Norton, 1958.

Peirce, Charles, S. S.: *Values in a Universe of Chance,* Selected Writings, Wiener, Philip, P. (ed.), Garden City: Doubleday, 1958.

Pelto, Pertti J.: *Anthropological Research: The Structure of Inquiry,* New York: Harper and Row, 1970.

PSYCHIATRY AND ETHICS

Pelz, Donald C.: "Creative Tensions in the Research and Development Climate," *Science,* Vol. 157, pp. 160–165, July 14, 1967.

Pfeiffer, John E., *The Emergence of Man,* New York: Harper and Row, 1969.

Pfister, Oskar: *Psychoanalysis and Faith: The Letters of Sigmund Freud and Oskar Pfister,* Meng, Heinrich and Freud, Ernst L. (eds.), New York: Basic Books, 1964.

Piaget, J. et al.: *Moral Judgment of the Child,* Glencoe: Free Press, 1948.

Piers, Gerhart and Singer, Milton B.: *Shame and Guilt,* Springfield: Charles C Thomas, 1953.

Platt, John R. (ed.): *New Views of the Nature of Man,* Chicago: University of Chicago Press, 1965.

Platt, John R.: *The Step to Man,* New York: Wiley, 1966.

Platt, John R.: *Perception and Change: Projections for Survival,* Ann Arbor: University of Michigan Press, 1970.

Polanyi, Michael: *The Study of Man,* Chicago: University of Chicago Press, 1959.

Polanyi, Michael: *Personal Knowledge,* New York: Harper and Row, 1964.

Polanyi, Michael: *The Tacit Dimension,* Garden City, Doubleday, 1966.

Popper, K.: *The Logic of Scientific Discovery,* New York: Basic Books, 1959.

Portmann, Adolph: *Animals As Social Beings,* New York: Viking Press, 1961.

Potter, Van Rensselaer: *Bioethics: Bridge to the Future,* Englewood Cliffs: Prentice-Hall, 1971.

Pribram, Karl H.: "The New Neurology: Memory, Novelty, Thought and Choice," in *EEG and Behavior,* Glaser, Gilbert H. (ed.), New York: Basic Books, 1963.

Pribram, Karl H., and Broadbent, Donald E.: *Biology of Memory,* New York: Academic Press, 1970.

Price, Derek, John de Solla: *Science Since Babylon,* New Haven: Yale University Press, 1961.

Proshansky, Harold and Seidenberg, Bernard (eds.): *Basic Studies in Social Psychology,* New York: Holt, Rinehart and Winston, 1965.

Pumpian-Mindlin, Eugene (ed.): *Psychoanalysis As Science,* Palo Alto; Stanford University Press, 1952.

Rabb, G.; Woolpy, J. H.; and Ginsburg, B.: "Social Relationships in a Group of Captive Wolves," *American Zoologist,* 7(2):305–311, May 1967.

Rader, Melvin: *Ethics and the Human Community,* New York: Holt, Rinehart and Winston, 1964.

Radin, Max: *Law As Logic and Experience,* New Haven: Yale University Press, 1940.

Rado, S.: "Emergency behavior, with an introduction to the dynamics of conscience," in *Anxiety,* Hoch, P., and Zubin, J. (eds.), New York: Grune and Stratton, 1950.

Ramzy, I.: "The Place of Values in Psychoanalysis," *International Journal of Psychoanalysis,* 46 (Part I):97–106, Jan. 1965.

Rank, Otto: *The Myth of the Birth of the Hero and Other Writings,* Freund, Philip (ed.), New York: Vintage Books, 1959.

Rantzen, H. B.: *Uncertainty, in Nature and Communication,* New York: Humanities Press, 1968.

Rapaport, David: "The Autonomy of the Ego." *Bulletin of the Menninger Clinic,* 15 (4):113–123, July 1951.

Rapaport, David: "The Theory of Ego Autonomy: A Generalization," *Bulletin of the Menninger Clinic,* 22(1):13–35, Jan., 1958.

Rapaport, David: "A Historical Survey of Psychoanalytic Ego Psychology," *Psychological Issues*, 1(1):5–17, Monograph 1, 1959.

Rapaport, David: *The Structure of Psychoanalytic Theory, A Systematizing Attempt*, Monograph 6, Vol. II, No. 2, New York: International Universities Press, 1960.

Raphael, D. D.: "Darwinism and Ethics," in *A Century of Darwin*, Barnett, S. A. (ed.), Cambridge: Harvard University Press, 1958.

Rapoport, Anatol: "Scientific Approach to Ethics," *Science*. 125:796–799, April 26, 1957.

Rapoport, Anatol: *Fights, Games and Debates*, Ann Arbor: University of Michigan Press, 1960.

Rapoport, Anatol: *Strategy and Conscience*, New York: Harper and Row, 1964.

Reagan, Charles E.: *Ethics for Scientific Researchers* (2nd ed.), Springfield: Charles C Thomas, 1971.

Redl, Fritz: *Controls from Within*, Glencoe: Free Press, 1952.

Redlich, Frederick and Freedman, Daniel X.: *The Theory and Practice of Psychiatry*, New York: Basic Books, 1966.

Reich, Charles A.: *The Greening of America*, New York: Random House, 1970.

Reid, John R.: "The Problem of Values in Psychoanalysis," *American Journal of Psychoanalysis*, 15(2):115–122, 1955.

Reik, Theodor: *Myth and Guilt*, New York: George Braziller, 1957.

Reik, Theodor: *Listening with the Third Ear: The Inner Experience of a Psychoanalyst*, New York: Farrar Straus, 1948.

Reiner, J. M.: *The Organism as an Adaptive Control System*, Englewood Cliffs: Prentice-Hall, 1968.

Rensch, Bernhard: *Evolution Above the Species Level*, New York: Wiley, 1959.

Reynolds, Vernon: *The Apes*, New York: Dutton, 1967.

Richfield, Jerome: "The Role of Philosophy in Theoretical Psychiatry," *Bulletin of the Menninger Clinic*, 17(2):49–57, March, 1953.

Richter, C. P.: *Biological Clocks in Medicine and Psychiatry*, Springfield: Charles C Thomas, 1965.

Ricoeur, Paul (trans. by Denis Savage): *Freud and Philosophy, An Essay on Interpretation*, New Haven: Yale University Press, 1970.

Ricoeur, Paul: *The Symbolism of Evil*, New York: Harper and Row, 1967.

Riesman, D.: *The Lonely Crowd*, New Haven: Yale University Press, 1950.

Riesman, D.: *Individualism Reconsidered*, Glencoe: Free Press, 1954.

Rioch, David McK.: "Psychiatry as a Biological Science," *Psychiatry*, 18(4):313–321, Nov. 1955.

Roazen, Paul: *Freud: Political and Social Thought*, New York: Knopf, 1968.

Robert, Marthe: *The Psychoanalytic Revolution: Sigmund Freud's Life and Achievement* (trans. by Kenneth Morgan), New York: Harcourt, Brace and World, 1966.

Roberts, Catherine: *The Scientific Conscience*, New York: George Braziller, 1967.

Roberts, Walter Orr: *A View of Century 21*, Claremont: Claremont Colleges, 1969.

Robinson, Paul A.: *The Freudian Left: Wilhelm Reich, Geza Roheim, Herbert Marcuse*, New York: Harper and Row, 1969.

Roe, A. and Simpson, G. G. (eds.): *Behavior and Evolution*, New Haven: Yale University Press, 1958.

Roe, A.: "Psychological definitions of man," *Classification and Human Evolution*, Washburn, S. L. (ed.), Chicago: Aldine, 1963.

Rogow, Arnold A.: *The Psychiatrists*, New York: G. P. Putnam's Sons, 1970.

Roheim, Geza: *Psychoanalysis and Anthropology*, New York: International Universities Press, 1950.

Roheim, Geza; Muensterberger, Warner; and Axelrad, Sidney (eds.): *Psychoanalysis and the Social Sciences*, Vols. I–V, New York: International Universities Press, 1947–58.

Romano, J. (ed.): *Adaptation*, Ithaca: Cornell University Press, 1949.

Romer, Alfred S.: *The Procession of Life*, Cleveland and New York: World, 1968.

Rosenblith, J., and Allinsmith, W. (eds.): *The Causes of Behavior: Readings in Child Development and Educational Psychology*, 2nd ed., Boston: Allyn and Bacon, 1966.

Rosenblum, Leonard A. (ed.): *Primate Behavior*, New York: Academic Press, 1970.

Rosenthal, Bernard G.: *Images of Man*, New York: Basic Books, 1971.

Rosenthal, David: *Genetic Theory and Abnormal Behavior*, New York: McGraw-Hill, 1970.

Rosenthal, Robert, and Rosnow, Ralph L. (eds.): *Artifact in Behavioral Research*, New York: Academic Press, 1969.

Rosenthal, Robert: *Experimenter Effects in Behavioral Research*, New York: Appleton-Century-Crofts, 1966.

Roslansky, J. D. (ed.): *Genetics and Future of Man*, New York: Appleton-Century-Crofts, 1966.

Roslansky, J. D. (ed.): *The Uniqueness of Man*, Amsterdam: North-Holland, 1969.

Roslansky, J. D. (ed.): *Creativity. A Conference*, in St. Peter, Minnesota, Amsterdam: North-Holland, 1970.

Rosner, Stanley and Abt, Lawrence (eds.): *The Creative Experience*, New York: Grossman, 1970.

Roszak, Theodore: *The Making of a Counter Culture*, New York: Doubleday, 1969.

Roth, John K.: *Freedom and the Moral Life*, Philadelphia: Westminster Press, 1969.

Rothblatt, Ben (ed.): *Changing Perspectives on Man*, Chicago: University of Chicago Press, 1968.

Rubenstein, Richard: *Morality and Eros*, New York: McGraw-Hill, 1970.

Ruesch, Jurgen, and Bateson, Gregory: *Communication: the Social Matrix of Psychiatry*, New York: W. W. Norton, 2nd edition, 1968.

Ruesch, Jurgen: *Therapeutic Communication*, New York: W. W. Norton, 1961.

Ruitenbeek, H. M. (ed.): *Psychoanalysis and Contemporary American Culture*, New York: Dell, 1964.

Ruitenbeek, Hendrik M.: *Freud and America*, New York: Macmillan, 1966.

Russell, C., and Russell, W. M. S.: *Violence, Monkeys and Man*, London: Macmillan, 1968.

Sachs, Hanns: *The Creative Unconscious*, Cambridge: Science-Art, 1942.

Sachs, Hanns: *Freud: Master and Friend*, Cambridge: Harvard University Press, 1944.

Sachs, Hanns: *Masks of Love and Life: The Philosophical Basis of Psychoanalysis*, Roback, A. A. (ed.), Cambridge: Science and Art, 1948.

Sahlins, M. D.: "The Social Life of Monkeys, Apes, and Primitive Man," in *The Evolution of Man's Capacity for Culture*, Spuhler, J. N. (ed.), Detroit: Wayne State University Press, 1959.

Saul, L. J.: *Emotional Maturity*, Philadelphia: Lippincott, 2nd edition, 1960.

Saul, L. J.: *Bases of Human Behavior*, Philadelphia: Lippincott, 1951.

Schafer, R.: *Aspects of Internalization,* New York: International Universities Press, 1968.

Schaller, G. B.: *The Mountain Gorilla: Ecology and Behavior,* Chicago: University of Chicago Press, 1963.

Scheibe, Karl E.: *Beliefs and Values,* New York: Holt, Rinehart and Winston, 1970.

Schilder, Paul: *Psychoanalysis, Man, and Society,* Arranged by Lauretta Bender, New York: W. W. Norton, 1951.

Schjelderup-Ebbe, T.: "Social Behavior of Birds," in *Handbook of Social Psychology,* Murchison, Carl (ed.), Worcester: Clark University Press, 1935.

Schon, Donald A.: *Technology and Change,* New York: Delacorte, 1967.

Schrier, A. M.; Harlow, H. F.; and Stollnitz, F. (eds.): *Behavior of Nonhuman Primates,* New York: Academic Press, 1965.

Schrödinger, Erwin C.: *Science, Theory and Man,* New York: Dover, 1957.

Schur, Max: *The Id and the Regulatory Principles of Mental Functioning,* New York: International Universities Press, 1966.

Schwebel, Milton (ed.): *Behavioral Science and Human Survival,* Palo Alto: Science and Behavior Books, 1965.

Schweppe, John S.: *Man: A Remarkable Animal: A Study of Man's Development and Interaction with His Environment.* Research and Education Fund, Chicago, 1970.

Scott, John Paul, and Fuller, John L.: *Genetics and Social Behavior of the Dog,* Chicago: University of Chicago Press, 1965.

Scott, John Paul: *Aggression,* Chicago: University of Chicago Press, 1958.

Scott, John Paul: "Hostility and Aggression in Animals," in *Roots of Behavior,* Bliss, E. L. (ed.), New York: Harper, 1962.

Sears, Paul B., "The Steady State: Physical Law and Moral Choice," in *Man Thinking,* Hastings, William Thomson (ed.), Ithaca, New York: Cornell U. Press, 1962.

Seidenberg, R.: *Posthistoric Man,* Chapel Hill: University of North Carolina Press, 1950.

Seidenberg, R.: *Anatomy of the Future,* Chapel Hill: University of North Carolina Press, 1961.

Seidenberg, R., and Cochrane, Hortence S.: *Mind and Destiny: A Social Approach to Psychoanalytic Theory,* Syracuse, New York: Syracuse University Press, 1964.

Shakow, David: "Ethics for a Scientific Age: Some Moral Aspects of Psychoanalysis," *The Psychoanalytic Review,* 52(3):335–348, Fall 1965.

Shapiro, H. L. (ed.): *Man, Culture and Society,* New York: Oxford University Press, 1956.

Sherwood, Michael: *The Logic of Explanation in Psychoanalysis,* New York: Academic Press, 1969.

Shinn, Roger: *Man: The New Humanism,* Philadelphia: Westminster Press, 1968.

Sidgwick, Henry: *The Methods of Ethics,* 7th ed., Chicago: University of Chicago Press, 1962.

Sills, D. L. (ed.): *International Encyclopedia of the Social Sciences,* New York: Macmillan, 1968.

Simmons, James R.: *The Quest for Ethics,* New York: Philosophical Library, 1962.

Simpson, George Gaylord: "Biology and the Nature of Science," *Science,* 139:81–88, Jan. 11, 1963.

Simpson, George Gaylord: *This View of Life,* New York: Harcourt, Brace, and World, 1964.

Simpson, George Gaylord: "The Crisis in Biology," *The American Scholar*, 36(3):363–377, Summer 1967.

Simpson, George Gaylord: *Biology and Man*, New York: Harcourt, Brace, and World, 1969.

Singer, C.; Holmyard, E.; Hall, A.; and Williams, T., (eds.): *A History of Technology*, Oxford: Clarendon Press, 1954–1958.

Singer, Marcus: *Generalization in Ethics*, New York: Knopf, 1961.

Sinnott, E. W.: "The Biological Basis of Democracy," *Yale Review*, 35(1):61–73, Sept. 1945.

Sinnott, E. W.: *Matter, Mind and Man*, 1st edition, New York: Harper, 1957.

Sinnott, E. W.: *The Bridge of Life*, New York: Simon and Schuster, 1966.

Sjoberg, Gideon (ed.): *Ethics, Politics and Social Research*, Cambridge: Schenkman, 1967.

Slater, Mariam K.: "Primate Parallels and Biocultural Models," in *Science and Psychoanalysis*, Vol. XII, *Animal and Human*, Masserman, Jules H. (ed.), New York: Grune and Stratton, 1968.

Sluckin, W.: *Imprinting and Early Learning*, Chicago: Aldine, 1965.

Smith, M. Brewster: *Social Psychology and Human Values*, Chicago: Aldine, 1969.

Smith, T. V.: *Beyond Conscience*, New York: Whittlesey House, McGraw-Hill, 1934.

Smith, T. V. and Debbins, William: *Constructive Ethics*, Englewood Cliffs, New Jersey: Prentice-Hall, 1961.

Snyder, Ross: *On Becoming Human*, Nashville: Abingdon, 1967.

Southwick, Charles H.: *Primate Social Behavior*, Princeton: Van Nostrand, 1963.

Spitz, Rene A.: *A Genetic Field Theory of Ego Formation—Its Implications for Pathology*, New York: International Universities Press, 1959.

Spock, Benjamin: *Decent and Indecent: Our Personal and Political Behavior*, New York: McCall, 1970.

Spotte, Stephen H.: *Fish and Invertebrate Culture. Water Management in Closed Systems*, New York: Wiley-Interscience, 1970.

Spuhler, J. N. (ed.): *The Evolution of Man's Capacity for Culture*, Detroit: Wayne State University Press, 1959.

Spuhler, J. N. (ed.): *Genetic Diversity and Human Behavior*, Chicago: Aldine, 1967.

Steiner, George: *Language and Silence: Essays on Language, Literature and the Inhuman*, New York: Atheneum, 1967.

Stent, Gunther S.: *The Coming of the Golden Age: A View of the End of Progress*, New York: Natural History Press, 1969.

Stephen, K.: "A Correspondence with Dr. Karin Stephen," *Science and Ethics*, Waddington, C. H., London: Allen and Unwin, 1942.

Stern, Karl: *The Third Revolution: A Study of Psychiatry and Religion*, New York: Harcourt, Brace and World, 1961.

Stevenson, Charles L.: *Facts and Values*, New Haven: Yale University Press, 1963.

Stone, Irving: *The Passions of the Mind*, Garden City: Doubleday, 1971.

Stone, Leo: *The Psychoanalytic Situation—An Examination of its Development and Essential Nature*, New York: International Universities Press, 1961.

Storr, Anthony: "Possible Substitutes for War," in *The Natural History of Aggression*, Carthy, J. D. and Ebling, F. J. (eds.), London: Academic Press, 1964.

Storr, Anthony: *Human Aggression*, New York: Atheneum, 1968.

Straus, E. W.; Natanson, M.; and Ey, H.: *Psychiatry and Philosophy*, New York: Springer-Verlag, 1969.

Sullivan, Harry Stack: *Conceptions of Modern Psychiatry* (2nd ed.), New York: W. W. Norton, 1953.

Sullivan, Harry Stack: *The Fusion of Psychiatry and Social Science*, New York: W. W. Norton, 1964.

Sutherland, John D. (ed.): *Psychoanalysis and Contemporary Thought*, New York: Grove, 1959.

Sykes, Gerald: *The Hidden Remnant*, 1st ed., New York: Harper and Brothers, 1962.

Szent-Györgyi, Albert: *The Crazy Ape*, New York: Philosophical Library, 1970.

Tarachow, Sidney: "Ambiguity and Human Imperfection," *Journal of the American Psychoanalytic Association*, 13(1):85–101, Jan. 1965.

Tavolga, William N.: *Principles of Animal Behavior*, New York: Harper and Row, 1969.

Tax, Sol (ed.): *Evolution After Darwin*, Vol. I: *Evolution of Life*, Vol. II: *Evolution of Man*, Vol. III: *Issues in Evolution*, Chicago: University of Chicago Press, 1960.

Tax, Sol (ed.): *Horizons of Anthropology*, Chicago: Aldine, 1964.

Taylor, Alfred Maurice: *Imagination and the Growth of Science*, New York: Schocken, 1967.

Taylor, Charles: *The Explanation of Behaviour*, London: Routledge and Kegan Paul, 1964.

Taylor, Gordon R.: *The Doomsday Book: Can the World Survive?* New York: World, 1970.

Teilhard de Chardin, Pierre: *Man's Place in Nature*, New York: Harper and Row, 1966.

Thorpe, W. H.: *Biology and the Nature of Man*, New York: Oxford University Press, 1962.

Thorpe, W. H., and Zangwill, O. L. (eds.): *Current Problems in Animal Behavior*, Cambridge: Cambridge University Press, 1961.

Thorpe, W. H.: *Learning and Instinct in Animals* (2nd ed.), Cambridge: Harvard University Press, 1963.

Thorpe, W. H.: *Science, Man and Morals*, London: Methuen, 1965.

Tinbergen, Nikolaas and the editors of *Life: Animal Behavior*, New York: Time, Inc., 1965.

Tinbergen, Nikolaas: *Social Behavior in Animals*, London: Methuen, 1965.

Tinbergen, Nikolaas: "On War and Peace in Animals and Man," *Science*, 160, June 28, 1968.

Tinbergen, Nikolaas and Falkus, Hugh: *Signals for Survival*, New York: Oxford University Press, 1970.

Titmuss, Richard M.: *The Gift Relationship—From Human Blood to Social Policy*, New York: Pantheon, 1971.

Toch, Hans: *Violent Men: An Inquiry into the Psychology of Violence*, Chicago: Aldine, 1969.

Toffler, Alvin: *Future Shock*, New York: Random House, 1970.

Torrey, E. Fuller (ed.): *Ethical Issues in Medicine*, Boston: Little, Brown, 1968.

Toulmin, Stephen E.: *The Place of Reason in Ethics*, Cambridge: Cambridge University Press, 1950.

Toulmin, Stephen E.: "The Logical Status of Psycho-Analysis," in *Philosophy and Analysis*, Macdonald, Margaret (ed.), Oxford: Basil Blackwell, 1954.

Toynbee, Arnold J.: *Change and Habit: The Challenge of Our Time*, New York: Oxford University Press, 1966.

Trilling, Lionel: *Freud and the Crisis of Our Culture*, Boston: Beacon, 1955.

Trilling, Lionel: *Beyond Culture*, New York: Viking, 1965.

Tullock, Gordon: *The Logic of the Law*, New York: Basic Books, 1971.

Valery, Paul: *History and Politics*, Vol. X of the *Collected Works of Paul Valery*, edited by Mathews, Jackson, New York: Pantheon, 1962.

Veszy-Wagner, L.: Review of *Progress and Revolution* by R. Waelder in the *International Journal of Psycho-Analysis*, 49(1):109–112, 1968.

Vickers, Sir Geoffrey: *Value Systems and Social Process*, New York: Basic Books, 1968.

Von Bertalanffy, L.: *Problems of Life: An Evaluation of Modern Biological Thought*, New York: Wiley, 1952.

Von Bertalanffy, L.: *Robots, Men and Minds*, New York: George Braziller, 1967.

Von Bertalanffy, L.: *General System Theory*, New York: George Braziller, 1968.

Von Bonin, G.: *The Evolution of the Human Brain*, Chicago: University of Chicago Press, 1963.

Von Mering, O.: *A Grammar of Human Values*, Pittsburgh: University of Pittsburgh Press, 1961.

Von Mering, O., and Kasdan, L. (eds.): *Anthropology and the Behavioral and Health Sciences*, Pittsburgh, University of Pittsburgh Press, 1970.

Waddington, C. H.: "The Relations Between Science and Ethics," *Nature*, London: 148:270–274, Sept. 6, 1941.

Waddington, C. H., Ewing, A. C., and Broad, C. D.: "Symposium on the Relations Between Science and Ethics," Proceedings of the Aristotelian Society, Vol. 42, pp. 65–100H, 1941–42; London: Harrison & Sons, 1942.

Waddington, C. H.: *Science and Ethics*, London: Allen and Unwin, 1942.

Waddington, C. H.: *The Ethical Animal*, New York: Atheneum, 1961.

Waddington, C. H.: *The Nature of Life*, New York: Harper & Row, 1961.

Waddington, C. H.: *Behind Appearance*, Cambridge: M.I.T. Press, 1969.

Waddington, C. H. (ed.): *Towards a Theoretical Biology*, Vol. III, Edinburgh: Edinburgh University Press, 1970.

Waelder, Robert: "The Problem of Freedom in Psychoanalysis, and the Problem of Reality Testing," *International Journal of Psychoanalysis*, 17:89–108, 1936.

Waelder, Robert: "The Principle of Multiple Function: Observations on Over-Determinism," *Psychoanalytic Quarterly*, 5(1):45–62, 1936.

Waelder, Robert: *Progress and Revolution: A Study of the Issues of Our Age*, New York: International Universities Press, 1967.

Waelder, Robert: *Basic Theory of Psychoanalysis*, New York: International Universities Press, 1960.

Waelder, Robert: "Psychoanalysis and History," in *The Psychoanalytic Interpretation of History*, Wolman, Benjamin B., (ed.), New York: Basic Books, 1971.

Wald, George: "Determinacy, Individuality, and the Problem of Free Will," in *New Views of the Nature of Man*, Platt, John R. (ed.), Chicago: University of Chicago Press, 1965.

Walker, Charles R. (ed.): *Modern Technology and Civilization*, New York: McGraw-Hill, 1962.

Wallia, C. S. (ed.): *Toward Century 21*, New York: Basic Books, 1970.

Wang, Hao: *Logic, Computers, and Sets*, New York: Chelsea, 1970.

Washburn, S. L.: "Speculations on the interrelations of the history of tools and biological evolution," in *The Evolution of Man's Capacity for Culture*, Spuhler, J. N. (ed.), Detroit: Wayne State University Press, 1959.

Washburn, S. L. and DeVore, Irven: "The Social Life of Baboons," *Scientific American*, Vol. 204, no. 6, pp. 62–71, June 1961.

Washburn, S. L. and Devore, Irven: "Social Behavior of Baboons and Early Man," in *Social Life of Early Man*, Washburn, Sherwood L., ed., Chicago: Aldine, 1961.

Washburn, S. L.: "Tools and Human Evolution," *Scientific American*, 203(3):63–75, Sept. 1960.

Washburn, S. L. (ed.): *The Social Life of Early Man*, Chicago: Aldine, 1961.

Washburn, S. L. (ed.): *Classification and Human Evolution*, Chicago: Aldine, 1963.

Washburn, S. L.; Jay, P.; and Lancaster, P. J.: "Field studies of old-world monkeys and apes." *Science*, 150:1541–1547, Dec. 17, 1965.

Washburn, S. L., and Hamburg, D.: "The Implications of Primate Research," *Primate Behavior*, DeVore, Irven (ed.), New York: Holt, Rinehart and Winston, 1965.

Washburn, S. L., and Hamburg, D.: "The Study of Primate Behavior," in *Primate Behavior*, DeVore, Irven (ed.), New York: Holt, Rinehart and Winston, 1965.

Washburn, S. L.: "Conflict in Primate Society," in *Conflict in Society*, DeReuck, Anthony and Knight, Julie (eds.), A CIBA Foundation volume, Boston: Little, Brown & Co., 1966.

Washburn, S. L. and Jay, P.: "More on tool use in primates," *Current Anthropology*, 8(3):253–254, June 1967.

Washburn, S. L. and Jay, P. (eds.): *Perspectives on Human Evolution*, New York: Holt, Rinehart and Winston, 1968.

Watts, A. W.: *The Two Hands of God*, New York: Collier Books, 1969.

Weigert, E.: "Human ego functions in the light of animal behavior," *Psychiatry*, 19(4):325–332, Nov. 1956.

Weigert, E.: *The Courage to Love*, New Haven: Yale University Press, 1970.

Weihofen, Henry: *The Urge to Punish*, New York: Farrar, Straus, and Cudahy, 1956.

Weiss, Paul and Weiss, Jonathan: *Right and Wrong: A Philosophical Dialogue Between Father and Son*, New York: Basic Books, 1967.

Weiss, R. F.; Buchanan, W.; Alstatt, L.; and Lombardo, J. P.: "Altruism is Rewarding," *Science*, 171:1262, March 26, 1971.

Wellisch Erich: *Isaac and Oedipus: A Study of Biblical Psychology of the Sacrifice of Isaac, the Akedah*, London: Routledge and K. Paul, 1954.

Wells, Donald A.: *The War Myth: The Rationalization of War-Making in Western Thought*, New York: Pegasus, 1967.

West, L. J.: "Ethical Psychiatry and Biosocial Humanism," *American Journal of Psychiatry*, 126:226–230, Aug. 1969.

Wheeler, W. M.: *Essays in Philosophical Biology*, Cambridge: Harvard University Press, 1939.

Wheelis, A.: *The Illusionless Man*, New York: W. W. Norton, 1966.

Wheelis, A.: *The Quest for Identity*, New York: W. W. Norton, 1958.

Whitehead, Alfred North: *Science and the Modern World*, New York: Macmillan, 1925; Lowell Lectures 1925.

Whorf, Benjamin Lee: *Language, Thought and Reality*, Cambridge: M.I.T. Press, 1956.

Whyte, Lancelot Law: *The Unconscious Before Freud*, New York: Basic Books, 1960.

Whyte, Lancelot Law: *The Next Development in Man,* New York: Henry Holt, 1948.

Wiesner, J. B., and York, H. F.: "National Security and the Nuclear Test Ban," *Scientific American,* 211(4):27–35, Oct. 1964.

Wilbur, George and Muensterberger, Warner (eds.): *Psychoanalysis and Culture,* New York: International Universities Press, 1965.

Williams, Roger John: *Biochemical Individuality,* London and Austin: University of Texas Press, 1969.

Winnicott, D. W.: "Psychoanalysis and the Sense of Guilt," in *Psychoanalysis and Contemporary Thought,* Sutherland, John (ed.), New York: Grove, 1959.

Wisdom, John: *Philosophy and Psychoanalysis,* Oxford: Basil Blackwell, 1953.

Wisdom, John: *Paradox and Discovery,* Oxford: Basil Blackwell, 1965.

Wolff, Peter H.: "The Developmental Psychologies of Jean Piaget and Psychoanalysis," *Psychological Issues,* Vol. II, No. 1, Monograph 5, New York: International Universities Press, 1960.

Wolff, Peter H.: "The causes, controls and organizations of behavior in the neonate," *Psychological Issues,* 5(1), Monograph 17, New York: International Universities Press, 1966.

Wolman, Benjamin B. (ed.): *The Psychoanalytic Interpretation of History,* New York: Basic Books, 1971.

Wolman, Benjamin B.: "Sense and Nonsense in History," in *The Psychoanalytic Interpretation of History,* Wolman, Benjamin B. (ed.), New York: Basic Books, 1971.

Woolpy, Jerome H.: "Socialization of Wolves," in *Science and Psychoanalysis,* Volume XII, *Animal and Human,* Masserman, Jules H. (ed.), New York: Grune and Stratton, 1968.

Wolstenholme, G. (ed.): *Man and His Future,* Boston: Little, Brown, 1963.

Wright, Quincy (ed.): *The World Community,* Chicago: University of Chicago Press, 1948.

Wright, Quincy: *A Study of War,* 2d. ed. Chicago: University of Chicago Press, 1965.

Wylie, Philip: *The Magic Animal,* New York: Doubleday, 1968.

Yankelovich, D. and Barrett, W.: *Ego and Instinct,* New York: Random House, 1970.

Yinger, John Milton: *The Scientific Study of Religion,* New York: Macmillan, 1970.

Zetzel, Elizabeth R.: *The Capacity for Emotional Growth,* New York: International Universities Press, 1970.

Zilboorg, Gregory: *Psychoanalysis and Religion,* Zilboorg, Margaret Stone (ed.), New York: Farrar, Straus and Cudahy, 1962.

Zuckerman, S.: *The Social Life of Monkeys and Apes,* New York: Harcourt, Brace, 1932.

Notes to Part II

Biographical Note

1. Levine, M.: *Pychotherapy in Medical Practice,* New York, Macmillan, 1942.

2. Levine, M.: "The Hippocratic Oath in Modern Dress," *Journal of the Association of American Medical Colleges,* 23:317, 1948.

The Diagnosis of Normality

1. Abraham, Karl: *Character Formation on the Genital Level of Libido Development. Selected Papers,* Hogarth, London, 1927, p. 407.

2. Alexander, Franz: "The Castration Complex in the Formation of Character," *International Journal of Psychoanalysis*, 4, 1923.
3. Meyer, Adolf: *The Meaning of Maturity. Our Children*, edited by Fisher and Gruenberg, New York, 1936.
4. Glover, Edward: "Die Normalität vom medizinsch—psychologischen Standpunkt," *Psychoanalytische Bewegung*, 4:536, 1932.

Dynamic Understanding of Human Behavior

1. English, O. Spurgeon, and Pearson, H. J.: *Emotional Problems of Living*, W. W. Norton, 1945.
2. Lilienthal, David E., member of the U.S. Atomic Energy Commission.

Bibliography to Part II

A Hippocratic Oath for Psychiatrists

Adams, Francis: *Hippocratic Writings*, Great Books, 10:1, Chicago: Encyclopedia Britannica.

Edelstein, Ludwig, and Emma J.: *Asclepius*, 2 Vols., Baltimore: Johns Hopkins Press, 1945.

Foxe, Arthur N.: "The Oath of Hippocrates," *Psychiatric Quarterly* 19:17–25, 1945.

Brugger, Thomas, and Frank, Alvin: "Peer Supervision as a Method of Learning Psychotherapy," *Journal of Comprehensive Psychiatry*, 3:47–53, February 1962.

Howey, M. Oldfield: *The Encircled Serpent*, New York: Arthur Richmond, 1955, pp. 89–90.

Levine, Maurice: "The Hippocratic Oath in Modern Dress," *Journal of the Association of American Medical Colleges*, 23:317, 1948.

Low, Barbara: "The Psychological Compensations of the Analyst," *International Journal of Psychoanalysis;* 16:1–8, 1935.

McLaughlin, James T.: "The Analyst and the Hippocratic Oath," *Journal of the American Psychoanalytic Association*, 9(1):106, January 1961.

Mead, Margaret: Personal communication, 1961.

Menninger, Karl A.: *Psychological Factors in the Choice of Medicine as a Profession*, Bulletin of the Menninger Clinic, 21:51–58, 1957.

Penfield, Wilder: *The Torch*, Little, Brown, 1960.

Racker, Heinrich: "Psychoanalytic Technique and the Analyst's Unconscious Masochism," *Psychoanalytic Quarterly*, 27:555–562, 1958.

Rogoff, Natalie: *The Decision to Study Medicine*, in the *Student-Physician*, ed. by R. K. Merton et al., Cambridge: Harvard University Press, 1957, pp. 109–129.

Sharpe, Ella F.: "The Psychoanalyst," in *Collected Papers on Psychoanalysis*. London: Hogarth, 1950, pp. 109–122.

Simmel, Ernst: "The Doctor Game, Illness and the Profession of Medicine," *International Journal of Psychoanalysis* 7:470–483, 1926.

Szasz, Thomas S.: "The Experiences of the Analyst," *This Journal* 4:197–223, 1956.

Wheelis, Allen: "The Vocational Hazards of Psychoanalysis," *International Journal of Psychoanalysis*, 37:171–184, 1956.

Zilboorg, Gregory: *History of Medical Psychology*, New York, W. W. Norton, 1941, p.22.

INDEX

abortion, and Hippocratic oath, 324
Abraham, Karl, 32, 272
adversary system, 162–163, 168
age
  as dimension in defining ethics, 46
  stages of life, 143–144
  see also generation gap
alcohol, effect on Ego, 184
Alexander, Franz, 256, 272
alliances, interpersonal, 34, 36
  audience-lecturer, 36–37, 39–40, 42–43, 106–108, 123–128
  as basic pattern of positive behavior, 35–36
  Ethicogenic, 224
  European Common Market, 116, 168
  I-Thou psychiatrist-patient, rebuttal of, 55–56
  mutual attention in, 44–45
  parent-child, 45–46
  reader-author, 21, 34, 36, 38–44
  see also therapeutic alliances
ambiguity, 121–122, 152–154
ambition, therapeutic, 331–332
ambivalence, 32
  effect on Golden Rule ethics, 199–200
animals, 56, 60–63
  avoidance of killing within species, 60–61
  baboons' response to danger, 64–66
  exhibitionism, 98
  fear of horses, 179–180
  importance of experiences in infancy, 63
  interaction with outside forces, 89
  -man differences, 90–91
  pecking order, 56–58, 95
  rats, competitive fighting of, 61
  responses to fear, 293–294
  social behavior of, compared with humans, 68–70
  social groups, 59–60
  studies of primates, 63, 64–66, 90
  survival of the fittest, 58–59
anxiety
  defenses against, 292, 296–303
  definition of, 295
Aring, Charles, 258
arithmetic, *see* mathematics
athletics, *see* sports

audience-lecturer alliance, 36–37, 39–40, 42–43, 106–108
  comparison with patient-psychiatrist relationship, 123–128
author, *see* reader-author alliance

baboons, response to danger, 64–66
battered children, 113–114
bees, 59, 61
behavior
  animal compared with human, 68–70
  six-point approach to study of individual, 304–309
  three-layer approach to understanding of, 292, 301–304
  see also animals; competition; defenses
birds, response to danger, 65
Body Has a Head, The, 134
Buber, Martin, I-Thou psychiatrist-patient relationship, 55–56

Cannon, Walter B., 82
case workers, hostility encountered in social work, 263–269
censorship, in writing, 25
childbearing, male envy of, 98–99
child-raising, 301–303
  "double messages," 235–237
  extreme words and attitudes, 117–118
  father-son alliance, 45–46
  father-son stilted conversation, 198
  Oedipal and Jobian attitudes, 155
  overly helpful father, 185–186
  see also children
children
  anxiety, 301–303
  battered, 113–114
  conscience, 275
  countertransference, 307
  dependency, 84–85, 143–144, 277
  Ego patterns, 189
  masturbation, 298–299
  narcissistic attitude, 279
  Oedipal and Jobian attitudes, 156, 157
  penis pride/envy, 98, 99
  projection defense, 62–63
  spoiled, 277
  unconscious hostilities, 268
  see also child-raising
chimpanzees, 66, 90